SLOW WALKS
IN
LONDON

A Visitor's Companion

SLOW WALKS
IN
LONDON

A Visitor's Companion

MICHAEL LEITCH

HarperPerennial

A Division of HarperCollinsPublishers

AKNOWLEDGMENTS

My thanks to members of many official bodies for help and information during my researches, in particular the London Tourist Board, London Transport, the Diocese of London, National Westminster Bank, and the Taxi Drivers' Association.

I am grateful to my late father for the opportunity to recirculate some of the remarks about London life in the first half of this century. Were he available to be asked, he would no doubt swear that all were true and faithful accounts.

A more general thank-you to the following for their advice and stimulating company at various stages in the book's evolution: Daisy Leitch and all at Reighton Road, Clapton; the duck-feeders of Kensington Gardens; the guides to Highgate Cemetery, and dutiful policemen and security guards everywhere, especially those who announced themselves with a tap on the shoulder and the perceptive opener, "Excuse me, sir, you seem to be taking notes."

Thanks also to Nora Harragin for her accurate and rapid feats with word processor and disk.

First published in Great Britain by Hodder & Stoughton.

HarperCollins books may be purchased for educational, business, or sales promotional use. For information, please call or write: Special Markets Department, HarperCollins Publishers, Inc., 10 East 53rd Street, New York, NY 10022. Telephone: (212) 207-7528; Fax: (212) 207-7222.

FIRST HARPERPERENNIAL EDITION

Library of Congress Cataloging-in-Publication Data
Leitch, Michael.
  Slow walks in London / Michael Lietch.
    p. cm.
  Includes index.
  ISBN 0-06-273101-7
  1. London (England)—Description—1981- —Guide-books.
  2. Walking—England—London.   I. Title.
DA679.L57 1992   91-55383

914.21
LEITCH
1992

92 93 94 95 96 ◆/MB 10 9 8 7 6 5 4 3 2 1

Ingram 4/12/93 13 00/7.54

CONTENTS

History notes; Transport – Underground, buses, trains, taxis; Telephones; Money and coaches; Opening times; List of public holidays; Clothing sizes; Watering holes; Toilets; What's on/further information; London by night; Quick London.

WELCOME!

Welcome to *Slow Walks in London*. I was born in London during the Second World War and spent the first thirty-three years of my life here. In the various conditions of schoolboy, student, bachelor, married man and novice father, I lived in flats and houses in West Kensington, Peckham Rye, Notting Hill, Chelsea, South Kensington, St John's Wood, Chiswick and St Margarets, Twickenham. For varying periods I worked in shops and offices in Oxford Street, Knightsbridge, the Strand, Fleet Street, Blackfriars and Covent Garden . . . and still do not feel overqualified to write about so vast a place.

Perhaps I am no worse than typical. Londoners tend to have amazing expertise about the district they live in, its back alleys and bus routes, and where they can buy a lettuce after dark. Then they stray into a neighbouring district – and they are lost. And yet, for all the missing pieces in their picture of the city, they are still Londoners.

This book is intended as much for them as it is for the visitor from afar. I hope it will encourage anyone who lives in London to go out and ferret in fresh quarters. London is filled with surprising corners, all waiting for the walker to look them up. For me, this time round, the hidden Georgian streets of Spitalfields were a particular delight, as was the bizarre switch from riding the ultra-modern robot railway through Docklands, to treading the murky Foot Tunnel that slopes under the Thames to Greenwich.

In the Topography section of the London Library there are yards of books about London, though not, let me suggest, one quite like this. Many other writers have walked the streets and reported on what they saw. My aim is similar, but behind the commentary I have tried to do something else: to unravel the city for visitors and residents in a way that is concise, illuminating and enjoyable.

Although maps can tell us much, the view at street level is a very different picture, and this has been my starting point. For newcomers and occasional visitors, often with limited time to spare, London has a dizzying range of things to see and do. How, though, to connect them up in the most interesting way possible? In this book, staying in one locality for each walk, I have pieced together twenty-four London routes which work gradually from Palace A to Tower B and also take in that special row of shops, that fascinating museum just down the steps and round the corner, and try to pass the doors of the most salubrious café or pub in the neighbourhood. In addition, eight walks cover the best to be seen in Windsor and Hampton Court, beside the sea at Brighton, in the university cities of Oxford and Cambridge, in the quiet rurality of Stratford-upon-Avon (well, perhaps it's not so quiet in the high season), and in the beautiful city of Canterbury.

Relax and take your time. The routes are planned and you have only to follow them. Some require just a few hours, others last all day, but none should be too taxing on the feet. London is very large and needs to be taken slowly, one piece at a time. It's a city for tortoises, not hares.

And good luck.

LONDON FROM A WALKER'S EYE VIEW

This section is a brief reminder for visitors about the advantages of being warm and comfortable throughout the day or however long you are away from your hotel or home base.

Britain is a nation of sixty million weather forecasters who retain their sanity by accepting that they will be right about as often as Halley's comet passes overhead. It is best to err on the side of pessimism. When the headlines in the tabloids scream, 'Phew, what a scorcher!' view this as proof that you will need a medium to heavy sweater. If the weather does turn warm, you can always tie the extra layer round your neck or waist.

Regard rain as a more or less constant threat. The most efficient means of keeping dry while walking around town is beneath the canopy of a folding umbrella. They are so much lighter and less bulky than raincoats – if you can get away without a coat.

Today I have been giving serious thought to what I shall wear tomorrow when I go to the Test match at Lord's. It is the 19th of June, it has rained every day for a fortnight and we are still running the central heating twice a day. Sitting in the open beneath Old Father Time for seven or eight hours is unlikely to do much for my suntan. I opt for a heavy sweater, corduroy trousers and a waterproof coat. The weather even influences my picnic selection: rather than cold beers, I shall take a bottle of fortifying red wine.

Here is a universal rule, as valid in Rome or Moscow as it is in London: very simply, look after your feet. Blisters are the curse of the slow-walking classes. Always wear strong, flexible, non-pinching shoes, preferably with soles and heels that give a little as they meet the pavement.

Some kind of bag is a good idea. I prefer the sort you can hang on yourself and more or less forget about. Use it to carry: the folding umbrella; camera and extra films; Travelcard; street map; notebook and pen, and, of course, your copy of *Slow Walks in London*.

Security These days it seems obligatory to add a warning about pickpockets and general security. London is not, by European standards, a particularly difficult or dangerous place, though visitors should be at least as vigilant as they are in their home town or nearest city. (Sometimes it is the 'I'm on holiday' tendency to loosen up that encourages a thief to fancy his chances.) Thieves and bagsnatchers are most active in crowded shopping streets, of which Oxford Street is the most notorious. Be wary also in Tube stations and on crowded trains.

Women with handbags on a long strap do well to wear the strap over the head and across the body with the flap or opening turned to face inward. The holster bag is now gaining in popularity. Designed to be worn under a coat or jacket and to fit beneath the arm, it may turn out to be the best deterrent yet against casual thieving.

Almost needless to say, leave good jewellery at home in a secure place. If you like to glitter, London teems with glamorous opportunities in paste, on sale anywhere from market stalls in Petticoat Lane to boutiques in South Molton Street.

THE GEOGRAPHY OF LONDON

London is undoubtedly big, the biggest city in Europe. Close to seven million people inhabit Greater London, and the Piccadilly Line of the Underground is 65km (40.5 miles) long from Heathrow Airport in the west to Cockfosters on the edge of North London.

By the Middle Ages London had two centres—the City, the original Square Mile enclosed by its wall, and Westminster, where in the eleventh century Edward the Confessor built his palace and founded an abbey church. The two centres were linked by the Strand, to the north of which lay open fields.

The first stone version of London Bridge was begun in 1176. It remained Central London's only bridge until 1738. On the south bank, Southwark became a thriving village with a reputation for theatres and arenas for bull and bear-baiting. Since Shakespeare's day and particularly after the railway arrived in 1836, South London has expanded into a vast and largely anonymous residential zone extending to the Kent and Surrey countryside which roughly begins after such places as Bromley, Coulsdon and Epsom.

North of the river, an important exodus from the City occurred after the Plague and Great Fire of 1665–6. The well-to-do hastened west and Charles II allocated land for building around Piccadilly, to the west of Charing Cross. This is now the centre of what is generally called the West End, which also covers the districts of Mayfair, Soho and Covent Garden.

Further west, the rural parish of Kensington attracted a new wave of residents when William III moved into Kensington Palace in 1689. Later it was developed rapidly in the first half of the nineteenth century. After the Great Exhibition of 1851 South Kensington became the chief museum centre in London.

Its southern neighbour is Chelsea, which grew steadily once the Royal Hospital was begun in 1682, and in the next century more and more streets and houses appeared on the Sloane-Cadogan estate. Upstream along the Thames, fishing villages at Hammersmith and Chiswich were absorbed by the expanding city.

Much the same happened to the north of the West End. Regent's Park was created by John Nash in the 1820s, and developers worked uphill to the villages of Hampstead and Highgate, neighbours across the broad expanse of Hampstead Heath.

The East End begins at Aldgate Pump, near one of the six original gates to the City of London. Beside the Thames it includes the old wharves and docks at Wapping, Limehouse and the Isle of Dogs, this last a long peninsula currently in the throes of massive redevelopment. London's shipping trade is now mostly handled downriver at the container terminal at Tilbury.

Maps A map of the Underground system is essential for getting around London, particularly since all the walks in this book originate at Underground stations. You can obtain the Underground map free of charge at any Underground station. The Route map for each walk carries details of the surrounding streets and should be a sufficient guide. For a general overview, newsvendors and bookshops sell a variety of folding maps and books of maps. One that is particularly easy to follow, thanks in part to its clever use of colour, is the indexed *London A–Z Street Atlas*, published by Geographers' A–Z Map Co.

Finding your way around may seem confusing at first, and using a street atlas with an index is one of the quickest ways to establish precisely where you are. Unless you have wilfully strayed to get away from main roads, a bus route will seldom be far off. The Tube network is broad and runs into almost every district except for most of South-East London, which is anyway criss-crossed with suburban railway lines feeding into the central termini. For further information about transport, see pages 376–8.

THE WALKS

Each Slow Walk opens with a Summary, then a Map and Route guide with street-by-street instructions, beginning at an Underground station. The essay which follows is suitable for reading either before you set off, as a form of briefing, or afterwards as a record.

The following symbols are used, mainly in the Route sections:

👁   Special visit recommended

⊖   Underground station

⇌   British Rail station

🏹   Suitable for a rainy day.

The following abbreviations are used in the Route sections:

N, NE, E, etc., to indicate directions

14C   Fourteenth century

All maps are drawn from north to south.

Walk 1

Piccadilly and St James's

The best of everything that money can buy – from potted meats to a beautiful hat. Window-shop in glittering arcades, visit Fortnum & Mason, Hatchards bookshop, an art show at the Royal Academy. See St James's Palace, the ducks in the Park, and the Georgian retreats of Clubland.

Allow   4-5 hours.

Best times   Not Sunday, when shops and arcades closed.

ROUTE

Begin at ⊖ Piccadilly Circus. Take 'Lower Regent Street' exit to **Eros statue**. Cross to Regent Street and take 3rd left into Vigo Street to Albany Lodge. Return to Regent Street, turn right and go through next arch into Swallow Street, then left into Vine Street and right to Piccadilly.

Cross to **St James's Church** and enter. At exit, turn left to Hatchards bookshop and Fortnum & Mason. Cross to Burlington House and **Royal Academy** ☜; open 10.00 to 18.00 (last tickets 17.30), closed Good Friday, 24-26 December. *Admission*.

Return to Piccadilly and turn right to Burlington Arcade. Walk through to Burlington Gardens and turn left to Old Bond Street, then left and right through Royal Arcade to Albemarle Street. Turn left and continue across Piccadilly to St James's Street. At foot, turn left round **St James's Palace** into Marlborough Road and cross The Mall to St James's Park.

Walk down to bridge and turn left. Bear left towards exit opposite Duke of York Steps. Go up steps to Waterloo Place and turn right into Pall Mall, then left through **Royal Opera Arcade** to Charles II Street. Turn left and keep straight on to St James's Square.

Turn right in square and exit up Duke of York Street to Jermyn Street. Turn left and then right through Princes Arcade to Piccadilly.

Walk ends here. Nearest refreshments in Red Lion pub, Duke of York Street, or The Gallery café in Simpsons, overlooking Jermyn Street. Nearest ⊖ Piccadilly Circus.

Piccadilly Circus

The great magnetism of this oddly shaped and perpetually overflowing junction is almost universal. If London were a country, then Piccadilly Circus would be its capital, the meeting-place not so much of fashion and culture as of people, the crowds of ordinary citizens who have flocked here to celebrate victories and festivals – and during the nights of the Blitz felt safer on the deep platforms and escalators of the Tube station than anywhere else. Each night up to four thousand came here with their blankets and pillows.

To follow the story of Piccadilly and its circus, stand beside the Eros fountain and look east towards Leicester Square and the crossroads where Coventry Street and Haymarket meet. This was the first part of

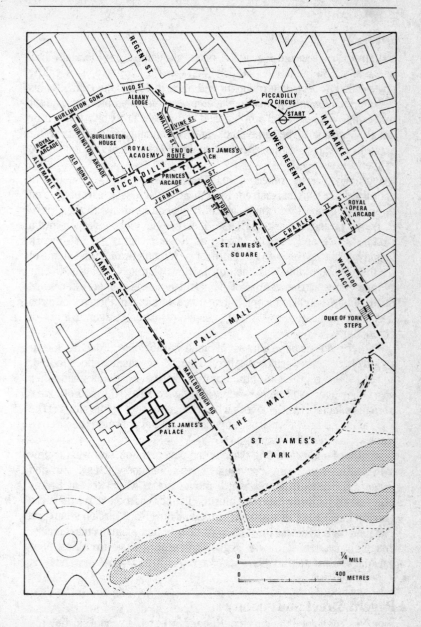

the street to be called Piccadilly, taking its name from Piccadilly Hall which stood on the north side. The hall was the property of a wealthy tailor called Robert Baker who moved there in 1612. One source of his fortune had come from making lace collars known as pickadils, and it was some waggish local who applied the name, probably to mock or irritate Mr Baker. The name stuck, and its meaning broadened to cover first the crossroads, then the road running west out of London on the 'waye to Readinge'.

Piccadilly Circus received its present shape in the nineteenth century. In 1819 John Nash cut Regent Street across it, part of his plan to unite Regent's Park, then called Marylebone Park, with the Prince Regent's palace at Carlton House. The crossing was enlarged into a circular space and became known as Regent Circus. In 1887 work began on carving the path of Shaftesbury Avenue through the slums of southern Soho to link with the equally new Charing Cross Road. This avenue, now at the centre of Theatreland, was named after Lord Shaftesbury the philanthropist. The 'Eros' fountain in Piccadilly Circus was also dedicated to 'Antony Ashley Cooper, Seventh Earl of Shaftesbury'.

Rather than sculpt an earnest likeness of the noble lord in frock coat and trousers, the sculptor Alfred Gilbert designed a fleet-footed, angelic figure representing the spirit of charity. Londoners had other ideas, however, and began calling the figure Eros (the god of love), perhaps mindful of all the lovers who arrange to meet on the steps of the fountain. The arrival of Eros, unveiled in 1893, confirmed the circus's place as the 'heart of the Empire'.

Another famous meeting-place is the pavement outside what is now Tower Records. Many previous generations knew it as Swan and Edgar's department store, which moved there when Regent Circus was first developed; the store closed in 1982. On the north side is the London Pavilion, originally a music hall and now Rock Circus, telling the story of rock and pop through wax figures and animatronics. Tacky images of Madonna, Bowie, Jagger and others wave from first-floor balconies. Time to move on.

Regent Street and Albany

John Nash designed the curve of Regent Street as a way of skirting the fashionable streets of St James's to the south. The Quadrant, as it is known, turns gracefully past the Café Royal on the convex north side and the sturdy colonnade by Air Street. The original Nash Quadrant included a broad colonnade on either side where shoppers could walk under cover; the roofs of the colonnades formed broad balustraded balconies for the lodgings above the shops. After the First World War the colonnades were removed to make the street wider, and the present scheme was finished in 1927.

Many of the shops are currently to let, though at the end of the curve Austin Reed and Aquascutum maintain their rivalry as outfitters to the still-solvent bourgeoisie. Beyond Aquascutum, Garrard 'the Crown Jewellers' usually have some stunning pieces in the window. I was recently mesmerised by a sterling silver statue of Desert Orchid, that beautiful grey steeplechaser of the 1980s, about to leap a fence. It was amazingly large, dwarfing the jewelled clocks and silver fish sets.

In Vigo Street the tailoring grows more exclusive: above the fluted wooden doorway of Gieves and Hawkes are three Royal Appointment shields. They are not the last of these sought-after badges that we shall see today.

Facing the top of Savile Row is Albany Lodge, set between the shop fronts of the Burlington Gallery. A very smooth gentleman in a tweed suit arrives, runs a plastic card through the security lock and vanishes inside the exclusive bachelor haven, composed of sixty-nine sets or chambers which Henry Holland created in 1803 from an earlier mansion known as Melbourne House. A long list can be compiled of the eminent politicians, actors and writers who have lived there, women as well as men: Dame Edith Evans and Margaret Leighton no less than Byron, Edward Heath and Terence Stamp.

In Swallow Street, pass Bentley's Seafood Restaurant and turn into Vine Street, best known from its position on the Monopoly gameboard. Continue past The Vine, a favourite watering hole – or step inside for a few minutes. I like its carpeted and panelled warmth, the reliefs of grape pickers behind the bar and the marvellous sports cartoons of Roy Ulyett which surround the room. In its way The Vine is the ultimate lounge bar, peopled at midday and after work by well-heeled commuters sporting regimental ties, managers and buyers from the smart local shops, women in twos and threes who might not go by themselves into an ordinary pub, and always one or two swarthy men in camelhair overcoats, big rings smouldering on their fingers.

Along Piccadilly

Cross Piccadilly at the nearby traffic lights. On the left is the elegant stratified front (1936) of Simpson Ltd, mainly known for classic menswear. Ahead is the fine parish church of St James's Piccadilly, designed by Wren and consecrated in 1684.

It has long been a fashionable church, a place of smart weddings and memorial services. Its history, and that of the surrounding streets, goes back to the Great Fire of 1666, and the Great Plague which preceded it. The well-to-do fled west to the healthier undeveloped lands beyond Charing Cross and King Charles II parcelled out land for building. Much of the land south of the 'waye to Readinge' was awarded to Henry Jermyn, Earl of St Albans, who built squares and streets such as St James's Square, Jermyn Street and Ryder Street. In 1940 the church was severely damaged in a bomb raid which brought down the steeple and one of the bells fell, eerily ringing, into the churchyard. Restoration was completed in 1954.

Enter through the Garden of Remembrance, dedicated to the courage of Londoners during the Second World War. The church has many artistic associations: William Blake was baptised here, and references to the church may be found in the writings of John Evelyn, Daniel Defoe and Sir John Vanbrugh. Wren designed the light and airy galleried interior so that 2,000 people could hear the service and see the preacher – a considerable innovation. The architect presumed it was 'the most capacious, with those qualifications, that hath yet been built'. There are notable works by Grinling Gibbons: the limewood altar carvings, the figures on the organ case and the white marble font (north aisle, beneath the gallery). A further attraction are the lunchtime recitals, currently on Thursday and Friday at 13.10.

Continue in Piccadilly past the headquarters of BAFTA (British Academy of Film and Television Arts), then the entrance to Princes Arcade, and arrive soon at Hatchards, Booksellers to Her Majesty the Queen: comfortable, spacious, large stock, knowledgeable staff – despite recent enlargements a visit to Hatchards still feels like shopping in an eighteenth-century house.

Into the eau-de-nil chandeliered and carpeted sumptuousness of

Fortnum & Mason, Grocers and Provisional Merchants to Her Majesty the Queen, established 1707. Follow your nose past chocolates and preserves, teas and coffees from every exotic location. Downstairs at the back a patient queue forms at lunchtime for seats in the Fountain Restaurant. Who goes upstairs at Fortnum's? They have many other departments devoted to millinery, lingerie, menswear and so on, but all the world seems transfixed by the potted charms of Gentleman's Relish and the glass jars of candied fruits on the ground floor.

From palate to palette. Cross the road to Burlington House and the Royal Academy. The courtyard is also the home of other learned societies – the Geological Society, Linnaean Society, Royal Astronomical Society, Society of Antiquaries. At its centre is Alfred Drury's statue of Sir Joshua Reynolds, the first President of the Royal Academy.

Founded in 1768, the Academy moved here in 1868 after periods in Pall Mall, Somerset House and the National Gallery building. The house is one of the great mansions which rose on the north side of Piccadilly in the 1660s. Under the Third Earl of Burlington, who built Chiswick House (see *Walk 24*), it was rebuilt about 1717 in the Palladian style by Colen Campbell. The large Italianate blocks on Piccadilly followed around 1870, and Sydney Smirke added a controversial third storey to the house in 1872 and exhibition galleries and schools in the gardens on the north side. There are regular special exhibitions in the seventeen main galleries, and an annual Summer Exhibition which has been a great social occasion for two hundred years. To see the new Sackler Gallery, opened in 1991, take the thin glass lift to the second floor, where a cool and airy glass-walled gallery has been cleverly inserted between the old buildings.

The Burlington Arcade is the best known of the luxury shopping arcades in and around Piccadilly, and was designed in 1819. Here shops sell cashmere by the hundredweight, silk shirts and pyjamas, monogrammed velvet slippers, jewellery, fine tobacco requisites, and singular items such as a shaving brush in pure badger, a silver camel or a bone china guardsman.

At the top is Cork Street, famous for art galleries. Turn left to the junction of Old and New Bond Street. The older part dates from the 1680s, when Sir Thomas Bond and other speculators acquired the land and built four new streets – Bond Street, Stafford Street, Dover Street and Albemarle Street. The development of New Bond Street followed in the 1720s. Famous international fashion names abound: Tiffany stands in Old Bond Street, next to Boucheron in New. Turn left past Loewe, Chanel and Gucci, and cut through Royal Arcade to Albemarle Street. Up on the right is Brown's Hotel, celebrated for its teas. Down on the left is Stafford Street, where the first Goat Tavern was built in 1686. The present house is recent (1958) and at lunchtime is crowded with separate schools of antique dealers and cockney clerical workers. The bar is sound on simple food, such as sausage and chips or a ploughman's lunch.

St James's Street and Palace

St James's Street is one of the two principal arms of Clubland, the other being Pall Mall. As such its best buildings are out-of-bounds to the ordinary public, though we may admire the superb central window of Boodle's at No.28 (John Crunden, 1776) which faces Henry Holland's Brooks's Club on the corner of Park Place. Also here are White's, at Nos 37-38, and the Carlton at No.69. Other clubs were once here and have departed, along with the coffee and chocolate houses which enjoyed a grand vogue around 1700.

Halfway down on the left is the Economist Building, three blocks set around a piazza reached by steps from the street. Its date is 1964, and it

is one of the few successful office buildings in London to emerge from that cube-obsessed decade. It is worth looking into the piazza to see the marvellously potty sculptures of bounding hares by Barry Flanagan.

St James's Street is home to some of London's most distinguished shops. Look for Lobb the bootmakers at No.9, Lock the hatters at No.6 (who devised the bowler as a hard hat for poacher-chasing gamekeepers), and Berry Bros & Rudd the wine merchants at No.3.

Ahead, guardsmen march out from sentry boxes in front of the beautiful small palace which Henry VIII built in mellow red brick on the site of St James's Hospital for 'maidens that were leprous, living chastely'. The gatehouse with flanking octagonal turrets leads to four courts – the Ambassadors' Court, Colour Court, Friary Court and Engine Court, though security requirements limit our viewing of them. After the burning of Whitehall Palace in 1698, St James's Palace was the main royal residence until George III moved to Buckingham House. Mary Tudor died here, and Elizabeth I and James I held court here. Charles I was kept prisoner in the palace before his trial and execution next day in Whitehall. Turn left around the gateway and beneath the arcade to find the Queen's Chapel on the other side of Marlborough Road. When built by Inigo Jones in the reign of Charles I it stood in the gardens of the palace and was the private chapel of Queen Henrietta Maria. In 1661 it was refurnished for Catherine of Braganza, Charles II's new Queen.

The Palace in more recent times has been the setting for several royal marriages, and the diplomatic custom continues of accrediting overseas ambassadors to 'the Court of St James's'. Continue along the open side of Friary Court towards the Mall and St James's Park.

Three other important houses arose within the palace precincts. To the west in Stable Yard is Lancaster House, known until 1912 as York House. The original seventeenth-century structure was rebuilt in 1825 by Benjamin Wyatt for the Duke of York, second son of George III, and now serves for state receptions and entertainments. Opposite is Clarence House, remodelled by John Nash for the Duke of Clarence. When he succeeded to the throne as William IV he continued to live there. It is now the home of the Queen Mother.

On the other side of St James's Palace is Marlborough House, built by Wren in 1709 for the Duchess of Marlborough and decorated with battle scenes from the War of the Spanish Succession. Edward VII lived there when Prince of Wales, and made it a gathering-place for the privileged and fashionable. It is now a Commonwealth centre and home of the Commonwealth Foundation.

St James's Park

To the left along The Mall is Admiralty Arch (1910) leading to Trafalgar Square and, at the far end of the Strand, the City of London, the original centre. To the right is Buckingham Palace, home of the monarch since Queen Victoria became the first royal occupant. Ahead across the trees is the tower of Big Ben at the Houses of Parliament. In this sprawling capital city, the physical links between monarchy, state and the business world are seldom so clearly felt as they are in the vicinity of St James's Park.

In the time of Henry VIII, St James's Palace stood outside London, very much a country house in grounds which became this park, surrounded by a wall. Elizabeth I held jousts and tournaments there and James I introduced a menagerie with hawks and camels, a tame leopard presented by the King of Savoy and an elephant from the King of Spain. Charles II extended the park and set about transforming Cowford Pool and the surrounding ponds into The Canal, where he strolled with his courtiers and dogs and fed the ducks. John Nash redesigned the park with the present irregular lake as its focal point. The concrete bridge dates from 1957, a poor replacement for the iron suspension bridge installed a century before.

All around, ducks and geese quack and screech for breadcrumbs and bold squirrels bounce across the grass to claim their share and be photographed. At the eastern end of the Lake is Duck Island. Nearby are the new Cake House, a pointed concrete pavilion, and the knoll where bands play on summer afternoons and evenings.

Turn back to The Mall, facing the brilliant cream range of Carlton House Terrace (1827-32) built by John Nash after demolition of the Prince Regent's palace, Carlton House. It was pulled down to help pay for the enormous costs of building and decorating Buckingham Palace (see *Walk 3*).

At the foot of Duke of York Steps is the Institute of Contemporary Arts (ICA), founded in 1947. Day passes admit visitors to its exhibition rooms, bar and café.

Climb the steps towards the massive column supporting Sir Richard Westmacott's statue of Frederick, Duke of York, second son of George III. As befits a former Commander of the British Army (1795-1809 and 1811-27), the Duke faces the War Office in Whitehall. Next in line is an equestrian figure of Edward VII by Sir Bertram Mackennal (1922).

Pall Mall runs across the end of Waterloo Place. The name comes from pell-mell, a stick-and-hoop game like croquet which Charles II liked to play. The street was laid out in 1661 and has always been fashionable, first as a residential street and then as the seat of many palatial clubs, among them the Athenaeum (here on the left), the Travellers', the Reform, the Royal Automobile Club and the Junior Carlton.

St James's Square

Turn right briefly to Farlow's Tackle Shop ('Suppliers of Fishing Tackle & Waterproof Clothing to HRH Prince of Wales') and enter Royal Opera Arcade, London's first. I think it has not been surpassed, a range of Regency shops, solid and dignified, lit by a chain of domed lights in the low roof. It was designed by John Nash and G.S. Repton and completed in 1817. Of the present shops, Peter Dale's armour collection is a highlight.

At Charles II Street, turn left across Regent Street to St James's Square, one of the principal elements of Henry Jermyn's development plan. It is very large and has seen much change of use, from fashionable residences near St James's Palace to business houses and embassies. Usually some portion is cordoned off while the latest interior-gutting refurbishment takes place. One long-term resident is the London Library in the north-west corner, which in 1991 celebrated its 150th anniversary with a grand drinks party in the gardens, around the statue of William III.

Leave the square by the northern entrance in Duke of York Street. Members of the London Library, business people, bricklayers and customers of the betting shop across the road all frequent the Red Lion at lunchtime, grabbing a square foot of bar space, shouting for beer and hoping the giant sausages and crab sandwiches are still on the menu. The bars glitter with excellent Victorian engraved glass and decorative mirrors. Our walk could well end here, or nearly so. If it must be tea, rather than drinks, then go up to Jermyn Street and in at the rear entrance to Simpson's. Their café, The Gallery, has tables overlooking Jermyn Street and supplies of Danish pastries for the hungry walker.

Finally, stroll westward along Jermyn Street: a chance to survey silk dressing gowns and shirts at Harvie & Hudson, delicious cheeses at Paxton & Whitfield, perfumes at Floris. Return to Piccadilly through Princes Arcade.

Walk 2

Whitehall and Westminster

Walk down Whitehall to see the Horse Guards, Banqueting House, Downing Street and Churchill's Cabinet War Rooms. Visit Westminster Abbey and, when Parliament is in session, follow the mazy progress of a debate in the House of Lords or Commons.

Allow   5-6 hours.

Best times   Monday to Friday.

ROUTE

Begin at ⊖ Charing Cross. At 'Trafalgar Square' exit, emerge by Nelson's Column and cross to Whitehall. Walk down past Treasury building and cross to **Banqueting House** on E side 👁; open 10.00 to 17.00 (last tickets 16.30), closed Sunday, Easter, Christmas week (reopens 2 January) and for special functions. To check, telephone 071-930 4179. *Admission*.

Cross to Horse Guards Arch for **Changing of Queen's Life Guard** 👁; Monday to Saturday 11.00, Sunday 10.00. Walk through arch to Horse Guards Parade and return to Whitehall.

Continue past Downing Street and Cenotaph memorial. Turn right into King Charles Street and at far end go down Clive Steps to **Cabinet War Rooms** 👁; open 10.00 to 18.00 (last tickets 17.15), closed 1 January, 24-26 December. *Admission*.

At exit, turn left along Horse Guards Road and continue through Storey's Gate. Cross Broad Sanctuary to **Westminster Abbey** 👁; *Admission* to Royal Tombs and Poets' Corner, open 09.00 to 16.00, Saturday 09.00 to 14.00, 15.45 to 17.00. Services only on Sunday. Leave by S door to Cloister and visit **Chapter House, Pyx Chamber and Undercroft Museum** 👁; open 10.30 to 16.30, closed 1 January, 24-26 December. *Admission*. Continue through Cloister to Dean's Yard. Turn right and right through gateway into Broad Sanctuary. Walk through gardens between Abbey and St Margaret's Church. Cross road to **Houses of Parliament** 👁; when in session, visit Chamber of either the House of Lords or House of Commons.

On leaving, walk round building to Big Ben. At river, cross Bridge Street to Boadicea statue and walk along Victoria Embankment. Just before Hungerford Bridge, turn left along Northumberland Avenue and 2nd right into Northumberland Street, where Sherlock Holmes pub.

Walk ends here. Nearest ⊖ Charing Cross.

Whitehall

At the head of Whitehall stands Le Sueur's bronze equestrian statue of Charles I, said by many to be London's finest. It was made in 1633 during the king's lifetime but not installed here until 1675, long after his death in 1649. During the Commonwealth (1649-60) it was sold to a brass merchant on condition he destroyed it. The man buried it instead, and at the Restoration the statue was presented to Charles II. The

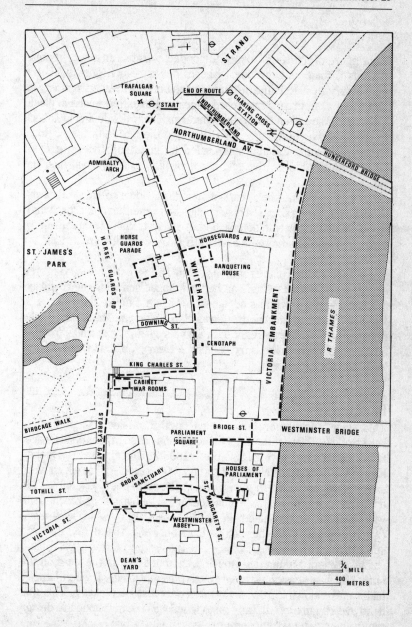

slight figure of the King looks with hooded eyes but an innocent smile towards Banqueting House, where he was beheaded. At the anniversary of his death, 30 January, flowers are placed against the plinth. On 12 February this year, a decaying wreath was still in place.

Cross to the pavement on the Whitehall Theatre side and look back up the slope to see Charles I rising above the façade of the National Gallery, Nelson's Column surrounded by lions and the spire of St Martin's-in-the-Fields, the gold hands of the clock bright against the blue dial.

Until 1931 the northern part of Whitehall, down to Horse Guards, was called Charing Cross, a distant allusion to the Eleanor Cross which stood there until it was demolished in 1647. It was on this medieval route to Westminster that Henry VIII carried out his great plans for Whitehall Palace.

The next section of the road was called The Streete and was entered on this side through a single-arched gatehouse spanning the roadway, the Holbein Gate, with its octagonal towers not unlike the front of St James's Palace, which the King was also building at the time. To the right – where now you see Sir John Soane's columns and frieze fronting Sir Charles Barry's Treasury building – Henry VIII had tennis courts built, and a cockpit.

Banqueting House

This solid block, oddly anonymous on the outside except for the balustrade on the roof, belongs to the second phase of Whitehall Palace, as planned during the reign of James I (1603-25) by Inigo Jones. By then Henry VIII's former Palace had some 2,000 rooms – all of which were later destroyed in a fire in 1698 when, so the story goes, a laundress laid out linen to dry too close to a charcoal fire. The blaze soon reached the wall hangings and engulfed the rest of the Palace, which was made largely of wood. Only the Banqueting House was saved, and this with some difficulty.

The present Banqueting House, begun in 1619, is the third on the site. The first version was 'old, rotten, sleight builded' when James I had it pulled down in 1606 and replaced by a stone building. This was destroyed by fire in 1619 and Inigo Jones was commissioned to design the building you may now enter.

Visitors to the Great Hall are offered an audio tour. It takes such a time to complete, and requires so many arduous gyrations that I am loath to recommend it. The sight of so many outwardly deaf tourists wheeling robotically about the hall also evokes uncomfortable comparisons with the stately masques which Ben Jonson staged here for the King and his Court.

In Stuart times the masque was an elaborate allegory, its purpose to portray the reigning monarchy in a perfect light. Performances continued in the Great Hall until 1635, when Charles I banned them for fear the smoke from the stage lights would damage the new ceiling paintings by Sir Peter Paul Rubens.

Rubens designed and with the help of many assistants painted these scenes on canvases which were fitted into an ornate framework prepared by Inigo Jones. The oval in the centre shows *The Apotheosis of James I*, and to each side are tumbling rows of cherubs rejoicing. The other large panels depict *The Union of England and Scotland* (north) and *The Benefits of the Government of James I* (south).

The principal event in the history of the building was the execution of Charles I. Conducted here from St James's Palace, he was led out through one of the windows on to a scaffold, its platform placed high and surrounded by black cloth so the crowd below would see only the upward rise of the executioner's axe and its sudden fall. However limited the view, one commentator called it 'the saddest sight England ever saw'.

Horse Guards Arch

From the Great Hall of Banqueting House, look through a window to Horse Guards Arch. In Henry VIII's day this area, and the Horse Guards Parade behind it, served as a tilt-yard for jousting. The Arch, built in the Palladian style and completed in 1758, is still the official entrance to the Royal Palaces, and for this reason it is protected by the horsemen of The Queen's Life Guard.

Each morning the New Guard arrives from Hyde Park Barracks at 11.00 (10.00 on Sunday). Two regiments alternately supply the Sovereign's Body Guard; they are the Life Guards and the Blues and Royals. The Life Guards wear scarlet tunics, a white helmet plume, white crossbelts and white leather breeches. The Blues and Royals wear blue tunics and a red helmet plume. Their crossbelts and breeches are also white, and both regiments wear identical steel cuirasses (breast and back plates) and black jackboots. In winter or bad weather they wear red or blue cloaks respectively to cover the rider and protect the haunches of the horse.

In the close confines of the courtyard there is tension as the Old and New Guards form up facing each other, the trumpeters on grey mounts, the other horses shiny black, their flanks gleaming like the boots and harness of the soldiers. A long silence, then a command is shouted, and responded to with piston-like precision. The Corporal-of-Horse posts the two mounted sentries in boxes facing Whitehall. When at last the changeovers are completed, the Old Guard rides out through the Arch and returns at a thoughtful pace along The Mall to Hyde Park Barracks.

Walk through the arch to see the great parade ground where the Sovereign's birthday is marked each year by the ceremony of Trooping the Colour. The palatial building with copper domes on the right is the Admiralty building; next to it is the Citadel, a modern fortress built in 1940 to provide a bomb-proof shelter for Admiralty staff.

Downing Street and Cenotaph

Continue along Whitehall, in Tudor times a narrow way flanked on the east side by Henry VIII's Privy Garden. At the far end of the garden was a gateway, King Street Gate; by the middle of the eighteenth century traffic pressures were too great and this and Holbein Gate were demolished. The road was widened and Whitehall joined up with Parliament Street, the end section which runs into Parliament Square. On each side are Government buildings. After Gwydyr House (the Welsh Office) the eastern prospect is dominated by the huge and bleak Ministry of Defence, a great white slab more suited to Ceaușescu's Bucharest than Whitehall. In front of it stand three of Britain's famous defenders: Field Marshal Slim, Sir Walter Raleigh and 'Monty'.

Downing Street is now screened off by the 'Thatcher Gates', ordered by the former Prime Minister in the interests of security. The street is named after Sir George Downing, a Member of Parliament who in about 1680 built the famous cul-de-sac of terraced houses which include No.10, residence of the Prime Minister, and No.11, where the

Chancellor of the Exchequer lives.

In the centre of Whitehall is the Cenotaph, national monument to 'The Glorious Dead' of both World Wars. It was completed in 1920 to the design of Sir Edwin Lutyens, and each year on the Sunday closest to the original Armistice Day (11 November 1918) wreaths are laid at a service attended by the monarch, senior politicians and members of the armed forces.

Churchill's War Cabinet Rooms

This fascinating museum displays the rooms as they were set out in 1940 for the War Cabinet – 9m (30ft) underground, a warren of chambers protected by a 1m (3ft) layer of reinforced concrete, from which Churchill ran the British end of the Second World War. An audio commentary, more succinct than most, is offered to visitors.

The British Government anticipated early that Hitler would direct an intensive bombing campaign against London, and these rooms were in operation from 27 August 1939. The Cabinet Room, viewed through a glass wall, is an extraordinary sight. On the far side, Churchill sat in the round-backed chair beneath the world map coloured heavily in British Empire pink. His Ministers and Chiefs of Staff sat round him in a tight rectangle of tables covered with blotting pads and metal ashtrays. A few feet above their heads, heavy red-painted girders provided extra support should the floors above collapse. More than a hundred meetings were held here up to the Japanese surrender in 1945. Nearby is a framed photograph of the War Cabinet of 1941: Arthur Greenwood (Minister without Portfolio), Ernest Bevin (Minister of Labour and National Service), Lord Beaverbrook (Minister of Aircraft Production), Sir Kingsley Wood (Chancellor of the Exchequer), Sir John Anderson (Lord President of the Council), Winston Churchill (Prime Minister), Clement Attlee (Lord Privy Seal), Anthony Eden (Secretary of State for Foreign Affairs).

Continue to The Dock, an uncomfortable dormitory for nights spent underground, and in the corridor see the Prime Minister's office, the Map Room and the Transatlantic Telephone Room. This is sparsely furnished with one black telephone on a desk, a candle, an inkstand and a red metal box labelled 'Cigarette Ends'; on the wall is a clock showing transatlantic times. This former broom cupboard was the world's first transatlantic hotline, linking Churchill to President Roosevelt in the White House.

In the Conference Room is a video show, and the tour also visits the BBC's outside broadcast equipment room, the Typing Pool with vintage machines on the desks, other War Map rooms and the Prime Minister's room, where Churchill slept in conditions little grander than an officer's dugout in the First World War.

The museum has a shop, a special access lift and full facilities for the disabled.

Westminster Abbey

The exit delivers visitors on to Horse Guards Road, facing St James's Park and a short stroll from the heart of Westminster. If it is lunchtime, a useful stopping-place is the Westminster Arms in Storey's Gate, with Storey's Wine Bar in the basement.

At the end of Storey's Gate, by the Methodist Central Hall, a broad view of Westminster opens out. Over on the left are the great West towers of the Abbey. To its left is St Margaret's, Westminster, parish church of the House of Commons. Beyond the Abbey are the Houses of Parliament. Closing the square ahead is the yellow stone building of Abbey Sanctuary, leading to Dean's Yard and Westminster School.

Cross Broad Sanctuary to the Abbey. This street takes its name from a tower that stood nearby, in which fugitives from justice could take refuge. It was a precarious right, which the authorities freely abused if they saw fit. In 1623 James I abolished all rights of sanctuary.

More than a thousand years of history are enclosed in Westminster Abbey, the national shrine, although its beginnings are obscure. There was certainly a monastic community here, and presumably a previous church, before Bishop Dunstan founded his community in about 960. A hundred years later Edward the Confessor established his palace at Westminster and set about rebuilding the abbey church, the West Minster, which had fallen into ruins. It was consecrated in 1065.

The building is primarily French Gothic in appearance, and combines elements from many early architectural styles: Saxon, Norman, Early English, Decorated and Perpendicular. In modern times the West towers were designed by Wren and completed by Hawksmoor in 1745, and the Victorian Gothic of Sir George Gilbert Scott is apparent in the restored Chapter House and the north transept.

William I (the Conqueror) was the first monarch to be crowned here, in 1066, and the tradition has continued to this day with hardly a break. The Abbey is rich in tombs and memorials to monarchs and great public figures, extraordinarily so in some of the eastern chapels where five or six kings lie buried almost side by side.

In the towering nave, the highest Gothic vault in England (31m/102ft) is carried on dark piers of Purbeck marble. Near the West door is the Tomb of the Unknown British Warrior, an unidentified body brought back from France and buried here on Armistice Day, 1920. Also commemorated in the nave are Isaac Newton, Winston Churchill, Clement Attlee, Franklin D. Roosevelt.

Bear left to the Musicians' Aisle, past the graves and memorials of Henry Purcell, Ralph Vaughan Williams, William Elgar and Benjamin Britten. Here an admission charge is collected to view the rest of the Abbey along a prescribed route.

To absorb the atmosphere, perhaps take a seat in the Statesmen's Aisle and look around, beneath the benign eye of Benjamin Disraeli or the sterner gaze of William Gladstone. Each hour prayers are said for the needs of the world. Ahead is the fine Lantern crowned by its vaulted roof, completed c.1500. The Choir and High Altar are the focus of Coronations and Royal Weddings; to the left are the imposing tombs of the Earl of Pembroke (d.1324) and Edmund Crouchback, Earl of Lancaster (d.1296). In the south transept is Poets' Corner, which we come to later.

Continue through the Ambulatory. On the left the Chapel of our Lady of the Pew leads to the Chapel of St John the Baptist. Next is the marble tomb of Queen Elizabeth I which she shares with her half-sister Queen Mary Tudor, framed by ten black marble columns inside the grille. At her neck the effigy of the queen wears a pickadil, one of the lace collars which inspired the naming of Piccadilly (see *Walk 1*).

The central chapel at the east end of the Abbey is the Lady Chapel. The banners of the Knights of the Bath hang above the choir stalls, their carved awnings surmounted by helmets and medieval devices: two carnival masks, a boar, a griffin, an elephant and castle. Henry VII and his Queen, Elizabeth of York, are buried behind the altar, as is James I. In front of the altar are the tombs of Edward VI and George II.

Follow the railed walkway to the tomb of Edward the Confessor, founder of the Abbey. Here too is the Coronation Chair made for Edward I; beneath its seat is the Stone of Scone, on which the kings of Scotland were crowned. Nearby are the tombs of five English kings: Henry III, Edward I, Edward III, Richard II and Henry V.

Return to the tomb of Mary Queen of Scots, put to death in 1587. Also buried here are King Charles II, King William III and Queen Mary II, and Queen Anne.

Walk through to Poets' Corner, where many important English writers are remembered: Geoffrey Chaucer, William Shakespeare, Samuel Johnson, Charles Dickens, T.S. Eliot, Gerard Manley Hopkins and Dylan Thomas. Beyond Poets' Corner, St Faith's Chapel is reserved for private prayer.

Cloister

Leave by the South door to the medieval cloister, begun by Henry III in about 1245, where eight abbots are buried. To see the Chapter House and treasures of the Pyx Chamber and Undercroft Museum, turn left through the brass rubbings display and round the next corner. Buy a combined ticket at the Chapter House and walk through to the monks' assembly chamber.

Completed in 1253, this was where the monks assembled each day, sitting on the stone wall benches to hear a reading from the Bible and deal with monastic business. To the displeasure of the monks, the House of Commons moved in here between 1362 and 1395. The room is a broad octagon, apparently founded on a single slim pillar and fan vault, deeply windowed on six sides and above the entrance, the lower walls decorated with now dark biblical scenes, some of them given c.1395 by John of Northampton, a monk of the Abbey, possibly to celebrate the departure of the politicians. Below in the first three bays to the left of the entrance runs a line of animals, variously captioned 'reynder, ro (roe deer), wild asse, tame asse, dromedary, kemeyl'. The beautiful red and gold floor tiles are thirteenth-century; here and there a brighter tile shows up, inserted during nineteenth-century renovations by Sir George Gilbert Scott. In this room are housed the rolls of honour of the Royal Army Medical Corps.

Turn left to the Pyx Chamber and Treasury. Once part of the Undercroft, it became a Royal Treasury guarded by a stout double door with six locks, introduced after a daring burglary in 1303. Standing on the floor is a massive fan-shaped medieval cope chest containing a gold cope of the seventeenth century, and in the showcases a collection of post-Reformation plate.

Of greatest interest in the Undercroft Museum are the funeral effigies. From the thirteenth century to the seventeenth an effigy of the monarch was carved, robed in full coronation regalia and placed on the coffin for the funeral procession or ceremony. Not all have survived, but those that have offer marvellously revealing portraits in the round of the long-dead. Some of the faces were taken from death-masks. The effigy of Edward III (d.1377) has a body of roughly carved wood and a face of plaster fixed to linen. The twist of the mouth on the right side may record a stroke which the king suffered before he died.

Later medieval effigies – those with heads and torsos mounted at living height on steel poles – had hands and heads of wood and a torso, arms and legs made of stuffed canvas or leather. The practice of displaying the royal effigy at funerals was abandoned after 1660, although effigies continued to be made, fashioned with heads and hands of wax which blend high realism with an other-worldly glow from the yellowy-green tinge of the wax. These later figures were placed near the tomb to impress visitors to the Abbey with their regal proximity. Other 'celebrity' figures on show, also made to attract visitors, are Admiral Lord Nelson and the statesman William Pitt the Elder. Today at royal funerals a gilt crown placed on a purple cushion serves to represent the monarch.

At the exit continue ahead through the Cloister. Here two modern plaques commemorate Edmund Halley, the second Astronomer Royal – this in a gold and black comet shape – and the global circumnavigators Sir Francis Drake, Captain Cook, and more recently Sir Francis Chichester.

Go out to Dean's Yard, where pupils of Westminster School pass to and from the school buildings in adjoining Little Dean's Yard. Return to Broad Sanctuary through the arch of Abbey Sanctuary. Pass through the gardens beside St Margaret's, and arrive in front of the Houses of Parliament.

Palace of Westminster

Members of the Houses of Lord and Commons have debated here in separate chambers for some six hundred years. The Palace was built as a royal residence for Edward the Confessor and the monarch and his court remained there until 1530. Then, after the fall of Cardinal Wolsey, that untiring palace-builder Henry VIII abandoned the cramped confines of Westminster for the Cardinal's luxurious complex at York Place, which the king turned into Whitehall Palace. In 1834 a fire destroyed almost all the buildings at Westminster and the present Houses of Parliament date from 1837. They were planned by Charles Barry, who called in Augustus Pugin to originate and supervise the Gothic ornamentation, which he did down to the last inkstand. Severe bomb damage in 1940-1 destroyed the House of Commons and it was rebuilt by Sir Giles Gilbert Scott in the spirit of Barry's design, though the decorative work is less exuberant than Pugin's.

Barry's vast structure is essentially one long building which contains the House of Lords, where the peers and bishops sit, and the House of Commons, the elected chamber, together with their lobbies, a Prince's Chamber, a Royal Gallery and many supplementary rooms. At each end is a famous tower. To the east is the Clock Tower of Big Ben, by which the nation sets the hour, and to the west is the imposing four-square mass of Victoria Tower, rising 122m (400ft) to the top of its flagstaff. At the centre of the building is the 91m (300ft) spire of Middle Tower, its lantern crowning the Central Lobby.

When Parliament is sitting, queues for the public galleries of the Lords and Commons form outside the door immediately across the road. That for the Commons is usually longer, indeed there may be no wait at all to visit Pugin's remarkable Chamber of the House of Lords. Debates there are pursued in a more muted vein than from the bright green benches of the Commons, now a familiar sight to news viewers on television.

Pugin's chamber is majestic. From a seat in the Strangers' Gallery, the eye travels to the Throne at the far end, from which the Queen reads her speech at the annual State Opening of Parliament. In front of the Throne is the Woolsack, where the Lord Chancellor or his deputy conducts the proceedings of the House as its Speaker.

The Government sit on the dark red benches on the left or Spiritual Side of the House, together with the bishops, and the Opposition face them on the Temporal Side. The business of the House can be difficult to follow, as assorted Lords stroll in and out, sit down for a few minutes and then amble off again. The debate continues, then a decision is needed. If it is not clear whether those saying 'Content' have outnumbered those saying 'Not-content' (or vice-versa), a Division is called. The Division bells are rung and the House divides. The 'Contents' file past the Woolsack and through the lobby on the Spiritual Side, and the 'Not-contents' go through on the Temporal Side. All this and more is explained in a useful leaflet given to visitors when they fill in their Strangers' Gallery form on the way in. A visit here is highly recommended, as much for the ordered civility of proceedings as for Pugin's Gothic feast of pinnacles, statues, frescoes, stained glass and panelling.

Back to Charing Cross

The walk could end here, in which case Westminster Tube station is nearby in Bridge Street. If the energy remains, stroll round towards Big Ben and the river. At the head of Victoria Embankment is Thomas Thorneycroft's statue of Queen Boadicea and her daughters (c.1850). Turn along by the boat pier facing the old County Hall building on the far side of the river, and continue past moored barges towards the red and black box frame of Hungerford Bridge carrying trains in and out of Charing Cross Station. Pass the golden eagle atop the Air Forces monument (1923) then the floating restaurants where many a good office party has been held on the *Tattershall Castle*, the *Hispaniola* and others. Our destination is another watering-hole, in Northumberland Street – the Sherlock Holmes, its roomy bar crammed with framed and showcased memorabilia of Sir Arthur Conan Doyle's deerstalker-hatted detective, including a huge bloodhound's head. Upstairs, on the walls of the passage to the dining room, are letters by the author and a drawing of himself as The Old Horse, pulling a cart loaded with copies of his life's work. Look in through a glass door panel to see a reconstruction of Holmes's study at 221b Baker Street. A deerstalker hangs by the door, a black bear rug occupies much of the floor, and on a table are his pipe and magnifying glass surrounded by a dusty clutter of personal belongings. Almost believable.

Walk 3

Queen and Country

> 'They're changing guard at Buckingham Palace -
> Christopher Robin went down with Alice.
> Alice is marrying one of the guard.
> "A soldier's life is terrible hard,"
> Says Alice.'

So wrote A.A. Milne in 1924. The ceremony goes on. When it is over, follow the Old Guard to Wellington Barracks and visit The Guards Museum. Look in at the Queen's Picture Gallery and see the Queen's horses and carriages in the Royal Mews. Finally, a walk through Green Park to Apsley House, former home of the Duke of Wellington, Napoleon's conqueror and national hero.

Allow   5-6 hours.

Best times   Wednesday or Thursday in summer. Look for a day when there is a Guard-changing ceremony *and* the Royal Mews are open (details overleaf).

ROUTE

Begin at ⊖ Green Park. In booking hall turn left and go up to street at sign 'for Buckingham Palace'. In Piccadilly, turn right through gates to Green Park. Walk across park to Queen Victoria Memorial and **Buckingham Palace.**

Queen's Guard is changed at 11.30: 1 May to 12 August, every day; 13 August to 31 March, every other day (to check, telephone London Tourist Board: 071-730 3488). No ceremony when 'very wet'.

Follow Old Guard along Birdcage Walk to Wellington Barracks and visit **The Guards Museum** ◉; open 10.00 to 16.00, closed Friday, 1 January, 24-26 December and certain ceremonial days (to check, telephone 071-930 4466). *Admission.*

Return along Birdcage Walk and bear left beside Palace in Buckingham Gate. Visit **The Queen's Gallery** ◉; open 10.30 to 17.00, Sunday 14.00 to 17.00, closed Monday (except Bank Holidays), Good Friday and Christmas Day. Gallery usually closes between mid January and late March each year (to check, telephone 071-930 4832, ext. 3351). *Admission.*

At exit, turn right to **Royal Mews** ◉; open 12.00 to 16.00: 1 October to 31 March, Wednesday only; 1 April to 11 July, Wednesday and Thursday; 17 July to 30 September, Wednesday to Friday. Opening times subject to alteration (to check, telephone 071-930 4832, ext. 3351). *Admission.*

To visit Apsley House, return to front of Palace and turn left along Horse Ride next to Constitution Hill. At Hyde Park Corner, take pedestrian subway to Exit 10 on island by Constitution Arch, then take Exit 7 to Exit 8 outside **Apsley House** ◉; open 11.00 to 16.50 (last tickets 16.30), closed Monday. *Admission.*

Walk ends here. Nearest refreshments across Knightsbridge at Pizza on the Park (afternoon tea served). Nearest ⊖ Hyde Park Corner.

Green Park and Buckingham Palace

In spring and summer an international crocodile winds downhill through the park, all sections of it heading for the Palace and a view of the most elaborate of the Guard-changing ceremonies. Across Queen's Walk to the left, the sleek mansions of Mayfair glow in the morning sun, and behind luxurious drapes late risers at the Ritz Hotel lift the covers on their first feast of the day.

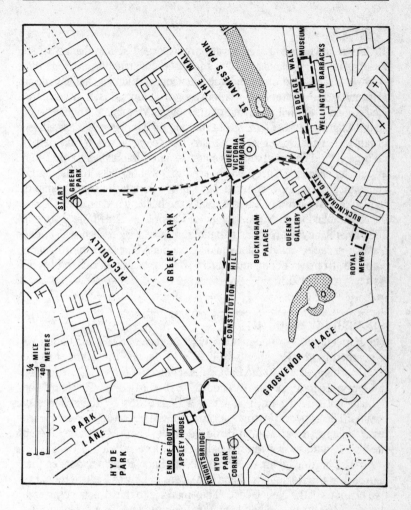

Charles II laid out this broadly sloping Royal Park in 1667, and later it became a popular ground for duellers, highwaymen and public celebrations. At 10.45 each morning the New Guard for Whitehall approaches along Constitution Hill, and to bellowed commands from the Corporal-of-Horse bears past the Queen Victoria Memorial and clops away along The Mall.

This large memorial to Britain's longest-reigning monarch (1837-

1901) was unveiled in 1911. It was part of a grand 'scenic change' which included the landscaping of The Mall, the construction of Admiralty Arch at its eastern end, and the refacing of Buckingham Palace in Portland stone. Queen Victoria, portrayed plump as in her later years, faces along The Mall, watched over by a gilt Victory.

Buckingham Palace grew out of one of George IV's grandiose dreams. He took over Buckingham House, acquired by his father George III in 1762, and in 1819 commissioned John Nash to expand it into a monarch's palace. Nash ran up gigantic bills to the great annoyance of the Government, particularly during the premiership of the Duke of Wellington, but eventually the building had progressed too far to be abandoned. Not until Queen Victoria ascended the throne in 1837 was it anywhere near habitable. Edward Blore had succeeded Nash as architect in 1830 and building continued for many more years. The east front was completed in 1847, and was later refaced by Sir Aston Webb in 1913.

Changing the Guard

The Palace is the permanent London residence of the Royal Family. It is guarded by the Regiments of Foot Guards, and these are changed each morning. At 11.10 the Palace detachment of the Old Guard forms up for inspection in the forecourt, to be joined at 11.15 by the detachment arriving from St James's Palace, led by their Corps of Drums. The two form up together to await the arrival of the New Guard from Wellington Barracks in Birdcage Walk. Five regiments make up the Foot Guards: Grenadier, Coldstream, Scots, Irish and Welsh.

At 11.30, the boom of drums along Spur Road announces the approach of the Regimental Band and Corps of Drums, behind them the two platoons of the New Guard. They march into the forecourt through the North Centre Gate and form up facing the Old Guard. During the next half-hour the action is gradual: the Palace keys are handed over, Ensigns patrol the forecourt and new sentries are posted. At 12.05 the Old Guard slow-marches out of the forecourt, breaks into quick-time and veers away to Wellington Barracks. Then the St James's Palace detachment of the New Guard marches away to its duties, lodging the Regimental Colour in the St James's Palace guardroom. Alone in the forecourt, the Buckingham Palace detachment marches off to its guardroom, ending the ceremony.

Guards' Museum

Follow the Old Guard back to barracks and visit this small museum which opened in 1988. The first Guards regiments came into being during the Civil War. While in exile at Bruges in 1656, Charles II raised His Majesty's Royal Regiment of Guards, known as Wentworth's Regiment after Lord Wentworth, its first Colonel. Within ten years the Royal Guards had precedence over all others.

In the museum see the functions of the various early regiments – the Grenadiers with their bombs, the pikemen of the Coldstreams, a musketeer of the Foot Guards (Grenadiers). Uniforms and memorabilia include the open pages of a Punishment Book and a cat o'nine tails, last used in 1850 on the unfortunate Charles Lacey who received fifty lashes and six months' imprisonment with hard labour. Written in fine copperplate is: 'Return of Killed and Wounded in the Action of Barrosa on the 5th of March 1811'. Examples are on show of early and recent bearskins, the distinctive tall headgear of the Guardsmen. Inside it, the head fits into a leather web of straps forming a skull cap; above this, a wicker frame keeps the bearskin rigid and in battle deflected sword blows.

Display cases recall the role of Guards regiments in the wars of Marlborough, the Napoleonic campaigns, the Crimean and Colonial Wars. By 1914 the glorious red of the tunic had turned to khaki for the static trench fighting. The survey of Guardsmen in action continues up to the Falklands War and will eventually cover the Gulf War.

The Guards' Chapel faces the museum. Dedicated in 1963, it replaced the old 1834 building which was destroyed by a flying bomb in 1944. Only the gilded mosaics of the apse survived and these are incorporated in the new structure.

Near the gate is the Guards' Shop, containing predictable books and souvenirs but where also, for a small donation, you may be photographed wearing a Guardsman's bearskin or a piper's bonnet.

Queen's Gallery

On the south side of Buckingham Palace, reached from Buckingham

Gate, is a former conservatory which in 1962 opened as a gallery showing pictures and treasures from the Royal Collection. Exhibitions are changed each year and run from late March to mid-January.

The recent show about Carlton House, George IV's extravagant London residence before he demolished it in 1827, brimmed over with fine art and fascinating objects. In the main room a vast portrait of George IV by Sir Thomas Lawrence was the dominating work, though not before you had passed a Rembrandt (*The Shipbuilder and his Wife*, 1633); two paintings by Stubbs (*The Prince of Wales's Phaeton*, and *Soldiers of the Tenth Light Dragoons,* both 1793). At the centre of the room were vast displays of gold and silver plate – perhaps recalling the table and room settings in the Royal Pavilion at Brighton (see *Walk 27*) – and round the walls priceless French furniture and clocks, among the latter a Negress Head Clock of 1790 which showed the time in the figure's eyes. At 12.58 the left eye said 'XII', the right eye '58'.

In the upstairs gallery, among the many Sèvres vases, jewelled cups, gold and tortoiseshell snuff-boxes and Oriental weapons was a fine Gainsborough (*Mrs Mary Robinson, c.*1780-1), several good Dutch seventeenth-century interiors and a group of watercolour drawings of interiors of Carlton House. In this Aladdin's cave, peace and orderliness are supervised by strolling attendants dressed in gold-braided top hats and frock coats with a red collar.

Royal Mews

The home of the royal coaches, and the horses that draw them, is announced by the massive pediment of the Riding House which rises above the Palace wall in Buckingham Palace Road. At its heart is an energetic relief of *Hercules Capturing the Thracian Horses*. The Riding House is by Sir William Chambers and dates from 1763-6. The quadrangular Mews, containing the stables and coach houses, is the work of John Nash and was completed in 1825.

From the entrance, go anti-clockwise to the east side where in summer the Gold State Coach is pulled out from beneath its canopy to catch the sun in the courtyard. It is the star of the horse-drawn fleet: made in 1762 for George III, it serves at Coronations and major royal events such as the Silver Jubilee procession to St Paul's Cathedral in 1977. It weighs 9 tons and is built on a framework of gilded palm trees, those at each corner crowned with lion's heads and branching to the central ornament of cherubs supporting the Royal Crown. The sculpted figures at the front proclaim through their conches the approach of the Monarch of the Ocean; those at the rear carry the Imperial *fasces* topped with tridents. Eight grey horses draw the coach, controlled by four postilions.

Continue to the Coach House where other state coaches gleam. The Irish and Australian State Coaches are now used alternately for the State Opening of Parliament. All these and the motor fleet are the responsibility of the Crown Equerry who runs the Royal Mews and organises the royal land transport for state occasions and special engagements.

Next are the stalls of the carriage horses: one line of Windsor greys and one of bays, mainly a modern version of the Cleveland Bay, paraded tail outward for public inspection. Notices warn not to go too close, and horses with a lively reputation are restrained by a strap across the front of the stall. Most are remarkably still and stately. Cardiff, currently the oldest, was born in 1969 and stands beside his younger stablemates Iceland and Barcelona. When visiting time is over, the horses are returned to stables in the next block.

'Lovely in there,' a kindly commissionaire with a remarkably horse-like lower dental arrangement told me. 'They got stables twice as wide as these stalls, and great big beds.' He shivered in the winter cold. 'They're warmer in there 'n what I am at home.'

The Museum/Tack Room is bathed in a warm odour of burnished leather despite the fact that everything on display is behind glass. Among the harnesses and saddles are the first used by the Princesses Elizabeth and Margaret.

The stable next to the bookshop has a further exhibition of small carriages – a pony landau, a donkey barouche, drags and sleighs.

Constitution Hill

If it is lunchtime, cross to Palace Street where the bow-fronted Phoenix pub serves buffet lunches from 12.00, or keep on to wine-bar fare at Carriages or Le Café.

From the front of Buckingham Palace, cross at the foot of Constitution Hill and follow the Horse Ride uphill through Green Park.

Towards the top of the incline, the mansions of Piccadilly converge from the right. Ahead is Constitution Arch (1828), designed by Decimus Burton and surmounted by the *Quadriga*, a weighty bronze group by Adrian Jones erected in 1912. Four prancing horses draw a chariot which a boy strains to control while a wreath-carrying figure of Peace alights behind him.

Apsley House, the London residence of the Duke of Wellington, is the colonnaded mansion in golden stone to the right, across the swirling traffic of Hyde Park Corner. On the island, pass the Machine Gun Corps monument by Francis Derwent Wood (1925). Nearby, J.E. Boehm's equestrian statue of the Duke of Wellington points at Apsley House. The plinth is guarded by soldiers of the four home nations: the 1st Guards, 42nd Royal Highlanders, 23rd Royal Welsh Fusiliers, 6th Inniskilling Dragoons.

Beyond the Wellington statue is the powerful First World War monument to the Royal Regiment of Artillery, its focus a rock-like stone howitzer.

Apsley House, The Wellington Museum

The Battle of Waterloo finished Napoleon and, for the time being, the French Army. The cost was appalling. The British lost a quarter of their force, 7,000 out of 28,000. Total Anglo-Dutch losses were 13,500 out of 69,000. Their Prussian allies lost 7,000 out of 70,000. The French lost more than 20,000 out of 71,000. It was the battle of giants needed to change the future of Europe, but no-one was more aware of the price of victory than the Allied Commander, the Duke of Wellington, who afterwards said that only a defeat was worse than winning.

It is the narrowness of the victory which helps to explain Apsley House and its contents. Although the Duke's military career had been thoroughly distinguished in earlier campaigns in India and the Spanish peninsula, Waterloo was the crowning achievement and this house bears witness to the tributes poured on the new national hero. The Duke went on to serve in high Government office, and was Prime Minister from 1828 to 1830. When he died in 1852, aged 83, one and a half million people lined his funeral route from Horse Guards to St Paul's Cathedral.

Apsley House was already in the Duke's family, the Wellesleys, when he bought it in 1817. It became his London residence and the address was nicknamed 'No.1 London'. In 1947 the Seventh Duke presented the house to the nation and it opened in 1952 as the Wellington Museum.

On the ground floor is the Plate and China or Muniment Room. Here are the Prussian Service of Berlin porcelain, originally of 420 pieces, presented to the Duke by King Frederick William III of Prussia; the Duke's orders, decorations and medals; a sword and dagger case including the court sword with three scabbards taken from Napoleon's carriage after the Battle of Waterloo. In the opposite corner from the door is the Duke's death mask. The largest single pieces are the silver-gilt candelabra and shield presented in 1816 and 1822 by the Merchants and Bankers of the City of London.

All through the house are paintings and sculptures, many of them given to the Duke or bought by him. Many others came from Joseph Bonaparte's hoard stolen from the Spanish Royal Collections. After the Battle of Vitoria (1813) Joseph was fleeing the field when a squadron of British hussars chased down his coach. On board were more than 165 paintings, cut from their frames and stretchers. The King of Spain allowed the Duke to keep his loot which, as a Spanish diplomat wrote, 'has come into your possession by means as just as they are honourable'.

An elegant staircase spirals upstairs past the colossal 'Graeco-Roman' statue of Napoleon Bonaparte by Antonio Canova. Originally commissioned by Napoleon in 1801, the 3.44m (11ft 4in) nude figure arrived at the Louvre in 1811 where it was kept behind screens because it was thought an embarrassment to the Emperor, who disliked the way the winged Victory in his right hand appeared to be flying away from him. The British Government enjoyed the joke and in 1816 bought the statue from Louis XVIII for 'less than £3000' and presented it to the Duke of Wellington.

To the left at the landing is a collection of mainly Dutch paintings including, in a row, *The Smokers* by Adriaen Brouwer, *A Musical Party* by Pieter de Hooch and *The Physician's Visit* by Jan Steen. Continue to the mirrored Waterloo Gallery with ornate gilded ceiling. Lift the cover of the portfolio on its stand to see Joseph Nash's 1852 picture of the Gallery laid out for a Waterloo Banquet, one of a series of reunions held by the Duke on Waterloo Day, 18 June, from 1830 to 1852.

The portfolio stands next to a famous Goya portrait of *Arthur Wellesley, First Duke of Wellington, on Horseback*. Above the nearby fireplace is a delicate *River Scene with Boars and Figures* by 'Velvet' Brueghel (Jan the Elder). Above the fireplace are three more landscapes by the same artist and nearby a *Pope Innocent X* ascribed to Velázquez. Above the main fireplace is an anonymous copy of the *Charles I on Horseback* by Sir Anthony Van Dyck which hangs in Windsor Castle.

Of battle paintings there are few, save in the next room which has the great panorama of Waterloo by Sir William Allan, recording the scene at 7.30 pm as the French Imperial Guard made its last desperate advance. Above it are portraits of four of Wellington's key commanders at Waterloo: Lords Hill, Somerset and Picton and Sir Henry Willoughby Rooke.

In the Dining Room is the astonishing plate used at the Waterloo Banquets, dominated by the silver-gilt Portuguese centrepiece crowded with metal palm trees, bundles of spears and running figures. Those June nights must have been heroic occasions.

Consider these manifestations of national pomp and power over a quiet cup of tea at Pizza on the Park, and maybe stroll down to Knightsbridge for a look at the shops. Harvey Nichols, a fashion leader, is not far away. And around the bend in Brompton Road is Harrods, visited in *Walk 18*.

Walk 4

Mayfair

A promenade through London's most exclusive residential quarter: grand houses and broad streets backed by a sustaining hinterland of mews and coach-houses. Window-shop among the boutiques, galleries and auction rooms of New Bond Street and stroll through Berkeley Square to the secluded maze of Shepherd Market, site of the original May Fair.

Allow   2-3 hours.

Best times   Not Sunday, when shops closed.

ROUTE

Begin at ⊖ Marble Arch. From pedestrian subway take Exit 3 to see the **Marble Arch** and return to subway, taking Exit 2 to arrive at top of Park Lane.

Facing S, take 1st left into North Row and 1st right along Dunraven Street (Lillie Langtry's house on site of No.19). Turn left into Green Street and continue to end. Facing battered remains of St Mark's, until 1976 the American Church in London, turn right along North Audley Street to Grosvenor Square.

The square has many **American connections** in addition to the Embassy building on W side. See statues of Eisenhower and Roosevelt and walk along N side to No.9 in NE corner, where John Adams lived.

Continue along Brook Street, turn right into Davies Street, passing Three Kings Yard on right. At Grosvenor Street turn left, where good coffee and croissants at Chalet Coffee Lounge, and continue to **New Bond Street**. Turn right past de-luxe outfitters and Sotheby's auction house, then right into Bruton Street (showrooms for guns, paintings and Rolls-Royces).

At **Berkeley Square**, cross gardens to far side and turn left. Keep on into Fitzmaurice Place which joins Curzon Street. Continue past Third Church of Christ Scientist to premises of Geo. F. Trumper, Court Hairdresser & Perfumer. Cross road and go through arch at No.47 to **Shepherd Market**.

Wander round shops and maybe stop to eat at one of the many restaurants, pubs and wine bars, Tiddy Dols the most famous. Walk ends here. Continue along White Horse Street to Piccadilly. Nearest ⊖ Green Park.

Marble Arch

For Londoners today, Marble Arch summons the picture of a nerve-jangling traffic circus, fearsome to negotiate. For Londoners in Hogarth's day, this was Tyburn, the chief place of public execution for some four hundred years until 1783. The condemned were driven in by cart and strung up on one of the top beams of a triangular gallows. The cart drove off and left them dangling, to the loud gratification of the surrounding mob and, of course, the nobs and wealthier necrophiles who watched from a special grandstand. Today the only reference to those gruesome days is Tyburn Way, the name of the road cutting

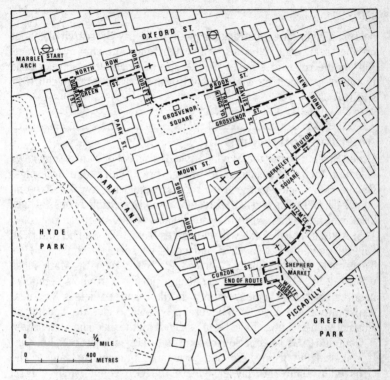

through the central island.

Marble Arch is modelled on the Arch of Constantine in Rome. It was designed by John Nash and set up in front of Buckingham Palace in 1827, then moved here in 1851 to stand in alignment with Park Lane and Cumberland Place. Its sooty elevations are indeed of marble, its eight columns decorated with florid capitals.

Across the road, at the edge of Hyde Park, is Speakers' Corner. Here all who wish to may sound their views, and usually do so on Sunday afternoon. The important principle behind the often loony rhetoric, namely the right to assemble here and demonstrate peacefully, was first recognised in 1872.

Park Lane defines the western boundary of Mayfair and has many elegant houses, immediately visible in the bow-fronted range after North Row. These are set back from the road and have their entrances in Dunraven Street. However fashionable, Park Lane is also very noisy, an eight-lane racetrack for most of the day. In search of calmer prospects, turn into North Row and right again into Dunraven Street. Across the road, at a house on the site of No.19, the actress Lillie Langtry – and well-known friend of Edward VII – lived between 1877 and 1880.

American Connections

Green Street typifies the Mayfair style of discreet opulence: long rows of silent Victorian mansions in orange brick with stone dressings. Behind rich drapes in the front rooms, candelabra twinkle. No-one comes or goes. The end of the street is closed by a gabled house in dark brick which stands next to the sad remains of the American Church.

St Mark's, North Audley Street, dates from 1825-8. The American Church moved away in 1976 and holds its services at Whitefield's Tabernacle in Tottenham Court Road. Since then St Mark's has wallowed in redundancy, its crumbling portico a tramp's refuge of huddled morning bodies, empty bottles and nameless puddles. Apparently there have been several proposals to give the building an alternative use, but all have been rejected by the planning authorities.

Continue to Grosvenor Square, one of the largest squares in London. It was laid out from 1725 and forms the principal holding of the Grosvenor Estate in Mayfair, where the Grosvenor family control some one hundred acres. Although the square remains a top-notch address, its sheer vastness gives it a chilly atmosphere, and the central gardens are distinctly lacking in charm. Perhaps the residents set too high a price on peace and privacy, mindful no doubt of those disquieting days when anti-Vietnam War protesters came in their thousands to demonstrate outside the US Embassy.

American connections with this square go back as far as US independence, though the present Embassy is fairly recent, completed in 1960. It spans the west side of the square and is fairly offensive to look at: the Capitalist version of a Totalitarian fortress, its different ethic symbolised by the lavish application of metallic gold facings, guaranteed to grate on any observing eye. Then there is the eagle, that dreadful attention-seeking bird, a feathered jumbo jet of a beast which squats on the Embassy roof.

If there is a humanising element in this part of the square, it comes from the statue of Dwight Eisenhower by Robert Dean, presented by the residents of Kansas City, Missouri, in 1989. It is intended to commemorate both D-Day (1944) and Eisenhower's inauguration as US President in 1953. The General, in military uniform, looks towards No.20 Grosvenor Square where he worked in 1942 when US Commander of the European Theatre of Operations, and in 1944 when he set up his Supreme Headquarters for the Allied Expeditionary Force.

In the gardens is a bronze statue of Franklin D. Roosevelt. It was unveiled in 1948 by Mrs Roosevelt on the third anniversary of her husband's death. It faces the memorial to the RAF Eagle Squadron, which consisted mainly of American airmen who joined up for action before the United States officially went to war after Pearl Harbor.

The house at No.9, in the north-east corner, is one of the few original buildings to survive. Here from 1785 to 1788 lived John Adams, the first American Minister to Britain after the Revolutionary War. A tablet recording his presence was placed here in 1933 by the Colonial Dames of America.

Walter Hines Page lived at No.7 when he was American Ambassador in 1913-18, and No.1 was formerly the American Embassy. It is now part of the Canadian High Commission.

New Bond Street

At the corner of Brook Street and Davies Street a *large* chandelier sparkles on the first floor of the Grosvenor Office, which manages the Grosvenor Estate for its owner, the Duke of Westminster, sometimes called the wealthiest man in England.

In Davies Street the curly iron balconies of Claridge's Hotel are painted in that unobtrusive shade of dove grey which signals to the very rich that this is their kind of pub. On the right is Three Kings Yard, a long mews recalling the old coaching days when the great houses of Mayfair needed a large equine staff to carry the owners hither and thither. At the far end is a handsome coach-house with clock tower, and beyond it is the Italian Embassy, its front entrance at No.4 Grosvenor Square.

Turn along Grosvenor Street past Jonathan Potter's Map Gallery. Avery Row, on the left, was once an interesting alley with small shops but is now undergoing a serious face-lift; happily, for residents and local office workers, its branch of Yates's Wine Lodge soldiers on. Things may change, but it is good to find that the Italian-owned Chalet Coffee Lounge in Grosvenor Street is as cheerful as ever, producing cakes and buffets for office parties – and hot croissants for winter walkers.

New Bond Street has a style of its own, ideal for the window-shopper who cares not what anything costs. Luxurious clothing abounds at Beale & Inman, Yves St Laurent and Herbie. Zilli has complete ensembles for the modern lounge lizard: fur-collared coats, long silk scarves and a cane to twirl. Look for a hat beneath the unicorn sign at Herbert Johnson. Nearby, flying its distinctive green flag, is Sotheby's famous auction house, founded in 1744. Across the road are turn-of-the-century paintings at The Fine Art Society.

In Bruton Street, around the corner, are Holland & Holland, sporting gun and rifle-makers since 1835, and other dealers selling vast abstract paintings. Gleaming Rolls-Royces and Bentleys are drawn up in the windows of Jack Barclay.

Take a turn through the gardens of Berkeley Square. The nightingale which may have sung there in the famous 1940 song ('I may be right, I may be wrong, but I'm perfectly willing to swear . . . ') has certainly departed, though the fine old eighteenth-century plane trees are still present. The range of houses on the west side is more or less all that survives of the original buildings, laid out in the 1730s and occupied by wealthy families who sought a town house in quiet leafy surroundings behind Piccadilly. No.45 was once the home of Clive of India, and the statesman George Canning lived at No.50, now the premises of Maggs Bros, dealers in rare books, manuscripts and autographs.

Shepherd Market

Continue through Fitzmaurice Place to Curzon Street, past Madison's Hotel and the Third Church of Christ Scientist to find the beguiling window of Geo. F. Trumper, Court Hairdresser and Perfumer. Admire the beautiful soft shaving brushes and the pots of shaving cream variously scented: almond, sandalwood, rose, coconut oil. They have manicure sets, silver perfume sprays and goat milk soap. I begin to wonder how customers of Geo. F. Trumper ever tear themselves away from their bathrooms.

The shop is a useful landmark because it stands opposite one of the entrances to Shepherd Market, which otherwise is not easy to find. Go through the arch at No.47, next to Bendicks chocolate shop, to find a remarkable village. This was where people celebrated the May Fair, a fifteen-day bash which began in the 1680s and soon acquired a reputation for outstandingly riotous, unbuttoned behaviour. It survived at least one banning before offended residents had it squashed for ever in 1764, by which time it had given its name to the entire new district springing up in the roads we have traversed between here and Oxford Street. Shepherd Market still has a name as a discreet rendezvous for expensive prostitutes.

Many of the buildings are now restaurants, pubs and coffee shops. One of the best-known is Tiddy Dols Eating House, on the corner of Shepherd Market and Trebeck Street. A good pub is Ye Grapes; its spacious room and open fire suggest an older, eighteenth-century atmosphere. Nearby are The Village ('Mayfair's coffee shop') and L'Autre wine bar. For practical purposes – of rest and refreshment, that is – our walk through Mayfair ends here, within a stone's throw of Piccadilly at the end of White Horse Street.

When in Mayfair, I like to know what is on at the Curzon Cinema, well known for its good programmes and luxurious seats. If the idea appeals, look up times in the *Evening Standard* or walk round to Curzon Street and see for yourself.

Walk 5

Soho

The West End's principal village, with long roots in craftsmanship, the restaurant trade, night life and 'the vice', all more or less visible today though the last two run at a reduced temperature.

Allow 3-4 hours.

Best times Not Sunday, when Liberty's is closed.

ROUTE

Begin at ⊖ Oxford Circus. At exit 'Oxford Circus & Regent Street', emerge in Oxford Street and turn right and right into Argyll Street. Walk down past London Palladium to **Liberty** ☜ ; open 09.30 to 18.00, Thursday open until 19.30, closed Sunday.

At exit, turn left and left down Kingly Street beneath arches. Turn left into Foubert's Place beneath the 'Carnaby' archway. Cross Carnaby Street and take next right along Newburgh Street. Turn right at Ganton Street and return to **Carnaby Street**. Turn left to end and left into Beak Street.

Keep straight on to Silver Place and turn left through Ingestre Place to Broadwick Street. Turn right to **Berwick Street** and right again, following the street market and continuing through Walker's Court to Brewer Street. Turn left to Wardour Street and right to St Anne's churchyard. Keep on down Wardour Street, cross Shaftesbury Avenue and turn left into Gerrard Street, now the centre of London's **Chinatown.**

At end, turn left through Gerrard Place, cross Shaftesbury Avenue and make a quick left-right to Frith Street. Continue past food shops, restaurants and Ronnie Scott's jazz club. In **Soho Square** turn left and walk round square to SE corner where House of St Barnabas-in-Soho, entrance in Greek Street ☜ ; fine Georgian house open Wednesday 14.30 to 16.15, Thursday 11.00 to 12.30. Chapel also open at these times, entrance in Manette Street.

Keep on down Greek Street. At Pillars of Hercules pub, turn left through arch to Manette Street and Foyles bookshop. Return to Greek Street and continue to Shaftesbury Avenue. Turn left to Cambridge Circus.

Walk ends here. Nearest refreshments (tea and pastries) at Maison Bertaux, 28 Greek Street, or Patisserie Valerie, 44 Old Compton Street. Nearest ⊖ Leicester Square.

Liberty & Co

At the top of Argyll Street the head of the roadway is usually straddled by Marto's handsome fruit stall (established 1932), making an appropriate customs post at one of the northern entrances to Soho, the district which cares for London's stomach.

On the left rises the great pediment of the Palladium, at its best when

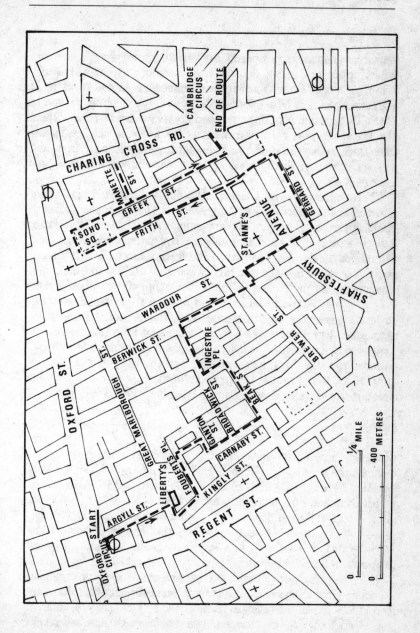

music hall and variety prospered. Walk down towards the 'Amsterdam Tudor' front of Liberty & Co. This entrance to Arthur Lasenby Liberty's store (founded 1875) gives immediate access to its most attractive rooms, where shoppers browse in the clubbish warmth of mock-Tudor wood panelling, moulded doorways and display cabinets that are almost *pieces* in their own right ('No, keep the scarves, I'll just have the cupboard, please'). The store was influential from the beginning, and in Italy the Art Nouveau movement was known as *Stile Liberty*.

There are two Liberty buildings, this one and the blocks in Regent Street, joined by a bridge over Kingly Street. The Tudor shop, made in the 1920s from the timbers of two fighting ships, shows off the classic Liberty look in fabrics and furnishings, womenswear, accessories and gifts, books, china and glassware. The Regent Street shop is a more down-to-earth emporium for menswear and kitchen and bathroom equipment. At the centre of the Tudor shop, the galleried atrium ascends to a hammerbeam roof, and oriental rugs draped over the gallery suggest the kind of bazaar that William Morris might have organised. Everywhere the famous colours of Liberty stand in co-ordinated ranges of scarf, handkerchief, sponge bag and address book. Wander round and return eventually, perhaps with your *de rigueur* purple bag, to our first entrance door. In the basement is a pleasant wood-panelled coffee shop serving good coffee in glass filter pots.

Carnaby Street

In Kingly Street pass under the Liberty arches, heeding the motto beneath the gilded clock: 'NO MINUTE GONE COMES EVER BACK AGAIN TAKE HEED AND SEE YE NOTHING DO IN VAIN.'

Kingly Street runs along the western front of Soho: on one side the store-backs of Regent Street, on the other a conglomeration of shops, pubs and restaurants. At No.19 is Harry's, the only non-Chinese eatery in Soho that is open all night. Turn into Foubert's Place, a paved overture to Carnaby Street.

I know a man who claims to have invented the term 'Swinging London', *circa* 1966. When he had this brainstorming idea, Carnaby Street was one of the principal clichés used by journalists to summon the essence of what had changed, what was new. Others, as I recall, were: The Beatles, Sandie Shaw's feet, David Bailey's photographs, Twiggy's looks and Mary Quant's designs. After a brief apotheosis as the leader of sharp fashion, Carnaby Street collapsed into a greasy souk crammed with tatty gear and tasteless souvenirs – plastic bowler hats, union jackwear, reproduction street and Underground signs. Collectors can still buy these in the open-fronted shops, along with enough flags, brooches and necklaces to supply their C-list friends with party presents for ever. A lonely survivor from older days is Inderwicks, the tobacconist founded in 1797 by John Inderwick who launched the vogue for Meerschaum pipes.

Parallel with Carnaby Street is Newburgh Street, an attractive cobbled way with neat renovated Georgian shopfronts aiming a considerable cut above those of their brassy neighbour. In Ganton Street, joining the two, flamboyant jewellery is enticingly displayed at The Great Frog. In Beak Street many premises were to let in the recessionary England of the early 1990s, though Anything Left-handed at No.65 is always of interest. New life has already come to Silver Place: for art, look in at Thumb Gallery and Kate Heller Gallery; there is old-style craftsmanship at Taylors the button specialist, and next door at Stephen Wells the frame-maker. Very bright flowers seek buyers at Manic Botanic.

Berwick Street Market and St Anne's Church

This old street market is as pongy and varied as ever: fruit and vegetables, Chinese umbrellas, handbags, flowers, fresh fish, nuts from the sack, fabric rolls, rugs and batteries. At the end is Walker's Court, the centre of London's greatly shrunken voyeur trade: Raymond's Revuebar, a tired Books and Mags shop, and transvestite larks around the corner at Madame Jo Jo's.

To the right in Brewer Street is Staines Catering Equipment, where chefs calm themselves before racks of knives, corkscrews, aluminium pans, giant colanders, a casually stacked mountain of ice buckets, skewers, meat hooks, ladles and tureens.

The fruit and vegetable market continues in Rupert Street, where the stallholders have developed an engaging form of adjectival hype to promote their stock. Thus: *Giant* Spanish Navals (*sic*), *Very Sweet* Nectarines, *Ripe* Avo's, *Jumbo* Asparagus, and, my favourite,

Fantastic Plums.

In Wardour Street I crossed St Anne's churchyard and met some lively ladies in the temporary hut of the Soho Society. They told me of plans to reopen the church, together with a new development of shops and offices and a museum of Soho life, commemorating the generations of native and foreign craftsmen and women who had settled there and made it such a distinctive quarter. I look forward to seeing their venture realised. It is more than fifty years since a wartime bomb destroyed the seventeenth-century church. The tower, a later addition rebuilt in 1803, survived the attack, and services were currently being held there in a first-floor chapel.

The journal of the Society, the *Soho Clarion*, brims with concern and affection for all who live and work in the area. It carries details of community schemes, political moves, new business ventures, results of the six-a-side football festival (Pizza Express beat Berwick Street Market in the final), and news of the next Soho Festival, usually held on the second Saturday in July when: 'There will be food from Soho's restaurants, music, books, jumble, entertainment, the spaghetti eating competition, the famous Soho Waiters' Race and much more!'

The garden of the churchyard stands five feet above street level. It had to be raised in order to pack in the bodies of the 60,000 former residents who are buried there.

Chinatown

High rents, devious landlords and the government's withdrawal of planning protection have radically pruned the old craft workshops which once abounded in Soho and provided a living for so many immigrant families. One area which has beaten the trend is busy Chinatown, on the south side of Shaftesbury Avenue, where the street sign for Wardour Street is also written in Chinese. The main highway of this new empire is Gerrard Street, entered beneath a Chinese gateway spanned by red and magenta banners and studded with light bulbs. Flags criss-cross the street and almost every frontage proclaims a restaurant, craft shop or grocery. For flavour, try Hong Kong Cultural near the far end, selling Chinese newspapers, books, bowls, fans, figurines, chopsticks and lanterns. Chinese shops continue in the piazza of Newport Place.

Frith Street and Soho Square

We have seen little so far of Soho's traditional restaurant life. In Frith Street it springs into view: Italian provision shops and restaurants, Alastair Little at No.49, just past Ronnie Scott's Jazz Club – a 1960s immigrant from Gerrard Street and the *QE2* of London jazz venues, open 20.30 to 03.00. Restaurants in Soho embrace almost every cuisine under the sun: Korean, Thai, Mexican, Hungarian, Greek, Spanish, Indonesian . . . all the way back to English.

Pubs in Soho can be a very personal matter, dictated as much by proximity to the office desk as by the company found there; décor tends to come a poor third. Thus for years I have been dropping into the Dog & Duck, on the corner of Bateman Street, rather than, say, the French or the Coach & Horses. It is mainly used by film people, though originally my crowd were from a publishers in Manette Street. It is small and narrow with a good gantry, much cut and engraved glass and darkly agreeable Victorian tiling in borders and panels. At the back, beyond the staircase which slants overhead, is a scorching open fire.

At No.6 is a plaque to William Hazlitt (1778-1830). The essayist died here and is buried in St Anne's churchyard.

Soho Square is the chief lung of this overcrowded quarter, its gardens a haven in season for sandwich-eaters and sunbathers. The quaint twentieth-century Tudor pavilion in the centre is the gardeners' refuge, and rolls of turf are neatly stacked against the walls; the building also conceals the ventilation shaft of an electricity station.

The name Soho was established before the square of that name was built in the 1680s. In the sixteenth century much of the area was farmland and foxes were hunted to the cry of 'So-ho!' or 'So-hou!' The first houses were the work of Richard Frith, and they were bought by noble and wealthy families. Despite much rebuilding since, the older Georgian roofline can still be seen above elegant houses on the north side.

In the south-west corner is a plaque to Sir Joseph Banks and other botanists who lived in a house on this site; meetings of the Linnaean Society were held here from 1821 to 1857. In the north-west corner is the nineteenth-century, rather Flemish-looking building of the French Protestant Church in London. A church was founded here in 1550 following Edward VI's grant of a charter to Huguenot refugees from France. On the east side of the square is the tall brick tower of the Roman Catholic Church of St Patrick. It stands on the site of Carlisle

House, occupied around 1760 by Mrs Cornelys, a former Viennese opera singer, courtesan and organiser of risqué masquerades.

On the corner of Greek Street is the House of St Barnabas-in-Soho, now a 'temporary home for women who have the necessary recommendations'. The house is open twice a week, and visitors are much impressed by the fine staircase, beautiful plasterwork and the panelled Council Chamber.

Greek Street

Continue along Greek Street, named after the Greek church which stood nearby. On the left are two famous Soho restaurants: the Gay Hussar, its name established under Hungarian chef Victor Sassie, and Au Jardin des Gourmets, a traditional, i.e. filling, French establishment.

At the Pillars of Hercules pub turn left through the arch into Manette Street, named after Dickens's Dr Manette who, in *A Tale of Two Cities*, lived there when it was called Rose Street. On the left are the twin apses of the Chapel of the House of St Barnabas, built in 1862 as a miniature reproduction of a French Gothic cathedral.

Here too is Foyles massive bookshop, notorious as the place where no customer can find a book, partly because the venerable store insists on stocking some of its shelves by imprint. If, therefore, you do not know who published what you are looking for, tough. The store would probably resist such accusations – if you could ever find someone to represent it – by pointing to the illuminated signs which list subjects in alphabetical order and their approximate whereabouts. Thus you scan through, for example, Travel Guides, Typography, Ufology, Urology, Veterinary, Virology . . . until you find the sort of thing you seek, and then must trek for miles trying to pin it down.

Across the road, the old northern sector of Foyles is now a Waterstone's. Though admittedly smaller, they do things in more style. There is carpet underfoot, and the displays exhibit a sympathetic feeling for the *shape* of books. Around the corner in Charing Cross Road is Collets, respected for its strength in the social sciences and its huge Russian and East European department in the basement.

Returning to Greek Street, and preoccupations gastronomic, the west side of the street contains, among other restaurants, La Bastide

(No.50) and L'Escargot (No.48), and on the east side is Maison Berteaux (No.28), purveyors of fine pastries since 1871. On the pavement outside No.29, you may see a grey-haired man glaring irritably up and down the street. Then he turns and vanishes for a minute or so inside the Coach & Horses, then he reappears on the pavement. He is Norman Balon, reputedly the rudest landlord in London. At the back of the bar his special brand of charm is celebrated in cartoons by Michael Heath for *Private Eye*, which held regular lunches upstairs. Although described by Richard Ingrams, former editor of the satirical magazine, as 'polite, kind and generous', Mr Balon is evidently content with his reputation and called his memoirs, published in 1991, *You're Barred, You Bastards*.

Walk 6 ☂

National Gallery and Covent Garden

Visit London's foremost picture gallery (Early Italian masters to Picasso). Move on to Inigo Jones's Church of St Paul, the 'actors' church', and the piazza and market buildings of Covent Garden. See the Museum of Transport in the old Flower Market and turn through narrow streets to Seven Dials, then on to the antiquarian dealers of Cecil Court. Finally tour the small rooms of the National Portrait Gallery.

Allow   All day.

Best times   Monday to Saturday; on Sunday National Gallery not open until 14.00.

ROUTE

Begin at ⊖ Charing Cross. At exit 'Trafalgar Square' rise to centre of square close to Nelson's Column. Walk up to **National Gallery** on N side square ☞; open 10.00 to 18.00, Sunday 14.00 to 18.00, closed 1 January, Good Friday, May Day bank holiday, 24-26 December.

At exit turn left towards Church of St Martin-in-the-Fields and bear round corner to St Martin's Place. Cross road by Edith Cavell statue and turn left up St Martin's Lane. On right, between Nos 55-56, go through narrow entrance to **Goodwin's Court**. Walk up to Bedfordbury and turn left to New Row. Turn right and cross to King Street. Entrance to **St Paul's Church** is on right, two doors before Essex Serpent. Walk through arch to church ☞; open 09.00 to 16.00.

Return to King Street and turn right to centre of **Covent Garden**, until 1974 London's principal market for fruit and vegetables. Explore boutiques and cafés in Fowler's central market building and stalls of Jubilee Market on S side. In SE corner is **London Transport Museum** ☞; open 10.00 to 18.00 (last tickets 17.15), closed 24-26 December. *Admission*.

Also in Covent Garden are animated puppets of **Spitting Image Rubberworks**, in Cubitts Yard off James Street ☞; 11.00 to 19.00. *Admission*.

Leave old market on E side and walk along Russell Street. Optional visit to Theatre Museum; open 11.00 to 19.00, closed Monday, Good Friday, 25 December. *Admission*.

Turn left up Bow Street past Royal Opera House to Long Acre. Turn left and right into Neal Street. At next intersection, bear left into Earlham Street. Continue to Seven Dials and keep straight on, past flower stalls on far side (still Earlham Street). Turn left down Tower Street, past Dobells jazz record shop, to Upper St Martin's Lane. Turn right, then at traffic lights bear left into Long Acre.

At corner of Stanford's map and travel book shop, turn right into Rose Street. Cross Floral Street towards blank wall and follow road to Lamb & Flag, a significant watering-hole; main entrance in alley.

At exit main bar, turn right and walk down to Garrick Street. Turn right and left into St Martin's Lane. Take 2nd right through **Cecil Court** to Charing Cross Road. Turn left to St Martin's Place and **National Portrait Gallery** ☞; open 10.00 to 17.00, Saturday 10.00 to 18.00, Sunday 14.00 to 18.00, closed 1 January, Good Friday, May Day bank holiday, 24-26 December.

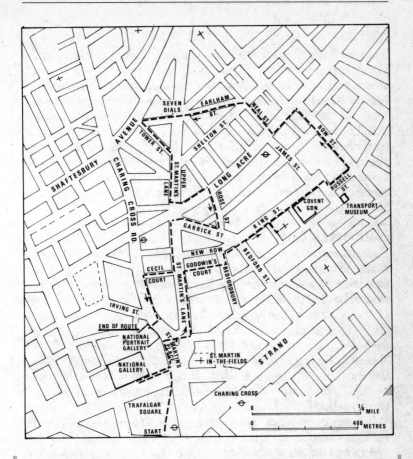

Walk ends here. Nearest refreshments in St Martin's Lane (Chandos pub, Mille Feuilles café, Pelican bar/restaurant, Peppermint Park). Nearest ⊖ Charing Cross.

Trafalgar Square

Arriving on the great island of Trafalgar Square, step through a huddle of oily disaffected pigeons lurking about before their next feed and photocall. Into the sky soars Nelson's Column, flanked by Landseer's four bronze lions. The monument was raised to commemorate Admiral Lord Nelson's most famous victory against the French fleet off

Trafalgar in 1805. The Corinthian column by William Railton is 44.2m (145ft) high and made of Devonshire granite; it was erected in 1839-42. Above it are a bronze capital cast from naval guns and the figure of Lord Nelson, by E.H. Baily, standing in full-dress uniform beside a capstan. Each year on Trafalgar Day, 21 October, the monument is decorated.

In London hearts, this is one of *the* public arenas for mass partying, particularly on New Year's Eve when Norway's annual gift of a tall Christmas tree makes a slender pyramid of lights. The base of Nelson's Column is also a popular rallying point and terminus for political meetings and marches, usually of a leftist or anti-war nature.

National Gallery

Looking around the square, laid out from 1840 on the site of the King's Mews, to the south is the Charles I statue at the top of Whitehall, and to east and west are the lumpish blocks of South Africa House and Canada House. Beyond the balustrade at the top of the slope is the broad front of the National Gallery (William Wilkins, 1832-8) with its central pedimented portico and dome *à la turque*, and minor minarets to each flank. From any angle the dome is extraordinarily modest, and often likened to a pimple. To the left of the main façade is the new extension, the Sainsbury Wing, which blends in neatly and politely and opened in 1991 to howls of disappointment from the architectural correspondents.

Walk up through the square towards the National Gallery. On the right, in a lampholder, is one of London's smaller police stations.

Although the Sainsbury Wing, which contains the oldest pictures on view, may be entered directly from the pavement, it is still a good idea to go in at the main entrance and there collect a floor plan and the latest *National Gallery News*.

Turn left and walk through Rooms 2-9. From the last of these, the Wohl Room, the best long view opens into the new wing: a line of diminishing arches, flanked in the vestibule by fat columns, all painted stone grey. On the left, a deep staircase runs down to street level.

For a chronological sequence, go left into Room 51. More intriguing, though, to follow the nave-like arches to the far end, advancing slowly on Cima de Conegliano's *The Incredulity of St Thomas*, restored and now light and bright with the figures' robes in vibrant green, red and orange, the flat grey wall of the painted background toning with the paler grey of the gallery wall.

This approach sets up other possibilities for cross-routes along other 'naves' which terminate in altarpieces and paintings. In Room 60 is another example of imaginative hanging: two *Virgins and Child* of the same period, by Raphael and Lorenzo Costa, face each other across the gallery.

Return to Room 51, containing the earliest and the latest in Renaissance art: Giotto's *Pentecost* (*c*.1306-12) and Leonardo's *The Virgin of the Rocks* (*c*. 1508) – two centuries apart and demonstrating two entirely different concepts.

The hang in the spacious top-lit studio-galleries allows good scope for setting sculpture alongside painted altarpieces and panels. One above the other are two works from the end of the thirteenth century: Duccio's *Jesus Opening the Eyes of the Man Born Blind*, and the large *Crucifix* in the style of Segna di Bonaventura, lofted on the wall as it would have been in the original church.

In Room 55 see wonderful horses of the fifteenth century: in Pisanello's glowing picture of *The Vision of St Eustace* – the stooping greyhound so like those in Uccello's *A Hunt in a Forest* in the Ashmolean Museum, Oxford. Then come Uccello's own *St George and the Dragon* and his *Battle of San Romano* – a frieze of heavy cavalry horses stamping and snorting across the foreground.

In Room 56 a Netherlandish room reminds us of the close parallels between North and South in the Renaissance. Here are paintings by Rogier van der Weyden and several Van Eycks, among them the compelling stillness of *The Arnolfini Wedding*.

Continue to zig-zag, room to room, looking for new visual comparisons. The marvellous treasures of this great collection include Mantegna's *The Agony in the Garden*; *Christ Crowned with Thorns* by Cima da Conegliano and Botticelli's *Mystic Nativity*. Arrive eventually at Cima's doubting St Thomas.

Beneath the main floor of the Sainsbury Wing is an agreeable brasserie; the principal shop is on the ground floor.

Work back to the main building and perhaps try one of the other groups of rooms. The West Wing (Rooms 2-13) has Italian, German and Netherlandish painting from 1510 to 1600 (Tintoretto, El Greco, Michelangelo, Titian, Veronese and others). The North Wing (Rooms

14-32) has French, Dutch, Spanish and Italian painting from 1600 to 1700 (Claude, Poussin, Vermeer, Rubens, Rembrandt, Velázquez, Caravaggio and others). The East Wing (Rooms 33-46) has paintings from 1700 to 1920. This includes many fine British artists – Gainsborough, Constable, Stubbs, Turner – and in Rooms 44-46 the museum's own collection of Impressionist and Post-Impressionist pictures is merged with the Berggruen Collection. Here are wonderful paintings by Cézanne, Van Gogh and Degas, all dominated by Seurat's *Bathers at Asnières*, the still figures white and glowing in the heat of the afternoon. Finally, a miscellany of Picassos has a room to itself (46).

St Martin's Lane

From the steps of the National Gallery turn to face the elegantly proportioned front and spire of St Martin-in-the-Fields, rebuilt by James Gibbs in 1722-4. Famous artists buried here include Nicholas Hilliard the miniature painter, whose works we may later admire in the National Portrait Gallery just across the road; Sir Joshua Reynolds, and the sculptor Roubiliac.

Cross St Martin's Place by the Edith Cavell monument (1920). George Frampton's severe statue commemorates the courageous nurse who was shot in Brussels in 1915 for helping refugees to escape through German-occupied Belgium. The woman and child on top of the granite pillar represent Humanity protecting the smaller states.

If refreshments are needed, they serve a cup of slightly stewed coffee in the upstairs Opera Bar of The Chandos pub on the corner, or wait for a better cup at Mille Feuilles in St Martin's Lane, where hand-made Belgian chocolates are to be gazed upon.

St Martin's Lane is one of the principal arms of Theatreland. Ahead is the London Coliseum, now the home of the English National Opera company, and on the left is the Duke of York's, the first theatre in the street, which opened in 1893.

A short way from the Coliseum, the bleak slit of Brydges Place is one of the narrowest and most uninviting alleys in London. Much more attractive is Goodwin's Court, entered between Nos 55 and 56 St Martin's Lane: an elegant row of black-painted, bow-windowed seventeenth-century houses, now turned into offices. At the Bedfordbury end, on the right, the panel suspended on chains is a reflector, used to increase the light in ground-floor rooms and once a common sight in London's alleyways.

From Bedfordbury, turn uphill to New Row, an interesting jumble of boutiques, bookshops and specialists such as James Asman for jazz records and Arthur Middleton, dealer in antique scientific instruments.

Cross to King Street, which formerly stood on the fringe of Covent Garden's fruit and vegetable market before it moved to Nine Elms, Battersea, in 1974. Then the street was lined with barrows, the gutters stuffed with discarded cabbage leaves and unwanted tomatoes, and car parking was supervised by a self-appointed comedian in a battered peaked cap. I worked at a publisher's office on the north side, where the staircase always reeked of orange peel; the landlords, who also occupied part of the building, were citrus fruit importers.

St Paul's Church

Just before the Essex Serpent, a former market workers' pub now converted to a wine bar – one of numerous gentrifications in this quarter – turn right through an arch to the churchyard and west door of St Paul's, the actors' church designed by Inigo Jones and consecrated in 1638. Perhaps the chief source of interest is the large number of plaques commemorating actors and theatre people. Among these and the well-known artists buried here are Sir Peter Lely, Grinling Gibbons, Thomas Rowlandson, Thomas Girtin and Ellen Terry. The church is also a prestigious venue for memorial services. Do not be surprised to find one in progress, or that a familiar face from cinema or television is singing a solo or reading the lesson.

The interior is essentially a simple rectangle – 'the handsomest barn in England', the architect promised his patron, the Fourth Earl of Bedford, who had not wanted to pay for anything much grander than a barn. The style is Tuscan with deep arched windows and golden stained glass in an abstract pattern flanking the pedimented reredos, and a round painting of the *Virgin and Child*. Alas the interior is not the original: a fire in 1795 destroyed all but the portico. However, the copy by Thomas Hardwick is said to be faithful to the original design.

Covent Garden

Return to King Street and continue to the piazza, originally laid out by Inigo Jones with colonnades on the Palladian model. Before joining the bustle in the old market buildings or paying heed to the buskers cavorting in front of St Paul's Church, turn to admire Inigo Jones's fine portico: only two central columns, and four in all, the broad eaves of the roof enclosing a recessed pediment – simple to the point of plainness, but daring too and marvellously effective in a country not known for temple-churches.

Then enter the market and browse among the boutiques beneath the pale blue iron and glass canopies. Inside are colourful stalls for children's clothes, knitwear, gewgaws, hats and ornaments, and rows of classier high-street shops – Thorntons Chocolates, an Elizabeth David Cookshop, Body Shop, shoes at Hobbs. There is open-air eating at pavement level and in sunken patios. On the south side is the more informal Jubilee Market Hall, where frocks and handbags hang out over the alleyways next to Chinese parasols and garish boxer shorts.

On the north side of the market, off James Street, the Spitting Image Rubberworks in Cubitts Yard is a very jolly show pouring scorn on the famous with an eighteenth-century bite and gleefulness. An expansion of the *Spitting Image* television series, it currently features the *Lickety Lick* game show with news presenter Sir Alistair Burnet in the chair, the Queen, Prince Philip and current political leaders. The display turns to technical demonstrations – how to make a latex foam mask, how robotics work, with press-button experiments which swivel heads, legs and eyeballs. Now is the time, if you so wish, to touch Madonna's rubbery belly button. Afterwards, they have souvenirs galore.

London Transport Museum

This is the latest home, opened in 1980, of London Transport's collection of trams, buses and Underground trains originally formed in the 1920s in the days of the London Omnibus Company. From the shop, move ahead past shiny red double-decker trams and vintage buses like the RTs on which I remember travelling to school, the engine throbbing like a motor boat.

A video at the first corner shows the 'Impact of Cheap Travel'. All around are fine models of stage coaches, horse-drawn omnibuses and trams, the display cases backed with photoboards showing street settings and a demonstration of the Gibson ticket machine which printed tickets on a blank paper roll and from 1953 ousted those highly collectable, coloured, pre-printed tickets which the conductor plucked from a wooden holder and punched with a hole to mark the fare limit.

On to an enclosed Tube exhibit celebrating one hundred years of Underground railways. There is a turn-of-the-century locomotive with a wooden carriage; a joystick for driving your own Tube through a tunnel and stopping it at the next station – if the schoolkids will ever let you have a go on it – and a great maroon steam engine with twin side boilers from the old Metropolitan Railway. This pulled open carriages on the Inner Circle before enclosed trains with electric traction arrived in service between 1901 and 1905.

The Frank Pick Gallery commemorates the work of London Transport's pioneering Design Manager. He commissioned outstanding posters from artists such as John Hassall, George Clausen, Laura Knight, Edward Bawden and others, urging the public to get away from it all and travel to 'Fresh Air and Sunshine', 'The North Downs', 'The Hop Gardens of Kent by Motor-Bus', 'Rugby and Twickenham by Tram'.

The route continues past a variegated fleet of shiny old trams and buses, and a green and cream open-air horse-drawn bus, one of Thomas Tilling's fleet serving 'Peckham & Oxford Circus'. It seated '10 in, 14 out', and on the upper deck passengers sat on a 'knifeboard', a long back-to-back seat running fore and aft along the roof. When it rained, they got wetter and wetter.

Bow Street, Neal Street, Seven Dials

Close to the Transport Museum is a large choice of lunch stops. Above the market is the Opera Terrace (entrance in Central Avenue), nearby is Tuttons Brasserie, and round the corner in Russell Street is the Brahms & Liszt wine bar and restaurant.

The chief occupant of Bow Street is the Royal Opera House, opened in 1732 as the Covent Garden Theatre. The present building was designed by E.M. Barry in 1858, its heavy cream portico of six Corinthian columns proclaiming its pre-eminence among London theatres (though a neighbour, the Theatre Royal Drury Lane, is visually more stupendous). Since the Second World War the Opera

House has achieved international repute for its grand productions of opera and ballet, and an extension programme in the 1980s has vastly extended its physical limits which now run the full length of Floral Street to James Street. The theatre's greatest problem is gearing its seat prices so that the ordinary public can afford them.

Across the road is Bow Street Magistrates' Court, which opened in 1740. Here the barrister and novelist Henry Fielding, who became magistrate in 1748, set up the first body of volunteer 'thief-takers' which grew into the part-time force known as the Bow Street Runners, precursors of the Metropolitan Police Force.

The next part of our walk is a ramble through the fashionable streets of refurbished Covent Garden. Neal Street runs north from Long Acre, specialising in healthy food and the appurtenances of designer living: smart clothes, tea- and coffee-making apparatus, neat lights at Artemide. At the intersection of five roads bear left into Earlham Street past the statue of a sleeping or grieving nude (a plaque would help us to decide). Arrive soon at the Cambridge Theatre and Seven Dials, a murderers' den in Dickens's day. Keep on past the flower stalls. On the left is the Dover Bookshop, selling only the output of the offbeat American list of Dover Books, an intriguing blend of art, engravings, crafts and ephemera. Around the corner in Tower Street is Dobells jazz record shop, a refugee from Charing Cross Road when the developers moved in and wrecked a fine idiosyncratic parade to the south of Cambridge Circus. In Upper St Martin's Lane, pass the dazzling glass frontage of Now and Zen's Chinese restaurant. It has been suggested that the bills are in proportion to the cubic footage from floor to towering ceiling occupied by each table; never mind, it looks fresh and beautiful.

Back in Long Acre, pause at Stanford's famous map and travel book shop and turn down Rose Street to find the Lamb & Flag pub. Main entrance to the bars is in the covered alleyway. This pub is one of my favourites for a few minutes' rest and recuperation; it is also a useful place to meet people in the West End, being only a couple of minutes from Leicester Square Tube station. If the downstairs bars are too crowded, go upstairs to the food bar and maybe take a table by the window. From such a peaceful vantage-point, it is hard to imagine how this pub once acquired a reputation for violence, along with a grisly nickname – the Bucket of Blood.

Down the slope to Garrick Street, emerging opposite the dingy, semi-rusticated front of the Garrick Club, named after the actor-manager David Garrick and ever-popular with publishers, politicians, theatre people and lawyers, whose *bons mots* seem to reach the gossip columns more regularly than those emanating from any other private club. Turn into St Martin's Lane. On the right are the Albery Theatre and the Salisbury pub, the latter a grand Victorian gin palace full of mirrors, marble and shiny brass, and a famous gathering-place for theatricals. Along the way are two old courts which connect with Charing Cross Road. St Martin's Court has the Motor Books shop and Sheekey's fish restaurant, and Cecil Court is a haven for collectors of antiquarian books, cigarette cards, coins, medals, prints and printed ephemera.

National Portrait Gallery

It is not embarrassed to call itself the finest portrait gallery in the world, and was founded in 1856 to 'collect the likenesses of famous British men and women'. The collection is grouped on five levels, and to view it chronologically go up to the Coronation portrait of Elizabeth I, take the lift to the top (2), walk down the steps to Level 4 and continue on Level 5. Those floors cover a period from the fifteenth century (House of Lancaster) to the early nineteenth (Industrial Revolution and Regency). Treasures and items of special interest include the Holbein cartoon of Henry VIII; the famous 'squashed' picture of Edward VI in distorted perspective (anamorphis) which the viewer can correct by placing an eye next to the indentation on the right of the frame; the 'Ditchley' portrait of Elizabeth I, and the 'Chandos' portrait of William Shakespeare. In various galleries lift the covers on the showcases to find small pictures and miniatures, among them Nicholas Hilliard's wonderful portraits of Elizabeth I, Sir Walter Raleigh and Sir Francis Drake. In '18th Century Arts' see portraits of Johnson and Boswell side by side, David Garrick and his wife, Lawrence Sterne and a self-portrait of George Stubbs.

On Level 3 ('Nineteenth Century') the chronology is rather back to front. The Queen Victoria room is at the furthest point and access to it may be blocked by a special exhibition requiring an admission charge. It could certainly be ordered better; lack of space is a pressing problem which the museum hopes to solve with a new development programme.

On Level 2 is a Royal Family room. Here are the Annigoni portrait of the Queen; Prince Charles and the Princess of Wales by Brian Organ; a charming study of the Princess Royal and others of Prince Philip, the Queen Mother and George VI. On this level and the ground floor are groups of personalities, politicians, sportspeople, actors and warriors, painted by artists as diverse as Bratby, Sutherland and Hockney. A feast of British faces.

Out on St Martin's Place, this walk concluded, discreetly survey your fellow passers-by. Is there really such a thing as a 'British face'? Can you see it in that newspaper seller over there, or in that pavement artist? How about that chap in the bowler hat, trying to hail a taxi – is he a British face? Or is it just the uniform, suggesting his nationality for him?

See what you think. The evidence is all about you.

Walk 7

Strand

Explore the old thoroughfare linking Trafalgar Square with the City. Delve into byways around the Adelphi and the site of Savoy Palace. Visit the Courtauld Institute Galleries in Somerset House, and the island churches of St Mary-le-Strand and St Clement Danes.

Allow 3 hours.

Best times Not weekends, when churches closed except for Sunday services.

ROUTE

Begin at ⊖ Charing Cross. Follow exit signs in station to 'Trafalgar Square' and then 'Strand (south)' and emerge in forecourt of railway station, where an **Eleanor Cross** marks the last stage of Queen Eleanor's funeral journey in 1290.

At E end forecourt, go down steps and right into Villiers Street. Take 2nd left into John Adam Street and turn right down Buckingham Street, and down steps to **York Watergate**. Turn left and left up next parallel street (York Buildings). Near top, turn right into underground tunnel of Lower Robert Street and follow past warehouses to river front of new Adelphi block.

Turn left along Savoy Place and at end block go up steps to Adelphi Terrace, where views of Cleopatra's Needle and the river. Return along Adam Street to Strand. Turn right and look into Savoy Court on right. Continue past Simpson's restaurant and turn right down Savoy Street to see Savoy Chapel (early 16C though much restored).

Back on Strand, walk on past Lancaster Place and on right visit **Courtauld Institute Galleries** ◉; open 10.00 to 18.00, Sunday 14.00 to 18.00. *Admission (free for members of London University and Friends of the Courtauld).*

At exit continue along Strand to see island churches of **St Mary-le-Strand** (James Gibbs, 1717) and **St Clement Danes** (Wren and Gibbs, 1682 and 1719).

Walk on past Law Courts to **Temple Bar** (now a Victorian monument in road marking W boundary of City of London). Walk ends here. Nearest refreshments in local hostelries such as Cock Tavern at 22 Fleet Street. Nearest ⊖ Aldwych (peak hours only); buses in Fleet Street go E to City and W to West End.

Charing Cross

Charing was a village on the western fringes of London when Eleanor of Castile, wife of King Edward I, died at Harby, Nottinghamshire in 1290. Her body was embalmed at Lincoln and then carried to London to be buried in Westminster Abbey. At each of the twelve resting places where the cortège stopped overnight, Edward I erected an Eleanor Cross.

The last of these was at Charing Cross. The original cross stood at the top of Whitehall, close to the present site of Le Sueur's statue of

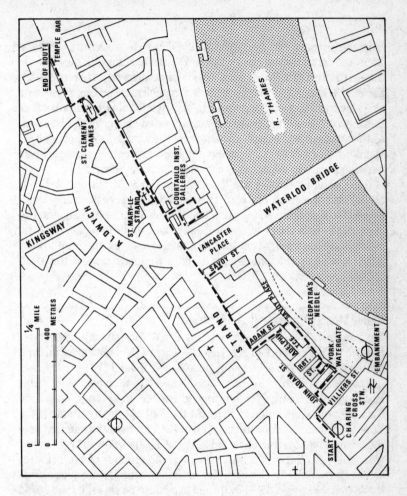

Charles I, until it was pulled down in 1647 and broken up. Before its destruction, the cross was the point from which all distances from London were measured. The present cross in the station forecourt was designed by E.M. Barry in 1863 from drawings of the old one; Barry also built the station hotel. The statues of Queen Eleanor are by Thomas Earp. Although not the most exciting of edifices – and the wire netting which traps the statues in their niches is an eyesore – the cross has a romantic history, now more than seven hundred years old.

In the earliest surviving map of London, which shows the city in 1558, the Strand linked Henry VIII's Whitehall Palace with the City. On the north side of the road, houses with gardens faced an open field. On the south side were mansions built for noblemen and bishops, with extensive grounds running down to the river. Some of the names of those great Tudor families are commemorated in nearby streets, such as Buckingham Street after the Dukes of Buckingham, while Somerset House was originally the palace of the Lord Protector Somerset, who governed the country for the nine-year-old King Edward VI.

Across the road today are the courtyard of St Martin-in-the-Fields (1724) and the head office of Coutts & Co., bankers to the Royal Family, whose founder set up in business in 1692 at 'the sign of The Three Crowns in the Strand'. The bank moved to the present building in 1904. It has been much renovated but preserves the pepperpot towers which were part of John Nash's original Regency blocks, the West Strand Improvements of 1831.

York Watergate and Adelphi

We turn down Villiers Street past York Place. More family connections here: the Villiers was George Villiers, Duke of Buckingham, who lived in a mansion called York House, demolished about 1670.

From John Adam Street, named after the architect, we follow Buckingham Street, which has a good eighteenth-century flavour, to the river, or rather, the old river. At the foot of the street stands the York Watergate. Before the building of the Victoria Embankment, and the Embankment Gardens, in 1864-70, the Thames flowed beneath this gate which gave access to the river from the grounds of York House.

The house at 14 Buckingham Street is interesting. A plaque records that Samuel Pepys (1633-1703) lived in a house on this site, and so did Robert Harley, Earl of Oxford (1661-1724), while in the present house, rebuilt in 1790, lived two nineteenth-century painters, William Etty and Clarkson Stanfield.

To the east of the next street, called York Buildings, was the old Adelphi. This was a grand speculative development of riverside houses built by the Adam brothers in the 1770s. The scheme included a Royal Terrace raised above large vaults which travelled underground into the hillside sloping down from the Strand. The vaults became Victorian wine cellars and coal stores, and eventually Royal Terrace was knocked down and replaced in 1938 by the anonymous commercial lump which has retained the Adelphi name. Fascinating, though, to wander into the old vaults along Lower Robert Street, now a shortcut favoured by taxi drivers, and emerge where the river used to run. In the Adams' day this was a busy wharf lined with small ships unloading, and loud with the noise of carters clattering their horses up to the waterside to collect and deliver.

Up above, from Adelphi Terrace, a good view extends over the Embankment Gardens to the river and the flanking bridges – Waterloo road bridge (1817) to the left and Hungerford rail and footbridge (1864) to the right. Ahead is Cleopatra's Needle, guarded by a pair of inward-facing sphinxes. The Needle, a granite obelisk weighing some 186 tons, dates from about 1475 BC. It was presented to Britain by Mohammed Ali, Viceroy of Egypt, and eventually towed from Alexandria to London in a special iron pontoon and erected here in 1878.

A plaque at No.8 Adam Street commemorates Sir Richard Arkwright (1732-92), industrialist and inventor of the water frame and spinning jenny, who lived in this house.

Strand and Savoy

The Strand passed into this century with a reputation for theatrical night-life, boisterous pubs, chop houses and restaurants. Theatres have stood on the site of the Adelphi Theatre since 1806 and the Vaudeville Theatre dates from 1870. It was the time of the music-hall song 'Let's all go down the Strand ('ave a banana)' and of the Gaiety Girls at the Gaiety Theatre, strolling the stage beneath parasols and displaying hour-glass figures which popped the eyes of Edwardian stage-door johnnies.

To the right in Savoy Court is another theatre, the Savoy, alas closed after a fire in 1990 destroyed its Art Deco auditorium. It was built in 1881 for Richard D'Oyley Carte who sought a special venue for putting on operas by Gilbert and Sullivan. The metallic frontage of the Savoy Hotel has a certain glitz, though little could match its grand beginnings in 1889, when César Ritz was manager and Auguste Escoffier directed the kitchens. Around the courtyard, plaques outline a much earlier period of glory, when a great mansion stood here, called Savoy Palace after a thirteenth-century Count of Savoy who owned the land. It survived one attack by the mob in 1377 but was brought down during Wat Tyler's Peasants' Rebellion of 1381. In 1505 it was rebuilt as a hospital for the poor. After various changes of use it fell into disrepair and was pulled down in 1816 to make way for the new road leading to Waterloo Bridge. All that remains of the hospital is the Savoy Chapel, entered on the far side of the gardens in Savoy Hill. It is curious in these sloping side streets, dominated by cliff-like hotel and commercial façades, to find a simple stone building, dedicated in 1510. In 1937 it became the Chapel of the Royal Victorian Order.

A sturdy survivor from the last century is Simpson's-in-the-Strand, which opened in 1848 as Simpson's Tavern and Divan and launched the custom of wheeling hot joints to its customers on a dinner wagon. The old building was demolished in 1900 and the present restaurant dates from 1904, a popular rendezvous for businessmen wanting a hearty traditional feed at lunchtime and never mind the waistline.

On the left in Wellington Place is the columned portico of the Lyceum, once a famous dance hall but now run into hard times, its doorways and capitals deeply encrusted with birdlime. In its better days it was the Royal Lyceum and Opera House, staging productions by Henry Irving which starred himself and Ellen Terry.

Courtauld Institute Galleries

In 1990 the Courtauld collection moved to Somerset House, together with the Courtauld Institute of Art for students of art history. Immediately the Galleries ran into controversy.

Critics said the rooms of Sir William Chambers's late eighteenth-century government offices were unsuitable for use as an art gallery. They were too hot, the plaster mouldings on the walls got in the way of the pictures, the conversion of the Great Room was a gimcrack disaster, there was nowhere to put the famous watercolours and drawings, and no room to display future acquisitions.

Much of this I agree with, though none of it would deter me from going in. The range and quality of the paintings make this a major collection, and the new location should undoubtedly attract more visitors than went to see it at its last, relatively obscure home in Woburn Square. It is based on the personal collection of Samuel

Courtauld, doyen of the textile family, augmented by later donations. The galleries are reached by a winding staircase. On the first floor are rooms devoted to Renaissance art, with a fine *Adam and Eve* by Cranach; later Italian art and Rubens; Tiepolo and Italian art of the eighteenth century; Impressionists and Post Impressionists.

The drawbacks identified by the critics are perhaps minor in themselves but together amount to something more serious. The pale green walls do not suit all the early pictures. A Van Dyck is awkwardly hung, high above a large fireplace. In Gallery 4, once the ante-room of the Royal Society of Antiquaries, the moulded wall panels have forced the Tiepolos into uncomfortable clusters. In Gallery 5 a small Seurat is virtually hidden behind the door. Gallery 6 is a dingy room which does nothing for the works of Cézanne, Toulouse-Lautrec and Modigliani, and Gauguin's *Haymaking* is hopelessly skied above the fireplace.

A sign warns that the stairs to the second floor are steep and slippery. A lift offers an alternative, but why not do something about the stairs? Gallery 7 shows eighteenth-century decorative arts and portraits and Gallery 8 has thematic exhibitions. This is the Great Room, and I do not at all like its instructional mélange, ranged in ugly booths around the walls and offering more commentary than picture across a bewildering span from fourteenth-century predella panels to Kokoschka. Press on though, and, whatever your feelings about Roger Fry and modern British abstract art – all squashed up together – do not miss the wonderful room of early Italian and Netherlandish paintings, including a landscape by Pieter Brueghel the Elder and other works attributed to the Master of Flémalle and Rogier van der Weyden.

Down again to the ground floor, where there is a bookshop and another winding stair down to a poky cafeteria.

The Lord Protector Somerset's original palace, completed in 1550, retained its royal connections until the eighteenth century. In 1775, after Queen Charlotte, wife of George III, had expressed a preference for living at Buckingham House, the old palace was demolished. The government offices which replaced it have been occupied by all sorts of bodies, from the Royal Academy to the Stamp Office and the Register of Births, Deaths and Marriages (which moved out in 1973). Today the Inland Revenue has the west wing, and at the far end of the courtyard is the Principal Registry of the Family Division of the High Court, where the public go in a steady stream to examine wills and grants.

St Mary-le-Strand

Many old streets and timber-fronted houses were lost at the turn of the century when the Strand was widened. The crescent of Aldwych opened a new route up to Holborn, and eventually the large blocks appeared which contain Australia House, India House and Bush House, centre of the BBC's External Radio Services. The parish church of the area is St Mary-le-Strand, a name going back to 1222. Before that, in 1157, Thomas Becket was appointed rector of a church on the site called The Nativity of Our Lady and the Innocents of the Strand; he remained rector until his martyrdom in 1170.

In 1549 the Lord Protector Somerset demolished the church to make room for his new palace and the parishioners moved to the Savoy Chapel, remaining there until the present church was opened in 1724. This is the first major work of James Gibbs and displays Italian Baroque influence in the treatment of the walls, plasterwork ceiling and domed porch, approached through a pretty garden where once an old maypole stood. The steeple reflects the style of Wren; in the Blitz it was twisted by bomb damage, and in 1983 dismantled and repaired. In 1984 the church became the official church of the Wrens (Women's Royal Naval Service), and a Book of Remembrance records the names of Wrens who have died in the Service from 1914.

St Clement Danes

Continue past the grim buildings of King's College. Ahead is a stern black statue of William Gladstone around which the vans of TV crews park while their reporters forage for scandal at the nearby Law Courts. Take shelter from the news-hounds in the Church of St Clement Danes.

Its history goes back to the ninth century when Danes who had married Englishwomen were allowed to settle in the district between Westminster and Ludgate. The present church was built by Sir Christopher Wren in 1682, and James Gibbs's steeple was added in 1719. The church was destroyed in the Blitz, though the walls and steeple remained above the rubble. The Royal Air Force launched an appeal fund and the restored church was reconsecrated in 1958 as The Central Church of the Royal Air Force.

This is also the 'Oranges and Lemons' church of the nursery rhyme. In March every year an Oranges and Lemons service is held here for children of the local primary school, and each day at 09.00, 12.00, 15.00

and 18.00 the bells play the old tune.

Inside, the atmosphere of the galleried building is very much that of an armed services church. The Welsh slate paving of the aisles incorporates more than 800 RAF badges. There are Squadron standards, eleven Books of Remembrance and memorials to special units such as the Polish squadrons which flew with the RAF in the Second World War. The carved pulpit is attributed to Grinling Gibbons, and nearby is a chair presented by the fighter ace Sir Douglas Bader. The walls of the crypt are studded with coffin plates from the time, up to 1853, when it served as a burial place. Other memorials include the bronze plaque of the Royal Air Force Escaping Society and the Battle of Britain Roll of Honour.

City Limits

To see the Strand to its end, continue past the Victorian Gothic Law Courts (see *Walk 8: The Inns of Court*), the timbered George pub, Twinings original tea and coffee premises and the Wig & Pen Club. In the centre of the road is a Victorian memorial designed in 1880 to commemorate the site of Temple Bar, a fine ceremonial gateway dating from the fourteenth century which straddled the road and contained a prison in the upper storey. The function of the gateway was to define the western limits of the City of London. It was rebuilt in the 1670s by Wren and finally removed in 1878 because it blocked the flow of traffic.

The present memorial is decorated with figures of Queen Victoria and Edward VII, and on top a bronze griffin from the City's badge. On the Strand side of the dusty plinth, a yellow arrow marks the centreline of the old gateway.

Walk 8

Inns of Court

All in a group, in courts and lanes to north and south of Fleet
Street, barristers and solicitors ply their trade. Visit Lincoln's
Inn, the Law Courts, Middle and Inner Temple. See also the
extraordinary collections in Sir John Soane's Museum, and
around the old heart of the newspaper world visit St Bride's
Church and Dr Johnson's House.
Allow   5-6 hours.
Best times   Not Sunday, Monday or bank holidays, when Sir
John Soane's Museum closed. Dr Johnson's House also closed
Sunday.

ROUTE

Begin at ⊖ Holborn. Turn left in Kingsway and 1st left in Gate Street, turning right at the corner to Lincoln's Inn Fields. Turn left along N side and at No.13 visit **Sir John Soane's Museum** 👁; open 10.00 to 17.00, closed Sunday, Monday, bank holidays. 1st Tuesday of month, opens evening 18.00 to 21.00.

At exit turn left and follow square round to gateway to **Lincoln's Inn**. See Library and Old Hall and visit Chapel. Turn S through New Square and go through arch to Carey Street. Turn left and right through Bell Yard to Fleet Street/Strand. Turn right to **Law Courts** and enter (first leaving camera at newsstand further on). Visit hall and selected court(s).

From Law Courts, cross Strand and enter Devereux Court. At Devereux Chambers, turn left to New Court of **Middle Temple**. Bear left past Hall and go ahead across Middle Temple Lane to garden next to Lamb Building. Continue to Crown Office Row and view of **Inner Temple Gardens**. Turn left to top of King's Bench Walk and turn left through gate to Tudor Street.

Continue to Dorset Rise and turn left. At Salisbury Square, go right through St Bride's Passage. Walk beside churchyard and at St Bride Foundation Institute turn down steps to road. Turn left and left up steps of St Bride's Avenue to **St Bride's Church** 👁. Visit church and crypts.

From church door, walk through to Fleet Street and cross road. Turn left and right into Bolt Court. Keep ahead to Gough Square and at No.17 visit **Dr Johnson's House** 👁; open May to September 11.00 to 17.30, October to April 11.00 to 17.00 (last tickets 15 minutes before closing time), closed Sunday. *Admission*.

At exit turn left through Pemberton Row and left via East and West Harding Streets to Fetter Lane. Turn right and 2nd left through Breams Buildings to Chancery Lane. Turn right and at corner of Southampton Buildings visit **London Silver Vaults** 👁; open 09.00 to 17.30, Saturday 09.00 to 12.30, closed Sunday.

Return to Chancery Lane and turn right to High Holborn. Walk ends here. Nearest refreshments at Cittie of York pub (opposite and to right). Nearest ⊖ Chancery Lane.

Lincoln's Inn Fields

At Holborn, one of the draughtiest Tube stations in London, emerge

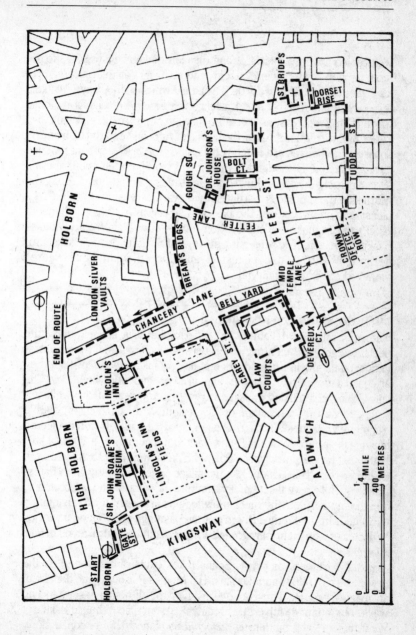

well cooled from the escalator and turn left down Kingsway. Take the next alley on the left, Gate Street, and turn right at the Ship Tavern. The alley by the Ship is Little Turnstile, which with Great Turnstile formed the old entrances to Lincoln's Inn Fields from Holborn. Only those with good reasons were let through the turnstiles, which also kept the cattle grazing in nearby fields from ambling into the fashionable square. The houses are much rebuilt since the first occupants moved here in the 1630s, though the mansion at No.66 (dated 1686) and the stucco frontages further down offer hints of earlier harmony. Along the north side the roofline is disrupted by upward extensions but there is a pleasing symmetry about the basically Georgian frontages. Numbers 12, 13 and 14 make a group by themselves – two plain-fronted houses flanking the eccentric projecting storeys of Sir John Soane's Museum, decorated with Gothic pedestals and topped with stone figures modelled on Athenian caryatids.

Sir John Soane's Museum

The museum is a delightful font of paraphernalia and paradox, the perfect eighteenth-century collector's showpiece and the smallest national museum in England. Its box-like rooms, some taller than they are broad or long, its nooks and alcoves and stairways, and the astonishing colonnaded passageway across the rear of the well, are hung and adorned with innumerable ancient statues and casts, marble fragments, plaques, urns, friezes, gargoyles, models for projected buildings – a new Whitehall, and various monuments, a 70m (230ft) Britannia, for instance, which Sir John Soane proposed to stand on top of Greenwich Hill. Under the guidance of enthusiastic attendants, panels open to reveal sets of architectural drawings and watercolours, and the mystery of why one is now looking at a giant fungus is quietly explained. In the Picture Room are the paintings of two famous series by Hogarth, the eight-part *Rake's Progress* and the four scenes of *The Election*.

In the basement or crypt, Soane takes exuberant revenge on the pretensions of fellow antiquarians. His Monk's Parlour is the domain of an imaginary monk, a man not overly given to self-denial, it seems. The walls are crammed with casts, medieval masonry from the old Palace of Westminster, and numerous *memento mori* including a bronze skull.

The monk, an Italian alter-ego of Sir John known as Padre Giovanni, lived in an adjoining cell, now a store cupboard. Through the parlour window are the ruins of an artificial cloister and the tomb of Father John, which in reality contains whatever is left of Fanny, a much-loved dog.

Sir John Soane, architect of the Bank of England and Professor of Architecture at the Royal Academy from 1806, lived in this house for twenty-four years up to his death in 1837. After his wife died in 1815 he lived there alone, accumulating more and more pieces for his collections, which with the house he eventually left to the nation on condition that they be kept 'as nearly as possible in the state in which Sir John Soane shall leave it'.

His wishes have been most honourably upheld. On the first Tuesday of the month the museum opens in the evening from 18.00 to 21.00, the rooms are lit by candles and candelabra and the atmosphere is stranger still, poetic as no other museum.

Lincoln's Inn

Continue round the gardens at the centre of the square. The sound of coughing through the bushes directs the eye to the unravelling spectacle of a cardboard village for dossers. Around the tennis courts and in bushes beside the railings are pitiful shacks made from cardboard packing cases, impromptu tents of plastic sheeting held down by looted milk crates. A sodden blanket dries on a bush, a T-shirt on a wire coathanger, attached to a tree branch, turns in the breeze. Along these dismal rows, the silence of the dead. How many men are hiding in the dark of those terrible shelters? Who looks after them?

On the east side of the square, turn in at the gatehouse of Lincoln's Inn. Founded in the fourteenth century, this is the oldest of London's four Inns of Court. The word 'inn', in this context, originally meant a hostel where barristers and law students lived in a community. As the administration of the legal profession has evolved, the Inns of Court are independent bodies linked federally to a Senate. To become a practising barrister, an applicant must find a position in a set of chambers attached to one of the Inns of Court where he or she then works and studies for his or her Bar examinations.

In England and Wales, most professional legal work is shared between barristers and solicitors. There are about 4,000 barristers, two-thirds of them in London, and 37,000 solicitors. While either may represent a client in one of the lower courts, only a barrister has the right to plead a case in the higher courts – the Crown Court, High Court and above. Barristers are a specialist élite and from their ranks are chosen the judges who preside in County Courts and the higher courts.

To the left of the gatehouse is the Library and Treasury, completed in 1845 with rows of tall chimneys in lattice brickwork, a lantern and cupola at the centre of the roof. To the right is New Square, built between 1682 and 1693, an orderly pattern of four-storey terraced houses around central gardens, faced on the north side with ornamental wrought-iron gates. On the far side is the Old Hall, completed in 'the fifth year of the reign of Henry VII' (1490). Nearby is the attractive stone vaulting of the Chapel undercroft, an open space designed as a meeting place for students, and for barristers and solicitors wishing to talk with their clients. The Chapel was designed c.1620, probably by Inigo Jones, and was much restored and enlarged in the next two centuries. Go up steps from Old Square to find solid ranks of pews in three rows running fore and aft, unlike the inward-facing pattern at Oxbridge college chapels. The east window is brilliant with heraldic glass bearing the arms of distinguished treasurers, and the corbels under the roof supports take the form of angelic busts of former preachers, gilt-winged and each holding his shield before him.

Outside by Stone Buildings (1780), the impressive long Classical block in Portland stone, a gardener runs his mower over the already immaculate lawn, sending up only the finest shower of bright green cuttings. The gardens are private but open to the public from 12.00 to 14.00 'for the enjoyment of rest and quiet'. This slightly pompous concession is made by order of the Under Treasurer to The Honourable Society of Lincoln's Inn.

In New Square, turn south past doorways emblazoned with nameboards listing the occupants, and leave through the archway next to Wildy & Sons, Law Booksellers. Beyond is Carey Street, home of the Bankruptcy Court and begetter of the expression 'to be in Carey Street', meaning at the very least that one is pushed for cash. To the right, bright silverware glitters in the window of The Silver Mousetrap and the Seven Stars pub is an old lawyers' watering hole with a panelled ceiling and prints of judges and barristers. Across the road is a private entrance to the Law Courts. We must go round to the front door in the

Strand, passing the Temple Bar memorial which marks the boundary of the City of London (described in *Walk 7*).

Law Courts

Cameras are not allowed in the Royal Courts of Justice, but may be left at the newsstand just along the road. The vendor makes a small charge for this and hands over a cloakroom ticket.

Go in to the main door, where Press teams and film cameramen seem perpetually in waiting, between signs which point to Barristers' Robing Rooms. After the security check, enter the huge vaulted hall, as big as a cathedral but austere in a way churches on this scale seldom are. The Law Courts were designed by G.E. Street and built between 1874 and 1882, marking virtually the end of the Gothic Revival period in large public buildings. It contains more than a thousand rooms and altogether about sixty courts which handle civil, rather than criminal, cases.

To left and right staircases lead up to the courts. In the centre of the marble floor are a map of the courts and a reading stand inscribed 'Daily Cause Lists', which identify the cases to be heard that day. For a closer look, choose a flight of stairs, say those leading to Courts 1-10, and walk along the gloomy stone corridor to the rear of the courts, where barristers and clients discuss, ponder and gossip to pass the time before they are called. Anyone may go in to sit at the back of a court which has benches marked 'Public'. Here in small panelled rooms, lined with the leather spines of legal books, the staid anti-dramas of English civil justice are played towards some distant conclusion. The judges and barristers in wigs and robes are impressively persuasive and firmly in charge on their home territory. The non-professionals look taut and overawed, trapped in their Sunday-best clothes. Imagine an eighteenth-century painting of the scene by Hogarth, and contemplate how little the routines seem to have changed.

Middle and Inner Temples

Lawyers and students acquired permission to start a hostel here in the early fourteenth century. The land had previously belonged to the Knights Templar, from which the name Temple derives, and is now the home of two Inns of Court. We enter Middle Temple from the alley of

Devereux Court, arriving in New Court, a pleasantly ordered development dating from the post-Fire years, *c.*1675. Continue to Fountain Court, where Shakespeare's *Twelfth Night* had its first performance. Pass the Tudor Hall and cross Middle Temple Lane, which more or less separates the two Inns, though not entirely. In the erratic network of lanes, alleys and courtyards, the legal people come and go, clerks weighed down by box upon box of documents, bundles of papers tied with string, making the ritual passage from chambers to court and back again.

The gardens of Inner Temple are closed to the public but the view across the broad sweep of lawns to the Embankment is free for all. Around the turn of the century the Royal Horticultural Society staged its annual spring show in these gardens, before moving in 1913 to the gardens of the Royal Hospital in Chelsea. In King's Bench Walk a fine terrace of chambers, designed for the greater part by Wren, parades along the east side of the gardens.

Go through the gateway to Tudor Street. Opposite the block called Temple Chambers is The Witness Box, a comfortable pub frequented at lunchtime by cockney clerks who talk airily of fast cars and shark fishing trips. Continue along Tudor Street which, with Bouverie Street, once contained the offices and press rooms of the *Daily Mail* and the *News of the World*. The vacant bays, where paper lorries formerly unloaded vast reels of newsprint, are now gaunt car parks. The *Observer* too had its offices in Tudor Street until the 1960s, a period when overmanning practices were rife throughout the industry. Then the paper moved to Printing House Square, where it already shared the presses with *The Times*. A man, whose sole job in Tudor Street had been to prevent fellow-workers from falling through a dangerous but necessary hole in the floor, was then found even easier employment guarding a non-existent hole in the new building.

St Bride's Church

Although many newspapers have moved away from Fleet Street, St Bride's will always be the printers' church. The relationship goes back to Wynkin de Worde, William Caxton's apprentice, who on his master's death in 1491 brought his press with movable type – the first in England – to a workshop next to St Bride's, where he knew he would find a literate and interested clientèle. Other printers moved in and for some 450 years Fleet Street and the Press were indivisible. The world's most famous newspaper street is now virtually defunct, overtaken by computer-driven methods which made the old premises redundant and also removed the need for central offices grouped in one part of London. Nowadays our national dailies are produced in semi-remote locations anywhere between Kensington High Street and Wapping. It is important, though, to remember the long history of life 'in the ink', and St Bride's is a quiet place to recall this past.

Churches have stood on this site since the sixth century AD. The sixth church here was destroyed in the Great Fire of 1666 and the new building was one of the fifty new churches designed by Wren. The tiered spire is particularly fine – 'a madrigal in stone' was one admirer's tribute to its tapering Italianate delicacy. In 1940 the church was destroyed by bombing. The rebuilding has proved significant in more than one sense. What we now see is a twentieth-century interior, but very much in the style of Wren. His galleries were not replaced, and the arrangement of pews is collegiate and inward-facing, not in eastward-facing rows as before. The altar too is markedly different, though the carvings in the towering reredos are strongly reminiscent of Grinling Gibbons. In all the new church is remarkably true to the ideals of our greatest Classical architect. The carpentry and ornamentation are an excellent testimony to modern craftsmanship, and the *trompe l'oeil* ceiling behind the altar is colourful and provocative. *Surely* the painting decorates a curved apse? It must do! The viewer is delighted to discover that the wall is flat.

Downstairs is a warren of crypts which only came to light after 1940 when the demands of reconstruction made it imperative to excavate the great forgotten underbelly which had been locked up and ignored since 1854. Then, after a plague of cholera had claimed more than 10,000 lives, Parliament banned any further burials in the City of London. After the war, to everyone's astonishment, a great burial maze was rescued from the past, making St Bride's more than a thousand years older than had been thought.

The old crypts are now reorganised into a main crypt where services are held and showcases document the many rare finds made on the site. Behind the altar, mirrors angle down to a Roman pavement, and all around are fragments of medieval wall. To the left of the entrance a partly raised walkway leads to the tiny medieval chapel, furnished with seats for no more than half a dozen, where office workers may snatch a few minutes' peaceful contemplation, seated safe beneath and far from the thump and roar of the piledrivers and diggers which reverberate through the parish, wrenching Fleet Street into a new phase of life.

Dr Johnson's House

Across the road in Fleet Street are two more dinosaurs: the old offices of the *Daily Express* (1931, known to *Private Eye* magazine as 'The Black Lubyanka') and to the left the *Daily Telegraph* (1930), distinguished by its coloured Art Deco clock. The alleys and courts around Fleet Street, and their taverns and coffee houses, were the haunts of many a famous writer in the eighteenth century – first Addison and Steele, then Johnson, Boswell and Goldsmith. The house at 17 Gough Square was occupied by Dr Samuel Johnson from 1749 to 1759, and is now preserved as a museum.

On the walls hang many portraits of the Doctor and his contemporaries, and interesting items of furniture include a narrow gout chair from the Old Cock Tavern. The furniture is thinly spread, though, and empty expanses of beige carpeting make an unfortunate barrier to summoning the spirit of the house where Johnson compiled his *Dictionary* in the garret. This is the most evocative room. Boswell said it was 'fitted up like a counting house' and in this low-ceilinged attic we can imagine the long desk where his staff of six clerks laboured side by side, standing up as was the practice then with office workers.

London Silver Vaults

In Chancery Lane we pass a gateway to Lincoln's Inn, next to the Chapel visited earlier. On the corner with Southampton Buildings are the underground rooms of the London Silver Vaults. Step down to the basement which is shared with the Chancery Lane Safe Deposit Company: two long marble corridors of shops dedicated to silverware, each housed behind a heavy strong-room door. Scores of small sparkling caverns purvey an unflagging collection of anything silver: teapots, candelabra, chalices, tableware, jewellery, clocks, decanter labels, snuff boxes – a bottomless inventory of desirable and costly treasures. Airless and four-square, it must be a strange place to work.

Continue up Chancery Lane to High Holborn. Beneath its striped awning – an apt conclusion to this tour of Legal London – the firm of Thresher & Glenny sells outfits for barristers, from gowns and neck bands to wigs in genuine horsehair.

Walk 9

Bloomsbury

The cosmopolitan quarter of scholarship, and of literary gatherings in the Twenties. Visit the Exhibition Galleries of the British Museum and stroll through leafy gardens into the central corpus of London University. See the Percival David Foundation of Chinese Art, the Thomas Coram Foundation for Children and the house to which Charles Dickens moved in 1837, now a museum.

Allow   All day.
Best times   Not Sunday.

ROUTE

Begin at ⊖ Tottenham Court Road. At exit marked 'Dominion Theatre, British Museum, Tottenham Court Road (East Side)', go up the steps beside the Dominion Theatre. Follow Tottenham Court Road and turn right in Great Russell Street. Continue to **British Museum** ⊚; Exhibition Galleries open 10.00 to 17.00, Sunday 14.30 to 18.00, closed 1 January, 29 March, 6 May, 24-26 December. *Donation requested.* Admission to British Library Reading Room is by pass only (except for brief visit, details below).

At exit turn left and continue to Bloomsbury Square. Turn left up Bedford Place to Russell Square. Walk through gardens and exit at NW corner to Thornhaugh Street. Walk through part of London University to Woburn Square and Gordon Square. Look round square and at SE corner visit **Percival David Foundation of Chinese Art** ⊚; open 10.30 to 17.00, closed Saturday, Sunday and bank holidays. At exit continue E to Tavistock Square. Go through gardens to NE corner and walk along Upper Woburn Place.

Turn right into Woburn Walk, right into Burton Street, left to Burton Place and right through the crescent of Cartwright Gardens. Turn right down Marchmont Street and walk through the Brunswick Centre. At Renoir Cinema, bear left to top of Brunswick Square and follow to **Thomas Coram Foundation** ⊚; Art Treasures open 10.00 to 16.00, closed Saturday, Sunday, bank holidays and when special conferences are taking place. *Admission.*

Turn left at exit and walk along path by football pitch to Mecklenburgh Square and turn right to Doughty Street. At No.48 visit **Dickens Museum** ⊚; open 10.00 to 17.00, closed Sunday and public holidays. *Admission.*

On leaving, continue along Doughty Street and keep straight on through John Street to Theobalds Road. Bear right across road to gardens of **Gray's Inn**, open Monday to Friday 12.00 to 14.30. Walk through to Gray's Inn Place. If gardens closed, walk through on parallel road to W (Raymond Buildings) and emerge at Inns of Court School of Law.

Turn left through Gray's Inn Place to Gray's Inn Square, the communal centre with Chapel and Hall. Turn right to South Square, containing the Library and Treasury, and continue past lodge to High Holborn.

Walk ends here. Nearest refreshments at Cittie of York pub, a prime

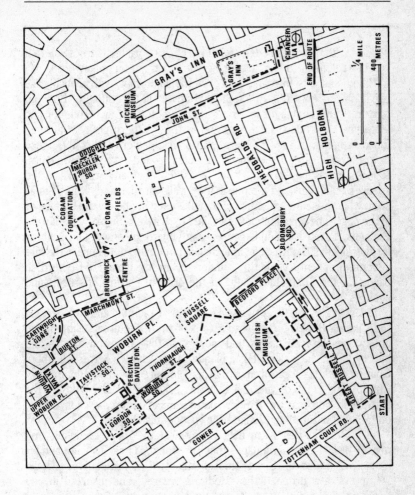

specimen dating from 1430 with a vast timbered bar and discreet panelled cubicles. Nearest ⊖ Chancery Lane.

Passport to Bloomsbury

Tottenham Court Road continues the northward line of Charing Cross Road as far as Euston, and specialises in video and hi-fi shops. To the west of the road junction is the grubbier end of Oxford Street, bordering the northern edge of Soho, a chain-store high street where it would be difficult to find something you could not buy elsewhere.

Bloomsbury, to the east, is an exceptional district, with probably the greatest concentration of intellectual power in the whole of London, nurtured and sustained in its northern sector by the students and lecturers of London University and in the southern part by an even more irregular army of scholars, publishers, dealers and coffee-house orators who cluster in the offices and cafés around the British Museum. It is a surprisingly green place, blessed with many well-preserved squares – and gardens the public may walk through and sit in. It is all somewhat museum-ish, much of the interest lying below the surface or in the past. The street names are a clue to this past. So many Bedfords, Russells, Tavistocks and Gowers, testifying to the power and alliance-forging skills of the Russell family which put down roots here in the late seventeenth century and then, under successive Dukes of Bedford, in particular the Sixth Duke, laid out the present pattern of streets and squares.

In Great Russell Street, just past the first rash of sandwich bars, is the Cinema Bookshop, a steadfast occupant of the area selling movie books, posters, postcards and glossy photos of screen heroes and heroines. On the wall here is a plaque to Mr Charles Kitterbell whom Charles Dickens located at No.14 and featured in 'The Bloomsbury Christening', one of the Tales in his *Sketches by Boz* (1837). Mr Kitterbell, you may remember, had an uncle, a 'cross, cadaverous, odd, and ill-natured' man called Mr Nicodemus Dumps:

' . . . Mr Charles Kitterbell was one of the most credulous and matter-of-fact little personages that ever took *to* himself a wife, and *for* himself a house in Great Russell-street, Bedford-square. (Uncle Dumps always dropped the "Bedford-square", and inserted in lieu thereof the dreadful words "Tottenham-court-road".)'

The snobberies attaching to where someone really lives in London are an ageless source of fun-poking. Dickens would no doubt have enjoyed the irony that, after the success of his *Autobiography of a Super-Tramp*, the author and wanderer W.H. Davies also settled himself at No.14, from 1916 to 1922.

At the crossing with Bloomsbury Street, look right to establish the position of *the* umbrella shop, James Smith & Sons, 53 New Oxford Street, its bright windows a parade of coloured brollies, sticks and parasols. (Never leave a James Smith umbrella on a train. It will be too irresistible to the finder and you will never see it again.)

In the next row on Great Russell Street are shops more characteristic of Bloomsbury: Collet's Chinese Bookshop, Arthur Probsthain Oriental Bookseller, a publisher's office and galleries selling Japanese prints and Roman coins.

British Museum

From the gateway, approach the great Classical portico, its pediment crowded with figures representing the forward march of civilisation. This was one of a series of major extensions designed by Robert Smirke between 1823 and 1866 to the original foundation initiated by the sale to Parliament at a generous price of Sir Hans Sloane's collections. Large-scale plans in the forecourt show the vast choice now available to visitors. Galleries on three levels offer various Antiquities, Oriental rooms, Prehistory and Romano-British History, Medieval, Renaissance and Modern, Coins and Medals, Prints and Drawings.

In the main hall collect a plan of it all and retire to one side to plot your course. The celebrated domed Reading Room is straight ahead. Visitors without a special pass may go inside for two or three minutes on the hour, 11.00 to 16.00.

From the hall a doorway on the right leads to the British Library Galleries, well worth a visit to see its fascinating collections of manuscripts and early books. The British Library is scheduled to complete its move to new buildings in Somerstown, next to St Pancras Station, by 1996 and changes are likely here from 1994 – though perhaps good old British lethargy and the traditional spirit of compromise will bring further slippage. After the move, the King's Library is due to house a permanent exhibition of European porcelain.

For now, go through to Room 30 to find the Manuscript Saloon. In showcases are English literary manuscripts from Ben Jonson to Philip Larkin, topographical drawings, prints, the Magna Carta and other historic documents – a marvellous trove and in itself worth at least half an hour. To the right, in a low-lit room with white blinds drawn, are wonderful illuminated manuscripts – the Lindisfarne Gospels, bibles, psalters, books of hours and calendars.

On the far side of the Manuscript Saloon is the King's Library, designed in 1823-6 by Robert Smirke for the library of George III, its volumes now lining the walls of the long and gracious room. In the main showcases are foreign-language manuscripts in Japanese, Hebrew, Persian, Arabic – including the Bible in Arabic – and maps and writing materials. Continue past Roubiliac's statue of William Shakespeare (1758), brought here from the actor David Garrick's villa at Hampton. On display nearby is Shakespeare's first folio of 1623, with a portrait head by Martin Droeshout. Then a copy of the Gutenberg Bible and early printed books from Caxton's period with other cases of Italian and German books, examples of music printing, bookbinding and the British Library philatelic collections in pull-out vertical trays.

The museum plan suggests a brief list of objects of special interest (including the Magna Carta and Lindisfarne Gospels, already seen). To find the others on the ground floor, go through the bookshop to Room 27 and turn right to 25. The Rosetta Stone is a slab of black basalt mounted in an iron surround to ward off the too-curious. It is inscribed with three different scripts – hieroglyphs, demotic Egyptian and Greek – and was found in 1799. Its decipherment in 1814 by Thomas Young changed scholars' understanding of early Egyptian scripts.

Turn left to Room 20 and go ahead to 8. If the Elgin Marbles in the Duveen Room are spectacular – a huge hall lined with friezes from the Parthenon, removed by Lord Elgin's agents and acquired for the British Museum in 1816 – then so is the Nereid Monument from Xanthos in the previous room (7): a meticulous reconstruction of the east front of a monumental Ionic temple tomb. So too are the Assyrian sculptures (17), long reliefs of war chariots carrying spearmen and bowmen, so often illustrated as the first known antecedents of the modern fighting tank. Here the room is fronted by a gigantic pair of winged bulls with bearded human heads from the gates of the citadel of Khorsabad (early eighth century BC).

The Portland Vase is in Room 14. The vase is made of two layers of glass, white inside blue, the white delicately carved with relief figures. The finest surviving piece of Roman cameo glass (first century AD), it was sold to the Dowager Duchess of Portland shortly after 1785 and placed on loan to the British Museum in 1910. In 1845 it was smashed, but has been convincingly restored.

Return by some improvised route to the entrance hall. For items of early British interest, go up to the first floor and tour Rooms 40 to 48.

Among the treasures of Roman and medieval pottery and plate are the Mildenhall Treasure (found in 1940) and the Sutton Hoo Ship Burial (found in 1939). This was probably the tomb of an East Anglian king of the seventh century AD, possibly King Raedwald who died in 624-5, and consists of shield remains, an iron helmet, axe-hammer, sword and chain-mail armour.

There is so much more to see, of course, but perhaps that is enough for now. Just as the Victoria & Albert Museum (see *Walk 18*) advises against trying to see everything in one go, so the British Museum deserves patience and return visits.

Bloomsbury Squares and Gardens

If at all hungry, eat now. Up around the University, where we go next, there is little on offer, so profit from the fare in and around Museum Street. Continue to the top of Bloomsbury Square, where a statue of the reformer Charles James Fox stands at the edge of the dusty gardens. The east side of this once-fashionable Georgian square was radically altered in 1928 by the gigantic iron and stone office block of the Liverpool Victoria Insurance Company. Follow the quiet rows of Bedford Place to the statue of Francis, Duke of Bedford, and turn into the broad gardens of Russell Square – a peaceful place with an all-year café, the grass occupied for the most part by students and solitary readers.

A green cabmen's shelter still thrives next to Thornhaugh Street. Inside, invisible to their client-persecutors, off-duty taxi drivers restore themselves with fry-ups and hot tea. At the house next to the traffic barriers is a plaque to the poet T.S. Eliot who worked here for the publishers Faber & Faber from 1925 to 1965. The house is now part of London University, and we walk through its grounds. The University is vast. Many of its buildings are concentrated here but there are colleges too in Kensington, the Mile End Road and as far away as Egham, near Windsor. Continue past the School of Oriental and African Studies, the architecture now gone from Georgian to twentieth-century slab on slab. A concrete avenue leads to narrow Woburn Square which is followed by Gordon Square.

This is the place chiefly associated with the Bloomsbury Set of writers, artists and thinkers. Several of the group lived at No.50 and in adjoining houses, among them Virginia Woolf, Clive Bell and Lytton Strachey. Their friend, the economist Maynard Keynes, occupied No.46 from 1916 to 1946. The gardens are especially pretty, laid out with winding paths, a good variety of trees and rose beds. On the west side, next to the range of blackened stone houses, is Dr Williams's Library, a centre of study for Nonconformists founded in 1729 and transferred to this building in 1890. Beside it is the University Church of Christ the King, begun in 1853 for the Catholic Apostolic Church and now in the care of the University. Its style is Gothic Revival. After the modest exterior the nave is surprisingly large; behind the altar window is a chapel with a richly painted timber roof.

Percival David Foundation of Chinese Art

This small museum of Chinese ceramics is attached to the School of Oriental and African Studies and opened in 1952. Its collection of some 1,700 pieces of wares from the Sung, Yuan, Ming and Qing dynasties (tenth to nineteenth centuries) is based on gifts by Sir Percival David and the Hon. Mountstuart Elphinstone.

Wander through the galleries on three floors and admire the delicate work, the soft and bold colours of the bowls, plates and vases, here the bust of an emperor, there an elephant flower-holder, then a row of seals, boxes and snuff bottles, a Ming ewer in the form of a dancing girl (sixteenth century), a Qing bowl painted with dragons in yellow and green enamels (nineteenth century), a Ming water pot in the shape of a recumbent elephant, decorated in underglaze blue and overglaze red enamel. The Elphinstone bequest of monochrome porcelains is shown by itself – a range of domestic objects in brilliant pink, green, aquamarine, browns and deep blue. See also the lovely Qing dishes, bowls and a teapot painted in *famille rose* enamels.

The craftsman's pride and piety are sharply reflected in the almost poetic inscription on the neck of a pair of vases known as the David Vases (1351):

THE FAITHFUL DISCIPLE AND MEMBER OF THE
JINGTANG SOCIETY, ZHANG WENJIN OF DEXIAO LANE
IN THE VILLAGE OF SHUNZHENG IN YUSHAN
DISTRICT OF XUNZHOU, IS HAPPY TO PRESENT AN

ALTAR SET OF AN INCENSE BURNER AND VASES AS A
PRAYER FOR THE PROTECTION OF THE WHOLE
FAMILY AND FOR THE PEACE AND PROSPERITY OF
HIS DESCENDANTS. RECORDED ON A LUCKY DAY IN
THE FOURTH MONTH OF THE ELEVENTH YEAR OF
ZHIZHEN. DEDICATED BEFORE THE XUNGYUAN
ALTAR OF GENERAL HU JUNGYI.

Woburn Walk

The arrangement of Tavistock Square seems formal after the more
pastoral atmosphere of Gordon Square. At the centre is a seated statue
of Mahatma Gandhi (1869-1948). On the north side of the square is
Adler House, Court of the Chief Rabbi. Near the headquarters of the
British Medical Association in Tavistock House is a plaque to Charles
Dickens who lived in a house nearby.

In Upper Woburn Place, on the corner by the New Ambassadors
Theatre, turn into Woburn Walk, a charming double row of black and
white bow-fronted Georgian shops now operating as cafés, antique
dealers and florists. The poet W.B. Yeats had lodgings here between
1895 and 1919, in which period he published the poems *The Wind
among the Reeds* (1899), *The Green Helmet and Other Poems* (1910) and
a number of plays.

Wind through to Cartwright Gardens – in summer the *thwick-thwuck*
of tennis balls rises from courts in the centre of the crescent – and turn
down to Marchmont Street. At the Marquis of Cornwallis pub, turn into
the extraordinary terraced complex surrounding the Brunswick Shopping Centre. In the piazza the receding stacks rise on both sides, offering marvellous greenhouse opportunities for apartment-dwellers. The
Brunswick Centre is by Patrick Hodgkinson (1969-72) and I judge it a
refreshing success. It has a relaxed atmosphere, conveying a sense
that people actually enjoy living there. It also has a good cinema, the
Renoir, right there by the shops – brilliant! A pity the Centre is beginning to age rather fast, however. Going scruffy at the corners, façades
streaked with grime – such is the premature fate of so many modern
schemes.

Thomas Coram Foundation

A statue of the kindly Thomas Coram (1668-1751) stands outside the headquarters of his Foundation. The great achievement of this former sea captain was to set up a Foundling Hospital in Lamb's Conduit Fields in 1739 to care for the hundreds of young children being abandoned in the streets of London by parents unable or unwilling to continue their responsibility for them. The building, completed in 1745, remained on the site until 1926 when it was demolished.

In the main hall is a model of the hospital, the Boys' Wing and the Girls' Wing flanking a central block. Here and on the stairway are statues and paintings mainly on the themes of foundling children, hospitals and biblical episodes. William Hogarth was one of the first governors of the hospital and presented it with his perceptive portrait of Coram which hangs on the first-floor landing. A doorway leads to the Court Room, reproduced as it once was on the ground floor of the old building. Hogarth persuaded several artist friends to give paintings and decorate the room. The ornate plaster ceiling is by William Wilton and around the walls the pictures include Francis Hayman's *Finding of the Infant Moses in the Bulrushes* (1746) and Gainsborough's *The Charterhouse from the Terrace* (1748).

Raise the cloths on the showcases to find an extraordinary display of tokens left with abandoned children admitted to the hospital between 1741 and 1760. The more typical bear the child's initials or name, for example 'John Cuthbert Born December the 20th 1757'. More stark is the bottle label which simply says 'Ale'.

The hospital moved out of London and was eventually closed when institutional care was seen as no longer appropriate. Today the Foundation concentrates on looking after children and young people who do not receive adequate statutory provision. The playground across the road in Coram's Fields is remarkable, operating under the splendid rule that no adult may be admitted to it without a child. The grounds also contain a children's farm, and one of the surprises of walking beside the boundary in Lansdowne Terrace is to be confronted by sheep loudly baa-ing.

From the Foundation building turn along by the all-weather football pitch, passing the Thomas Coram Nursery on the left. Not all the children who play in Coram's Fields are little angels. At the end of the footpath three boys arrive on a luggage trolley marked 'King's Cross Station', which they abandon and jog away to their private Gazzaworld.

Dickens Museum

Officially it is called Dickens House Museum, on the reasonable grounds that Charles Dickens lived here with his family between spring 1837 and winter 1839, when they moved on to a grander house at 1 Devonshire Terrace, near Regent's Park (since demolished). To me, however, it is more of a museum than a house, crammed as it is with memorabilia from all periods of the writer's life, from the lawyer's desk at which he worked as a fifteen-year-old clerk in Gray's Inn to a range of kitsch objects which celebrate his fame as a novelist. In the Morning Room, for example, you can find Dickens sculpted in sugar for an anniversary cake, a gruesome model of the Maypole Inn (from *Barnaby Rudge*, which he began to write in this house) and an enormous Dickens family tree tracing members from 1785 to 1972.

This 'wide world of Dickens' approach differs hugely from the quiet intimacy of Carlyle's House in Chelsea (see *Walk 16*) which has aimed at presenting a Victorian author's home as he lived in it, and has largely succeeded in that aim, and in allowing the author's personality to come through. Here, although there are genuine associations with Dickens – he completed *Pickwick Papers* and wrote *Oliver Twist* and *Nicholas Nickleby* while living at 48 Doughty Street – it is not known for certain whether he wrote these books in the room now called The Study or in some other room. Around the house, furniture has been assembled to suggest the way things may have been. Some of the pieces were owned at some time by Dickens and some are supplementary period-pieces. There are too many question-marks for those in search of authenticity. Others, however, may submit happily to the deluge of Dickensiana on view.

The house is the only one of Dickens's London residences to have survived. It was saved from threat of demolition by the Dickens Fellowship, renovated and opened as a museum in 1925.

Gray's Inn

As a supplement to the other three Inns of Court visited in *Walk 8*, stroll through the gardens of Gray's Inn and walk through Field Court to Gray's Inn Square, a red-brick quadrangle which reflects the closed world of lawyers, at each doorway the names of the occupants of the various chambers painted on a board, as is also the custom on staircases at Oxford and Cambridge colleges. In South Square are the Library and

Treasury and in the centre a statue of Francis Bacon, a student of the Inn in 1586 who rose to become its Treasurer in 1608-17. Charles Dickens worked at an office in this square and located the lawyers of *Pickwick Papers* in chambers nearby.

Our walk ends just past the lodge in High Holborn. For its architecture as much as the refreshing drinks on offer, call in at the main bar of the Cittie of York, formerly Henekey's Long Bar, now a Samuel Smith pub – a lofty room with vats and barrels on a gallery above the bar. The inn dates from 1430 and was restored in 1923. On the far side of the great drinking concourse are panelled cubicles for four, places of discretion where lawyers may exchange confidences with their clients. Downstairs in the corridor leading to the Barnaby Rudge Cellar are enlarged photographs of the old days at Samuel Smith's Yorkshire brewery. They include a steam delivery dray, *c.*1918, and document the old and grisly custom of leading heifers into the yard and posing them with grinning brewery employees. Then they were hauled off and killed to provide the workers with their bumper Christmas dinner.

Walk 10

St Paul's and Barbican

Stroll uphill from Blackfriars to explore Wren's masterpiece, St Paul's Cathedral. Discover the Norman parish church that escaped the Great Fire. See Smithfield Meat Market and the Barbican complex. Finish at the excellent Museum of London.
Allow All day.
Best times Not Monday, when Museum of London closed, or Sunday when part of St Paul's Cathedral closed.

ROUTE

Begin at ⊖ Blackfriars. Turn right past flower stall to Queen Victoria Street and turn right. Cross by old *Times* building and turn left up St Andrew's Hill. On right, visit **Church of St Andrew-by-the-Wardrobe** 👁 ; open 08.00 to 18.00.

At exit continue up hill, turn left in Carter Lane and right along Creed Lane. In Ludgate Hill, turn right and visit **St Paul's Cathedral** 👁 ; open 07.30 to 18.00, in winter closes 17.00. *Admission*. Crypt and Treasury open 09.30 to 16.25, Saturday opens 11.00, closed Sunday. Upper galleries open 09.45 to 16.15, closed Sunday. *Admission*.

From steps by west door, turn right and right through St Paul's Churchyard. At New Change, turn left and cross to St Martin's-le-Grand and Aldersgate. Take 2nd left in Little Britain, bearing right and then turning right through Bartholomew Close, passing Butchers' Hall on left. Return to Little Britain and turn right to West Smithfield.

At Tudor-style gateway, walk through to **Church of St Bartholomew the Great** 👁 ; open 08.00 to 16.30, Friday opens 10.45, Saturday closes 20.00, closed Sunday except for services.

Return to West Smithfield and turn right. Turn right into Cloth Fair to see No.41 and return to West Smithfield. Turn right and continue through Grand Avenue of **Meat Market**, then right along Charterhouse Street, through Charterhouse Square and along Carthusian Street to Aldersgate. Turn right to Barbican Tube station and take stairs up to footbridge crossing to Barbican. Follow yellow signs to **Barbican Centre**. Keep on down steps, across piazza and down steps to Theatre entrance. Collect leaflets and explore (many opportunities for lunch).

From front of Theatre, turn left along Lakeside Terrace to boundary with Guildhall School of Music and Drama. Go up North Stair and across Gilbert Bridge. At end, take public lift down to 'Street' and walk across to **Roman wall** beside E end Church of St Giles Cripplegate.

Return as far as rectory and turn right past Crowders Well pub (also good for lunch) and right along Wood Street. At St Alphage Garden turn left to **Roman and medieval wall** in garden. Go back to end of road, cross and go up steps to podium. Turn right and cross footbridge, and follow signs to **Museum of London.** At far end of Thomas More Highwalk turn left along John Wesley Highwalk to museum entrance 👁 ; open 10.00 to 18.00, Sunday opens 14.00, closed Monday except bank holidays. *Donation requested*.

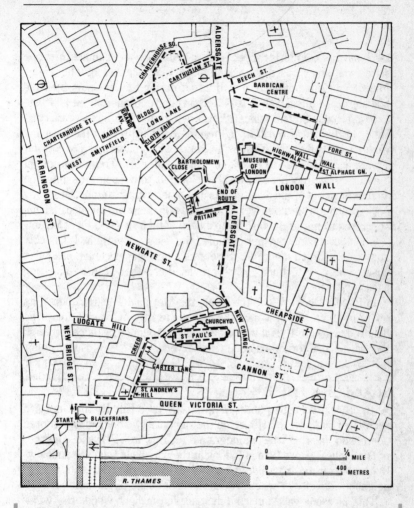

Walk ends here. Nearest refreshments in Museum Café on next level down from main entrance. Nearest ⊖ Barbican (return along John Wesley Highwalk and follow highwalks more or less parallel with Aldersgate).

Queen Victoria Street

At the Tube station the way past the sweet perfumes of the flower stall leads to Queen Victoria Street. The building opposite, panelled in green slate, was known as the 'chicken shed' to employees of The Times Publishing Company who moved into it during the 1960s as their old building was demolished. *The Times* had been published at this address, Printing House Square, since 1785, when for the first three years of its life it was known as the *Daily Universal Register*. In 1974 the company was taken over by the Thomson Group, which published *The Sunday Times,* and moved up to Gray's Inn Road. Later *The Times* was bought by Rupert Murdoch and forcibly relocated to Wapping despite the violent protests of the print unions and others who hated both the way new production methods were imposed upon them *and* the idea of being separated from the clubbish atmosphere of their beloved Fleet Street.

The *Observer* newspaper occupied the wing to the right. It has now gone to Battersea, and Fleet Street as a newspaper centre has fallen apart. The new technology has prevailed and there can be no going back.

In Puddle Dock, beside the river, the Mermaid Theatre opened its doors in 1959, the first new theatre in the City of London for three hundred years. In 1981 it was rebuilt and surrounded by offices, though the original auditorium has been preserved.

St Andrew's Hill

At the Baynard Castle pub, turn up St Andrew's Hill. By the Georgian rectory of St Andrew's House on the right are two fine old flat-fronted postboxes bearing the monograms of Edward VII and George, presumably V. Here turn in to look at the parish church of St Andrew-by-the-Wardrobe, now a double parish with St James Garlickhythe, its neighbour downriver where the garlic boats used to unload.

This pleasant galleried church, panelled in light wood, the white tunnel-vaulted ceiling of the nave decorated with finely detailed wreaths, is guild church to the Worshipful Companies of Blacksmiths, Mercers and Parish Clerks, and to the Worshipful Society of Apothecaries. Their banners jut from the gallery fronts together with those of the City and Diocese of London. The name of the church goes back to the fourteenth century when the Great Wardrobe, formerly kept in the Tower, was brought to Blackfriars. The Great Wardrobe was the name of the department in the Royal Household responsible for looking after the King's stores. These, in particular the robes of state, swelled greatly in richness and number during the reign of Edward III (1327-77), a man of flamboyant tastes who founded the knightly Order of the Garter and once had to pawn the Crown Jewels to bail himself out of debt.

Churches have stood on this site since 1240 or earlier. The medieval church was destroyed in the Great Fire of 1666 and rebuilt by Wren in 1685-95. Incendiary bombs in 1940 brought down most of the building, which was restored and adapted before it reopened in 1961. The church also acts as host to the Orthodox Church of India; each Sunday members of some forty-five families come here to worship in the Malayalam language.

St Paul's Cathedral

Walk up the hill to Carter Lane, and by the Rising Sun pub turn along Creed Lane, narrow and shady, taking its name from the writers of religious texts who lived and worked there. At the junction with Ludgate Hill, step into the sunlight and turn to face the dramatic spectacle of the west front and dome of St Paul's. The great Cathedral spans the top of the hill from the pavement up to the heavens. Wren's masterpiece, majestic and unforgettable. Broad steps rise to the paired columns of the double portico and the pediment deeply incised with Francis Bird's relief of the *Conversion of St Paul*. To either side are the great west towers, harmonising with both the verticals of the portico and the roundness of the dome, and terminating in gilded copper pineapples.

The Great Fire consumed Old St Paul's and this building arose between 1675, when the foundation stone was laid, and 1710. Wren received his final payment, after much wrangling, a year later. By then he was seventy-nine years old and had been involved with renovation and building projects at the Cathedral for forty-eight years. In the closing phases, his enthusiasm undimmed, the venerable architect was winched up to the lantern in a basket to supervise the works.

Cross the road and walk past the railed-off statue of Queen Anne to the Cathedral door. Many find the interior less imposing, even cold, compared with the exterior. Looking towards the high altar, two almost contrary styles meet the eye: the unadorned stone of the nave, flanked by severe marble and bronze monuments, suddenly catches fire at the crossing and in the domed ceiling of the choir which is covered in a profusion of gold and coloured glass mosaics, the Victorian-Byzantine addition of Sir William Richmond.

Here on the left is a towering monument to the Duke of Wellington, by Alfred Stevens, almost touching the top of the nave arch. To the right, in the south aisle, is Holman Hunt's *The Light of the World* (1904), the artist's life-sized replica of the smaller original – painted fifty-one years earlier – which hangs in the chapel of Keble College, Oxford. Christ knocks on a door which represents the human soul. The lantern in His hand sends a glowing aura across His robes and face, its warmth suggesting not so much lamplight as golden rays from the embers of a fire. The picture illustrates the lines of Revelation III: 20, inscribed thus on the frame:

BEHOLD I STAND AT THE DOOR AND KNOCK IF ANY MAN
HEAR MY VOICE AND OPEN THE DOOR I WILL COME
IN TO HIM AND WILL SUP WITH HIM AND HE WITH ME.

Continue to the crossing and there look up into Thornhill's painted dome, decorated with eight monochrome frescos illustrating the life of St Paul. This dome is the innermost of three. Outside it, a brick cone rises to support the lantern, ball and cross, and outside the cone is the familiar dome of wood coated with lead which we see from the street. The scale is huge, as is the size of the void. While the top of the cross is 111m (365ft) from the cathedral pavement, the eye of the inner dome is only 65m (214ft) high.

In the north transept the great marble urn of Francis Bird's font is stoutly impressive, surrounded by public monuments to war heroes. Sir Thomas Picton, who fell at Waterloo, receives the largest tribute. To one side is the Regimental Chapel of The Middlesex Regiment. In the western arch next to the font a bannerless staff commemorates the loss of the regiment's colours to invading Japanese forces in Hong Kong in 1941. Only the crowned silver tip of the staff has survived.

Walk through the ambulatory to the ornate black and gold wrought-iron gates by Jean Tijou. Nearby is Henry Moore's eloquent *Mother and Child* (1984). The slanting figure of Mary cradles the Child in a smooth hollow in which the two are at once united and somehow miraculously separate.

Standing next to the high altar, its canopy carried on fluted and twisted columns of oak, look back along the choir, the wooden stalls subdued save for the exuberant if faded carvings by Grinling Gibbons, who also decorated the organ case. The brightly coloured saucer domes of the ceiling and the surrounding spaces carry Sir William Richmond's interpretation of the *Benedicite*: 'O all ye works of the Lord, bless ye the Lord.'

The high altar and canopy, or baldequin, are modern and commemorate overseas Commonwealth troops who fell in the two World Wars. In the apse behind the high altar is the American Chapel, dedicated to US serving men and women based in Britain who lost their lives during the Second World War. Return along the south ambulatory. The effigy of the poet John Donne (1573-1631) is one of the very few which survived the Great Fire.

In the south transept, the doorway to the crypt is guarded over by an appropriate *memento mori*: three skulls in a cartouche. At the foot of the steps turn right past marble tombs and tablets to the third recess on the right. This is Painters' Corner. Sir Christopher Wren is buried here: on the wall beside his tomb, inscribed in Latin, is the famous declaration: 'Reader, if you seek his monument, look around you.'

The artists buried here include Sir Joshua Reynolds, Sir Thomas Lawrence, J.M.W. Turner, Lord Leighton and Sir John Millais. The grandest tombs in the crypt are those of the Duke of Wellington and Lord Nelson. Wellington's is a mighty block of black Cornish granite flecked with chrome yellow. Nelson's black marble sarcophagus, raised up high, was originally made for Cardinal Wolsey almost three hundred years earlier, but was not granted to the Cardinal after he fell from favour with Henry VIII.

The Treasury has good eighteenth- and nineteenth-century plate and the extraordinary Jubilee cope made for the Queen's Silver Jubilee of 1977, decorated in gold thread and silk with the spires of seventy-three churches and the cathedral.

Look also for the Great Model, demonstrating the second of Wren's Post-Fire designs. This followed a Greek Cross version which the City authorities rejected, feeling it lacked the necessary size and grandeur. As part of his campaign to sell the next design, Wren had this masterpiece of seventeenth-century joinery created. So keen was he to show off the interior as well as the exterior details, he attached the floor to brass pulleys so it could be let down, allowing visitors to stand inside the model. Unfortunately, the clergy decided the Great Model design was 'not enough of a cathedral-fashion'. Wren hastily produced his Warrant design, and in 1675 won authority to start building. He was by then thoroughly sick of royal and other committees and vowed 'from that Time . . . to make no more models, or publicly expose Drawings, which . . . did but lose Time and subject his Business many Times, to incompetent Judges'.

The extent of his rage may be measured by the differences between the Warrant design, which had a modest dome surmounted by a tiered and tapering steeple, and the cathedral he actually, defiantly, built.

Return to the crossing. In the south aisle the intrepid may wish to go up high. Everyone should, if possible, try to make it to one or other of the galleries. The way up is initially very easy: a broad and shallow wooden staircase spirals almost to the Whispering Gallery. Here look down from a wall bench to the floor of the crossing. The acoustics at this level grant that a message whispered to the wall will travel round and be heard on the far side of the gallery, some 43m (140ft) away. Look up through the eye of the dome. There by the lantern is the inner Golden Gallery. It seems very small, and very very high. A compromise for faint hearts is this: take the next staircase up to the Stone Gallery, which tours the drum just above the level of the windows.

This next stage is via an enclosed spiral staircase. At the top you step out to a broad pavement encircled and protected on the outside by a tall balustrade some 2.2m (7ft) high. There are benches to rest on and a 360-degree panorama of London to admire.

It is not easy to find a high-up view in London. In some places, the Telecom Tower is one, security fears have overcome other interests and the public is firmly excluded. Here on St Paul's the balustrade is too thickly built for a continuous view but the fragmented picture is rewarding. First is the prospect east to the financial districts of the City, the Sixties slabs and the Post-Modern jokes, and the NatWest Tower, at 183m (600ft) formerly the tallest building in Europe, now overtaken in that respect by Canary Tower in the Isle of Dogs (244m/800ft), its snowcap pyramid topped by a flashing aerial warning light. Best of all are the Wren churches: immediately below are St Vedast and St Mary-le-Bow, at either end of Cheapside, pointing delicate spires out of the City canyons.

Further round, see the flaming gilt urn on top of the Monument (its balcony *may* be visited, see *Walk 11*), next to the towers and high-level footbridge of Tower Bridge. Upriver are the smaller towers of Cannon Street Station and its railway bridge next to the road crossing of Southwark Bridge. Then along to the twin bridges at Blackfriars and the great bend leading through red and black Hungerford Bridge to Westminster. Alas, all the Parliamentary buildings save Victoria Tower are obscured by the Shell Building. Next is a long view over the roof of the nave and between the west towers of the cathedral to the curve of Fleet Street, the Telecom Tower (which in happier times had a revolving restaurant at the top) and the gilt figure of Justice, sword and scales in hand, atop the Old Bailey, the Central Criminal Court.

For the very intrepid, an open staircase leads up to the outer Golden Gallery at the base of the lantern.

Little Britain and the Butchers

Turn through St Paul's churchyard by the Chapter House and keep on through the gardens to the Edwardian column which marks the site of St Paul's Cross, once an 'outdoor pulpit' like Speaker's Corner in Hyde Park, where anyone could come and air their regrets and dreams.

At New Change, cross by the florist's to St Martin's-le-Grand, which until recently housed the headquarters of the General Post Office. Keep on past Postman's Park and the Church of St Botolph-without-Aldersgate – meaning that it was built outside the old city gate – and then, with the rotunda of the Museum of London ahead, turn left to Little Britain.

On the right is Bartholomew Close, where the Worshipful Company of Butchers have occupied various versions of a hall they first moved into in 1885 and which was bombed in both World Wars. Behind its modern façade the old ways go on, symbolised by the portrait of a prize bull in the front hall. Back in Little Britain, the way leads past St Bartholomew's Hospital on the left to the circus of West Smithfield and the shrine of English butchery, Smithfield Market. Housed in a Victorian market building, its main arched entrance has dragons in the spandrels and in the pediment are the arms of the City of London.

St Bartholomew the Great

The greatest surprise in this quarter lies just to the right, through a Tudor-style gateway. The timbered upper part is of unknown date, restored to look like this in 1932. The stone arch beneath is even more interesting, for this once stood at the west end of a vast cruciform church. From here the nave extended in ten bays all the way to the present entrance and beyond.

St Bartholomew's is very old, founded in 1123 as an Augustinian priory by Rahere, a reformed courtier at the court of Henry I, and completed in the sixteenth century. At the Dissolution of the Monasteries, Henry VIII ordered its destruction. Sir Richard Rich pulled down the nave and the Norman transepts and was preparing to do the same to the choir when local residents intervened, pleading for it to be left to them as a parish church. Sir Richard relented but took over the Lady Chapel and turned it into a house for his own use. Then, most extraordinary of all, on the night of the Great Fire of 1666 the flames raced through the City but the wind changed when they reached Pie Corner some three hundred metres away. Protected also by the city wall, St Bartholomew's was saved. Through this one stroke of fortune the building became by some five hundred years the oldest parish church in the City of London.

In the nineteenth century the church was saved from decay, two shorter transepts were added and the apse restored in Norman style. The nave is still a wonder to behold. Up in the side galleries the triforium arches are supported by triple columns with geometric capitals. At the centre of the south side is the mullioned oriel window behind which one of the priors, William Bolton, had his quarters. From here he kept an overseeing eye on his monks in the choir and on the offertory box at the shrine to Rahere beside the high altar. Walk round the vaulted ambulatory and look back through the forest of stout and ancient columns. In the north aisle is a famous verse in the tablet to John and Margaret Whiting. She died in 1680 after the couple had lived together in the parish '40 years & upwards':

Shee first deceas'd. Hee for a little Try'd
To live without her, lik'd it not & Dy'd.

Before leaving, walk out to see the one surviving arm of the old monks' cloister. Not so surprisingly, this is the church of the Butchers' Company who hold a special service here on Common Hall Day in September.

Meat Market and Charterhouse

In West Smithfield, turn briefly along Cloth Fair which takes it name from the medieval Bartholomew's Fair which was an important market and fair for drapers and cloth merchants until it was banned in 1855 for rowdiness and debauchery. The poet laureate Sir John Betjeman lived at No.43, a small house with its front door in Cloth Court. Number 41, next to it, has coloured panels beneath the projecting windows and is the oldest house in the street, though now much restored.

Turn up through the arcade of Grand Avenue, where the odour of meat hangs in the air and in side arcades are butchers' stalls with low aluminium counters, heavy meat scales and dozens of empty hooks. The market is officially open until midday but usually packs up between ten and eleven o'clock.

On the far side bear right past the market pub, the Smithfield Tavern, licensed to open its doors at 06.30, and continue to Charterhouse Square. To the left are the buildings of Old Charterhouse, originally a Carthusian monastery and later home to a school for poor boys and a hospital or retirement home for poor gentlemen. The school expanded into the well-known public school which in 1872 moved to Godalming. Pensioners still live in the old buildings and part of the grounds are now occupied by the Medical College of St Bartholomew's Hospital.

Barbican

At Aldersgate Street, steps by the Tube station lead up to a footbridge to the Barbican. This vast residential complex was launched in the late 1950s on 14 hectares (35 acres) of ground bombed virtually flat in World War II. The arts and conference centre arrived later and was opened in 1982. Londoners still find the angular maze of walkways, or 'highwalks' as they are known here, the proliferation of steps and broad breezy piazzas about as familiar as a housing estate on Mars. They goggle at the soaring storeys and alarming balconies of Lauderdale Tower, one of three skyscraping blocks more than 122m (400ft) high. It *is* somehow futuristic, though the long horizontal window-box gardens do much to soften the hard edges. Keep on down steps and past Butler's Wine Bar, and down more steps to the Theatre entrance. Outside it a broad terrace is covered with canopied tables in blue, red and green and a regiment of fountains spurts vees of water in the rectangular lake. Ahead, figures crossing on a distant walkway suggest a scene from *Metropolis*, or is it just another working day in Robotsville, EC2?

In the foyer a directory points the way to nine floors of theatre, concert hall, cinemas, art galleries, terraces, cafés and restaurants. For free entertainment, there are regular lunchtime concerts on the terrace or in the foyer.

When ready to leave, go out to Lakeside Terrace and turn left to the boundary with the Guildhall School of Music and Drama. Go up North Stair to Gilbert Bridge which crosses the lake to the Church of St Giles Cripplegate and, beyond it, the City of London School for Girls. From the balcony at the end of the highwalk, a fragment of the old city wall can be seen next to the east end of the church. Take the lift down to 'Street' and walk across to it.

This part of the wall is now Route Point 14 of the London Wall Walk organised by the Museum of London. The stones are from the north wall of a square Roman fort which jutted outwards from the main defences; it dates from about AD 120. To the right is the foot of one of the medieval bastions. These projected into a ditch, now represented by a lily-covered moat in which large goldfish swim. Battlements and towers were added between the thirteenth and fifteenth centuries and formed the southern boundary to the churchyard of St Giles. These were pulled down in 1803, by which time the wall was seen mainly as an obstruction – and also a source of building material for other structures.

To see another piece of Roman wall, follow the Route to Wood Street. At the corner of St Alphage Garden, a plaque marks the site of an old city gateway, Cripplegate, demolished in 1760. Along here, a larger section of the city wall stands in a partly sunken garden. The lower part is Roman, built when ground-level was some 3m (10ft) beneath the present street-level. The upper section has inserts of decorative red brickwork added in 1477 in the time of Mayor Joceline.

Return to the corner of Wood Street and go up steps to the podium. The street called London Wall is noisy and unlovely, so take the nearest footbridge and follow signs through the Barbican apartment blocks on the south side of St Giles Cripplegate, arriving eventually at John Wesley Highwalk which runs directly to the white blocks of the Museum of London. Along the way, look down to the Tudor-style hall of the Ironmongers' Company.

Museum of London

This excellent museum opened in 1975 and combines the collections of the old London Museum, latterly in Kensington Palace, and the Guildhall Museum. In the shop near the entrance are useful guides, including a plan which selects sixty-six items of interest. Displays are arranged in spacious galleries on two levels around a central courtyard. Wander through from Prehistoric to Roman, Saxon, Tudor and modern times.

Each period is amply illustrated with objects and reconstructions, such as the Roman kitchen and living room, and special treasures such as the sculpture fragments from the Roman temple of Mithras excavated in Walbrook, and the fascinating Cheapside Hoard of sixteenth- and seventeenth-century jewellery. Look through a window in the Roman gallery to see a further section of the old city wall. Of particular interest to Slow Walkers may be the models which recur: the wooden bridge in Roman times, with wharves and river boats; the medieval river at the entrance to the Fleet, dominated by Bridewell Palace and Baynards Castle, both long vanished; Henry VIII's grandiose Whitehall Palace as it was in c.1650; and the dramatised diorama of the Great Fire, with commentary based on the words of Samuel Pepys who observed it.

Down the ramp by the gold Lord Mayor's coach of 1757 – which is still rolled out each year to carry the new Lord Mayor through the City to swear his oath of office in the Law Courts. In the Late Stuart gallery is a cutaway model of Wren's St Paul's, showing the upper galleries where you may have stood earlier in the day. In the Eighteenth Century gallery, see architectural models of Classical London as interpreted by James Gibbs, William Kent and Sir William Chambers, and a costume cabinet with beautiful silk dresses made from materials woven by Huguenot craftsmen in their Spitalfields workshops (see *Walk 12*). Move on to life-size reconstructions of Victorian shops and offices – a tobacconist, a barber, a bank manager's office, an import shipping office, a grocer, a tailor, and the corner of a public bar.

From the twentieth century is an ornate Art Deco screen and lift car, installed in Selfridges store in 1928. Then the wonders of radio ('the wireless') and furniture just like we had at home! There, my goodness, is the Thirties radiogram we stood plants on (I think it conked out before I was born); my grandparents' telephone with the long earpiece suspended from a hook; the ducks that flew across our dining-room wall, and the very mangle that wrung out our washing on Mondays. Wartime London is evoked mainly through the fine photographs of George Rodger, Bert Hardy and Bill Brandt. Finally, an exhibition of treasures and trinkets has ornaments from Roman times to 1920s chokers and plastic finery from the Fifties.

The museum has a shop, a café with terrace on the next level down, and offers full facilities for the disabled.

Walk 11

Monument and City

Survey the City from the top of the Monument, and walk up to Leadenhall Market. At the financial heart, visit the Bank of England Museum and continue to Guildhall, centre of London's civic government for more than a thousand years.
Allow   3-4 hours.
Best times   Monday to Friday.

ROUTE

Begin at ⊖ Monument. Turn right in Fish Street to the **Monument** (1671-7), commemorating the Great Fire. Take the stairway to the top ☞; open weekdays 31 March to 30 September 09.00 to 18.00, 1 October to 30 March 09.00 to 16.00, May to September open Saturday, Sunday 14.00 to 18.00 (last tickets 20 minutes before closing time). *Admission.*

Continue left down Monument Street, past Pudding Lane where the Fire started (see plaque on corner). At foot, turn left in Lower Thames Street facing old Billingsgate Fish Market. Continue past rear of Custom House and turn left up St Dunstan's Hill. Keep ahead to old Church of St Dunstan-in-the-East and after tower turn right through garden in former nave, destroyed in Blitz. At far side, go left up St Dunstan's Hill and cross to Mincing Lane, past Plantation House on left. At Fenchurch Street turn left and right along Cullum Street. At top, go ahead through arch of Beehive Passage to **Leadenhall Market.**

Explore market shops (coffee at Croissant Express). Leave market along Whittington Avenue and turn right in Leadenhall Street to look at new Lloyd's building.

Turn W along Leadenhall Street to Cornhill. On left see St Michael's Church and note position of Simpson's Tavern in Ball Court. Continue to Bank, where Bank of England, Royal Exchange and Mansion House dominate the crossing of six roads at the centre of the City. Turn right at screen wall in front of Bank of England and left down Bartholomew Lane to **Bank of England Museum** ☞; open 10.00 to 17.00, Sunday and bank holidays 11.00 to 17.00, closed Saturday.

At exit, turn left to Lothbury and left. Keep on into Gresham Street and at Basinghall Street turn right to Guildhall Buildings (1st left). Arrive at **Guildhall** ☞; hall open 10.00 to 17.00, October to April, closes Sunday, also closed 1 January, Good Friday, Easter Monday, 25-26 December and for some civic occasions. To check, telephone 071-606 3030.

From front of Guildhall bear right across courtyard to Aldermanbury and turn right to **Guildhall Library**; open 09.30 to 17.30, closed Sunday. Inside, 1st door on left admits to **Clock Museum** ☞; open 09.30 to 16.45, closed Saturday, Sunday.

Walk ends here. Nearest refreshments, walk S along Milk Street to The Magogs pub, with Micawbers wine bar in basement. Nearest ⊖ Bank.

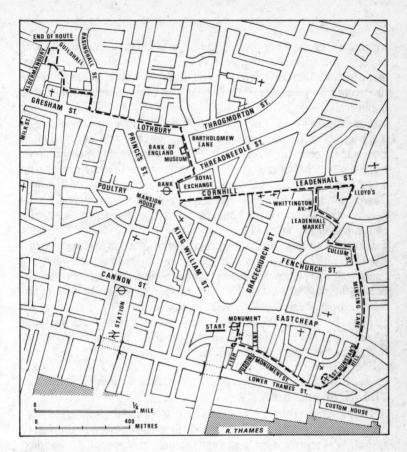

Monument

Christopher Wren designed this huge Doric column as a memorial to the Great Fire of 1666. The Act of Parliament which called for the 'Column or Pillar' declared its purpose was 'the better to preserve the memory of this dreadful Visitation'. Wren made it 61.5m (202ft) high, this being its distance west from Pudding Lane where the Fire started.

Some essential statistics about the Great Fire: it burned for three days, razing the medieval City which consisted largely of timber buildings packed together in a maze of narrow streets and alleys. It destroyed 87 out of 109 City churches, 44 livery halls and more than 13,000 houses. That only nine lives were lost was something of a miracle. After the Fire, there could be no going back. A new City was needed, and it must be made of stone. So, from the 'dreadful Visitation' came Wren's Classical churches and a new St Paul's, followed in the next century by the flowering of Georgian London beyond the City's boundaries.

The climb to the viewing platform is steep, narrow and continuous up 311 steps. On the way, some window ledges are at a happier height than others for taking a quick rest. The viewing platform is not large, but since 1842 has been caged-in, to stem the flow of unfortunates who were jumping off it. Fine views extend over the City and towards Tower Bridge and HMS *Belfast*, and along the river by the neighbouring Church of St Magnus the Martyr. Far to the west, Big Ben is just visible at Westminster.

Who caused this terrible Fire? In search of a scapegoat, we turn down Monument Street and at the corner of Pudding Lane find the answer. A wall plaque stands near the site where the fatal spark caught hold in the shop of Thomas Faryner, the King's baker. Nature, in the form of a dry summer which by 2 September had turned the wooden city to a tinderbox, allied to a strong wind which that night blew the flames rapidly from street to street, secured the fate of some 160 hectares (400 acres) within the City walls.

The River and the City

At the foot of the road is Lower Thames Street and the converted shell of the old Billingsgate Fish Market which in 1982 moved to the Isle of Dogs. For centuries Billingsgate and Queenhithe were the chief landing points for fishing boats putting in to London. Billingsgate became supreme because of its better position on the seaward side of Old London Bridge, whose narrow arches were difficult to navigate. The market building dates from 1874 and is by Sir Horace Jones. On top of the pediment are a nereid or maidenly sea creature, and pairs of entwined fishes.

The next long block is the unprepossessing rear of Custom House, continuing the control of customs levies which began in London more than a thousand years ago. Turn up St Dunstan's Hill and keep on ahead to Wren's tower at St Dunstan-in-the-East, dating from 1697. Step past the padlocked gates and the block behind the tower, and turn through the churchyard. The medieval nave survived the Fire but had to be rebuilt in 1817. In the Blitz, only Wren's tower escaped destruction. Now the nave is a handsome garden framed by restored Gothic Revival arches through which ferns and creepers freely twine.

From St Dunstan's Hill is a first view of the monstrous new fortress in Mincing Lane – Minster Court – combining pink stone and black windows in retrogressive tribute to Modernists of a previous age, men such as Gaudí and Berlage, who had a lot more style about them. Mincing Lane is *the* historic trading street for tea, cocoa, coffee, rubber and spices, which in former times were barrowed here from the river. Plantation House, on the left, was until 1973 the home of the London Commodity Exchange, now a block away in Mark Street.

From Fenchurch Street turn into Cullum Street. At the second bend is Bolton House (1907), dressed in pale-coloured tiles with a leafy frieze; at ground level the principal shop is Jones the Bootmaker (established 1857). At the top of the road take to Beehive Passage and come upon one of the most extraordinary architectural conflicts in London. 'My lords, ladies and gentlemen!' as a boxing presenter might put it, 'on your left, friendly old Leadenhall Market by Sir Horace Jones, with lovely iron arcades in dark red and cream. On your right, the Monster from Outer Space, a nightmare in stainless steel, the new Lloyd's building by Richard Rogers and Partners!'

On the outer wall of the new insurance market, rows of glass-walled lifts swarm up and down like mechanised fleas, transferring clerks and brokers to the level of their choice. Step into the market which now deals mainly in fish, meat, fruit and vegetables, with attendant pubs and wine merchants. Office workers crowd the pavement outside Croissant Express, taking their elevenses *en plein air*.

To find the front of Lloyd's, go along Whittington Avenue and turn right in Leadenhall Street. It is a fantastic building, its height defined by a series of fourteen bucket-shaped projections stacked up at intervals around it. As at the same architect's Pompidou Centre in Paris, the service pipes, lifts and concrete supports are strung round the exterior. Beside the front entrance, the Lloyd's porter in his traditional livery of red coat and black top hat with buckled gold band, stands in a hard-edged glass-walled box and looks hopelessly out of tune with his surroundings.

Tours of the building are no longer possible for security

reasons. Turn west along Leadenhall Street. At the junction with Bishopsgate there is a good view of the supremely bland NatWest Tower (1980, Sir Richard Seifert and Partners), of which all that will ever be said was that it used to be the tallest building in London.

In Cornhill, a canyon of banking and insurance, the architectural interest is slight. On the left St Michael's Church is a pleasant refuge where the dusty colours hang of the Stock Exchange Battalion of the 10th Royal Fusiliers (City of London Regiment). A church stood on this site before the Norman Conquest, and the present building was redesigned by Wren in 1672 and heavily restored in 1858-60 by Sir George Gilbert Scott. In the reign of Henry VII (1485-1509) the patronage was bought by the Worshipful Company of Drapers which still retains the gift of the living. Other companies which hold their annual Election services here are the Woolmen, the Master Mariners and the Guild of Air Pilots and Air Navigators.

At the sign to Simpson's Tavern step into Ball Court, where the former chophouse provides outstanding value at lunchtime. The alleys and courts off Cornhill were once a centre for coffee-houses where commodity dealers and other traders conducted their business. At Mr Garroway's Coffee House, in Exchange Alley, the Hudson's Bay Company held its first fur auction in 1672.

Bank

Three grand porticos of the City establishment look onto this triangular junction, where in summer office workers bask and gasp in the sunlight. This central part of the City is so overcrowded with buildings, it is one of the few open spaces they can sit in without being expected to pay. Immediately to the right is the Royal Exchange, conceived in Elizabethan times as a great trading centre and opened by the Queen in 1570. The present building, the third on the site after fires destroyed the first two, dates from 1844; in the pediment the inscription asserts confidently that:

THE EARTH IS THE LORD'S AND THE FULLNESS THEREOF

with the implicit message that the Earth existed chiefly for the benefit of England's merchant class. The building continued as the Royal

Exchange until 1939 and now is partly occupied by the Guardian Royal Exchange Assurance Co.

Facing it is the fine screen by Sir John Soane surrounding the Bank of England, the Government's bank, the inner part rebuilt in 1921-37 by Sir Herbert Baker when the bank needed to expand upwards. In the pediment sits the 'Old Lady of Threadneedle Street' holding a model of the building.

To the left is Mansion House, official residence of the Lord Mayor of London. The Corinthian portico, completed in 1753, is by George Dance the Elder. The two principal rooms inside the building are the Ball Room and the Egyptian Hall, used by the Lord Mayor for official banquets.

Bank of England Museum

In 1988 the Bank of England opened this small museum dedicated to its history and the evolution of banknotes. The first room is a reconstruction of Soane's banking hall, the Bank Stock Office, completed in 1793. The fifty-nine gold bars in the Rotunda are, alas, facsimiles, but the Bank Note Gallery has the real stuff, from the hand-written receipts of the seventeenth century, issued after the Bank was founded in 1694, to the near-forgeproof notes of today. Here in showcases are their ancestors of not so long ago: the brown ten-shilling note and the 'white fiver', the inter-war £1 and 10s., banded with type and looking rather like Post Office vouchers, and the larger, more elegant notes of earlier centuries. The Bank has a good collection of silver – cups, wine coolers, candlesticks and sconces – and another of Roman remains excavated during the inter-war rebuilding. Most impressive of these is a large piece of mosaic floor, wonderfully preserved.

Guildhall

This ancient medieval hall has been much restored since the first Lord Mayor of London was installed here in 1192. He and his sheriffs are still elected and admitted to office in the vast and impressive chamber. The present oak-panelled roof is the fifth on the site, decorated with the shields of the eighty-four Livery Companies of the City of London. The banners of the 'Great Twelve' – the most powerful medieval guilds – hang from the walls. In order of precedence they are the Mercers, Grocers, Drapers, Fishmongers, Goldsmiths, Skinners, Merchant Taylors, Haberdashers, Salters, Ironmongers, Vintners, Clothworkers.

On the left-hand side facing the dais, next to the Wellington Monument, is a list of important trials held in the Guildhall, including those of Lady Jane Grey and Archbishop Cranmer. The statues of Gog and Magog, legendary giants whose effigies were regularly paraded at medieval fairs, are replacements for those destroyed in 1940. Gog wields a mace and Magog is armed with a halberd.

The crypt beneath the hall is the most extensive medieval crypt in London. It is rarely open to the public but you may be lucky if you ask at the main entrance. The eastern half is particularly fine, supported by stout pillars of blue Purbeck marble.

Clock Museum

At the entrance to Guildhall bear right across the courtyard, facing the Church of St Lawrence Jewry, and turn right around the new west wing (1974) in Aldermanbury. Here is the entrance to Guildhall Library and Clock Museum. The Library specialises in maps, manuscripts, prints and books about London and is open to members of the public who have specific inquiries to make.

The Clock Museum is a major horological collection. The display exhibits clocks and watches and other time-keeping devices gathered since the foundation in 1631 of the Worshipful Company of Clockmakers. There are pocket sundials, astrolabes, travelling clocks, fine jewelled pieces and skeleton clocks whose every movement is bared to view. There are marine chronometers, a gas-operated clock and a Chinese celestial clockwork globe. Close this walk to the restful ticking of the longcase clocks, on parade at the end of the room, the chorus led by a Thomas Tompion design of 1672.

Opposite in the hall, the Guildhall bookshop has books on every corner of London, posters, prints and packs of historic playing cards.

Walk 12

Spitalfields

East End markets on a Sunday morning – Petticoat Lane and down to Whitechapel. The Bangladeshi shops in Brick Lane. Huguenot weavers' houses near the old Spitalfields Market. Step into the shadow of Jack the Ripper, and step out of it to join the geese and goats at Spitalfields Farm.

Allow   4 hours.
Best time   Sunday morning.

ROUTE

Begin at ⊖ Liverpool Street. Take the exit to the British Rail station and at the far end of the concourse go up the escalator to Bishopsgate. Cross the road and turn left to **Middlesex Street** (**Petticoat Lane**) 👁; market open Sunday 09.00 to 14.00; smaller market open weekdays around lunchtime.

Walk to end, also exploring stalls in side streets. At Whitechapel High Street, turn left past Bloom's Jewish restaurant to **Whitechapel Art Gallery** 👁; open 11.00 to 17.00, Wednesday until 20.00, closed Monday.

At exit turn left and left through Osborn Street to Brick Lane. Turn left along Fashion Street to Commercial Street. On right are Hawksmoor's **Christ Church** and the old Spitalfields Market. Also nearby is Ten Bells pub, its walls documenting the deeds of Jack the Ripper, infamous Victorian murderer.

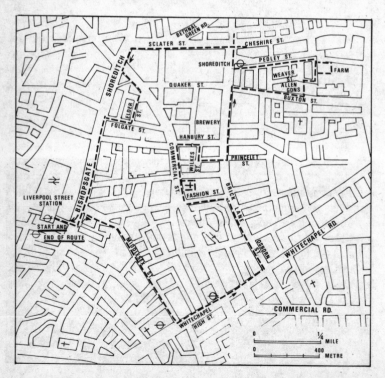

Go up Commercial Street and turn right along Hanbury Street to No.28, opposite the scene of the second Ripper murder. Turn down Wilkes Street past old weavers' houses. Turn left to Princelet Street. At No.19 is Spitalfields Heritage Centre, behind the house a galleried synagogue built after 1870 by Jewish refugees.

Keep on to Brick Lane and turn left to Truman's Brewery. Turn right into Buxton Street, passing vacant lots and a grassy field. Just before children's playground, turn left along path beside Allen Gardens, then right in Weaver Street to **Spitalfields Farm** ☜; open 09.30 to 17.30, closed Monday.

On leaving farm, turn right and left along Pedley Street to Shoreditch Station. Keep ahead in alley to **Brick Lane**. Turn right under bridge to market ☜; open Sunday 09.00 to 14.30. Explore market stalls here and to right in Cheshire Street. Turn left through **Sclater Street market** ☜; open Sunday 09.00 to 14.00.

Continue to merger with Bethnal Green Road. Turn left into Shoreditch High Street and left into Commercial Street. Turn right down Elder Street and right into Folgate Street. Continue to Bishopsgate and turn left to Liverpool Street Station.

Walk ends here. Nearest refreshments at top of Middlesex Street. Nearest ⊖ Liverpool Street.

Petticoat Lane

The entrance to Middlesex Street faces the new Broadgate development, a self-important confection which looms over and partly straddles Liverpool Street Station. The style is anyone's guess: Post-Modernist, of course, but in it are mixed hints of Thirties-Egyptian and Greek Thomson's Glasgow, and in the glasshouse gables, I suppose, a rather limp-wristed salute to Decimus Burton. *Quelle salade*!

Petticoat Lane was once a thriving market for second-hand clothes, and this probably explains its popular name. On the map it is Middlesex Street, as it has been called officially since 1832. Although a smaller market operates here at lunchtime on weekdays, Sunday morning is definitely the time to go. Apart from old clocks, watches and jewellery, and a few antiques, everything is new, and a bargain to boot. Side by side are stalls selling cosmetics, antique jewellery and astoundingly cheap padded wax jackets; then an outpost of Tubby Isaacs's seafood empire has prawns, whelks, cockles and mussels by the pint. Across the way are Mary Quant socks, jazzy bath towels and leather belts. Soon we meet the first orator. Seated on an upturned plastic milk crate, he slowly empties the contents of a maroon cloth bag on to his table. Thin golden necklaces and pendants lie curled round each other as the orator intones his pitch:

'Over one 'undred pounds worf of *stolen* jewellery. *Stolen!* 'Ere, put it away before the police come.' (The preview over, he slips the jewels back in the bag. Now for the bargain.) 'I won't charge yer 'arf price fifty, not forty not firty. I won't charge yer twenty. I'll charge yer ten. *Stolen!*'

In an average morning he must go through that routine literally hundreds of times. A few stalls along, a china seller limbers up for the day. One of the great acts in street market theatre, he and his colleagues sell dinner sets and tea sets by the basket. Good china sellers are not afraid either to jerk the whole lot up in the air, and catch it all without a single breakage, or to smash an entire basketload on the pavement in feigned anger when buyers fail to come forward.

Stalls continue all the way down to Whitechapel High Street, and side roads to the left are jammed with vendors of leatherwear, lingerie, shirts and skirts, toys, games and gadgets – anything from the Amazing Clucking Chicken, which really does make a very good cluck, to the Amazing Wash-Matik International, which apparently cleans your car while you just stand there.

Amble through the crowd. By mid-morning the main alley between the stalls is so packed, forward progress is measured by the inch, like shuffling out of a football ground. Nor is it just the density of the throng. People *want* to move slowly, like moonwalkers, apparently weightless and definitely mesmerised. After all, if you come to Petticoat Lane, you don't want to miss anything. I agree. I think it is the best, certainly the most professional, street market in London.

Turn along Whitechapel High Street. At the corner of Goulston Street is a larger Tubby Isaacs stall, emblazoned in several places with the slogan 'World Famous Jellied Eels'. Keep on past Aldgate East Station. The next landmark is Bloom's, which calls itself the 'World Famous Kosher Restaurant'. Neither of these claims is fanciful; they *are* world-famous. Each day Bloom's draws a full attendance from locals, tourists, and workers and business types from the City. Long ago is the day when I had my first gedempte meatballs and potato latkas in there.

Whitechapel Art Gallery

The Whitechapel Art Gallery is one of the best small art galleries in London, and a beacon of culture for East Enders. The Art Nouveau building was designed by C.H. Townsend and completed in 1899, twelve years after the foundation in nearby Mile End Road of the People's Palace Technical Schools. This, with the East London Technical College, brought facilities for education and recreation to local working men, and later became Queen Mary College, part of the University of London. Slowly, and most notably after Jewish refugees from Europe arrived in the East End from around 1870, people began to pull themselves upwards, though most had to do it by their boot straps.

The gallery was refurbished and reopened in 1965. In the long white room are temporary exhibitions of modern paintings and sculpture. Recent exhibitors include the Swiss sculptor Martin Disler and two Americans, the auto-photographer Cindy Sherman and the abstract expressionist Richard Diebenkorn. Upstairs, past the café and audio-visual room, the Upper Gallery is regularly used for community art projects involving schoolchildren and artists who work in local schools. On the ground floor is a good bookshop, run by Zwemmer's of Charing Cross Road.

Brick Lane and Old Spitalfields

Spitalfields has been home to three waves of immigrants, and Brick Lane is a centre for the latest arrivals who have come here over the last thirty years from Bangladesh. Their mosque in Brick Lane was originally built in 1742 as a chapel for Huguenots, the French Protestant refugees who were the first immigrants, and later was used as a place of worship for the Jews who settled in the area in the nineteenth century. The street abounds with Indian and Bangladeshi restaurants and special food shops selling groceries and oriental sweetmeats. At the Modern Saree Centre the window is bright with mannequins in sparkling sarees.

In Fashion Street, to the left, is the battered remnant of an extraordinary building. The Arcade, by Abraham Davis, dates from

1905 and looks like a vestige of Edwardian India, now recolonised by Bangladeshi merchants who use the shops as warehouses for food and garments. Step round a pallet of vast gourds, avoid the rising mounds of cardboard boxes and wrapping paper and arrive soon in Commercial Street.

Spitalfields grew up around the nursery fields attached to a priory and hospital founded in 1197 and known as St Mary Spital. The community increased rapidly after 1685, when Louis XIV of France revoked the Edict of Nantes. The Huguenots, suddenly deprived of their religious and civil liberties, fled to England, Holland and other countries with a Protestant tradition. Many of those arriving in London were trained weavers and chose Spitalfields, which already had a name in the silk-weaving trade, as the place to start a new life. From this period come the distinctive weavers' houses of Spitalfields, their attic windows built specially large to admit maximum daylight to the long workshops in the roofs.

Christ Church is easily the mightiest building in the neighbourhood. It was designed in 1720 by Nicholas Hawksmoor and served the twin purposes of providing a place of worship for the Huguenot community and of asserting the power of the Church of England in an area noted for its Nonconformist factions. Above the great Tuscan columns of the portico rises a massive tower and spire. The interior is a vast rectangular temple of brick and stone, a little battered from the passing of time but powerful and solid. Columns dividing the main body from barrel-vaulted side arcades climb to terminate in ornate capitals and cornices, the coffered vaults and ceiling decorated with plaster roses. The chancel arch is bold and straight in the Roman style, surmounted by the royal arms flanked by a lion and unicorn.

Across the road is the old market building. Specialising in vegetables and fruit, especially bananas which ripened in its heated cellars, it was first established in 1682. The present building dates from the 1860s. The market recently moved to a new site in Leyton and various plans to redevelop the 4.2 hectare (10.5 acre) site are under discussion. Locals most fear a crushing invasion by bankers and brokers advancing from the Bishopsgate flank on the far side. They are surely right to have such fears, for the impact on rents is certain to be least favourable to those who actually want to live in Spitalfields, not just work there.

Jack the Ripper

On the corner of Fournier Street is the Ten Bells pub. Marie Kelly, sixth victim of Jack the Ripper, was last seen in this bar before a rent collector found her horribly mutilated corpse in a house at 26 Dorset Street, now White's Row car park.

The pub used to be known as the Jack the Ripper until women's groups forced a change of name. Little else has altered. The Victorian bar is decorated with a grisly necrophiliac display which documents the Ripper's activities. In 1888 he killed six women in three months, all in the Whitechapel area. Most were prostitutes, but the murderer's true motives went with him to the grave, for he was never caught. What most appalled and terrorised the inhabitants of this poverty-riddled neighbourhood was the Ripper's methods: first he killed by strangling, then he carved up the bodies with a finesse and vigour suggesting not only a maniac but one also skilled in surgery. Who would be next to fall under his scalpel?

On the walls of the bar, by the way, partly masked by Ripper ephemera, are some good tile pictures in Dutch patterns, and one of life in old-time Spitalfields called 'Visiting a Weaver's Shop'.

In Hanbury Street, around the corner, the Ripper's second victim, Annie Chapman, was found in a yard now built over by Truman's Brewery. The yard stood opposite No.28. Someone has chalked a large white M on the wall, and circled it.

Georgian Houses

From Hanbury Street, turn down Wilkes Street. Here are fine rows of weavers' houses with broad and beautiful carved Georgian doorways. When young professionals began moving into this area a few years ago, buying up the eighteenth-century houses, they were labelled rather sneeringly as the 'new Georgians'. Number 19 is shiny red and freshly restored, and No.13 is quite staggeringly decrepit.

At No.19 Princelet Street, on the left, is the Spitalfield Heritage Centre, a community body which studies the history of immigration in the area. Once the home of a Huguenot silk weaver, in 1870 it was acquired by Jewish refugees. Go in to see the fascinating synagogue which they built in the garden, immediately behind the main house and joined to it. It was designed in the East European style with a ladies' gallery. No less extraordinary is the house itself. It needs restoring, but the dark panelled passages and elegant doorways have a magical stillness about them, the authentic feel of Georgian London as it was more than two hundred and fifty years ago.

Return to Brick Lane and walk up to Truman's Brewery. Its origins go back to the seventeenth century when it was known as the Black Eagle Brewery. Under the Truman family it became famous for its porter and in the late nineteenth century was the world's largest brewing company.

Spitalfields Farm

Head away from the city, or so it seems, past the vacant lots in Buxton Street to Allen Gardens and a ramshackle urban farm. This community project, staked out beside the railway at Shoreditch, makes a wondrous place of calm for town kids in baseball caps and shell suits to come and look at goats and sheep, and maybe help groom the shire horse. There are pens for geese, rabbits and hens as well, and the farm runs a programme of craft and farming activities. There is a café in a brightly painted shack which serves farm brunches on Sunday. Old farm carts stand about, cows and horses graze, and orange marigolds sprout from a wheelbarrow.

More Markets

Brick Lane street market begins just round the corner from Shoreditch Station and runs up to Bethnal Green Road, spilling over in side streets, each with a different cast to its merchandise. Brick Lane is fruit and vegetables, loud with cockney traders who bellow the bargains from beside their stalls. An old lavender seller sits on a box waving fragile sprigs more in hope than expectation. A youth freelances with a tray of mushrooms which he shakes under your nose. 'Wan' any mush?' he cries.

In Cheshire Street to the right the main theme is electrical goods, which does not mean you could not find a tea towel, a leather jacket or a pound of cherries. The joyous mixture continues to the left in Sclater Street: get your pond fish food and doggy chews, a fishing rod, workboots, a box of eggs, a tracksuit. As the morning turns to afternoon the tide of market débris rises. Keep on beside the railway carried on arches towards the terminus at Liverpool Street. Under the railway, outright poverty shows itself at a second-hand clothes market. The traders lean with sad eyes against the wall, their crumpled stock in a heap on the pavement where it has been thumbed through all morning and dropped again, discarded.

Finally, off Commercial Street, head south along Elder Street which has fine Georgian houses at the far end. Now within touching distance of the City, and to some extent already absorbed by it, to judge from the many company name plates on the doors, these houses are spick and refurbished. At No.32 is a plaque to Mark Gertler (1892-1939), the painter of nudes and still lifes who lived in the house. Born in Gun Street on the other side of Spitalfields Market, he spoke only Yiddish until the age of eight, and later was sent to the Slade School by the Jewish Educational Aid Society. In some ways, a typical East End beginning.

Around the corner in Folgate Street are more Georgian houses. Number 18 is outstanding. The owner has restored and maintained it in its original style, when it was the home of a Huguenot silk weaver and his family. The house is open on the first Sunday in the month in the afternoon, and for special evening performances which recreate its history.

For rest and refreshment, the wine bars at the top of Middlesex Street are available but inevitably crowded at Sunday lunchtime. For somewhere quieter, and a seat, keep on to Liverpool Street and turn right to the Great Eastern Hotel.

Walk 13

The Tower of London and Shakespeare's Southwark

Visit the famous Norman stronghold and take the launch from Tower Pier to HMS *Belfast*. On the Southwark side of the river tour the London Dungeon and the Operating Theatre Museum, take lunch at the galleried George Inn and visit the Shakespeare sites near Bankside.

Allow   All day.
Best times   Not Sunday.

ROUTE

Begin at ⊖ Tower Hill. At exit, turn left down steps and go through tunnel to Tower of London moat. Turn right and follow line of Moat around by Devereux Tower at corner and down towards river and **Tower** entrance 👁; open March to October 09.30 to 18.30, Sunday 14.00 to 18.15 (last tickets 17.00); November to February 09.30 to 17.00, closed Sunday (last tickets 16.00). *Admission*.

Return to exit and turn left to Tower Pier. Ferry launch to HMS *Belfast* leaves from moorings on bankside of pier. **HMS *Belfast*** 👁: open 20 March to 31 October 10.00 to 17.00, 1 November to 19 March 10.00 to 16.00. *Admission* (buy combined ticket for launch and ship tour).

Leave ship and follow gangway to river walk flanking new London Bridge City development. Turn right to vast open-fronted arcade of Hay's Galleria and walk through it to Tooley Street. Turn right and cross to **London Dungeon** 👁; open Easter to September 10.00 to 17.30, October to March 10.00 to 16.30. *Admission*.

At exit, turn left and left under railway in Joiner Street. At St Thomas's Street, turn right to tower of old church and visit **Operating Theatre Museum** 👁; open Monday, Wednesday, Friday 12.30 to 16.00. *Admission*.

On leaving, turn right to Borough High Street and left to **George Inn Yard**, where London's last galleried coaching inn serves lunch until about 15.00.

Return to Borough High Street and turn right. At St Thomas's Street cross left to Bedale Street and go right through Green Dragon Court and under railway to **Southwark Cathedral**. For entrance at SW door, go left around churchyard by arcades of Borough Market.

At SW door turn right to Cathedral Street and right to St Mary Overies' Dock where trading schooner **Kathleen and May**; optional visit, open 10.00 to 16.30, Saturday-Sunday 11.00 to 16.30, closed weekends October to March. *Admission*.

Turn left along Pickford's Wharf to see rose window of old Banqueting Hall in Winchester Palace. Continue in Clink Street past Clink Exhibition on site of old Bishops' prison (not worth the *admission*). Facing yard of Anchor pub, turn left and right along Park Street, where plaque to Shakespeare's Globe Theatre. Continue under railway and turn right at Bear Gardens to **Shakespeare Globe Museum** 👁; open 10.00 to 17.00, Sunday 14.00 to 17.30. *Admission*.

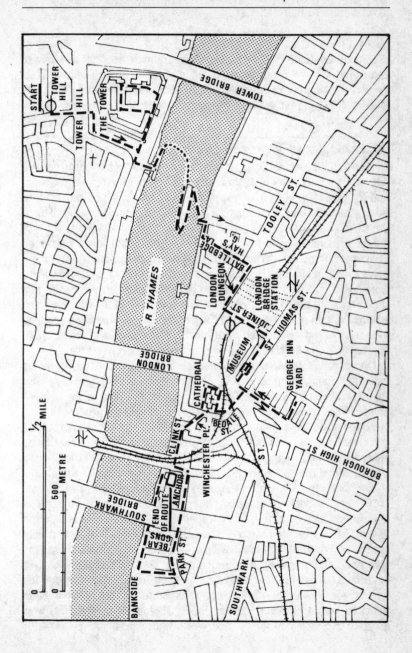

At exit, continue on Park Street to Emerson Street and turn right to river and observe progress on building of new Globe Theatre. Walk ends here. Nearest refreshments at Anchor pub (right along Bankside river walk). Nearest ⊖ London Bridge.

Tower Hill and Tower of London

Close to the Tube station is an impressive chunk of ancient City wall. The Roman part rises to 4.4m (14ft), the level of the old sentry walk, and is made of blocks of ragstone with tile courses inserted to strengthen and bind the structure. Above it the medieval wall rises to 9m (30ft).

One of London's first Norman castles was a timber fort constructed in a corner of the Roman wall. In 1078 William the Conqueror ordered a great tower of stone to be built which would not only frighten dissident Londoners into submission but also deter invading armies. Such was the success of the White Tower, which soared to 27m (90ft) high and was made with walls 4.6m (15ft) thick at the base, it spawned so many extensions and a moated outer wall that from the west side, approaching the entrance, the original tower is barely visible.

On the bridge to Byward Tower, a Yeoman Warder in full Beefeater rig is explaining the niceties of a public execution long ago: ' . . . and then he takes the head and sticks it on top of the pike of the nearest soldier. This soldier then has the *privilege* of leading the procession . . .' No-one faints, but this kind of 'living narrative', history in very small selective bite-sizes, is not for me. Besides, this walk is going to be anatomical enough anyway, what with the torture rooms of the London Dungeon and the surgeons' knives at the old Operating Theatre!

Continue ahead between the inner walls, passing the Bell Tower (1190) and arriving at Traitors' Gate, the river entrance for hapless prisoners. Once admitted, few escaped. The Tower's role as a prison and place of execution lasted down the centuries. It was certainly established by 1305, when Sir William Wallace, the Scottish insurgent, was executed there by hanging, drawing and quartering. The last person to be beheaded in England was Lord Lovat, who suffered his fate at the Tower in 1747. Numerous State prisoners have been detained within its walls, the last being Rudolf Hess, the Nazi who escaped to England in the Second World War.

Here turn left to the Bloody Tower (1225). Printed copies are kept in this tower of Sir Walter Raleigh's *History of the World* (1614) and his *Counter Blast to Tobacco* which he wrote while a prisoner there, locked up for twelve years. Go up through the tower and return to ground level via Raleigh's Walk.

Continue uphill past a fragment of the original bailey. High on the right stands the great inner keep. Look out for vast ravens and hear their throaty caw, like a saw cutting through a plank. The ravens are the sole survivors of a menagerie which was transferred to Regent's Park Zoo in 1834.

Keep an eye here on the crowds, and if the way is reasonably clear go straight ahead to the Jewel House. Here you may see one of my favourite heritage-industry signs, pointing the way to 'Toilets Torture Instruments Education Centre'.

The Jewels Tour begins with a vast gilt wine cooler of 1829, maces, swords of state, flagons, silver heralds' trumpets, and standards, orders, ribbons and robes including those of the Order of the Garter – the gold buckled garter and magnificent robes of dark blue velvet – and the deep gold of the Sovereign's Coronation robes. Continue down into a concrete dugout and choose to travel round the Crown Jewels chamber either on the lower level next to the showcases or in more leisurely fashion on the upper level behind. 'There is no stopping in the lower level,' the warders' voices constantly remind us, and we shuffle round like prisoners of war and squint as best we can at the crowns and swords and other royal regalia.

At the exit, turn left to find the Oriental Armoury and Heralds Museum and on the far side of the courtyard the Museum of the Royal Fusiliers. While I would never seek to *hurry* anyone, I feel the Tower is such an impersonal place, and always so overcrowded, that a reasonably quick visit lasting an hour or so is about right.

If you agree, turn right to Tower Green, where the execution block still stands. Seven prisoners were beheaded here, five of them women. Two were wives of Henry VIII, Anne Boleyn and Catherine Howard. At the far end of the green, the Queen's House adjoins the Yeoman Gaoler's House, in which Lady Jane Grey was imprisoned. She was executed at the block when she was sixteen years old, and had been Queen of England for nine days. At 11.30 each morning, a Guard Mounting ceremony takes place on Tower Green, and sentries are posted outside the Queen's House and the guardroom.

Return to Byward Tower, where the Ceremony of the Keys is enacted every evening at ten o'clock. A party of four Guardsmen accompany the Chief Yeoman Warder and lock the West Gate and those at Middle Tower and Byward Tower. The guard salute 'The Queen's keys' and the Chief Yeoman cries, 'God preserve Queen Elizabeth'. He then takes the keys to the Resident Governor at the Queen's House, and the Tower sleeps safe for another night.

HMS *Belfast*

The engine of the low open launch throbs into action, and from the shelter of Tower Pier the boat reverses into the tideway and swings in an arc across the river to the landing-stage of the great cruiser. Here is a superb vantage point for looking at Sir Horace Jones's Tower Bridge, which opened in 1894. The bascule bridge welcomes visitors, by the way, who may prowl the glass-enclosed walkways and inspect the engine room.

Aboard HMS *Belfast* (1939), the Royal Navy's largest-ever cruiser, follow the yellow arrows forward under cool sun canopies to the forward gun turret. Here a map demonstrates the range of the six-inch guns – up to 22.6km (14.1 miles), a range which easily encompasses all the Slow Walks in London and would even land a shell on Hampton Court too. Then go up on the bridge, high above the river, and look over the side at the twin Bofors gun mountings on the deck below. Up again to the Flag Deck where visual signalling was carried out using flags or lamp projectors for long-range communication.

Below in the Operation Room is an audio-visual show of *Belfast* attacking a radar contact which turns out to be a German battlecruiser and five escorting destroyers. Amid the thunder of her guns, *Belfast* scores damaging hits. Nor is this fantasy, for in 1944 she was in the cruiser squadron which attacked and slowed the German battleship *Scharnhorst* off the Norwegian coast, where she was later torpedoed and sunk.

The tour (self-guided) continues through the Compass Platform and the Bridge Wireless Office. (When shinning down narrow companionways, grip both railings and step down facing forward.) Bells ring: it is eight bells of the forenoon watch (midday), the time when sailors went to dinner and received their tot of rum. See the Admiral's sea cabin and sea pantry with its remarkably civilised china cups and saucers. The whole ship was restored as a museum and opened in 1971. The reconstructions are fine on detail. In the NAAFI shop, the stock includes bath buns and forgotten brands of cigarettes such as Black Cat and Gold Flake, along with packets of Rinso washing powder, Zubes for sore throats and Paragon the zinc oxide plaster.

In the capstan machinery space, men slung hammocks from special iron bars and prisoners were kept in two punishment cells. Among other displays: the modern messdeck; the sick bay where a dummy sailor is about to be parted from his appendix; the vast galley with lines of coppers, fryers and ovens. Close to the end of the visit, clamber below through the boiler room and engine room – and try not to crack your head.

London Dungeon

On land again, turn along the river walk and go through Hay's Galleria, a huge arcade developed from the old dock at Hay's Wharf. This area around Tooley Street, Southwark, was once known as 'London's Larder' from the mass of riverside warehouses which stood here and have only recently been converted to general business use. Now a fun shopping mall with brasseries and restaurants, Hay's Galleria sports a centrepiece in the form of a colossal kinetic ship sculpture, more Emmett than Tinguely, entitled *The Navigators* and designed by David Kemp in 1987. It spouts water, its paddle wheels turn and the superstructure includes an astrolabe, a long chimney stack and giant harpoons.

The London Dungeon in Tooley Street is the world's first medieval horror museum. The experience is a little expensive, but to give them credit there can be few forms of torture they have not recreated with waxworks and models. Hanging, drawing and quartering is routine stuff here. See what you think of the hot-water ordeal, being hanged at Tyburn or boiled to death, stretched on the rack, branded and left to rot in a gibbet iron. The display includes a reconstruction of the Great Fire, in which you stand in an old City street while rafters crackle and crash about you. Mainly for students and the young, who of course love the Gothic atmosphere.

Operating Theatre Museum

In this fascinating and serious small museum, we see the Operating Theatre as it was used between 1822 and 1862. It was rediscovered in 1956 and is the only known theatre of its type to have survived from pre-Victorian times.

Enter from the back of the 'standings', U-shaped rows where students from the United Borough Hospitals of St Thomas and Guy's leant on wooden rails as the patient, a woman from one of the wards of St Thomas's Hospital, was brought in. Blindfolded, to spare her the embarrassment of seeing an audience of men, and the sight of the surgeon's instruments laid out in readiness, she was laid on the wooden operating table at centre-stage. She would also not see the Latin motto on the wall above, meaning 'From compassion, not for gain'.

In privileged seats around the table sat visiting surgeons and eminent guests. Before 1847 there were no anaesthetics, so the patient was given a strip of leather to bite on. Amputation was the most common form of operation, carried out swiftly and with skill; a leg might be severed in one minute. Beneath the table a box of sawdust was used to catch blood as it ran off the table. The floor of the theatre is false, laid on joists which rest on the true floor; the space between was packed with more sawdust to prevent any seepage of blood from staining the ceiling of the church below.

On display in the museum in the next room are contemporary surgical instruments – perforators, forceps, scalpels, a carbolic steam spray for killing bacteria and grisly pictures of Victorian operations.

Borough High Street

The courts on the east side of the street were a centre for coaching inns, places where passengers stayed before journeying out to Kent and the Continent. George Inn Yard is the third in line after King's Head Yard and White Hart Yard, and is now the only galleried coaching inn left in London. Today only one timbered wing remains. In Shakespeare's day the whole courtyard was enclosed by galleries, and travelling players performed in the central arena. Just down the road is the site of the Talbot Inn which, until it was rebuilt in 1676 after a fire, was known as the Tabard. It was from here that Chaucer's pilgrims set off for Canterbury to worship at the shrine of St Thomas Becket.

Southwark Cathedral

A church stood here before 1066, known as St Mary Overie and later as St Saviour. It is the oldest Gothic church in London, and became a Cathedral church in 1905, when the first Bishop of the new Diocese of Southwark was enthroned.

In the south aisle is the reclining figure of William Shakespeare, whose brother Edmund was buried here in 1607. The whereabouts of his grave is not known but a stone in the paving of the choir commemorates 'Edmond'. In the north transept is the tomb and recumbent figure of the apothecary Lockyer, who died in 1672. His long epitaph includes these heroic lines:

His virtues & his PILLS are soe well known
That envy can't confine them under stone.

Here to the east, through a glass wall, look into Harvard Chapel, usually reserved for prayer and meditation. The chapel commemorates John Harvard, founder of Harvard University, who was born in Southwark in 1607.

The Clink

Continue to St Mary Overie's Dock, where the *Kathleen and May* is moored, a three-masted 240-ton, 28m (98ft) trading schooner built in 1900 and now owned by the Maritime Trust. Her presence is a reminder of the old right of parishioners of St Saviour's parish to land goods free of toll.

In Pickford's Wharf see the old rose window, gleaming white in a section of old wall. This was part of the Banqueting Hall of Winchester Palace, residence of the Bishops of Winchester whose medieval see extended up to the Thames. The palace occupied some 28 hectares (70 acres) and a principal courtyard stood on the site of the present Winchester Square. Along Clink Street is the Clink Exhibition of 'Clink Prison and the Bishop of Winchester's licensed brothels of the Bankside'. The tone is prurient and, inside, the nudge-nudge wall panels about courtesans and the 'stewes' are not really worth the entrance fee.

What *is* interesting is that the Bishops of Winchester kept a private prison near this site which was known as 'the Clink', a term which spread to describe prisons at large. Thus, in 1835, the maritime novelist Frederick Marryat wrote: 'We've a nice little clink at Wandsworth.' This part of Southwark also served as an entertainment centre, not only in the sense that it offered theatres and bear-baiting arenas but also a great warren of brothels or 'stewes'. This word originally meant steaming baths, then took on a similar relationship to the knocking shop as the sauna and massage parlours of today.

Shakespeare's Southwark

In Park Street, opposite the offices of the *Financial Times*, a relief plaque marks the site of a famous theatre:

HERE STOOD GLOBE PLAYHOUSE OF SHAKESPEARE
1598-1613

Continue under Southwark Bridge where a new grey marble office block covers the site of the Rose Theatre. It was discovered in 1989 and the excavated remains should eventually go on public display in the basement. Look out for signs.

The next alley is Bear Gardens, in Shakespeare's day a place of torment for bulls and bears. In this street is the Shakespeare Globe Museum which shows plans of the new International Globe Theatre which it is hoped will one day open on Bankside. It is planned as a reconstruction of the original Globe, in form a 'wooden O' with spectators looking down from roofed galleries onto a central stage. Here too are many models of the old theatres – the Rose, the Swan, the Hope, the Curtain and the Globe, and a diorama looking across the river to Southwark and showing, in a row, the Globe, the Bear Gardens and the Swan.

Upstairs is a full-size replica of a seventeenth-century indoor playhouse, now used for shows by professional companies and students. Five rows of pews surround the five-sided projecting stage. Go up to the gallery and look over the stage from the upper level. In the next room are occasional exhibitions on a Shakespearian theme.

Finish this walk on Bankside, beside the building site of the new Globe Theatre. The project needs a lot of money before it can be built. I wish it well. Southwark needs more than shopping malls and spooky museums if it is to enjoy a true rebirth.

Across the river is a fine view of St Paul's, rising above the warehouses and office blocks. Up by the lantern, tiny figures inch their way round Golden Gallery. For refreshment and a gentle review of the day, walk along Bankside to the Anchor. A pub has operated on this spot since about 1513 and the present building dates from 1775. Dr Johnson is evoked here, and very likely drank here. His friend Henry Thrale owned the local brewery in Park Street and gave Dr Johnson a room in his house nearby, where he wrote part of the *Lives of the Most Eminent English Poets* (1779-81).

Walk 14

Lambeth Walk

Into the transpontine heartland, pausing first at the cultural enclave on South Bank. Among the day's bouquet of more or less fragrant attractions: Lower Marsh street market, the excellent Imperial War Museum, the pub where Charlie Chaplin last saw his father, a seventeenth-century garden, and the story of Florence Nightingale, the 'Lady of the Lamp'.
Allow All day.
Best times Not Monday or Saturday. Reasonably early start recommended, reaching Museum of Garden History in good time before it closes at 15.00 (open until 17.00 on Sunday).

ROUTE

Begin at ⊖ Embankment. At station concourse turn right to Victoria Embankment then right and up steps and across Hungerford Bridge. Go down to terrace by **Royal Festival Hall**, look inside for leaflets and turn left beside river.

At end terrace go down steps to National Film Theatre Bar and Restaurant (good coffee stop). Turn right and up steps to **Hayward Gallery** and **Museum of the Moving Image** ☜; the latter open 10.00 to 20.00, Sunday and bank holidays October to May closes 18.00 (last tickets 1 hour before closing), closed Monday, 24-26 December. *Admission.* Go in now or save for another day.

At exit turn left and follow road to Belvedere Road. At railway bridge ahead, turn left along Concert Hall Approach beside former studio of Feliks Topolski, now open 17.00 to 20.00 (Monday to Saturday) as the artist's 'Memoir of the Century'.

Bear right under the railway and cross York Road towards Waterloo Station. Bear left beside the arches in Mepham Street and continue to Waterloo Road. Turn right past the station and opposite the Old Vic theatre turn right in Baylis Road and bear right through **Lower Marsh street market**.

At the end of the market turn left in Westminster Bridge Road. Bear right along St George's Road and turn right into Lambeth Road by entrance to **Imperial War Museum** ☜; open 10.00 to 18.00, closed 1 January, 24-26 December. *Admission.*

At exit turn left along Lambeth Road. On corner of Kennington Road is Three Stags pub (with Charlie Chaplin associations). Continue almost to the river and turn in at **Museum of Garden History** ☜; open 11.00 to 15.00, Sunday 10.30 to 17.00, closed Saturday and from second Sunday in December to first Sunday in March.

Cross road by bridge and turn right along Albert Embankment, opposite Houses of Parliament. At Westminster Bridge go up steps and turn right. Follow road around St Thomas's Hospital and turn into hospital grounds at sign to **Florence Nightingale Museum** ☜; open 10.00 to 16.00, closed Monday, Saturday, 1 January, Good Friday, Easter Sunday, 25-26 December. *Admission.*

Walk ends here. Nearest refreshments across Westminster Bridge. If warm, try café terraces in St Stephen's Parade, close to Big Ben. Nearest ⊖ Westminster or Lambeth North.

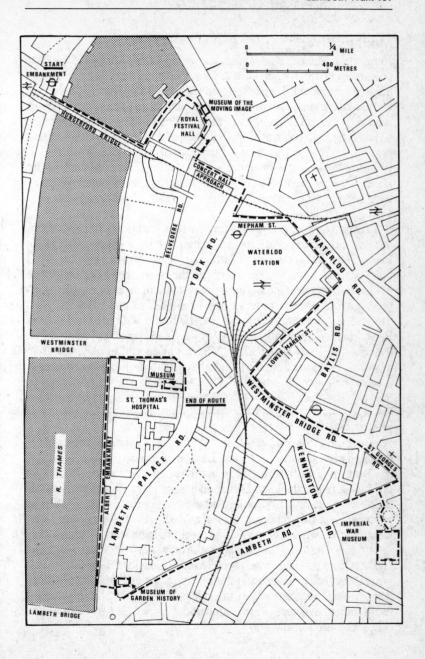

Monet's River

Hungerford Railway Bridge, also known as Charing Cross Bridge, was completed in 1864 when Claude Monet was aged twenty-four, and a hard-up art student. He painted many of his famous views of the bridge, with steam trains puffing across and sunlight reflected in the river, around the turn of the century between 1899 and 1904. Plainly, though, he had long been captivated by this reach of the Thames. When he first came to London it was to avoid the Franco-Prussian War of 1870-1. From that visit came beautiful scenes such as *The Thames and the Houses of Parliament* (1871) for which, again, the vantage point must have been close to Hungerford Bridge, perhaps from a barge moored by the Embankment.

The footway being on the northern side of the bridge, our best views are down-river to the City which stands astride Waterloo Bridge. St Paul's Cathedral is the focus of attention, flanked by faceless towers of the post-war period. The clump of three on the far left are the residential towers at the Barbican; close to them, from this angle, is the rare sight of a Wren spire which has survived – St Bride's, Fleet Street. The tallest tower to the right is the HQ of the National Westminster Bank. Immediately ahead is Cleopatra's Needle (erected 1878), described in *Walk 7* and which Monet was careful to eliminate from nearly all the views in which it could have figured, presumably because it broke up his composition.

South Bank

We head now towards the first post-war attempt to rejuvenate the bomb-shattered districts of South London. This was the site chosen for the Festival of Britain of 1951, officially a new-age commemoration of the 1851 Great Exhibition. Less grandiose in scope, it was an immense success with a public still emerging from under the clouds of wartime hardship – petrol rationing was abolished only the previous year, identity cards were still carried and meat rationing went on until 1954.

The Royal Festival Hall, ahead, is the only survivor of that wonderful junket. Other buildings which symbolised the shape of the future were a giant Dome of Discovery and the Skylon, a super-thin vertical ellipse which jabbed optimistically at the clouds. Such a pity that they pulled those other buildings down after the Festival – the Skylon was converted into ashtrays.

There was a lot of rain that summer, but eight million people surged to these terraces to gawp at sculptures by Moore, Hepworth, Epstein and others. They danced as they had not danced since VE-Day in 1945, the men in trilby hats and raincoats and the women (then known as ladies) in dresses that owed more to the austere policies of Sir Stafford Cripps, the skeletal-featured Chancellor of the Exchequer, than they did to the New Look dictates of Christian Dior.

The Royal Festival Hall is now joined as a concert centre by the neighbouring blocks of Queen Elizabeth Hall and the Purcell Room, opened in 1967 and built in the later Brutalist style as part of the South Bank arts complex, together with the Hayward Gallery. 'Bunkers' or 'cultural ghettos', their opponents call them. They are certainly bleak, and on a cold windy day no joy to walk past. They have more integrity, however, than the monster of 1958 which soars on the other side of Hungerford Bridge – the Shell company's headquarters, in a style you might call Financial Totalitarian.

Outside the Festival Hall is a colossal head of Nelson Mandela by Ian Walters, erected in 1985 by the Greater London Council. For its bizarre blend of humanitarian and loony-left initiatives, the GLC was later disbanded under Mrs Thatcher's rule, leaving London without a central governing body, and, as such, doomed to lag behind its European counterparts.

At the door for box office and coffee shop go into the Festival Hall and collect leaflets about forthcoming events. The Review Restaurant, on Level 3, has wonderful views over the river. Outside on the terrace is *The Cellist* by Siegfried Charoux, which I seem to remember as one of the more outrageous exhibits at a Royal Academy Summer Exhibition around 1959. Further along are the fluid stainless steel pipes of *Zemran* by William Pye (1972).

Museum of the Moving Image
This new museum is wedged beneath the Hayward Gallery (well worth a visit when a good show is on) in a surrounding forest of concrete disguised as the grey beams of some Cubist log store.

The show starts in a black and white optical-tiled vestibule with early experiments in moving and static images: shadow plays, peepshows, the zogroscope, camera obscura and magic lantern. Then a demonstration of Robert's Fantascope, a magic lantern mounted on a wheeled carriage to move up to and away from a translucent screen. Then the evolution of cameras to study and present movement, through Muybridge's horses and Marey's photographic gun. Then the flick-pictures of Edison's Kinetoscope and What-the-Butler-Saw.

There are screenings of the Lumière brothers' pioneering *cinématographe* from which more or less everything followed, leading to the rise of Hollywood. The very young are invited to enact a Western shoot-out scene, directed by a real ac-*tor*. Walk through to the museum's main cinema and see compilations of extremely small clips from famous movies – best for those with an attention-span of less than three seconds – and later be interviewed by an on-screen Barry Norman or read *The News at Ten* to camera, then step outside the booth and watch yourself at work.

It is all flashy enough, and technically up to date as it should be, and evidently popular with children. And if you want to read up in a potted way on some aspect of the cinema, there are miles of photoboards to scan for information. What the museum lacks, compared with its smaller and much more modest equivalent at the Palais de Chaillot in Paris, is the personal contribution of enthusiastic and committed guides and the consequent scope for intellectual engagement. If that is seen as too austere these days, or élitist, then the museum planners should reconsider. Here they have made too many sacrifices to easy entertainment.

The museum has a large shop, refreshments next-door in the National Film Theatre, and wheelchair access through most of the displays.

Lower Marsh

Facing the ramp up to Waterloo Station, take to scruffy Mepham Street beside the railway arches, where rich coffee smells flow out from Drury's shop. Further on is the Hole in the Wall, a famous pub in these parts. At lunchtime the large back bar, improbably panelled like a chalet, is a heaving noisy place popular with workers in suits and overalls alike, and the trains rumbling overhead transmit gentle vibrations through the floor and up the customers' legs.

Continue past the While U Wait Hand Car Wash to an unimposing stretch of Waterloo Road next to the station, brief comedy provided by the kitsch frontage of Caesar's American Take Away. Inside the windows a row of nine Persil-white columns with frieze instantly evoke the fish and chip parlours of ancient Rome. The thing about South London (pronounced 'Sarf Lah-'n by proper locals) is not to expect too much. A lot of it is very bleak, a vast jigsaw of forbidding council flats and long grey rows of suburban villas which for me symbolise the barren boredom of British Sundays long ago, when the height of public entertainment was watching a band of the Boys Brigade march by; on a really brilliant Sabbath the leader would strut past twirling his mace, fling it in the air and drop it.

At the next corner is the Old Vic, opened in 1818 as a house of melodrama. Since then it has served many branches of theatre, from temperance music hall to opera, ballet, Shakespeare, and Christmas productions of *Toad of Toad Hall*.

At this crossroads we turn right to a well-known local street market which took root long ago down the side turning of Lower Marsh, off Baylis Road. Its stalls offer the usual mix of bargain frocks and washing powder, nighties and T-shirts, Christmas cards in May, Alice bands and sunglasses, fluffy toys and a strong line in shiny silver-look trays and candleholders and other lovely stuff to stick on your mantelpiece. In Streets pub they will do you a fair cup of coffee along with pints of the usual.

Imperial War Museum

Turn in through the rose gardens towards the towering dome and portico of the old lunatic asylum, the way more than adequately signposted by two massive 15-inch naval guns, developed for the Queen Elizabeth Class battleship of 1912.

The museum moved here in 1936 from South Kensington, occupying the central block of what had been the Bethlehem Royal Hospital. Its collections survey the history of warfare since August 1914, and recent renovations have vastly enhanced its public appeal.

The Large Exhibits Gallery is an immense galleried hall with space for half a dozen fighter planes and flying bombs to hang in the air from cables. On the ground are field guns, trucks and tanks, from the First World War Mark V cut open on one side to show the hellish compartment in which the crew of eight drove the vehicle and operated its cannon and machine guns. A German one-man submarine (1944) and an Italian 'human torpedo' (1941) flank *Tamzine*, one of the smallest of the civilian boats used in the Dunkirk evacuation of 1940.

On Floor 1 are more guns and the cockpit sections of three Second World War aircraft. Here you can get closer to the suspended aircraft and check the technical data on panels around the gallery. Floor 1, the main art gallery floor, is divided into two sections, one for each World War. In the 1914-18 part are many famous pictures including John Nash, *Over the Top* (1917); Paul Nash's blasted tree stumps in the heavily ironic *We are Making a New World* (1918); Stanley Spencer, *Travoys Arriving with Wounded at a Dressing Station at Smol, Macedonia, September 1916*; Sir William Orpen, *Harvest 1918*. In the later gallery are works by Rodrigo Moynihan, *Medical Inspection 1943*; Spencer on location in Port Glasgow, *Shipbuilding on the Clyde* (1946); Evelyn Dunbar, *Land Army Girls Going to Bed* (1943), and an evocative view by Sir Muirhead Bone of *St Bride's and the City after the Fire, 29 December 1940*.

On the Ground Floor there are galleries for temporary art exhibitions, for example showing First World War posters, a period rich in Expressionist graphics. Also here is the John Singer Sargent Room, dominated by his panorama of blinded men – *Gassed, 1918*.

The most adventurous presentations are on the Lower Ground Floor. Begin by buying a ticket for the Blitz Experience. Check the time written on the ticket, which may be for several performances ahead. If you have to wait, take a tour through the other galleries covering various aspects of the two World Wars, illustrated with a lively range of posters, videos, weapons, uniforms and ephemera. The Trench Experience is a remarkable walk through a slice of trench on the Somme in 1916, eavesdropping on soldiers chatting during a smoke break. Look through periscopes to the enemy lines and see a raiding party prepare to go over the top, the air filled with the stench of drifting gunpowder.

The Blitz Experience happens every ten minutes and lasts for eight. It is declared unsuitable for under-fives and the nervous. If you are the latter, perhaps reflect that they do seem to let everyone out afterwards. It would be unfair to reveal what happens in S Shelter. Before going in, candidates for the next air-raid sit apprehensively back to back on a metal mesh-seated bench, about as comfortable as riding in one of the army lorries upstairs. Suddenly, the call to action, and nervously in you troop.

The museum has a shop, a licensed café and disabled facilities.

Lambeth Road

Opposite the museum is the house at No.100 where William Bligh lived. The commander of the *Bounty* is buried at the far end of the road in the churchyard of St Mary-at-Lambeth.

For lunch, perhaps call in at the Three Stags on the corner of Kennington Road. The food is pure cardboard but the room is large with the atmosphere of a dormant cockney boozer that stages live music from Ray and Trevor on Friday and Saturday nights, and coach parties are welcome. Charlie Chaplin was born in Lambeth in 1889 and a newspaper cutting on the wall claims that this pub was the last place he saw his father. If so, he would still have been a young boy since Chaplin senior, himself a music hall entertainer, died when Charlie was eight or nine. Both would probably recognise the yellowed wallpaper on the ceiling of the bar.

Along on the left is Lambeth Walk, site of an unpretentious street market made famous in Lupino Lane's musical *Me and My Gal*, first performed in 1937, which featured a song and dance about 'doing the Lambeth Walk'. The pub of the same name features a sign with a pair of Pearlies, the costermonger 'royalty' who dress up in black suits of light decorated with hundreds of mother-of-pearl buttons. At one time the Pearly Kings and Queens were a kind of trade association looking after the interests of costermongers; today they sport their wonderful outfits to raise money for charity.

Museum of Garden History

This interesting project opened in 1983 as a means of saving the redundant church of St Mary-at-Lambeth from demolition and to celebrate the work of the two John Tradescants, distinguished plant collectors and royal gardeners to Charles I, both of whom are buried in the churchyard.

In the nave of the old church, information panels survey gardening styles, tools, and favoured plants of famous gardeners. This basic exhibit is to be expanded when a planned upper gallery is built. Book treasures include John Tradescant's catalogue, the *Museum Tradescantianum or A Collection of Rarities preserved at South Lambeth near London* (1656), and a campaigning booklet for Second World War allotmenteers entitled *Cloches versus Hitler*.

Stroll through the small seventeenth-century garden in the churchyard. The central knot garden is complete, though the borders have still to be planted to their full potential. Further screening from the rumble of Lambeth Road traffic would also be a good idea. Captain Bligh rests in the taller of the chest tombs, the Tradescants in the other, distinguished by the bushy trees carved at each corner.

The museum has a shop and a café.

Albert Embankment

Cross to the riverside, passing the gateway of Lambeth Palace, since the twelfth century the London residence of the Archbishop of Canterbury. The Tudor gatehouse was completed in 1501.

By the river wall the smell of old muddy water brings back a memory from long ago. An old Motor Torpedo Boat of Second World War vintage had moorings between this wall and the pier, and I, a keen Sea Scout, spent many weekends on board. We learned to crew whalers on the tideway, rowing up to the Houses of Parliament and back beside Millbank with neither a care nor the dimmest sense of the history all around us. As London schoolboys we took it all for granted – so there was the boat, and over there was the Palace of Westminster . . . so what? We were much more concerned to wave at passing girls on Lambeth Bridge and to hear stories of what some bold spirit had recently seen and done at the Biograph, the local fleapit in Vauxhall Bridge Road.

The view across to the great sweep of Parliament is very fine for all my ancient ingratitude, and the awnings on Riverside Terrace mark the enviable spot where Members of Parliament entertain their guests to tea.

Florence Nightingale Museum

Beneath the Nightingale School of Nursing, which Florence Nightingale founded in 1860 at St Thomas's Hospital, is a museum dedicated to the life of this exceptional woman. As the displays make clear, she is best known for the pioneering years when she cared for soldiers in the Crimean War, but her achievements were far richer and more varied. Hating a life tied to society she dedicated herself to one of obscurity and toil. She freely criticised many nineteenth-century institutions, campaigning and drawing up plans for improved army barracks and civil hospitals. She brought better standards of sanitation and irrigation to help the people of India in their fight against disease and famine. At home she won recognition and better conditions for nurses and midwives and worked tirelessly in the fields of district nursing and health care.

The museum offers a prescribed route surveying her life, illustrated with personal possessions, costumes and jewellery, a Victorian nurse's uniform and a set of William Simpson's lithographs of the Crimean War. At about the halfway point a small cinema shows a twenty-minute video.

At the end of our walk, the best chances for tea and other refreshments lie across Westminster Bridge, either at the cafés in St Stephen's Parade by Big Ben or at the Westminster Arms in Storey's Gate, which has a wine bar in the basement.

Walk 15

Queen Anne's Gate to Tate Gallery

A tour of little-known historic streets in Lower Westminster, through Smith Square and Victoria Tower Gardens to the Tate Gallery and its fine British and International collections.
Allow   3-4 hours.
Best times   Monday to Saturday; on Sunday Tate Gallery not open until 14.00.

ROUTE

Begin at ⊖ St James's Park. On the platform, take the exit marked 'Park and Broadway'. At barrier, turn left and cross Petty France to **Queen Anne's Gate**. At next corner, street continues to right in facing rows of elegant early 18C houses, many with decorative wooden canopies. Plaques commemorate famous occupants.

Continue past Queen Anne statue to end. Turn right down Dartmouth Street to Tothill Street. Turn right to Broadway and bear left past Tube station block. On left is New Scotland Yard.

Cross Victoria Street to **Strutton Ground street market**. Walk through and turn left along Great Peter Street. See parish church of St Matthew, now fused to neighbouring buildings. Turn left into Great Smith Street. Pass old Public Baths and Washhouses and turn right by Church House bookshop into Little Smith Street. At Tufton Street, look left for gateway to Dean's Yard (see *Walk 1*). Then turn right past ecclesiastical outfitters, cross Great Peter Street and turn left along Dean Trench Street to Smith Square, dominated by St John's Public Hall, a Baroque church now converted to a concert hall. Look in at box office for leaflets.

Leave square via Dean Stanley Street and cross Millbank to Victoria Tower Gardens. Walk up to Gothic fountain and turn right. Continue beside river on Millbank to **Tate Gallery** ☞ ; open 10.00 to 17.50, Sunday 14.00 to 17.50, closed 1 January, Good Friday, May Day bank holiday, 24-26 December.

Tour galleries of British and International art, including Turner collection in Clore Gallery. Walk ends here. Nearest refreshments in museum. Nearest ⊖ Pimlico (right at exit, along Millbank, across Bessborough Gardens, turn right then left into Drummond Gate and follow round to Tube station).

Queen Anne's Gate

From the Tube station cross to Queen Anne's Gate and walk along beside the vast overground bunker which contains and protects the Home Office. At the next corner, the Baroque building on the left (No.36) is the headquarters of the National Trust. Beyond black iron gates is a grassy bank down to Birdcage Walk and St James's Park.

Look along the main part of the street. It was once divided by a wall where the present street narrows; the close on this side was called

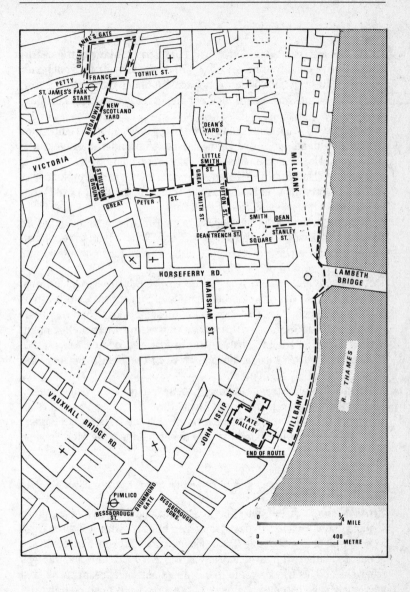

Queen Square, that on the other was Park Street. Many of the nearby houses are of Queen Anne period (*c*.1704) and have slender-columned porches with carved wooden canopies. All along the southern row, small white grotesque heads look out above the ground and first-floor windows.

Proximity to Westminster attracted many politicians and statesmen to this street and one, Lord Palmerston, was born here, at No.20, in 1784. Lord Haldane, the philosopher and statesman, lived at No.28 in 1907-28; William Smith, MP, an early nineteenth-century pioneer of religious liberty, lived at No.16, as did Admiral of the Fleet Lord Fisher in 1904-10, when he was First Sea Lord.

At the old boundary of the closes, opened in 1873, a statue of Queen Anne stands close to the wall behind railings. Next to her is a redundant street sign, its legibility not so much erased as left for London's natural resources of soot to obscure.

At the far end, at No.1, a plaque to Sir Edward Grey, Foreign Secretary, faces the office of the Director of Public Prosecutions (Nos 4-10). An old pub, The Two Chairmen (meaning sedan chair carriers), established *c*.1756, closes the street and we turn down Dartmouth Street. Here at No.11, sharing the orange-red door colour of the Earlybirds food bar, is the headquarters of the Fabian Society, the democratic socialist movement.

Back in Tothill Street-Broadway, bear left past the Tube station block. This mighty pile, No.55 Broadway, is the headquarters of London Regional Transport. Soon on the left we pass New Scotland Yard which houses the administrative departments of the Metropolitan Police.

South of Victoria Street

Cross Victoria Street into the more raucous purlieus of Strutton Ground, now a paved pedestrian street but still with its old market selling fruit and vegetables, bargain clothes, kitchen and electrical goods. My father went to school in Victoria, *circa* 1914-17, and this was where he and his friends came to buy doughnuts and cream horns, and something called 'itchy-koo powder', presumably from some departed joke shop, which they took away in small tins and dropped down the necks of classmates. In a local pub during those wartime days, he remembered, orders for sausage and mash were shouted up the hatch with the cry 'Two Zeppelins in a cloud!'

At the next corner turn left in Great Peter Street, opposite the large blocks of flats initiated by the Peabody Trust. George Peabody, an American philanthropist, endowed a fund in 1862 that was used to build large estates for the poor of London. The style of these 'Peabody Buildings' is repeated in many inner districts, from Spitalfields (the first) to Camberwell.

Continue past the Elephant & Castle pub, with its unusually jolly sign – the Elephant is at the seaside and wears a red bowler hat, dark glasses and a white bathing dress covered in crimson stars; three sand-castles complete the allusion. Arrive shortly at St Matthew's parish church, its Victorian tower fused to the modern building next door, Trevelyan House, which contains the Lord Chancellor's Department. The church lives on, despite a fire in 1977 which destroyed most of it. Look inside to see how the new, smaller church, rebuilt in 1984, retains the atmosphere of the old.

At the crossing with Marsham Street, look right to see the brown brick 'Byzantine' building of the Ninth Church of Christ Scientist. Many other religious institutions are concentrated in this dingy but fascinating quarter. Turn up Great Smith Street to the Abbey Community Centre, occupying the site of the old Westminster Public Baths and Washhouses, and next door the Westminster Public Library. Turn down by Church House, the Church of England administrative centre where both Houses of Parliament met for a time in the Second World War after a massive night raid in May 1941 damaged both chambers in the Palace of Westminster.

At Tufton Street, look left to the gateway to Dean's Yard, leading to Westminster School and the Abbey (see *Walk 1*). Ahead is Faith House, with choirboys' robes in the window; inside the porch a gilded arch shows the way downstairs to the showroom of Watts & Company, Ecclesiastical Furnishers to HM Queen. Nearby in Tufton Street is the august timber front of J. Wippell & Co., established in the ecclesiastical garment business since the eighteenth century, in the window a frozen procession of white, black and purple raiment. Then comes the headquarters of the Mothers' Union, inaugurated in 1876, a tablet in the wall dedicated to Mary Sumner, the founder. Continue past the rear of the 'Byzantine' church to the offices of the Corporation of the Sons of the Clergy, and here turn left to Smith Square.

Thomas Archer's huge Baroque church, completed in 1728, dominates the modest proportions of this square in a manner rarely found in London; St-Sulpice in Paris may be the nearest in spirit, particularly in the way one is so suddenly confronted with such vast façades and soaring corner towers. Now known as St John's Public Hall, it was converted after being severely bombed in the Second World War and is an important concert venue, famous for its BBC lunchtime concerts and also running a full evening programme. Look in at the box office for a leaflet about the current month's activities. If it is lunchtime, the Footstall restaurant is open from 10.00 to 17.00 on weekdays.

On the north side of the square is an attractive row of Queen Anne houses, c.1726. On the south side, well within glowering distance, are Transport House, HQ of the Transport and General Workers' Union, and the Central Office of the Conservative Party, where the true-blue flag always flies.

Millbank

Leave the square by the east side (Dean Stanley Street) and go down to the river which lies across the surging traffic of Millbank on the far side of Victoria Tower Gardens. Straight ahead is the Anti-Slavery Monument, an exuberantly roofed Victorian Gothic fountain with marble columns and four basins. It commemorates the emancipation of slaves in the British Empire.

Continue by the river wall, away from Victoria Tower and the Houses of Parliament. At low tide, a broad spread of dark Thames mud, liberally inset with stones and rubble, decorates the foreshore. On the far side are the towers of Lambeth Palace and the dark blue painted shacks of Lambeth Pier.

The gardens continue for a while on the other side of Lambeth Bridge, then follows an unlovely vista of concrete office blocks on the south or Vauxhall bank and the no less horrid pile of Millbank Tower on this side. At last the friendly columns and pediment of the Tate Gallery's portico come into view.

Tate Gallery

The Tate is widely thought of as London's principal modern art museum. So it is, but it also contains an important British collection which goes back to Elizabethan times. One way to summarise the contents of the Tate Gallery is to say that there are three principal divisions: British art from 1550 to the present day; International art since the Impressionists; and the Turner Collection in the Clore Gallery. The first two merge in the modern period, and some rooms are changed each year to emphasise different aspects of the collection. Several special exhibitions are usually on view in the central galleries and elsewhere.

If you collect a gallery plan at the entrance and then walk through to the Rotunda, there are seats where you can get your bearings and work out a route. To see the British galleries, walk up to the far end and begin at Room 1. Between here and Room 11 or thereabouts is a marvellous assortment, in roughly chronological order, of Tudor and Stuart artists; the age of Hogarth, and the art of the Industrial Revolution set close to the elegant portraiture of Gainsborough and the drama of Stubbs's animals. Some backtracking is inevitable to maintain the chronology, and it would help if the room numbers were displayed in the rooms themselves as well as on the gallery plan. The collection continues with sporting and genre pictures; William Blake and Samuel Palmer; the Romantic landscapes and visions of John Martin, Fuseli and William Dadd; the natural landscapes of Constable and the brilliant Bonington.

Room 9 is a curious conjunction of nineteenth-century academic painting and the Pre-Raphaelites. Side by side with Landseer's *Sleeping Bloodhound* and James Ward's *Spaniel Frightening Ducks* are the brooding intensity of William Morris's *La Belle Iseult*, the dramatic colouring of Millais' *Ophelia* and the Symbolist works of Rossetti and Burne-Jones. Somewhere at the crossroads between the two is William Dyce, also an admirer of Raphael: *Madonna and Child* and *Pegwell Bay, Kent*, pictured on the day the comet went over.

Some of these rooms are subject to change, but there will probably be a selection of high-gloss Victorian pin-ups by Lord Leighton, Alma-Tadema and Poynter and the softer, lyrical figures of Albert Moore and Whistler. Around the turn of the century the leading artist in Britain appears to be J.S. Sargent. The full meaning of this dismal thought is brought home in the next room, where the first paintings of the International Collection reveal the astonishing brilliance of the

Impressionists and Post-Impressionists, since 1870 or so light years ahead of the plodding academics at work in Britain.

To restore faith in British art, it can be helpful at about this point to walk across to the Turner Collection in the Clore Gallery and there admire the brilliance of possibly our greatest painter, an important precursor of the Impressionists.

The Modern rooms are more prone to change than the earlier British groupings. The collection includes fine Impressionist works by Camille Pissarro and Monet; Gauguin in his Pont Aven-Nabis phase and in Tahiti; Van Gogh at Auvers; the revolutionary reworkings of reality by Cézanne and Matisse; the Post-Impressionist pictures of Bonnard; Fauvism and Cubism – Picasso, Braque, Léger; the Camden Town Group; Stanley Spencer; and various representatives of British and International abstract painting and sculpture, from Nicholson and Hepworth to Pollock, Newman and Rothko.

The gallery compensates for its somewhat out-of-the-way location by having a good restaurant (open 12.00 to 15.00, closed Sunday) and a coffee shop. There is a museum shop and good facilities for the disabled.

Walk 16

Chelsea

Charming, privileged, artistic, quaint – Chelsea, the 'village of palaces', is an admirable place to wander. From King's Road turn down to Wren's Royal Hospital, home of the Chelsea Pensioners. Visit the National Army Museum, the Physic Garden, and Carlyle's House in Cheyne Row, where the essayist and historian lived from 1834 until his death in 1881.
Allow   4-5 hours.
Best times   Wednesday and Sunday, April to October, when Physic Garden open. Carlyle's House also closed in winter. See detailed timings overleaf.

ROUTE

Begin at ⊖ Sloane Square. At exit, walk ahead to **King's Road**. Take 3rd left into Royal Avenue. At end, turn right into St Leonard's Terrace and 1st left into Durham Place leading to Ormonde Gate.

Enter grounds of **Royal Hospital** 👁; open 10.00 to 12.00, 14.00 to 16.00, Sunday 14.00 to 16.00. Walk ahead from gates and turn left through College Court. Exit in far corner to Figure Court; Great Hall and Chapel are through central door on left. To find Museum, continue through Figure Court to Light Horse Court; Museum is on far side of East Road.

Exit to Royal Hospital Road and turn left. Continue to **National Army Museum** 👁; open 10.00 to 17.30, Sunday 14.00 to 17.30, closed 1 January, Good Friday, May Day bank holiday, 24-26 December.

At exit, turn left to **Physic Garden** at 66 Royal Hospital Road 👁; open approx. 25 March to 21 October, Wednesday and Sunday only, 14.00 to 17.00. (To check timings, telephone 071-352 5646.) *Admission*. If closed look through gate in Swan Walk.

Walk to end Royal Hospital Road and continue through Cheyne Walk, crossing Oakley Street. At King's Head and Eight Bells, turn right into Cheyne Row. **Carlyle's House** is No.24 👁; open April to end October, Wednesday to Sunday and Bank Holiday Mondays, 11.00 to 17.00. *Admission*.

Walk up Cheyne Row and keep on to Glebe Place which dog-legs twice on its way to King's Road. Walk ends here. Turn right to return to Sloane Square. Nearest refreshments all around, or continue to Peter Jones. Nearest ⊖ Sloane Square.

Sloane Square

From the Tube station walk ahead past the flower stall and W.H. Smith's bookshop to the far side of the square and the top of King's Road, marked by the smoothly curving curtain wall of Peter Jones, the Chelsea person's department store, second only to Harrods in the upper-crust wedding list trade. From its fifth-floor coffee shop views extend over the square to the Royal Court Theatre, home of the English Stage Company, and beyond to the brick and stone banded campanile of Westminster Cathedral. To the left, round the corner in Sloane Street, is another favoured store, the General Trading Company.

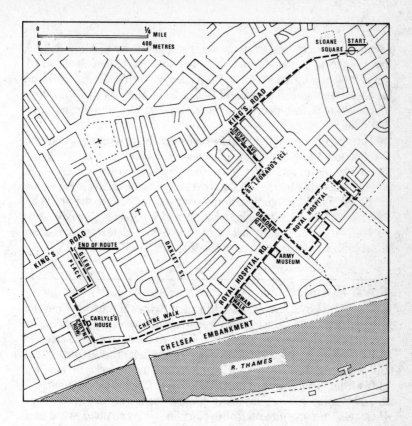

In 1712 Sir Hans Sloane, President of the Royal Society, bought the Manor of Chelsea. He is perpetuated in the many Sloane and Hans street names in the area, as is his son-in-law, Lord Cadogan. Sloane Square is also the centre from which distances and status are judged in the world of Sloane Rangers, members of the old-money set whose habits and assumptions are hilariously categorised in *The Official Sloane Ranger Handbook* by Ann Barr and Peter York.

King's Road

If it seems quiet, think of it more as a village high street. This is what it always was, and what it reverts to when the weekend parade of window-shoppers and style-freaks has passed by. King's Road is famous for its boutiques, but no longer sets the tone as it did in the Sixties of Mary Quant. After the Duke of York's Territorial Army headquarters, the shopfronts of Blazer and Chipie give a foretaste of the *boutiquerie* which occurs in more concentrated form further down the road.

Turn into the beautiful broad expanse of Royal Avenue, created in 1694 to join the Royal Hospital to King's Road. It is said that James Bond lived here, and I can vouch that *The Servant* was filmed in and around one of the houses on the west side. During the freezing winter of 1962-3 I had a room across the way and remember the arc-lights shining well into the evening, and in a closing scene Wendy Craig rushing out of the house and embracing a tree, defeated by the evil manoeuvres of Dirk Bogarde in the title role.

Royal Hospital

At the end of Royal Avenue look through the gates of Burton's Court for a broad view of Sir Christopher Wren's hospital or retirement home for old soldiers, founded by Charles II in 1682. At the centre of the complex is Figure Court, the oldest section. To the left of the dome is the Chapel, to the right the Great Hall, an arrangement similar to that used in the front quadrangles of many Oxford and Cambridge colleges.

Today some 400 In-Pensioners of the British Army live at the Royal Hospital. They are organised on military lines in six companies and are a familiar and popular sight in the neighbourhood, going about in their distinctive uniform – navy blue in winter and scarlet in summer – with a cap bearing the initials 'R.H.'.

Enter at the Chelsea Gate and shortly turn into College Court, added by Wren in 1687-8. Walk straight through, past doorways carved with the words 'Cook' and 'Butler' on the lintels and go through a door to Figure Court. The side wings flanking the Hall and Chapel serve as dormitories for the In-Pensioners and look out to the broad sweep of the gardens running down to the river. In the centre is a statue of Charles II by Grinling Gibbons, the Dutch-born sculptor best known for his marvellous wood carvings which decorate many buildings of the Wren period. On the far bank of the Thames, the forlorn hulk of Battersea Power Station, a famous landmark, awaits its conversion to a new use.

In the Great Hall the panelling is inscribed with the names of battles fought by the British Army between 1660 and the Falklands War. It was here, according to his wishes, that the Duke of Wellington's body was laid after his death in 1852. For five days thousands filed past the coffin before the Duke was taken for burial in St Paul's Cathedral. The large mural at the far end shows Charles II on horseback; it was begun by Antonio Verrio and completed by Henry Cooke. On the dining tables are large leather jugs, known as 'black jacks', once used for bringing up beer from the cellars.

Cross the octagonal vestibule to the Chapel. The main decorative element is the painting of *The Resurrection* in the half-dome of the apse, carried out by Sebastiano Ricci who came to London hoping to win the competition to decorate St Paul's Cathedral but landed this commission instead. The choir stalls, though modern, are worth a look to see the copy of Grinling Gibbons's private mark, an open pod of peas, the one he is said to have used to sign jobs for which he had not been paid. To the left of the altar is the Royal Book, recording members of the Royal Family who attend on Founder's Day. On the other side is the King's Chair, made at the request of George VI after a bomb destroyed the Infirmary building in 1941. The King, visiting the Hospital, found two of the original beams in the rubble and asked for this chair, and the small table facing it, to be made from them.

To visit the Museum, continue into Light Horse Court, named after the old cavalrymen who once occupied it, and cross East Road. In its Long Gallery and Medal Room are maps and mementoes donated by members, and case after case of service medals which In-Pensioners bequeathed to the Hospital or which remained there when no relative came forward to claim them.

In May each year the grounds of the Royal Hospital make a fine setting for the Chelsea Flower Show.

National Army Museum

This museum opened in 1971. Its founding collection came from the Royal Military Academy at Sandhurst and its purpose is to survey the history of the British Army from the time of the early militia units up to the First World War. There is some coverage of events after August 1914, though this is primarily the role of the excellent Imperial War

Museum (see *Walk 14*).

In the Weapons Gallery the display takes the visitor through the history of swords, pikes and muskets. Press buttons for a step-by-step graphic demonstration of how early firearms worked, then see the fearsome fat-barrelled machine-guns developed by the firms of Gatling, Maxim and Vickers, and the weapons of the modern gas-masked infantryman, prepared for the wider horrors of nuclear, biological and chemical warfare.

A new permanent gallery on the first floor looks at the glamour and the grimmer aspects of army life in the struggle against France from the Revolution to the Battle of Waterloo, also at the work of the colonial garrisons, struck down more by disease and decay than the ructions of dissident locals. There is a diorama of the field of Waterloo at 7.15 pm, a brave attempt by Captain William Siborne, who assembled it between 1830 and 1838, to show the massing of 140,000 men at the climax of the battle. Nearby is the skeleton of Napoleon's horse, Marengo, captured after Waterloo by a British officer.

The Story of the Army continues, charting the khaki years from Flanders to the Falklands and Gulf Wars. At the walk-in trench exhibit, the earnest commentary competes with the recorded chatter of machine-gun fire. Tread muddy duckboards and squint through a periscope for a forward view of stunted trees and the invisible enemy. Continue to the present day and finish the tour in the Uniform and Art Galleries.

The museum has a café, a shop and facilities for the disabled.

Physic Garden

At the crossing with Tite Street several blue plaques are visible on the red-brick mansions, most notably one for Oscar Wilde who lived at No.34 from 1884 until 1895. Here he wrote, among other works, *The Picture of Dorian Grey* (1891), *Lady Windermere's Fan* (1892) and *The Importance of Being Earnest* (1895).

After Oxford's Botanic Garden (see *Walk 28*) the Chelsea Physic Garden is the oldest in England, founded in 1673 by the Society of Apothecaries to grow plants with medicinal applications. Within its 1.4 hectares (3.5 acres) are the oldest rock garden in Europe, begun in 1772, a herb garden, and among the many rare and exotic plants is the largest olive tree growing outdoors in Britain. The marble statue at the central meeting point of the paths is of Sir Hans Sloane, who presented the gardens to the Society of Apothecaries. The Society commissioned the statue from John Rysbrack and it was erected in the garden in 1737.

Cheyne Walk

At the river, bear right to walk beside the admirable row of tall riverside mansions in Cheyne Walk. The novelist George Eliot died at No.4 in 1880. Then in residence at No.16 was Dante Gabriel Rossetti, whose house was a meeting-place for artists and writers. The poet Swinburne stayed there and regular visits were paid by Oscar Wilde, George Meredith and William Morris.

Intriguing garden arcades run all the way to the pavement from the front doors of some of the houses. At the alley passing beneath No.24 a sign announces that this was the site of Chelsea Manor House. Henry VIII had it built in 1536 and gave it as a wedding present to Catherine Parr, the wife who outlived him. It was demolished in 1753 after the death of the last occupant, the ubiquitous (around here, anyway) Sir Hans Sloane. Beyond the end wall of the now-private mews, the old garden lives on with mulberry trees said to have been planted by Queen Elizabeth I. On the wall a notice directs all drivers to *walk* their horses while passing under the archway.

Level with Albert Bridge, ignore the sign pointing right up Oakley Street to Carlyle's House. You can go that way, but it is better to stay on Cheyne Walk. Cross Oakley Street and step round the pert-bottomed *Boy on a Dolphin* statue (David Wynne, 1975). In the continuation of Cheyne Walk look for a gap in the railings and go through to see the bronze statue of Thomas Carlyle by Sir Edgar Boehm (1882). The seated essayist looks out with shrewd amusement at the traffic barrelling by, in sharp contrast with the calm broad river beyond.

A good lunch stop is on the corner of Cheyne Row – the King's Head and Eight Bells, once frequented by Carlyle and the artists James McNeill Whistler and Walter Greaves. Both these men painted Henry Holland's wooden Battersea Bridge, just a few steps away; one of Whistler's famous versions, *Old Battersea Bridge: Nocturne Blue and Gold* (*c.*1870), is in the Tate Gallery collection.

Carlyle's House

A stone medallion of Thomas Carlyle is positioned above the front windows of this gloriously dingy house, preserved as it was when the writer and his wife lived there, and now looked after by the National Trust. The Carlyles came to London from Craigenputtock in Scotland. They settled here in 1834 and Thomas Carlyle died in the front sitting room in 1881. By that time he had become a revered thinker and writer, and in this house wrote his most famous works, *The French Revolution* (1837) and *Frederick the Great* (1857-65). His wife Jane, now acknowledged as an exemplary letter writer, described her new house thus:

'We have got an excellent lodgement, of most antique physiognomy, quite to our humour; all wainscotted, carved and queer-looking, roomy, substantial, commodious, with closets to satisfy any Bluebeard . . . '

It is a delight to wander through the panelled rooms, amply furnished with pictures and personal treasures. Above the piano in the Sitting Room is a painting of the room with the Carlyles in it. Jane Carlyle was disappointed with the result and wrote: 'The dog is the only member of the family who has reason to be pleased with his likeness.' The dog, Nero, is buried in the garden; alas, some heartless collector has stolen his headstone.

The Carlyles took breakfast in the Back Dining Room. In the closet leading off it is a bronze cast of Carlyle's hands, made by Sir Edgar Boehm. In the Entrance Hall, along the staircase and in the upstairs rooms are many pictures of Carlyle, a testament to the stature he won in his own time, even if he is little read today. He was drawn and painted by, among others, Whistler, Millais and Greaves, and photographed by Julia Margaret Cameron.

The basement kitchen is a marvellous relic of life before electricity. Until 1852 all water had to be pumped from a well beneath the floor; cooking was done on the black cast-iron saddleback range, and in a domed portable oven known as a 'hastener'. This room was where the maidservant slept – provided, that is, Carlyle did not require it for smoking his pipe, in which case she had to wait in the scullery until he went up to bed.

On the first floor is the Library or Drawing Room, where the Carlyles received their guests. The reading chair, fitted with swivel and book-rest, was presented to Carlyle on his eightieth birthday. In Mrs Carlyle's bedroom is the 'red bed' in which she was born and which they brought down with them from Scotland. In the adjoining dressing-room are Carlyle's washstand and enamel hip-bath. His own bedroom was upstairs, in the area now allocated to the custodian's flat. Finally, go up to the Attic or Garret Study, which in his quest for a silent work-room Carlyle got the firm of Cubitt to build for him. Here he wrote *Frederick the Great*. Beside the books and manuscripts are showcases filled with the author's personal possessions: his cigar case, letter scales, clay pipes and travelling inkwell.

King's Road: A Second Slice

Continue along Cheyne Row. Around the next corner, at 22 Upper Cheyne Row and 'not a gunshot' away, as Carlyle once wrote, lived his friend the critic and essayist Leigh Hunt. Keep on to Glebe Place, one of the prettiest streets in Chelsea, a mixture of white cottages, small houses and gabled red-brick studios, all owned, it seems, by assiduous windowbox gardeners. Ivies, pansies, ferns and small flowering shrubs flow in a river of vegetation all the way to King's Road.

Features of the King's Road – among the semi-outrageous fashion shops and just plain expensive antiques galleries – are Chelsea Old Town Hall, now in part the public library; the Chelsea Potter, an attractive building but a grotty pub; the statued portico of The Pheasantry, no longer a private club; and the Markham Arms, if it ever recovers from its latest refit. For all the zeal of the developers – and one does rue the passing of some King's Road institutions such as the premises of Thomas Crapper, Sanitary Engineers – the village atmosphere that is *mostly* found here, though never on Saturdays, has changed remarkably little in the last thirty years. And for that we can be truly thankful.

Walk 17

Royal Kensington and Parks

Enjoy the civilised tumult of Kensington High Street and seek out the charming palace where the future Queen Victoria was born. Walk through Kensington Gardens to Long Water, and at the Peter Pan statue turn towards the Serpentine Gallery and the Royal Albert Hall.

Allow   4-5 hours.

Best times   Any day; on Sunday Kensington Palace not open until 13.00.

ROUTE

Begin at ⊖ High Street Kensington. Leave Tube station through shopping arcade and turn right in **Kensington High Street**. At Derry Street, turn right to entrance (at No.99) leading up to eccentric Roof Gardens on top of old Derry & Toms department store. Tour gardens (the Tudor Rose, the Spanish, etc.), salute the flamingoes and return to High Street.

Turn right to traffic lights and left up Kensington Church Street. Bear right through Lancer Square to York House Place, and turn right to **Kensington Gardens and Palace**. To enter Palace, walk ahead up gentle rise to Broad Walk and turn left. Go in at far end of building to see Court Dress Collection and State Apartments ☞; open 09.00 to 17.00, Sunday 13.00 to 17.00 (last tickets 16.15), closed 1 January, Good Friday, 24-26 December. *Admission*.

At exit, see Sunken Garden and Orangery, open as a tea room April to September. From Orangery, walk E across Kensington Gardens, keeping Round Pond to the right. At far side of pond, where paths intersect, bear right at signpost pointing to 'Serpentine Gallery'. Then take next-left path towards large equestrian statue (*Physical Energy* by G.F. Watts). Continue to Long Water; **Peter Pan statue** is in dip to left beyond wooded enclosure.

From here, turn right to end of bridge separating Long Water from The Serpentine, where refreshments available in new 'tented' restaurant. Then turn SW along path to **Serpentine Gallery** ☞; open 10.00 to 17.00.

Turn S towards **Albert Memorial**. Walk round and cross Kensington Gore to **Royal Albert Hall**. Ticket Shop is to right at Door 9. From there see decorated front of Royal College of Organists, then continue to rear of Hall. Go down steps beside a lesser-known Albert memorial, commemorating the 'International Exhibition' of 1851, to Prince Consort Road.

Turn left past Imperial College to Exhibition Road. Turn right to Science Museum.

Walk ends here. If energy permits, continue with *Walk 18: Museums and Harrods*. If rest and recuperation are the first priority, walk down Exhibition Road to South Kensington Tube station where good choice of cafés and restaurants: Daquise (Polish) and Dino's (Italian) in station block, or Bistro Vino and Bistro Rivoli opposite on S side. Nearest ⊖ South Kensington.

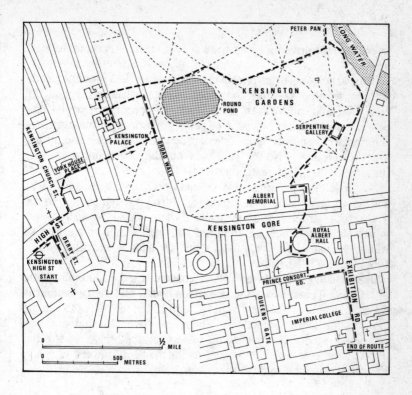

High Street and Roof Gardens

There is an eccentric vigour about 'High Street Ken' which has easily survived the decline of its retailing empires – that grand old interlocking triumvirate of Barker's, Derry & Toms and Ponting's, where you could buy everything, spend half a day ambling from one department to another and only have to brave the open air once for the short dash across Derry Street.

Perhaps it is only shopping habits which have changed, not people. The inhabitants of those Thirties and Victorian apartment blocks surrounding the High Street are no doubt as well-connected as they always were, though now they buy their groceries at Marks & Spencer and carry them home, instead of ordering them in Barker's capacious food hall (gone) and then returning home to receive them, several days later, from the driver of a smart van decorated in red, yellow and black stripes.

The old store buildings remain in place, more or less, and fine palatial warehouses they are too. The upper floors of what was, until 1973, Derry & Toms – above the present Marks & Spencer and British Home Stores – now serve as offices. One delightful curiosity to survive these refurbishments may be found by going down Derry Street and turning in at the entrance to No.99. Take the lift to the sixth floor and step out through the Art Deco restaurant to the Roof Gardens.

To the left lies the 'English Woodland Garden', with pools for ducks and, more improbable still, flamingoes. Stroll through an arch to the Tudor rose garden and discover also a white-walled 'Spanish' garden where the palm trees are tethered with ropes against the English winds. A Union Jack flying from a flagpole adds a colonial flavour – Gibraltar in W8, perhaps.

This usually deserted wonderland, conceived in the 1930s for clients of Derry & Toms, is open during office hours, and the restaurant is open to the public on Sunday from 12.30 to 15.00; the rest of the time it is used for private functions. The views over London are alas restricted, though by standing on the hump-back bridge next to the door to the restaurant you can see the museum towers of South Kensington and the dome of the Albert Hall.

To Kensington Gardens

Continue along the High Street. Barker's has retained the far section of its old store, and the rest of the building is occupied by other shops and the offices of the *Evening Standard*, itself the sole survivor of a trio of London evening newspapers which the street vendors used to announce as '*Star, News* an' *Standud!*'

Turn up Kensington Church Street, past the parish church of St Mary Abbots, founded in the twelfth century by the Abbot of Abingdon and much rebuilt, most recently in 1872 by Sir George Gilbert Scott. Bear right through an arch to Lancer Square, a shopping development in the Lego style of architecture, and after the outdoor café in the piazza turn along York House Place. Cross Kensington Palace Gardens, pausing to view the great orange brick and stone mansions, several occupied by embassies, which have earned the road the nickname

'Millionaires' Row'. Ahead through the railings is Wren's porticoed entrance to the west side of Kensington Palace.

The way-in for members of the public is at the diagonally opposite corner. To reach it, walk into Kensington Gardens past the statue of William III of Orange and go up the rise to Broad Walk. The ample sheet of the Round Pond stretches out ahead, a later addition to these gardens which originally were the grounds of Nottingham House, a Jacobean mansion bought by William III in 1689. The King, a keen landscape gardener, was anxious to move away from Whitehall Palace, whose low-lying riverside location did his chronic asthma no good at all. He commissioned Sir Christopher Wren to enlarge and convert Nottingham House to provide State and Private Apartments for himself and Queen Mary II.

The gardens were first opened to the public by George II, who allowed his subjects to stroll there on Saturdays, and the Broad Walk became a fashionable place to promenade and be seen. In the reign of William IV the gardens were opened all through the year.

A polite but unusually intimate bond links members of the Royal Family and the people of this quietly distinguished neighbourhood. It is reflected in the inscription beneath a statue of Queen Victoria in Broad Walk. It was sculpted by Princess Louise, her sixth child, and was erected in 1893. The inscription reads:

HERE IN FRONT OF THE PALACE WHERE SHE WAS
BORN AND WHERE SHE RESIDED UNTIL HER
ACCESSION, HER LOYAL KENSINGTON SUBJECTS
ERECT THIS STATUE, THE WORK OF HER DAUGHTER,
TO COMMEMORATE FIFTY YEARS OF HER REIGN.

Kensington Palace

Now on view at the Palace are the State Apartments on the first floor, overlooking Kensington Gardens, and the Court Dress Collection and some other rooms on the ground floor. Leading from the entrance hall, dimly lit galleries show court dress from the eighteenth and nineteenth centuries, then the visitor enters the columned Red Saloon, where Queen Victoria held her Accession Privy Council on 20 June 1837.

Continue through the Saloon of 1870 to the North Drawing Room, principally furnished with a large bed. This is where, on 24 May 1819, the future Queen was born, after her parents, the Duke and Duchess of Kent, had moved to the Palace in 1818. In a display case nearby, see the tiny coronet of a countess, the eight silver balls on tall points reminiscent of a birthday cake for one.

The Court Dress collection moves into the present century, a sumptuous array of dresses in silk satin trimmed with diamanté and lace, and embroidered with silk, chenille, pearls and bugle beads. It reaches a dramatic finish with what may still be called The Wedding Dress, that exuberant cream confection of bows and puff sleeves and extravagant train worn in 1981 by HRH The Princess of Wales and now lent by her to the collection.

Return through the entrance hall and shop and go up the oak-panelled Queen's Staircase (1691) to Queen Mary's Gallery. The warmth of the panelling suggests several things: a domestic atmosphere, calm and refined, and a preference for the small-scale over the grand effect – a country-house atmosphere rather than a palatial one. The beautiful carved mirrors are by Grinling Gibbons.

Queen Mary's Closet is the first of a series of private living rooms. Next are a tiny dining room with two high-backed chairs, a drawing room and the Queen's Bedchamber. The rich hangings and bedspread of the tall four-poster are original; the dazzlingly ornate writing cabinet, decorated with marquetry inlay and semi-precious stones, is a later import, from a purchase by George IV (he of the super-opulent Brighton Pavilion – though, oddly enough, but then perhaps it is not so odd, Queen Mary herself had possessed a similar cabinet more than a century before).

Go back through the Queen's Drawing Room to enter an altogether grander set of State Apartments: these were designed in 1718-20 by Colen Campbell for George I, and decorated by William Kent. Our route through these rooms is somewhat in reverse order, beginning with the Privy Chamber. Originally, visitors reached this small and rather private audience chamber by climbing the King's Staircase and entering through the ante-room called the Presence Chamber.

The Privy Chamber is hung with tapestries woven at Mortlake and representing three months of the year. The ceiling is by William Kent and depicts Mars and Minerva in a central ellipse. Windows here look out over Clock Court, part of Wren's earlier conversion scheme.

The Presence Chamber has a richly carved overmantel in pearwood, probably by Grinling Gibbons. The ceiling by Kent is remarkable – the earliest example in England of arabesque decoration in the Pompeian manner. Bright red diagonal bands lead from a central roundel of Apollo in his chariot.

The King's Grand Staircase is an extraordinary reworking by Kent of Wren's panelled design. There are black Irish marble steps and a wrought-iron balustrade by Jean Tijou (1696), and the dominant feature is the series of *trompe l'oeil* paintings of recognisable court servants and others, painted looking over a balustrade as though at arriving visitors.

On, next, to the King's Gallery, a long room designed to display the finest paintings in the Royal Collection. Some are very large indeed, such as the fleshy *Satyrs and Sleeping Nymphs* by Rubens. Above the fireplace is a wind-dial designed by Robert Morden in 1694. The pointer is connected by a system of rods to a wind-vane on the Palace roof; when the wind changes, hear it creak as it swings to a new position.

Continue through to Queen Victoria's airy bedroom which looks over the gardens by the Princess Louise statue. It was in this room that she was woken in the early hours of 20 June 1837 to hear that her uncle, William IV, had died; she went downstairs via the ante-room to meet the Archbishop of Canterbury and the Lord Chamberlain.

The King's Drawing Room contains a monstrous four-sided clock, and in the former Council Chamber are a stupendous carved ivory throne and footstool, presented to Queen Victoria by the Maharajah of Travancore on the occasion of the Great Exhibition of 1851, and an interesting canvas with Prince Albert inaugurating the Exhibition in Hyde Park. Around the room are other fascinating heavy objects from the 'Exhibition of the Industry of All Nations' and the International Exhibition of 1862: a jewel cabinet in the form of a pagoda, and a table fountain with three silky-backed horses and a four-dog centrepiece.

Finally, the Cupola Room, tall and square, the principal state room in the Palace, for which William Kent designed massive fluted Ionic pilasters supporting a Roman entablature, grand marble doorways and a ceiling painted with octagonal coffers in blue and gold. The coffers diminish in size towards the central panel enclosing the star of the Order of the Garter. The effect is mystifying. Is there a dome or is it all an illusion? In fact the ceiling rises only 1m (3ft) from edge to centre.

Out via the Queen's Staircase to the Sunken Garden and the beautiful Orangery, built in 1704 and used by Queen Anne as a 'summer supper house', and where some twenty orange trees still live. In summer it is open as a tea-house and restaurant. In the circular rooms at each end are huge marble vases made originally for Hampton Court; the pine and pearwood carvings above the arches are by Grinling Gibbons.

Across the Park

Strike out across the flat acres of Kensington Gardens, passing the curved octagonal basin of the Round Pond, built in 1728 to form the centrepiece of a large lawn encircled by trees, now a favourite place for model boat sailors. To find the Peter Pan statue, bear left towards G.F. Watts's equestrian statue, *Physical Energy* (1904), and walk down to Long Water, known in the eighteenth century as The New River after the River Westbourne was dammed at the eastern end of the Serpentine.

After boat sailing, the second most popular ritual in these gardens is feeding the ducks and geese which gather in front of the Peter Pan statue – a motley fleet of mallard, tufted ducks, Canada Geese and the occasional red-crested pochard. The statue of J.M. Barrie's eternal boy is by George Frampton and was erected in 1912. He stands on a tree stump decorated with spiralling elves, fairies, birds, rabbits, mice, and a single snail.

From here, either walk round Long Water and cross back by the Serpentine bridge, or turn right beside the lake. On the far side, the great white pelvic structure is *The Arch* by Henry Moore (1979).

The road crossing the lake divides Long Water from the Serpentine and Kensington Gardens from Hyde Park. To the east of the bridge is the Lido, where lunatic swimmers take dips at all seasons and rowing boats are for hire. For refreshment, try the tent-roofed New Serpentine Restaurant (closed Monday) or its neighbour the more modest Waterside Café.

The Serpentine Gallery, built in 1908 by Sir Henry Tanner as a tea-house, was reopened in 1972 by the Arts Council. It has four good-sized rooms for showing paintings and sculpture and runs regular exhibitions.

Turn south, crossing the Flower Walk laid out in 1843, towards a massive Post-Modernist tower which turns out to be the weathertight cladding which masks the Albert Memorial. It is part of a seven-year cleaning and repair project begun in 1989. George Gilbert Scott's extraordinary national memorial to Prince Albert, who died in 1861, is 53m (175ft) high and incorporates the central figure of the Prince by J.H. Foley, along with dozens of other figures around the base. It was opened to the public in 1872; the Prince was installed four years later after a first version was found unsatisfactory. The memorial is well worth a closer look, and essential for students of High Victorian decorative art, but for the time being visitors must make do with the explanatory display boards fixed to the scaffolding.

Walk round to the Royal Albert Hall, the second great monument to the Prince, begun in 1867 as the 'Hall of Arts and Sciences' and much enjoyed by Londoners as a venue for sports events, dances and concerts, most notably the annual Promenade Concerts or 'Proms' which moved here in 1941 after the Queen's Hall, Langham Place was bombed. For a century the hall suffered from a notorious echo, eventually resolved to general satisfaction in 1968.

On the west side of the Albert Hall stands the splendid façade in

maroon and cream plasterwork of what since 1904 has been the Royal College of Organists. Designed in the early 1870s by Lieutenant H.H. Cole of the Royal Engineers, the building was intended for the new National Training School of Music, hence the plaques of famous composers and dedications to the musical virtues of 'MELODY', 'RHYTHM', 'HARMONY' and, rather squashed in, 'COUNTER·P$^{\underline{T}}$'.

To the rear of the Albert Hall is another feast of Victorian architecture – the mansion flats of Albert Court; the Prince Albert monument of 1863, designed to commemorate the Great Exhibition and moved here in 1899 from the gardens of the Royal Horticultural Society; the dark red blocks and Norman towers of the Royal College of Music, and behind these a copper dome belonging to the Natural History Museum.

Continue down the steps to Prince Consort Road and walk along beside the imposing front of the Imperial College of Science and Technology, established in 1907 and incorporating the Royal College of Mines, the Royal College of Science and the City and Guilds College.

At Exhibition Road, developed from the profits of the Great Exhibition, turn towards the Science Museum, which arose as a repository for the scientific collections of the Victoria and Albert Museum across the road.

Here, if unfed and unwatered for some hours, walk down past the museums to Cromwell Road and cross to South Kensington. Comfortable cafés and restaurants are to be found by the maroon-tiled Tube station, built c.1868 by the Metropolitan and District Railways; see Route section for details.

Walk 18 🕊

Museums and Harrods

The great Victorian museums of South Kensington – Natural History, Science, and Victoria & Albert (applied art and design) – are here combined with an inspection of merchandise at the store which began life as Mr Harrod's grocery shop.
Allow   5-6 hours.
Best times   Not Sunday, when Harrods closed.

ROUTE

Begin at ⊖ South Kensington. Go up steps to station arcade and turn left. On street, turn right and walk round station block past Dino's restaurant. In Thurloe Street, turn left up Exhibition Road.

At Cromwell Road crossing, turn left to **Natural History Museum** 👁: open 10.00 to 18.00, Sunday 11.00 to 18.00, closed 1 January, Good Friday, 24-26 December. *Admission* (free Monday to Friday 16.30 to 18.00, Sunday and bank holidays 17.00 to 18.00).

At exit, turn left to Exhibition Road and left to **Science Museum** 👁; open 10.00 to 18.00, Sunday 11.00 to 18.00, closed 1 January, 24-26 December. *Admission* (free 16.30 to 18.00).

At exit, turn right and cross road beside **Victoria & Albert Museum**. Main entrance round corner in Cromwell Road 👁; open 10.00 to 17.50, Sunday 14.30 to 17.50, closed 1 January, May Day bank holiday, 24-26 December. *Admission* (said to be voluntary, but they do not mean it).

On leaving, turn left to Thurloe Place which merges with Brompton Road. On left at junction is **Brompton Oratory** (the Oratory of St Philip Neri); open 06.30 to 20.00.

Continue along Brompton Road to centre of Knightsbridge. On right, Beauchamp Place has interesting boutiques. Further along on right is **Harrods** 👁; open 09.00 to 18.00, Wednesday closes 20.00, closed Sunday.

Walk ends here. Nearest refreshments in store. Nearest ⊖ Knightsbridge (next to store at top of Hans Crescent).

South Kensington

At the Tube station a murky tiled subway leads off towards the museums: useful for guiding parties of schoolchildren beneath the heavy traffic of Cromwell Road, but generally grim. To see a little of South Kensington, turn left through the station arcade beneath the wrought-iron sign of the old railway company. Extraordinary to think that this section of the world's first underground railway, the line between Paddington and South Kensington, has been running for more than 120 years – it opened in 1868, the year when both Disraeli and Gladstone served as prime minister.

Ahead, Onslow Place swings away to the Fulham Road; to the right is the Old Brompton Road and all around are pubs and late-night cafés.

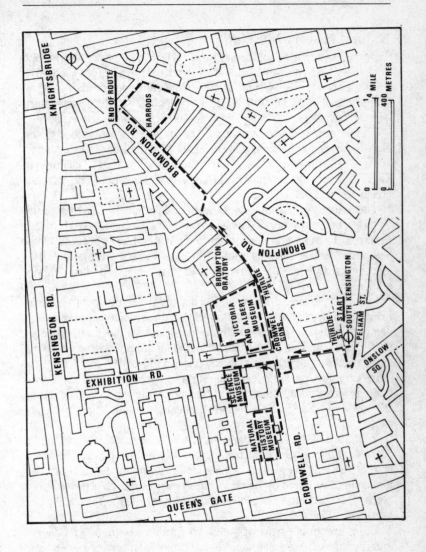

For an immediate cup of coffee, walk round the station and put in beneath the yellow awning at Dino's, or round the block at Daquise or Turbino.

Natural History Museum

Turn into the foot of Exhibition Road and walk up past the print and booksellers to Cromwell Road. On the left rises the pale blue and yellow brick palace of the Natural History Museum, designed by Alfred Waterhouse and opened in 1881, and, connected to it, the squat eastern wing in blue glass (1977) housing various technical departments.

This is now a double museum. The main entrance admits to the Natural History collections, also referred to as the Life Galleries, and a separate entrance in Exhibition Road admits to the Earth Galleries, in effect the new name for the old Geological Museum. The two are connected and one ticket is valid for both.

The admission charge includes a useful brochure with a map of the galleries on four floors. These cover something in excess of 1.6 hectares (4 acres), grouped in and around Waterhouse's beautiful nave-like central hall terminating in stained-glass windows which establish its identity as a centre of learning rather than, say, a de-luxe railway station.

Fun and spectacle are now as much a key to the museum's style as overt, lead-by-the-nose education. Some exhibitions are permanent, some temporary. If the brochure does not suggest an order of preference, then surrender and be lost among the wondrous columns and arches carved in tiny detail with birds and leaves.

In 'Creepy Crawlies', learn the survival secrets of ants and diving beetles, look through binoculars at the jaws of the wind scorpion, enter the world of Spiders & Co. ('Can you hear with your hair? Arachnids can!')

In 'Return of the Living Dinosaurs', a model Maiasawa gazes fondly into a nest of nineteen eggs busting out with hatchlings, watched by a rival attraction, the swivelling head and neck of a steel dinosaur, its movements operated by visitors from an overhead control panel. From out of the walls, the cries of two million years ago: 'Yaaargghh . . . grerkk . . . glubble!'

The museum is particularly pleased with its new Ecology Gallery, entered through a moonlit rainforest. It projects an ambitious overview for the twenty-first century of all the concerns which have inspired the Natural History and Geological collections since their first assembly deep in the nineteenth century. Now with film and video, and dramatic walkways across a glass-walled chasm, the visitor can study the whole ecological picture – how forms of life survive and conquer, how rocks change, how a leaf traps sunlight and food chains perform and how the incursions of bulldozing mankind threaten the future of the planet.

The upper galleries are more staid. The Mammal Balcony offers a zoo of the stuffed; the Darwin exhibition explores natural selection. At the top of the central stairway is a slice of Giant Sequoia from a tree born in 557, just before 'St Columba brought Christianity to the Scots'. All history since then is outlined across the 4.5m (14ft) diameter of the slice, until the tree was cut down in 1892, eleven years after the museum opened.

The museum offers copious shopping opportunities, a restaurant, café, picnic area and baby facilities.

Science Museum

The National Museum of Science and Industry has long roots founded in a variety of scientific collections which first came together in 1856 at the 'Brompton Boilers'. These and additional collections then briefly formed the science section of the new Victoria & Albert Museum, which opened in 1909, and were moved across the road to their present site in 1913.

Much renovation and extension have followed, and the present galleries reveal a semi-sophisticated hybrid which covers a vast range of subjects presented in an almost disconcerting variety of styles. The current pressures on museums to entertain as well as inform have yet – on the face of it – to be accepted here with conviction – though the problems of the Science Museum are enormous.

In part they go back to the museum's origins. From the entrance you go through the uninspired Exploration of Space (surely this could be more animated?) to an old-fashioned transport museum. It contains, among other exhibits, a Glasgow tram, early motor cars and steam locomotives. The pride of the collection are *Puffing Billy* of 1813, the oldest steam locomotive in existence, and Stephenson's *Rocket* of 1829. Both came from the collections of the old Patent Office Museum and were acquired in 1884. They are priceless objects in the history of land transport and are presented 'straight', with no flashing lights or 'chuff-chuff' sound effects. As a result, they receive little attention.

However, on the first floor, young children converge enthusiastically on the Launch Pad Gallery. This is a science playground for, as the name suggests, getting the young involved with scientific principles. Here they can carry out all sorts of simple experiments – be weighed in a 'giant steelyard', do a car drag test, work a bubble pump, and so on.

Most other sections on this floor have little obvious appeal for children of primary or early secondary age, say up to thirteen years. Exhibits deal in classic museum fashion with such topics as plastics, gas, agriculture, meteorology and time. At the far end is 'Food for Thought', the Sainsbury-sponsored exhibit on the science of food – how it is made, measured and sold – with plenty to sniff and peer at, and buttons to press. Here young teenagers with clipboards buzz about under the supervision of teachers. Again, it seems that the more lively display has won a bigger audience.

Whereas the Natural History Museum has gone full-tilt for a rock 'n' roll approach, at least on the ground floor, the Science Museum shows a reluctance to abandon its more austere look-and-read techniques. More money would no doubt help them.

The museum has shops, a coffee shop, and ramps for the disabled.

Victoria & Albert Museum

This much-loved museum is frank about its problems. It is the 'home of the world's greatest collection of applied art and design'. It has seven miles of galleries and so 'you are advised *not* to try and see everything in one go'. As to precisely what it contains, a former director, Sir Roy Strong, once explained that there was no 'central thread that animates these discrepant if marvellous collections . . . For over a century the Museum has proved an extremely capacious handbag.'

Although the present museum, designed by Aston Webb, was not opened until 1909, its origins go back to the Museum of Manufactures (1852) which with the collections of the School of Design were brought to the 'Brompton Boilers' in South Kensington in 1857. Treasures rapidly accumulated under Sir Henry Cole, the first director, and all were finally rehoused in Aston Webb's grand terracotta brick building, topped by a central tower which terminates in an imperial crown.

At the information desk beyond the entrance, collect a plan of the various levels and perhaps plot your own route. Below I suggest an enjoyable hour's worth which takes in the Raphael Cartoons; Great Bed of Ware; European furniture and sculpture; the Constable collection;

the old Art Nouveau refreshment rooms, and treasures of Northern and Medieval Europe. This is one of many possible options, and pays scant homage to the museum's Islamic and Oriental collections.

To find one of the museum's grander treasures, go left through the shop and along the flanking corridor lined with Indian sculptures (47B-47A). In Room 48A, seven Raphael Cartoons survive from the ten New Testament scenes prepared for the Sistine Chapel at the request of Pope Leo X. Each is a full-size painting in colours and size (akin to watercolour), executed in 1515-16. In 1623 they were bought by the future Charles I for the new tapestry works at Mortlake where several sets were woven with different borders. At the end of the room are Bernini's sculpture *Neptune and Triton* (1622) and a three-part fresco of the *Nativity* by Perugino (1522).

Continue left up the steps to the Great Bed of Ware (2), one of England's first purpose-made tourist attractions. It was built *c.*1590 for an inn at Ware, Hertfordshire. Its frame, as big as a room, measures 3.23m (10ft 6in) wide and 3.30m (10ft 10in) long. It is made of oak and there are painted inlays at the bedhead. The story goes that, on 13 February 1689, it was occupied by twenty-six butchers and their wives.

In the next rooms to the right (1C-1A), are seventeenth- and eighteenth-century furniture, tapestries, jewellery and plate, then in 21-21A European Sculpture (1500-1600) beginning with Canova's *Sleeping Nymph*. The sculpture collection travels across one side of the central Costumes Gallery and continues with medieval works.

Turn left to Italian treasures of 1400-1500 (20-17). Early on, an amazingly intricate *Crucifixion*, with a *Nativity* in the predella, is from an altarpiece carved in pearwood for Sant' Agostino, Piacenza. There is much to see in stone and terracotta reliefs, altar crosses and maiolica.

For the Constable landscapes, turn left after Room 17 towards the Lunch Room and take the rather wobbly, booming lift to Level 6, an airy modern gallery at the top of the building with good views south across the domes and towers of the museum to Chelsea and the chimneys of Lots Road Power Station. On the walls and central panels is a fine selection showing the artist in his early years and at the height of his powers in small and large canvases, sketches and drawings. See *Flatford Mill from a Lock on the Stour*, cloud and tree studies, sketches from Hampstead and Brighton, studies of foliage and another of poppies.

The V & A houses the national collection of British watercolour painting, and in neighbouring rooms, low-lit to guard against fading, are such works as John Nash, *Porch at Montacute, Somersetshire*; J.M.W. Turner, *Entrance to the Chapter House, Salisbury Cathedral*; and Thomas Girtin, *On the Wharf*. Works are rotated to display the full collection over a period of time; it contains many jewels, and quite a number of very moderate pieces.

Return to Level 1 and go through to Room 12, where a prominent work is della Robbia's terracotta rondels of *The Labours of the Month* (c.1450-6). Turn left at Room 13 to find the glorious Morris, Gamble and Poynter Rooms, originally the museum's refreshment rooms and a controlled riot of Art Nouveau decoration. The room by William Morris is green with bending plaster boughs and twigs, and delicate pale stained-glass windows. At the centre of the group, the room by James Gamble is a Falstaffian chapel supported by gold and white ceramic columns and half-surrounded by an apse rich in stained glass bearing inflammatory quotations and mottoes:

THE · FAT · STUBBLE · GOOSE · SWIMS · IN · GRAVY · AND · JUICE · WITH · THE · MUSTARD, or
HOT ROLLS AND HOT TOAST: COLD PIGEON PIE (ROOK) AND COLD BOIL'D AND COLD ROAST: SCOTCH MARMALADE JELLIES COLD CREAMS COLDER ICES BLANCMANGE WHICH YOUNG LADIES SAY SO VERY NICE IS.

The Edward Poynter room is calm and library-like, a Dutch kitchen masquerading as a grill room with masses of blue tile pictures.

After this extraordinary explosion of Art Nouveau, Liberty Style or what you will, continue through the early Italian rooms and turn right to 27 – Northern Europe (1450-1550). Here is a fine limewood carving of *Christ Riding on an Ass* (South German, c.1510-20), and a treasury of smaller pieces in boxwood, silver gilt and gilt bronze – medallions, inkstands, table clocks, powder flasks, beakers and chalices.

At the small Spanish room (1450-1550), it is impossible to speed past the huge School of Valencia altarpiece with scenes from the life of Sant Jordi (St George), patron saint of Catalonia. Turn right here through Room 24 (Europe, 1100-1450) and left through Room 43 – the superb Medieval Treasury (Europe, 400-1400) – to return to the information desk and exit. In the former gallery is the *Soissons Diptych* (late 13C), a finely detailed ivory relief. In the latter are the *Lorsch Bookcover* (9C), a Carolingian gospel book with ivory figures of the Virgin and Child, St John the Baptist and Zacharias; and the *Erpingham Chasuble* (*c.*1400), made of Italian silk with English embroidery.

The museum has a shop, restaurant, lunch room, and facilities for the disabled.

Harrods

It is the outstanding pile in the neighbourhood. The green of its awnings is a colour in its own right – say 'Harrods green' and shoppers of the Western world know what you are talking about. Its façades are no less distinctive – rusticated, pilastered, garlanded, the colour of crabmeat. At the corner of the building, look up to see four monstrously large Royal Appointment shields. Though overstated, they proclaim the identity of the place: Harrods supplies members of the present Royal Family with china, glass and fancy goods, provisions and household goods, men's outfits and saddlery. 'Top that,' is the message of the shields.

Turn in at the first main entrance, leading to 'Fashion Jewellery'. In the next room to the left is the opulent 'Egyptian Hall' selling upmarket glassware amid fat columns incised with hieroglyphics. Return and go left to find the Meat & Fish Hall, most famous of Harrods' departments, where in a corner two mermaids preside over the magnificent fish display, renewed each morning; the mosaic ceiling portrays hunting scenes (by W.J. Neatby); the fish counters are overhung with swagged nets decorated with fish, lemons and crustaceans, and clusters of pheasants adorn the game and poultry section. Doorways lead through to 'Bakery, Tropical Fruit & Nut', and to 'Floral, Fruit & Vegetables' – which has charming leaf reliefs on the ceiling with citrus fruits and pink roses. From these rooms, other doorways indicate 'Charcuterie' and 'Confectionery & Pharmacy'. Somewhere in the east, in 'Cosmetics & Perfumery', a piano tinkles. Cross the white marble floor towards the escalators and collect 'Your Guide to Harrods' from the nearby information desk.

Harrods, so big it has dispensed with the original Mr Harrod's apostrophe, began in 1849 as a grocer's shop serving the villagers of

Knightsbridge. From groceries the shop branched into perfumes, patent medicines and stationery. Now they say there is nothing you cannot buy here. The main part of the present building dates from 1901-5.

If you have no particular place to go, try 'China & Glass' on the second floor. A spectacular cluster of rooms begins with 'International Crystal & Glass' – black-walled, grey-carpeted, with displays for Daum, Lalique, Saint Louis, Baccarat, Bohemia, Swarovski and other manufacturers. A recent special item was a Lalique cactus table priced at £33,500, which everyone walked past without a blink between them. Next is the 'British Crystal Room', with Tudor, Stuart, Tyrone, Edinburgh, Thomas Webb, Royal Brierley. To the right is the 'Waterford & Wedgwood Room', then through to 'International Porcelain'. Ahead is another room for Royal Worcester, Spode and Aynsley, and off this another for Royal Doulton.

It is all much expanded since I worked here, a penniless ex-student wheeling round for a direction in life. My old department, 'Earthenware', has been upgraded to 'Informal Tableware' and is terribly smart, devoting many shelves to the smooth French products of Villeroy & Boch and Gien, and old familiar names such as Mason's Ironstone, Poole and Johnson Brothers. No chamberpots any more, I see. (White and sturdy they were, with *reliable*-looking handles.)

From here you can go through to Harrods Bookshop, as famous among booksellers as almost any in London. And from there, well, refreshment may be called for. A glance at the store guide reveals no less than eleven restaurants, cafés and bars, scattered between 'Lower Ground' and '4' – some in the vicinity of toilets and some not.

Walk 19

Marylebone

Pay a visit to Britain's most popular tourist attraction (Madame Tussaud's) and another to London's least-known cultural jewel (the Wallace Collection). In between, the leisured prosperity of Marylebone High Street.

Allow   5 hours.

Best times   Any day; on Sunday, Wallace Collection opens 14.00. Early start recommended.

ROUTE

Begin at ⊖ Baker Street. At exit turn left to **Madame Tussaud's and London Planetarium** 👁 ; open 10.00 to 17.30, summer opens 09.00, closed 25 December. *Admission.*

At exit, turn left. By York Gate, cross Marylebone Road and turn right into Marylebone High Street where plaques mark a former residence of Charles Dickens.

Continue past old church garden containing Charles Wesley monument and keep on past shops and restaurants to Thayer Street. Turn right at Hinde Street to Manchester Square and visit **Wallace Collection** in mansion on N side 👁 ; open 10.00 to 17.00, Sunday 14.00 to 17.00, closed 1 January, Good Friday, May Day bank holiday, 24-26 December. *Donation requested.*

On leaving, walk ahead round gardens to Duke Street. At Wigmore Street, turn left, cross James Street and turn right in St Christopher's Place, passing smart boutiques to Gee's Court and Oxford Street. Walk ends here. Nearest refreshments all around, best in previous streets and South Molton Street. Nearest ⊖ Bond Street.

Marylebone Road

At the station exit ignore the sign to the Sherlock Holmes Museum, an essentially bogus set-up in that its given address, 221b Baker Street, never existed outside Arthur Conan Doyle's imagination until some entrepreneurs stuck the number on an appropriate fanlight in Baker Street and began charging visitors rather heavily to 'meet' Mr Holmes and Dr Watson. Less unctuous, and free, is the collection at the Sherlock Holmes pub in Northumberland Street (see *Walk 2*).

Walk past a row of tacky souvenir shops beside the throbbing traffic of Marylebone Road, a major artery linking the City with the M40 motorway to Oxford and Birmingham.

Madame Tussaud's

The celebrated waxworks has been in this area since 1835 and now draws more than 2.5 million visitors a year, more than any other attraction in Britain. By mid-morning the queue at the door is dauntingly long, so it's best to be there around opening time.

The museum's founder, Marie Tussaud, learned to model wax

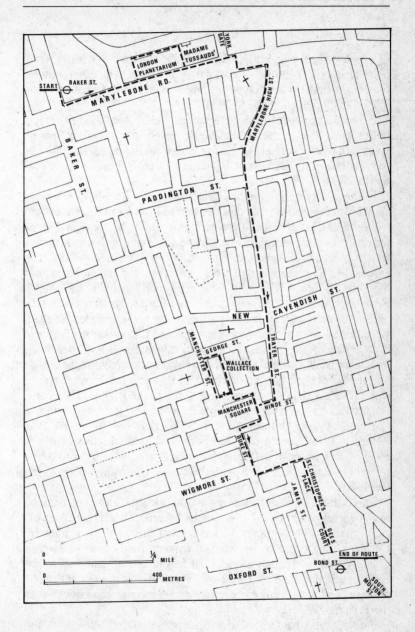

figures from her uncle Philippe Curtius, and inherited a collection from him which she later brought to Britain and toured in a travelling show for more than thirty years before settling in Baker Street. The museum moved to its present home in 1884.

If you plan to visit the Planetarium as well, a combined ticket is a better buy. Rise in the lift and be delivered into a kind of Spanish courtyard where Mañuel the waiter ('He's from Barcelona') is stationed to greet you with a drinks tray, but unfortunately is about to topple over the railings into a lily pond.

In the courtyard is a motley group of mainly British sporting and showbiz personalities, the kind the tabloids call by nickname or first name only: Gazza, Shilts, Lester, Daley, Both, Martina, and some fading lights such as Kojak, Scargill and JR. The way leads through a tented avenue to a celebration of two hundred years of waxworks. The earliest is a Sleeping Beauty (1765), featuring Madame du Barry, last mistress of Louis XV, who was later guillotined in the French Revolution; her portrait was made from life by Madame Tussaud's uncle. An exhibition of heads no longer on show includes Keegan, Khrushchev, Byron, Nureyev, Churchill and Cilla. Nearby, Fergie in her wedding dress receives much attention, and there's a video showing how Jerry (Hall) was measured and her waxwork made, this alongside shelves full of eerie anonymous hands, feet and other bodily parts.

Sound Stage 1 is the movie section: figures of Brando, Hitchcock, Bogart and the fourth wax Monroe I have seen portrayed with her skirts billowing over the grating in *Seven Year Itch* (there are twin sisters in Paris, Amsterdam and Barcelona, and who knows where else). Continue past a faintly depressing line of stars considered bankable today – Joan, Michael, Sylvester, etc. – and go down to the Great Hall.

This is the room of kings, queens and statesmen. Cries of recognition from overseas visitors: 'Si, c'est Marie Antoinette!' and 'Ach, Mozart, ja'. Signs say 'Photography Welcome' and many go for it eagerly. Germans wait in line to be snapped making ironic gestures at poor Chancellor Kohl. Thank goodness our Royals are cordoned off so no-one can actually stand next to them. This does not prevent ingenious attempts with long-focus cameras to frame Japanese housewives with the Prince of Wales.

Finally, the Chamber of Horrors, where Hitler attends at the dungeon door. The most frightening thing in these gloomy galleries is other people who blunder around in the semi-dark and scream. Tableaux of executions are a little grim, admittedly, and a demonstration of how the US authorities disposed of Gary Gilmore, as recently as 1977, seems in questionable taste. Then a Jack the Ripper Street and other scenes of famous murderers at work: Christie, Crippen and George 'Brides in the Bath' Smith. There is more, but that is probably the best of it.

The corridor lands visitors in a refreshment room, and from there a 'Space Trail' leads up to the Planetarium. Inside the dome a half-hour show tracks through the heavens, the journey marred by the introduction of two birds with silly voices, brought in to liven up the presentation. Clearly, the Planetarium has little respect for the attention span of its average visitor. I would like to think they have got this slightly wrong.

Marylebone High Street

The Marylebone Road should now be completely clogged, the roadway with buses, taxis, cars and delivery vans, the pavement with a hundred-yard crocodile queuing for the waxworks and dozens more customers arriving by the minute. Feeling glad that you came early, cross the road opposite the columned portico of the parish church of St Marylebone (originally known as St Mary by the Bourne, after the stream better known as the Tyburn).

At Ferguson House, on the corner with Marylebone High Street, a large plaque shows Charles Dickens surrounded by characters from six novels he wrote while living at a house on the site. This was No.1 Devonshire Terrace, Regent's Park, to which he moved in 1839 from Doughty Street (see *Walk 9*). Round the corner an inscription on the wall records that he lived here until 1851 and then sorrowfully wrote, 'I seem as if I had plucked myself out of my proper soil when I left 1 Devonshire Terrace and could take root no more until I return to it.'

Along the road in the old church garden is a monument to the Methodist Charles Wesley (1707-88), brother of John, who wrote many hymns, among them 'Love divine, all loves excelling' and 'Hark, the herald angels sing'. Also buried here are the painter George Stubbs and the architect James Gibbs.

At the next bend the High Street begins in earnest with a good blend of shops, pubs, brasseries and restaurants, and flowers on the pavement at Gainsborough's and Weymouth's. Outside No.33 (next to the offices of BBC Magazines) is a lamppost from the old music hall which stood here at the entrance to Marylebone Gardens, an eighteenth-century pleasure ground with assembly rooms for concerts. Across the road at No.83 Daunt Books has a long, inviting travel book department at the rear of the shop.

There *is* a different atmosphere about this pleasant street. Some might call it 'villagey', but that is surely too sentimental. It is more that of an intimate small town, and quite remarkable for being only yards away from the metropolitan turmoil of Oxford Street. At Hinde Street we turn right to Manchester Square. On the left, at Hinde Street Methodist Church, students of Trinity College of Music give free lunchtime concerts on Thursday at 13.00.

Wallace Collection

Sir Richard Wallace was the illegitimate son of the Fourth Marquess of Hertford. They and the Third Marquess were jointly responsible for building up this brilliant collection of paintings, furniture and *objets d'art* which Sir Richard's widow bequeathed to the nation in 1897. It came to London in 1872 from Paris, where Sir Richard lived for many years, and was installed at Hertford House, a family property which was specially converted for the purpose.

The collection is surprisingly large. Broadly, *very* broadly, it is worth saying that the ground floor contains the furniture and the first floor the paintings. Thus, if you first tour the ground floor and feel the paintings are a little dull, this is because the best is yet to come: room upon room of quite splendid pictures, and in Gallery 19 one of the most perfect viewing galleries in the world, hung with no less than seventy canvases.

On both levels there are two circuits, one inside the other, the outer one touring a courtyard. On the ground floor are sumptuous displays of furniture, glass and ornament: Sèvres porcelain with its brilliant ground colours of green, *bleu céleste* and the deep *beau bleu*, and exquisitely painted pastoral scenes. There are chased gilt clocks on pedestals combined with vases and statues of Carrara marble; desks and secretaires with plaques in Sèvres porcelain; Japanese lacquer cabinets; thick Bohemian glass, Syrian ivories, Italian maiolica, bronze statuettes, Limoges enamel pictures, miniature wax relief portraits – the grouping in each room carefully done to lead from one art form to another and so reveal, for example, how the art of portraiture is expressed in so many other ways than with paintbrush and pen. Galleries 5-7 contain Sir Richard Wallace's remarkable collection of European arms and armour, one of the finest in the world. For me the best paintings on the ground floor are in Gallery 10 – a brilliant group by Richard Parkes Bonington (1802-28) who might have become Britain's greatest painter had his working life not been so dreadfully short.

Continue up the Grand Staircase with its eighteenth-century French balustrade of forged iron and bronze, chased and gilt, to find a sea of Bouchers all around – *The Rising* and the *Setting of the Sun*, the *Autumn* and *Summer Pastorals*, the *Rape of Europa* and *Mercury Confiding the Infant Bacchus to the Nymphs*. In Gallery 13 are views of Venice by Guardi and Canaletto. In Galleries 15-18 are Dutch and Flemish masters of the seventeenth century – a profusion of canvases by van Ruisdael, Rubens, van Ostade, de Hooch, Gabriel Metsu, Terborch, Steen, Willem van de Velde the Younger, and Rembrandt's *The Artist in a Cap*.

Gallery 19 is an amazing room. Above the main arrangement of pictures is an upper row of still lifes and hunting scenes, including fourteen by Jan Weenix who specialised in the genre as court painter to the Elector Palatine Johann Wilhelm. Beneath this frieze of upended hares and sparkling peacocks the most famous canvas is the glorious *Laughing Cavalier* by Frans Hals. Elsewhere are Titian's vibrant *Perseus and Andromeda*, Poussin's *Dance to the Music of Time*, Rubens's *Rainbow Landscape* flanked by Van Dyck's full-length portraits of *Philippe le Roy* and his wife *Marie de Raet*, the *Lady with a Fan* by Velázquez and a group of portraits by Reynolds, Gainsborough, Lawrence and Romney.

The next room has French paintings of the early-mid nineteenth century, one wall dominated by Ary Scheffer's *Paolo and Francesca*, its languorous theatricality prefiguring the Symbolists. In Gallery 21 is an outstanding collection of French eighteenth-century paintings and furniture. Of the former, the many by Watteau compel attention, down to the tiny *Gilles and his Family*. There is another group by Fragonard, including his famous *The Swing*, and seven pictures by Greuze. Continue through the outer galleries, then the inner loop which leads back to the Bouchers on the landing. Truly, the Wallace Collection can have few rivals in luxury, beauty and refinement.

To Oxford Street

Walk across to the railed gardens, where the overgrown waving trees and shrubs are not quite up to Fragonard but refreshing just the same. At Wigmore Street turn and cross James Street which has café terraces on the widened pavement. St Christopher's Place has many smart boutiques – Whistles, The Hat Shop, children's shoes at Buckle-My-Shoe, more clothes at Charli. At Under Two Flags they stock model soldiers, military books and prints. Keep on through Gee's Court to Oxford Street, our terminus for today.

The great emporium in this feverish boulevard is Selfridges, to the right. Across the road are more boutiques in South Molton Street, and for music collectors the HMV store is always worth a browse.

Walk 20

Little Venice to Regent's Park

Further delights of 'village London' beside the Grand Union Canal. Detour to Lord's Cricket Ground, rejoin the canal and follow it to the Zoo. See the Nash terraces beside Regent's Park and walk through the Flower Garden to Park Crescent and Portland Place.

Allow All day.

Best times Any day, though Lord's tour not available Sunday morning.

ROUTE

Begin at ⊖ Warwick Avenue. At exit, walk up Warwick Avenue to triangular pool of **Little Venice**. Turn left along Blomfield Road beside canal, continue to main road and cross to Aberdeen Place/Cunningham Place.

At St John's Wood Road, turn right to **Lord's Cricket Ground,** entrance at Grace Gates ☞; tours at 12.00, 14.00, some days also at 10.00, 16.00, not Sunday morning or big match days (to check, telephone 071-266 3825 or 071-289 1611). *Admission*.

At exit turn left, cross Wellington Road and walk past St John's Wood Church. In Prince Albert Road, continue to Charlbert Street then cross to Regent's Park and at Charlbert Bridge descend to canal path, open 07.30/08.00 until 1 hour before dusk. Walk on to 2nd bridge (Primrose Hill Bridge), go up to Outer Circle and turn left to main entrance to **London Zoo** ☞; open 09.00 to 18.00 (last tickets 17.30, animal houses close 17.45), closed 25 December. *Admission*.

Follow recommended route, or some other of your own devising, and return to exit at main gate. Turn right and walk round Zoo to park at Broad Walk. Bear left towards Gloucester Gate and first of **Nash terraces**. Continue past Cumberland Terrace, turn left at Cumberland Place and right through arch to Chester Terrace.

At end, turn back into park at Chester Walk Gate and fork left to the Flower Garden. At Dolphin fountain, turn left along Broad Walk to exit park. Cross Outer Circle and turn left and right to Park Square East, where Daguerre's old Diorama building.

Continue to Marylebone Road and Park Crescent. At top Portland Place – the northern end of Nash's grand street scheme – look down towards BBC and Regent Street.

Walk ends here. Nearest refreshments, try Masons Arms (1st left in Devonshire Street). Nearest ⊖ Regent's Park.

Little Venice

At the Tube station exit, face away from the slate-grey needle spire of St Saviour's church and the green cabmen's shelter and walk, oddly enough, uphill towards the water. At Little Venice three branches of canal converge around a willow-shaded island. The branch ahead goes down to Paddington Basin beside the railway station; the others belong to the Grand Union Canal which to the left runs to Regent's Park,

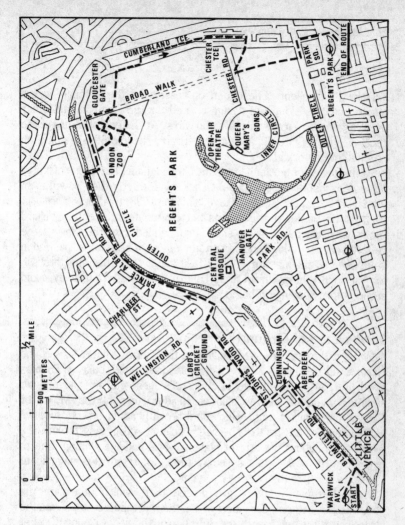

eventually joining the Thames at Limehouse, and to the right meanders through West London to Birmingham and the North.

The prettiest part is over by the boat station of the London Waterbus Company which from 31 March to 30 September runs hourly trips to London Zoo or Camden Lock. The flower-bedecked narrowboats, the blue and white iron bridge and the sheet of still water make one of the most picturesque and peaceful scenes in all of London.

Turn left along Blomfield Road, where two rows of boats and barges are moored, some brilliant with plants and clearly lived in, others curtained and silent. The queen of vessels on these canals is the narrowboat, its elongated design shaped for carrying coal and other bulk cargoes on narrow inland waterways. At the end of the road the canal disappears into the Maida Vale Tunnel, beneath the tea pavilion perched on the bridge.

At the angle of Aberdeen Place and Cunningham Place is one of North London's most distinctive pubs. Crockers, formerly the Crown, is an effusively decorated Victorian tavern built in 1898. It is not as pure as it was; in the Sixties it still had its perfect nineteenth-century billiard room with vast dusty green shades suspended over the tables. The coffered ceiling in that room is nonetheless very handsome, painted in gold, caramel and maroon. After a Test match at Lord's, spectators in the know skirt the crush at Lord's Tavern and come here to analyse and argue before heading off home.

Lord's Cricket Ground

Turn in at the famous gates dedicated to 'William Gilbert Grace The Great Cricketer (1848-1915)'. This splendid ground, built by Thomas Lord in 1814, is the home of England's most elegant and difficult summer game. It serves also as headquarters of the MCC, or Marylebone Cricket Club, which until recently administered the laws and running of the game. The MCC colours of egg and tomato are famous throughout the cricket-playing world and the waiting time to become a member – and so enjoy the comforts of the magnificent Pavilion – is currently twenty-two years.

Now, fortunately, there are guided tours which penetrate the hallowed Long Room, the museum and the real tennis court. From the Grace Gates the tour passes the club shop of Middlesex County Cricket Club, the resident county club representing an administrative area which has vanished but whose boundaries in North London are tattooed in the memory of every true cricket fan.

Go in at the rear of the Pavilion and up to the Long Room. Two rows of seats and high stools face the broad windows overlooking the velvet green of the pitch. This view also highlights the Lord's slope, a remarkable fall of 2m (6½ft) from the Grandstand on the left to the Tavern and Mound side on the right. The other walls are filled with paintings of the great and worthy – W.G., Bradman, Gubby Allen, Plum

Warner, and a display of bats used by famous stroke players such as Trumper, Hobbs, Hutton and Compton.

In the museum is an excellent display of equipment ancient and modern, portraits and paintings, the Ashes urn and the sparrow which Jehangir Khan killed in flight while bowling for Cambridge University in 1936, here stuffed and mounted on the ball that did the damage. The paintings of cricket grounds well convey the idea that this game is a way of life by itself. In one of them, a panoramic view includes the Prince of Wales standing beside his wife Princess Alexandra while ogling Lillie Langtry and various society ladies he evidently knew better than he would have cared to say.

Walk through to the Real Tennis court. This is a bewilderingly complicated racket-and-ball game, played on a court which imitates a medieval cloister with sloping roofs known as penthouses on three sides. The server hits a heavy iron-cored ball along the side roof and each player then tries to bury the ball in some awkward corner. Only nineteen such courts now remain in Britain. Real tennis is the ancestor of modern lawn tennis, the rules for which were first drawn up at Lord's in 1875 by the MCC.

In summer visitors can see the Indoor School which has excellent facilities including a bowling machine which delivers balls at up to 100 mph. Then take a lift to the top of the Mound Stand, tented summer architecture at its best. To the right is the Nursery End and the new Compton-Edrich Stand, named after Middlesex's 'Terrible Twins' whose *annus mirabilis* was 1947. When it opened in 1991 the admirable Denis Compton said, 'Fancy naming a stand after me and Bill and not putting a bar in it.' Ahead is the Grandstand, surmounted by the figure of Old Father Time, and to the left is the imperious terracotta and white frontage of the Pavilion. A perfect arena for the very best of games.

Canal Walk

From the Grace Gates, turn left opposite the huge temple of the Liberal Jewish Synagogue. At the corner of Lord's is a sporting frieze by Gilbert Bayes called *Play Up, Play Up, and Play the Game* (1934) after Sir Henry Newbolt's stirring poem *Vitai Lampada* in which:

There's a breathless hush in the Close tonight –
Ten to make and the match to win –

The somewhat rigid figures in the frieze faithfully epitomise the old Corinthian virtues of fortitude, fairness and cold showers. Continue past the battered but handsome façade of St John's Wood Church, designed by Thomas Hardwick and completed in 1814. Then come the brick and stucco cliffs of Prince Albert Mansions, the greenhouses of Regent's Park visible over the fence on the right.

At the end of this fence, turn into the park and beside Charlbert Bridge drop down the embankment to the Grand Union Canal. The canalside walk is peaceful and pleasant, the trees overgrown and agreeably scruffy; close your ears to the noise of traffic and you could be many miles from London. When the deer and antelope terraces loom ahead, go up to Primrose Hill Bridge and cross to Outer Circle and the red-bannered entrance to the Zoo.

London Zoo

This old and venerable zoo first opened in 1828. Alas it is under threat and may have to close. Although it recently came ninth in the list of Britain's top tourist attractions, attendances are down on what they need to be. Zoos, moreover, are under fire from conservationists and a further swing in the public mood may provoke a terminal crisis or compel London Zoo to turn itself into a 'conservation centre', whatever that may mean. We must see.

The Zoo recommends a route for visitors, though to follow it would mean backtracking to the deer, camels and giraffes that we have already seen from the road. An alternative way, fitting well with lunchtime needs, is to take the path by the Apes and Monkeys to the refreshment places grouped around the fountain in Barclay Court. On a warm day it is pleasant to eat outside despite competition for your slice of pizza from wasps and scraggy mendicant pigeons. While here, look at your Events Guide (handed out at the entrance) to check when the various attractions take place: the Gorilla Encounter, Elephant Weighing, Penguin Feeding, and so on.

After lunch, perhaps stroll down past the gibbons rolling on the grass with their young to see the rhinoceros impassively chewing sycamore branches tossed to it in bundles by a keeper. One afternoon, after watching the sea lions cope with several buckets of fish, I walked to the elephant moat to see four bleary-eyed residents roll and tumble in their muddy pool, tromboning wheezily, before the keeper threw water over them and scrubbed their backs with a broom.

Near the southern perimeter is Lubetkin's famous penguin pool, built in 1936, elegant like the set of a stage musical with spiralling ramps and shallow steps to conduct the tottering penguins down to the water. After the Big Cats, turn past Three Island Pond and its pretty flamingos, and return to the entrance by the chimpanzees and tangle-haired orang utans.

Regent's Park

Follow Outer Circle past the Zoological Society buildings and veer into the park, towards the first of Nash's great terraces, announced by the bright maroon pediment at the end of the block. This is Gloucester Gate, one of an impressive series of terraces designed in the 1820s by John Nash as part of his Regent's Park development scheme linking Carlton House and Regent Street to a palace for the Prince Regent in what was then known as Marylebone Park. The palace was never built, but the basic plan has survived: an Outer Circle road enclosing 197 hectares (487 acres) of parkland with a large ornamental lake, flanked on three sides by elegant if oversized stucco terraces.

The line of these terraces is broken by the Danish Church and St Katharine's Hall. Once part of a charitable foundation called St Katharine's by the Tower, which moved here in 1825 to make way for the building of St Katharine's Dock, these buildings were made over to the Danish church in London during the First World War. The Gothic chapel is by Ambrose Poynter and dates from 1829.

Walk along beside Cumberland Terrace, newly refurbished and one of the most imposing of Nash's blocks, though I have reservations about the colour, reminiscent of Cornish ice cream. For a closer look, turn up Cumberland Place to the monumental arched entrance to CHESTERTERRACE, the name emblazoned in the frieze in poorly spaced capital letters. Strolling through here gives a good impression of Nash's plan: close to the centre of London he created a park *and* a countryside setting for the occupants of all these grand terraces which he positioned facing away from the rest of town and looking inward over the lake and gardens. He had also planned to build more than fifty villas in the park, scattered about and screened by trees. That would have been too much, and it is undoubtedly a good thing that only eight of these were completed. Perhaps, too, it would have been a little too perfect to have had yet more ice-cream façades running along the north side of the park. They were planned, and were to have been called Munster Terrace and Carrick Terrace. Instead, the land was allocated to the new Zoo. My own feeling about all these terraces is that they are very grand to be sure, but overwhelming too, if not actually over the top in terms of city living appropriate to the 1990s. I would certainly not want to live there.

Reeling a little from cream paint syndrome, return to the park at Chester Walk Gate and the ordered beds of the Flower Garden. At the Dolphin fountain (Alexander Munro, 1862), turn left along Broad Walk to the edge of the park.

In Park Square East is the home of the Diorama Trust, an arts project based on the central octagon which once housed the revolving auditorium of Louis Daguerre's 'Palace of Light'. Modelled on its predecessor in Paris, the London Diorama opened in 1823 and was an instant hit with the public. Two great picture screens showed palace interiors, a cathedral or some piece of Romantic scenery. The operators used shutters and filters to create an illusion of movement, of things appearing and disappearing. When one episode was complete, and day had turned into night, or Mount Etna had finished erupting, the auditorium swung through seventy-three degrees to point the audience at the second screen.

Current plans are to restore the building and install a Museum to the Diorama, together with a theatre, cinema and workshops. A worthy project, particularly since this is the last surviving version of Daguerre's various Diorama buildings.

Cross Marylebone Road to Park Crescent, one of the most elegant parts of Nash's scheme. Two grand sweeping curves of Ionic-columned façades converge at the top of Portland Place, a broad boulevard laid out by Robert and James Adam around 1788 and later absorbed by Nash into his great triumphal way. Although spoiled by too much redevelopment, Portland Place at least retains its breadth, and with that an air of spaciousness uncommon in London's West End.

Walk 21

Hampstead

A tour of Hampstead and its glorious open Heath. Visit Keats House, stand high on Parliament Hill, go through the Woodland Area to see the art treasures at Kenwood. Return via the Spaniards Inn and Vale of Health.

Allow All day.

Best times Any day except odd days when Keats House and Kenwood closed (see Route).

Note Paths on the Heath can be muddy, even in summer, so wear waterproof shoes or boots.

ROUTE

Begin at ⊖ Hampstead. Turn left down Hampstead High Street and left into Flask Walk. Continue ahead in Well Walk. See old well at entrance to Well Passage and turn right through Gainsborough Gardens to far side. Continue along Heathside to East Heath Road.

Turn right, the Heath to either side, and descend to Downshire Hill and turn right. At corner by St John's Church, turn left down Keats Grove to **Keats House** ☞; open 10.00 to 13.00, 14.00 to 17.00 or 18.00 in summer; open afternoon only in winter, closed 1 January, Good Friday, Easter Saturday, 1 May, 24-26 December.

At exit, turn right to South End Road. Cross to gravel path and turn left uphill, then bear right on to **Heath** next to sunken Hampstead Ponds. At 2nd pond take crossing to right and follow footpath uphill to left of main path. Go over the crown of the hill, down to a cycleway and up again on the other side through a small oak wood. Cross next field and bear right through gap in hedge to next field. Go up to benches at top of **Parliament Hill** for excellent views over London.

Return to gap in hedge and bear gently NW towards Sports Ground (see map). Turn left around its borders and right at the drinking fountain. Continue up a rise to a bridge across a lily-strewn lake. Take the next right down a half-hidden narrow path which dips under trees, cross a short bridge and go briefly uphill. At the top is a junction of many footpaths. Behind railings a sign announces the 'Woodland Area'. Go ahead along an often muddy path which curves right between fences. At the fork where a rhododendron separates the paths, go left and follow gently downhill to lake. Turn left across bridge to broad park where cream mansion of **Kenwood** stands at the top of a rise.

Take steps up to left of Orangery (left-hand wing). Go left through bower next to Orangery and walk round to front of house ☞; open Good Friday or 1 April (whichever is earlier) to 30 September 10.00 to 18.00, 1 October to Maundy Thursday or 31 March (whichever is earlier) 10.00 to 16.00, closed 24-25 December. Visit fine art collection (Iveagh Bequest) and return to front entrance.

Follow path left to Hampstead Lane. Turn left to **Spaniards Inn**, on top of hill after Winnington Road. Continue along Spaniards Road, Sandy Heath on the right. At the junction with North End Way is Jack Straw's Castle. Cross to Whitestone Pond and turn left down East Heath Road past Royal Free Hospital, then left down **Vale of Health** to extraordinary cluster of houses entirely surrounded by heath. Walk

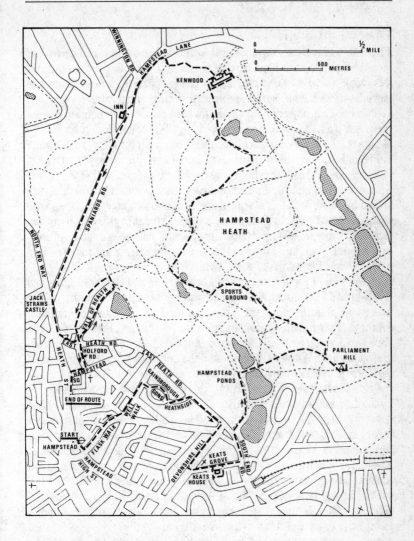

through to end, turn left and follow country path which leads back uphill to East Heath Road.

Cross to Holford Road and turn right in Hampstead Square to Heath Street. Turn left towards Tube station. Walk ends here. Nearest refreshments all around.

The Spa on the Hill

There is much to see and admire in the streets to east and west of
Heath Street and the High Street, almost a town tour by itself, but for
this walk I have chosen to add a large portion of Heath to the
ingredients. Enough, in fact, to bring us within range of the wonderful
eighteenth-century paintings at Kenwood. So, it's an open-air day for
the most part, best done in dry weather. When it's dreich on Hampstead Heath, the footpaths under the trees soon dissolve to sludge.

From the Tube station turn almost immediately into the paved way of
Flask Walk. After the shops are rows of delightful houses: bow-
windowed eighteenth-century frontages, then a startling cubic shape in
brown brick at No.29, prefacing a line of curiously gabled cottages with
bushy front gardens, artfully unkempt. This street says much about the
character and appeal of Hampstead: calm on the surface, pretty,
expensive to buy into, the kind of bourn which graduate middle-class
professionals like to make their own.

At the foot of the hill, the old red-brick Wells and Camden Baths and
Wash-houses sound an appropriate watery note. The healthy spring
waters of Hampstead were first exploited in the late seventeenth
century, not long after refugees from the Plague and Fire of 1665 and
1666 had arrived to swell the population of the village. The physician to
the Wells, a Dr William Gibbons, said the spring in Well Walk produced
chalybeate water of the finest quality, as good as water from Tunbridge
Wells. (Chalybeate, by the way, means 'impregnated with salts of
iron'.) Londoners poured up the hill to taste it and flasks filled with it
descended the hill by the cartload, to be sold in taverns around Fleet
Street and Covent Garden. A fashionable spa took root, its focus the
spring and a Great Room which stood nearby and contained an
assembly room for concerts and dances and a pump room for taking the
waters. The vogue lasted for about twenty-five years from 1700, until
ruffians and gamblers ruined it. A second spa near Burgh House – Dr
Gibbons's Queen Anne residence, now in part a local-history museum –
had a brief existence before the low-lifers moved in and it too closed
down. A rather dismal Victorian fountain now marks the site of the
spring, at the entrance to Well Passage. The water in the basin is
stagnant-green and the plate warning us not to drink it has a redundant
air. I would not like to see a dog put his tongue in that stuff.

The sign on the gate to Gainsborough Gardens says 'Private', and it
may be prudent not to march through the pretty sunken gardens at the

centre. To right or left around the oval, the gardens are fringed with rose bushes, laurel, holly and fine mature trees – oak, horse chestnut and maple – forming a Romantic woodland walk in the spirit of a Constable painting. He, for a time, lived near the spring at No.40 Well Walk, and wrote of Hampstead, 'I love every stile, and stump, and lane in the village; as long as I am able to hold a brush I shall never cease to paint them.'

At the far side, a first view of the open Heath, rolling away from the fine shuttered villas of Heathside. Follow the route to Downshire Hill and turn past the attractive stucco front of the chapel of St John's, completed in 1823, and walk down Keats Grove.

Keats House

When the poet John Keats came to live at Wentworth Place in 1818, it was as the guest of his friend Charles Brown who lived in one of two then separate houses sharing a common garden (the eastern part, to the left). The other house was owned by Charles Dilke who the following year let it to a Mrs Brawne, a widow with three children. Her elder daughter, aged eighteen, was Fanny, whom Keats had met some months earlier. She and Keats became engaged but the poet, realising he had tuberculosis, went to Rome to find a cure and in 1821 died there at the age of twenty-five.

In the light airy rooms are paintings and documents, and in the library a collection of letters by Keats and other treasures. In this house he wrote 'On a Dream', 'La Belle Dame sans Merci' and the odes 'To Psyche', 'On Melancholy', 'To a Nightingale', 'On a Grecian Urn' and 'On Indolence'.

Upstairs is Keats's bedroom, furnished with a 'tent-bed' such as he may have slept in. In the basement are the white-painted kitchens of the two houses, and on the Keats side a wine cellar fitted with whitewashed brick compartments. Outside in the garden is a drooping plum tree, successor to the one Keats sat beneath when composing his 'Ode to a Nightingale'. Inspiration for the poem, according to Charles Brown, came after a nightingale nested near the house. The story beneath a painting in the collection adds the idea that, after an evening with friends at the Spaniards Inn, Keats went out and was later found lying entranced on a bank listening to the song of a nightingale.

Parliament Hill

From South End Road, take to the Heath by Hampstead Ponds and follow the route to the top of Parliament Hill (97m/319ft). Here a marvellous panorama opens out across the whole of London. An annotated map beside the footpath picks out the most prominent buildings and others you may strain to recognise. The seasons of the year play a part in this, for although the map takes heed of the clumps of trees immediately ahead, in summer they grow thicker and broader and mask rather more of the view. Usually visible through the two main gaps are: to the left, the NatWest Tower and the City, and the dome of St Paul's; to the right, the television mast at Crystal Palace, Victoria Tower at the Palace of Westminster and the London Telecom Tower.

Across the Heath

The route to Kenwood is a gentle progress over undulating fields and along footpaths which bend past the Sports Field, and over a bridge crossing a lily pond where panting dogs swim and retrieve sticks from the water. Footpads and highwaymen were regular denizens of the Heath in former times, and even today all that flutters in the bushes at night is not birdlife. By day, however, it is open and peaceful. Joggers jog, and walkers make their own beelines through copses and up grassy slopes, criss-crossing on their individual paths. Through the Woodland Area the way is lined with holly and rhododendron and shaded by taller trees. Over bushes to the left glimpses of the cream south façade of Kenwood come into view.

At the lake a sign points right to the Open Air Stage. We go left across a bridge where a broad park opens out, and at the top of the slope stands the great house of Kenwood. Between 1764 and 1769 Robert Adam extended a brick villa of *c*.1700, adding a third storey and the Library wing on the right to balance the Orangery on the left. At the front, on the far side, he built a great portico, and clad the whole in gleaming stucco.

The Iveagh Bequest at Kenwood

Head across the park, boggy in places, and walk up the shallow steps beside the Orangery. To enter the house, walk through the bower and around to the front. The great attraction of Kenwood today is not so much the house as the magnificent collection of paintings which Edward Cecil Guinness, 1st Earl of Iveagh, installed here and bequeathed to the nation in 1927.

From the Hall, go left past the Great Stairs to the Ante Chamber. From the Venetian window is a fine view across the park. To the left, and not quite visible from here, is the Open Air Stage where summer concerts are held from June to September. The paying audience sit on chairs or on the grass on this side of the lake and look across the water to the orchestra; non-payers can usually get near enough from the Heath to hear the music but probably will not be able to see anything.

This room was an ante-room to the Library and also the vestibule to the dressing-room of Lord Mansfield, the Lord Chief Justice, who commissioned Adam to convert the house. On the walls hang paintings by Angelica Kauffmann. The eighteenth century is not the only period represented at Kenwood, but works from that time predominate.

The long Neo-Classical Library is a perfect long gallery running into apses at each end, where the bookshelves stand. It was intended also as a grand reception room and on the north wall, in place of windows, mirrored recesses reflect the view across the park and expand the interior space.

Turn right through the Ante Chamber to the Dining Room Lobby. This and the Dining Room were added later in 1793-6. Look up to the circular balustraded balcony and central skylight. Paintings by Boucher include *Landscape with Figures Gathering Cherries*. In the Dining Room are Lord Iveagh's finest paintings, led by Rembrandt's *Self Portrait* of *c*.1663: a marvellous mature work, its drama concentrated in the face of the artist, the body sketchy and mysterious, though the brushes in his hand are held in a firm geometric pattern. Nearby is Vermeer's *Guitar Player*, which seems untypical compared with his works in the Rijksmuseum, Amsterdam, and a fine fiery picture by Frans Hals, *A Man with a Cane*.

Continue through Lord Mansfield's Dressing Room, now decorated with pictures by Gainsborough and Reynolds, to the long Breakfast Room. Here are paintings by Gainsborough, Cuyp, and a fascinating view of *Old London Bridge* (1630) by Claude de Jongh, the Tower rising in the distance above the wharf houses.

In Lady Mansfield's Dressing Room is an exhibit tracing the history of Kenwood and a cabinet of exquisite Chinese porcelain. Next, in the

Housekeeper's Room, are splendid views of Rome by Pannini and of Venice by Guardi. In the Orangery (in the eighteenth century a kind of rich person's greenhouse) are some excellent portraits by Gainsborough of *Lady Brisco*, angular and with an imperious coiffe of stiff powdered hair, and *Mary, Countess Howe*, wearing infinitely detailed robes and a pearl necklace.

Turn through the splendid Music Room and go up to the first floor which is usually reserved for special exhibitions. Back at ground level, walk out to the south terrace to find, beyond the Library, the Cold Bath, favoured in the eighteenth century for medicinal bathing. In the former Service Wing are the Old Kitchen and Coach House, the latter converted to a rather institutional café. From this end of the terrace, look across the lake to the curving lines of the Open Air Stage.

Spaniards Inn

A short road walk brings us to this famous watering hole, my choice for a lunch stop. Built in the late sixteenth century, its Spanish connections are cloudy now, but may relate to a Spanish ambassador to the Court of James I who stayed there before it was an inn. Its most dramatic moment, apart from the days when Dick Turpin the highwayman stabled his horse across the road in the toll-house, came in 1780. A party of Gordon Rioters, on their way to cause havoc at Kenwood, were delayed by the landlord who kept them drinking until the soldiery arrived and disarmed them. The landlord was allowed to keep the rifles and they are on display in the saloon bar. Today the quarry tiles are vinyl and the furniture is brewer's quasi-rural, but late on a weekday lunchtime the low-ceilinged rooms are pleasantly quiet. The food bar operates until 15.00.

To the Vale of Health

Spaniards Road is noisy, I am afraid, but, with one further rural loop, we are on our way back to town. To the right on the Sandy Heath side the bank falls away dramatically into a gully steep enough for boys to fix a rope to a tree and swing out over the void with the abandon of chimpanzees. Keep on to the fork, where Heath House stands next to North End Way. Across the road, Jack Straw's Castle is a famous old coaching inn, named after one of the leaders of the Peasants' Revolt (1381) who hid in a building on the site until he was found, captured and executed. Unfortunately, the pub is closed during the afternoon.

Cross to Whitestone Pond, a broad shallow expanse where carters and coachmen watered their horses after the long climb up from London. From East Heath Road, turn suddenly down a winding country road to the Vale of Health, an extraordinary enclave of houses surrounded by the Heath. Once a marshy swamp, it was successfully drained and has been home to generations of fortunate families and a number of artists and writers. Leigh Hunt lived there, John Constable sketched and painted nearby, and D.H. Lawrence moved to No.5 Byron Villas in 1915.

Our walk is nearly done. Return by a grassy slope to East Heath Road and continue to Christ Church, then turn through Hampstead Square to Heath Street. The Tube station lies just down the hill. Stroll past the boutiques, art galleries, pubs, cafés, brasseries and restaurants – individual enterprises which give Hampstead a distinctive and stylish mark. I am entirely with the residents who rose up recently in eloquent wrath when it was proposed to install a McDonald's just down the road.

Walk 22

Highgate

Up on the heights of North London, enjoy the elegant houses and pretty Pond Square, and visit the fascinating Victorian wilderness of Highgate Cemetery.
Allow   4-5 hours.
Best times   Any day, but more tours of West Cemetery at weekends.

ROUTE

Begin at ⊖ Highgate. At exit to Archway Road, turn right and go up steps. Turn left and cross Archway Road and take next right up Jacksons Lane. At Southwood Lane, cross to Park Walk footpath and arrive in North Road beside The Wrestlers pub.

Turn left to end and cross to Highgate West Hill. At The Flask pub turn left along South Grove to Pond Square. Turn right down Swains Lane to **Highgate Cemetery** 👁; East section open November to March 10.00 to 16.00, April to October 10.00 to 17.00 (last tickets 15 minutes before closing). *Admission*. West section open for guided tours on the hour, November to March 12.00, 14.00, 15.00, April to October 12.00, 14.00, 16.00; on Saturday-Sunday every hour 11.00 to 15.00 November to March, 11.00 to 16.00 April to October. First Saturday in August and October, open for unaccompanied visits. *Admission*.

At exit, turn left and right into Waterlow Park. Bear left up a rise, cross bridge over lake and walk uphill to Lauderdale House. Turn right down Highgate Hill to **Whittington Stone** at foot, on pavement just before Whittington Stone pub.

Walk ends here. Nearest refreshments not recommended. Nearest ⊖ Archway.

The Wrestlers

On the edge of woodland, walk up a steep flight of steps from the Tube station. The hilliness of Highgate may come as a surprise. Few roads run on the flat for long, and many fall away at almost unnerving angles.

Turn up Jacksons Lane, initially a red-brick Victorian street of flats and houses, some with top-storey balconies on which it would be interesting to breakfast, weather permitting. After the modern blocks, squeeze into the bollarded single-lane bottleneck at the top of the road – an oddly rural way, as is the footpath on the far side of Southwood Lane. Emerge in North Road by The Wrestlers, today a fairly unremarkable pub but one which claims attention with an unflagging list of feats and features.

It dates back to 1547. It is the highest pub in London. Dick Turpin the highwayman not only used it, he had his own tunnel which ran from the cellar to a place unknown, said to be Jack Straw's Castle on the far side of Hampstead Heath. It also guards the tradition of the Highgate Oath, a quaint custom going back to 1623 which requires strangers or

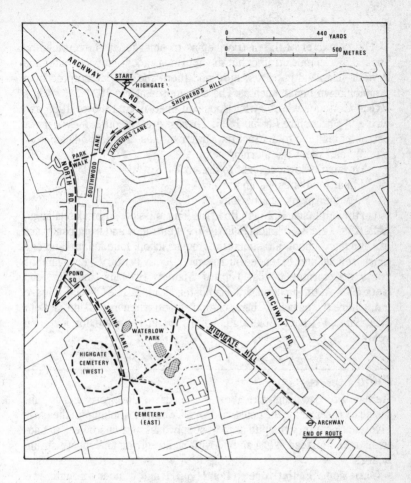

volunteers to 'Swear on the Horns'. The ceremony is practised twice yearly in March and August. In the bar is a script of the proceedings which apparently involve much saluting of maids or kissing of the horns. More amusing, no doubt, when you've had one or two.

Across the road are the elegant and still impressive High Point apartments, designed in 1938 by Lubetkin and Tecton. Turn left and at No.92 find a plaque to Charles Dickens who stayed there in 1832. Dickens has an unusual posthumous connection with Highgate, as we shall see later.

The character of the district begins to emerge. It is overbuilt and spoiled by too much traffic, but the housing is good – rows of older and newish villas and cottages, here and there the line interrupted by a grander town house such as The Sycamores at No.19. Next door is Byron Cottage, where A.E. Housman lived from 1886 to 1905 and wrote 'A Shropshire Lad' in 1896. There were, of course, few cars or petrol fumes then to distract the author of these reflective lines:

When I meet the morning beam,
Or lay me down at night to dream,
I hear my bones within me say,
'Another night, another day'.

On the other side of North Road the long mass of red-brick buildings, hitherto doorless, culminates in the main entrance and front courtyard of Highgate School, a distinguished boys' school founded in 1565 and much rebuilt and extended in the nineteenth century. Two famous poets are former pupils, Gerard Manley Hopkins and Sir John Betjeman. At the junction with Hampstead Lane is The Old Gate House inn, where the essayist Charles Lamb stayed when in 1831 he came to visit Samuel Taylor Coleridge, who lived in Highgate for nineteen years.

Pond Square

Across the road, Highgate West Hill leads to the pretty Flask pub, which has braziers in the courtyard for all-weather drinking. In the early eighteenth century the pub used to supply flasks for customers to take over to Hampstead Wells and fill with health-giving chalybeate spring water.

Turn along South Grove to Pond Square and wander through. The ponds at the centre of this picturesque triangle were filled in back in 1864. The present mixture of buildings is varied and full of interest: pretty cottages and town houses, the Pond Square Chapel (Highgate United Reformed Church) and, next to each other, the Highgate Literary & Scientific Institution and The Highgate Society. The former has a library and reading room and runs day and evening classes. Look in at the timber-roofed hall, frozen in some distant age: a small stage at one end, dusty busts on the wall and a ragged frieze of framed prints and paintings. Also the stern injunction: 'CHILDREN MUST BE UNDER

STRICT SUPERVISION OF THE ADULT RESPONSIBLE'. Clearly, a house of self-improvement, and it's meant to be painful!

Highgate exudes a small-town worthiness which may in part stem from its nonconformist institutions. Long ago the City of London banned the opening of non-Anglican chapels within a five-mile radius of the City. Highgate then found particular favour with Dissenters looking for somewhere respectable to settle.

Perhaps sit on the terrace of Groves Café on the corner and watch the world come and go, tracking past the shops in the sloping High Street.

Highgate Cemetery

Swain's Lane drops deep into a Victorian netherworld furnished with shrouded urns and angels, broken columns and obelisks of marble. Through a padlocked gate an early vista unfolds of overgrown footpaths and silent tombs climbed over by ivy and fern and shaded by rampant trees. Follow the high wall down to the latticed yellow chimneypots of the lodge to Waterlow Park. Just beyond are the entrances to the East and West Cemeteries.

On the left, the East Cemetery is open and may be wandered at random. This is the later part, opened in 1857. Buy a plan at the gate from one of the Friends of Highgate Cemetery who now tend its acres. Point 39 is the most popular destination with visitors: the fierce bust atop the tomb of Karl Marx (1818-83), inscribed:

WORKERS OF THE WORLD UNITE

and

THE PHILOSOPHERS HAVE ONLY INTERPRETED THE WORLD IN VARIOUS WAYS · THE POINT HOWEVER IS TO CHANGE IT

Turn back a few metres and go up a footpath on the right to find the simple granite obelisk to the novelist George Eliot (1819-80). To return to the entrance, keep on up the path and turn left by the perimeter along a track past ivy-covered tombs and thick bushes. Having twenty minutes to spare before the next guided tour of West Cemetery, I spent most of that time tugging at undergrowth and ivy in search of No.55, the tomb of Sir Leslie Stephen, Bloomsbury man and father of Virginia Woolf, but got nowhere.

West Cemetery is wholly fascinating, the Victorian burial ground *par excellence*, now overlaid with a Romantic tangle of bounteous Nature. The Cemetery opened in 1839, one of seven commercial ventures started around the outskirts of London – West Norwood, Nunhead and Kensal Green are others – because inner-city churchyards were overfilled and unhealthy, the constant prey of graverobbers. Highgate was run by the London Cemetery Company and until the 1950s was landscaped and kept in good shape by a team of up to twenty-eight gardeners. Then profitability ceased and decline set in, and the cemetery was rescued in 1975 by the Friends of Highgate Cemetery who took over both plots and maintain them as best they can.

The tour begins from the Anglican chapel – the neighbouring one is for Dissenters, which here applies to all non-Anglicans – and follows one of various loops which the guide selects in advance. The guide explains the history of the place, and alerts visitors to some of the symbolism applied to the tombs: a broken column – a life snapped off; inverted torches – a life extinguished; the memorial on a plinth of three steps – representing Faith, Hope and Charity; clasped hands – a meeting in the hereafter; a shrouded urn – a body covered over.

Surprisingly perhaps, for a place so large, the cemetery contains fairly few very famous people. Most of those are either in Westminster Abbey or the crypt of St Paul's Cathedral. This the Dickens family found out the hard way when they tried to carry out the novelist's wish to be buried quietly at Highgate. 'No,' said Queen Victoria, who wanted him in Westminster Abbey.

The layout is one of winding paths and other tricks of perspective to increase the sense of grandeur. Follow through to an arch flanked by stout Egyptian columns and enter the Egyptian Avenue lined with above-ground burial chambers, and continue through the Circle of Lebanon where the novelist Radclyffe Hall is buried (1886-1943). From the top of the steps at the far side, look back across the circle to the huge Cedar of Lebanon which crowns the design.

The largest monument in the cemetery is nearby, that of Julius Beer (1836-80) who in 1870 bought the *Observer* newspaper (his wife Rachel owned *The Sunday Times*). Thought *nouveau riche* in his lifetime, and being Jewish besides, Beer failed to make his desired mark on sniffy high society. In death, though, he was determined to outdo them all. John Oldrid Scott was commissioned and he designed a huge tomb modelled on that of King Mausolus at Halicarnassus, which was one of the Seven Wonders of the ancient world. Peer upwards through the grille to see the domed mosaic ceiling.

Among the other tombs are the large sleeping lion atop George Wombwell (1777-1850) who ran a travelling menagerie; the Rossetti family tomb, from which Dante Gabriel retrieved a sheaf of poems from beside the head of Elizabeth Siddall, seven years after her death; the Maple family, of the Tottenham Court Road furniture firm; Charles Cruft, the dog-biscuit magnate and founder of the famous pedigree dog shows; and F.W. 'William' Lillywhite (1792-1854), the cricketer. Close to the entrance are some moderns: Philip Harben, the first television chef; Patrick Wymark the actor; and Professor Jacob Bronowski, a great populariser of science on television and author of *The Ascent of Man*.

Waterlow Park

Turn through Waterlow Park and bear left up a rise, aiming for the cream-coloured mansion on top of the hill on the far side of the lake. Cross the bridge and eventually go up steps between two beheaded stone eagles. The entrance to Lauderdale House is at the front, set back a little from Highgate High Street.

This is one of several mansions built in Highgate in the sixteenth century by wealthy men who sought somewhere healthier to live than the cramped medieval streets of the City. Another, Cromwell House, stands across the road at No.104, and was built a little later, in about 1638. Lauderdale House is now a centre for local arts and crafts exhibitions. Sir Sidney Waterlow presented it to London County Council in 1889, together with the park named after him.

Whittington Stone

Turn down Highgate Hill towards Archway. At Dartmouth Park Hill are the towering green domes of St Joseph's, Church of the Passionist Fathers, its great rose window thickly spoked like a tractor wheel.

The Whittington Hospital and the Whittington & Cat pub give early warning that we are approaching the stone erected here in 1821 to honour London's most famous Lord Mayor, whose life is still celebrated annually in the pantomime season. Just before another pub bearing his name, the Whittington Stone, it stands on the pavement in an oval railed enclosure – a simple stone with the Mayor's large cat on top, an addition of 1954. The inscription reads:

> SIR
> RICHARD WHITTINGTON
> THRICE LORD MAYOR
> OF LONDON
> 1397 – RICHARD II
> 1405 – HENRY IV
> 1420 – HENRY V
> SHERIFF – IN 1393

Tradition has it that young Dick Whittington was resting at this spot, having decided to run away from town, when he heard Bow Bells call to him: 'Turn again, Whittington, Lord Mayor of Great London.' He did, and the British acting profession is profoundly grateful to him.

Walk 23 ⤤

Docklands and Greenwich

A scenic ride above the quays of East London's newly converted Docklands, a walk beneath the Thames and a tour of Greenwich and its outstanding attractions: the *Cutty Sark*, National Maritime Museum, Queen's House, the pretty park and the Old Royal Observatory.

Allow   All day.

Best times   Docklands Light Railway may be closed some weekends. A bus service operates along the route at those times, but the views are less good. To check, telephone 071-222 1234.

ROUTE

Begin at ⊖ Tower Hill. At exit turn left for Tower Gateway Station on the Docklands Light Railway. Special ticket needed (Travelcards and other passes may be valid if they cover the right zones; check at Information Office). Book to Island Gardens; the journey may involve changing trains at Crossharbour.

At Island Gardens walk through to river wall and look across to best view of Wren's **Royal Naval Hospital** (now the Royal Naval College). At glass-domed rotunda take lift down to **Greenwich Foot Tunnel** and walk across to far bank.

Emerge from second lift by **Cutty Sark**, world's last surviving tea clipper ☜; open 10.00 to 17.00, closes 18.00 in summer, Sunday and Good Friday opens 12.00, closed 24-26 December. *Admission*. Good idea to buy Day Passport here to all main Greenwich attractions.

Gipsy Moth IV, Sir Francis Chichester's round-the-world sailing ketch, is in its own dry dock on far side of Foot Tunnel entrance; open April to September 10.00 to 18.00, October 10.00 to 17.00, Sunday opens 12.00. *Admission*.

Walk up past Gipsy Moth pub to Greenwich Church Street and turn left along Nelson Road and Romney Road to **National Maritime Museum** ☜; open 10.00 to 18.00, Sunday 12.00 to 18.00, closed 1 January, Good Friday, May Day bank holiday, 24-26 December. *Admission*.

Exit on side facing park. Lunch available nearby at The Bosun's Whistle cafeteria or The Gloucester pub near park gates in King William Walk. Continue across park and uphill to **Old Royal Observatory** ☜; open as for National Maritime Museum. *Admission*. Visit Flamsteed House and Meridian Building.

Return down grassy slope to **Queen's House** at centre of colonnades ☜; open as for National Maritime Museum. *Admission*.

Continue to **Exhibition Building** in east wing ☜; open as for National Maritime Museum. *Admission*.

Return along Romney Road and right down King William Walk to Greenwich Pier. Walk ends here. Nearest refreshments all around. To return to central London, either cross river again to Docklands Light Railway or take boat to Charing Cross or Westminster.

Another option is to take a one-hour cruise downstream to Thames Barrier; open 10.30 to 17.00, Saturday-Sunday 10.30 to 17.30. *Admission*. Boats from Greenwich Pier every 1¼ hours; last boat 16.15.

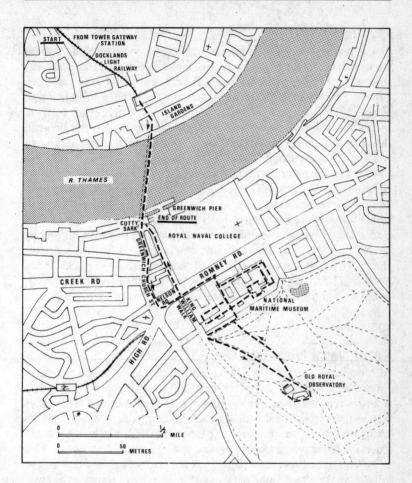

Docklands Light Railway

This intriguing little railway is expanding fast to meet the big demand anticipated for public-transport links as the riverside and docks of East London are rejuvenated. While this is going on, there will be some disruption to weekend services. Travellers can check in advance by telephoning 071-222-1234.

The driverless two- or four-car trains have panoramic windows at front and rear, and nip at a lively pace along an elevated track towards the great pointed cap which surmounts Britain's tallest building, Canary Tower (244m/800ft). Broad views over the docks begin at Limehouse Basin. After Westferry the train swings through a right-angle to West India Quay and Canary Wharf, where the station lies directly beneath the great fifty-storey hulk of the Tower. Oddly, from a distance the size of it is not overwhelming. The old docks on the Isle of Dogs cover such a vast area, architectural writers may end not by criticising the monotony or blandness of Canary Tower but by suggesting that it should have been made twice as tall.

The new Post-Modernist blocks around Canary Wharf I find astonishingly feeble. Where a city like Dallas makes its impact by pitching its glass towers close and stacking them high in a dense, shadowed forest of green and blue and baby pink, those of Dockland are too low and dispersed, too tentative to start a drama. Quite fun, though, to see in their mirror-glass walls the reflection of your train as it ripples through.

Royal Naval Hospital

At Mudchute comes a vision of the past – the solemn domes of Wren's Royal Naval Hospital, best seen from the riverside gardens after the train has reached its terminus. This was the view of it that Wren most admired, a symmetrical and audacious pattern which depends for its completeness on the illusory properties of a fifth block, the distant Queen's House which fills the central space.

This majestic Classical scheme took the place of a manor house built in 1427 by Humfrey, Duke of Gloucester, brother of Henry V. He was the great book collector whose library went from here on his death to form the founding collection of the university library at Oxford, which later became the Bodleian Library (see *Walk 29: Oxford 'B'*).

The manor house at Greenwich grew into a palace and three Tudor monarchs were born there: Henry VIII, Mary I and Elizabeth I. The distant house in the middle is the key to the whole plan now on view. Queen's House, designed by Inigo Jones, was begun in 1616 for Anne of Denmark, wife of James I, and finished in 1640 for Henrietta Maria, wife of Charles I. By the Restoration the waterside palace had begun to crumble, and King Charles II commissioned Inigo Jones's pupil, John Webb, to design the King's House as an extension to the old palace. King Charles's Block, on the right at the waterfront, arose between 1663 and 1667. Little then happened until Queen Mary, in 1692, ordered the planning of a naval hospital on the site, an equivalent to the old soldiers' hospital in Chelsea (see *Walk 16*) which had been founded ten years earlier by Charles II. Queen Mary further directed that the new blocks should not prevent Queen's House from remaining visible from the river, hence Wren's split plan inserting a colonnaded avenue between the two rear blocks. Most of the old palace was then demolished. Vanbrugh succeeded Wren as architect and the final building was completed in 1742. Although impractically grand for a hospital, it survived as such until 1869 and in 1873 became the Royal Naval College, the name by which it is known today.

Greenwich Foot Tunnel

This immensely useful piece of Edwardian engineering opened in 1902. Two lift shafts, housed at ground level in brick rotundas with glass domes, are sunk about 18m (60ft) down and joined by an immense tube consisting of a flagged pavement and curved tunnel walls glazed with 200,000 tiles in best lavatorial white. The 'bog' impression is fortified by an odour of disinfectant which seems to wax strongest around the lifts but never entirely fades.

The usefulness of the Foot Tunnel, originally created for dockworkers living south of the river, is greater than ever, since it now links the Tube-starved inhabitants of Greenwich with the Docklands Light Railway and gives them faster access to workplaces in the City and East London, as well as the new offices opening in Docklands.

Cutty Sark

She was built in 1869 and is the world's last surviving tea clipper. She worked the tea trade from China until 1877 and then, after the opening of the Suez Canal made steam-powered vessels more effective on the China run, was switched to the wool trade from Australia. In the 1880s she made several notably fast passages, including one in 1887-8 of sixty-nine days from Newcastle, New South Wales to the Lizard. A chart near the entrance to the ship museum shows her progress on a voyage in 1885: London to Sydney, 1 April to 20 June.

Clippers, so-called because they 'clipped' the wind, were much admired for their lean lines – the sharp rake of the stem and the overhanging counter stern shaving the area of hull in contact with the water and increasing the vessels' speed through it. The *Cutty Sark* served in the wool trade until 1895, was sold to Portuguese owners and eventually was acquired and brought to her specially constructed dock at Greenwich in 1954.

Walk through the history exhibition in the upper cargo hold and go down to see the figureheads. These wonderfully painted ladies of the sea project their comforting bosoms inward along both sides of the lower hold. There are male figureheads too, though sailors tended to favour females, believing that a carved woman with naked breasts could calm a storm at sea. All are watched over through a well by Nannie, the *Cutty Sark*'s original figurehead. The ship's name means 'short chemise', and comes from a poem by Robert Burns. Nannie was a witch and chased a Scottish farmer on his grey mare. The farmer escaped but Nannie snatched at the horse's tail and pulled it off, and is portrayed grasping it in her left hand.

Then climb the companionway and walk the deck planks plugged with ribs of tar to make them waterproof. Look in at the deckhouses to see a wax cook peeling potatoes and the ship's carpenter in his workshop, and the cramped box in which twelve seamen slept in bunks and took their meals.

Into Town

On the far side of the Foot Tunnel entrance is *Gipsy Moth IV*, the trim 16m (54ft) ketch in which Sir Francis Chichester in 1966-7 made the first solo voyage around the world by an Englishman. His plan was to beat the sailing times of the old clippers. He sailed non-stop from Plymouth to Sydney in 107 days. On his successful return to the Thames he was knighted at Greenwich by the Queen, who dubbed him with the same sword that Elizabeth I had used in 1581 to knight Sir Francis Drake aboard his ship the *Golden Hind*, just a short way up-river at Deptford.

At the other Gipsy Moth, the pub on the dock, they serve filter coffee as well as the usual drinks. Continue towards the spire of St Alfege's Church, rebuilt by Hawksmoor in 1712-18. Greenwich Church Street is crowded with restaurants and antique shops, and an alley on the left leads through to the Arts and Crafts Market. Turn along Nelson Road, named after the Admiral who in 1805 lay in state in the Hall of the then Royal Naval Hospital. Continue past the Dreadnought Seamen's Hospital and the naval cemetery where some 20,000 former inmates of the Royal Naval Hospital were buried between 1749 and 1869.

National Maritime Museum

The main collections of this fine museum, which opened in 1937, are housed in the west wing, completed in 1809 and joined to the Queen's House by an elegant colonnade. Exhibitions are changed periodically. The Upper Level currently shows Discovery and Sea Power 1450-1700 and Ships of War 1650-1815. Spacious and well arranged, the galleries display ship models, globes, sea charts, uniforms, portraits and marine paintings. Among the many famous canvases are John Bettes the Younger's portrait of *Elizabeth I*; the South German School *Battle of Lepanto, 1571*; the marvellous heraldic English School *Spanish Armada, 1588: An Engagement between the English and Spanish Fleets*; the Netherlandish picture of the same battle showing the *Launch of the English Fire Ships off Calais, 28 July*; and Sir Peter Lely's *Peter Pett and the Sovereign of the Seas*.

On Middle Level see the Age of Nelson and Napoleon, with J.M.W. Turner's patchily brilliant *Battle of Trafalgar* (mysteriously, he has painted the principal ship in profile, and worked in a view of its stern as well, defying the laws of perspective), and de Loutherbourg's *Battle of the First of June 1794*. At Lower Ground Level is the magnificent Neptune Room, dominated by the vast presence of the restored paddle tug *Reliant* (1907) which visitors can wander through and see the great pistons driving the portside wheel. Next to the tug's after section is the elegant Thames steam yacht *Donola* (1893), its cabin table set for a stylish tea party.

In the Barge House nearby are Queen Mary's open shallop (1689) and a ten-oared Admiralty barge of the eighteenth century used by Lords Commissioners of the Admiralty when visiting ships and dockyards on the river. At the far end of the room, and much more decorative, is Prince Frederick's State Barge (1732), designed by William Kent and decorated by James Richards, Grinling Gibbons's successor as Master Carver to the Crown. Sleek and golden it is, from the streamlined dolphin prow to the luxurious upholstered 'coach' or cabin at the stern.

The museum has a shop, a children's play area and limited facilities for the disabled. For lunch there is The Bosun's Whistle, the museum's own 'café-restaurant' in an adjoining block. In reality this is a slightly grim self-service cafeteria. A better choice may be The Gloucester pub, 100m away on the edge of the park at the top of King William Walk. It is no oil painting, but has a big room, a bar menu, and on some evenings live music and exotic dancers of either sex.

From hereabouts, strike inland and uphill through the leafy park. When the gradient gets steep, turn and draw sustenance from the riverscape. For centuries Greenwich and the neighbouring up-river borough of Deptford were at the centre of British naval affairs. Deptford was a thriving dockyard in the reign of Henry VII (1485-1509); in 1609 the English East India Company built its own dockyard there, and it was also the headquarters of the Victualling Board, responsible for supplying the Royal Navy with food, rum and clothing.

Old Royal Observatory

In Greenwich Park itself, connections with navigation and the sea were established in 1675 when Sir Christopher Wren designed the Royal Observatory at the top of the hill for John Flamsteed, the first Astronomer Royal.

On the wall by the gateway is a fascinating 24-hour galvanic metallic clock (1851), one of the earliest electrically driven public clocks, which shows Greenwich Mean Time throughout the year. Here too are the Ordnance Survey benchmarks of length, a series of bars with D-shaped endpieces which define standard Imperial measurements from 'one British yard' down to three inches.

Entrance to the Observatory is beside the statue of General James Wolfe, a gift of the Canadian people erected here in 1930. Wolfe, a resident of Greenwich, was brought back to the family house after his death at the Battle of the Plains of Abraham, Quebec (1759), and was buried in St Alfege's Church.

From the ticket desk, cross the courtyard where the Meridian line of Longitude 0° marks the division between the Eastern and Western Hemispheres. On the far side, stairs in Flamsteed House lead directly up to Wren's splendid Octagon Room, used for stellar observations between 1676 and 1820. The astronomers moved their telescopes from window to window and stood them out on the balconies. From here Flamsteed made the observations for his star catalogue, *Historia Coelestis Britannica* (1725).

Downstairs are exhibits on the measurement of time, including John Harrison's fascinating marine timekeepers which operate with vertical bar-balances connected by taut wire coils which swing hypnotically towards and away from each other. Down again to Precision Timekeeping, the room loud with the clank of ancient pendulums. Set your watch by the Radiocode clock and see a reproduction of Congreve's rolling-ball clock in which a brass ball zigzags through a track like a backgammon board and tips the balance each time it reaches an end.

The museum's prescribed tour leads next through the simply furnished apartments of the Astronomers Royal, and on via the garden to the Meridian Building, where Flamsteed worked in the Quadrant Room and the Sextant Room.

One final curiosity: on the roof of the Octagon Room a red ball is mounted on a mast. Installed in 1833 to alert shipping on the Thames, it was one of the world's first visual time signals. It still works. Shortly before 13.00 local time each day the ball is raised to the top of the mast and drops on the hour.

Queen's House

Take to the grassy slopes on the far side of the Wolfe statue and stroll down through the park. Arrive at the museum colonnade and go beneath the arch into the cobbled courtyard of Queen's House. When the house was built, it spanned the old carriageway between Deptford and Woolwich.

The recommended route on the museum plan suggests visitors cross the Great Hall to the ticket desk, where Acoustiguides are available, then return through the hall and take the elegant Tulip Staircase up to the first floor.

The Queen's House is newly restored and reopened in 1990. The designers have had a feast, leaving us much to think about. The wall hangings, fireplaces, furniture, light fittings and much else are new, designed by modern craftsmen to suggest the house as Henrietta Maria, widow of Charles I, might have known it when she lived there in 1662. The first impression is of a garish mistake – but then why not? When the furnishings were new, they must have shone with the bright golds, greens, blues and oranges that we see today. Joined with these, moreover, are many original elements which have survived and been cleaned and painted: doorways, beams, the wonderful ceiling of the Queen's Chamber and the marble floor of the Great Hall.

So, a brilliant merging of new and old? Not entirely. Several discordant elements stand out. The ceiling of the Queen's Chamber is one: so beautiful, and so real, it gleams with a patina of age that sets it at odds with the fake furnishings beneath. It is too good for them. I would also quibble about the fake marbling effects – ripples of grey paint on white surfaces – which are no better than tricksy restaurant décor. Worst of all, though, is the ceiling of the Great Hall. The original Gentileschi paintings of the *Arts and Sciences* (1636) were removed nearly three hundred years ago at the request of the Duchess of Marlborough and then installed on the ceiling of the saloon at her new London residence, Marlborough House, for which purpose they had to be cut down to fit the available space. Impossible, therefore, to reimport the originals. In their place now are a set of dreadfully crude laserscan reproductions which look like early colour xeroxes. Seen from close-up, as is unavoidable when you are standing on the gallery, the full import of the Duchess of Marlborough's cultural vandalism pings you straight in the eye.

For all those criticisms there is yet much to admire. The gracefulness and symmetry of the rooms, matching sets on either side of the house for the King's and the Queen's Presence Chamber, Anteroom, Privy Chamber, Chamber, Closet and Bedchamber. Go out to the magnificent Loggia, take a seat and maybe contemplate the view across the sloping park and up to Flamsteed House, the walkers and their dogs criss-crossing on a web of footpaths. A perfect place, much more satisfying than its downstairs equivalent, the Orangery, which is disappointingly short of orange trees. Also on the ground floor is the Maritime Museum's excellent collection of Netherlandish marine paintings of the sixteenth to eighteenth centuries. The two Willem van de Veldes, father and son, may even have had a studio in the Queen's House, after they left Amsterdam in 1672 and joined the service of Charles II who paid them an annual retainer to record sea-fights.

The museum's third block, the east wing, is due to become a Special Exhibition Centre, mounting a series of thematic shows drawn from the museum's impressively large store of collections.

Our walk is done. On the way back to Greenwich Pier, via King William Walk, take the alley by The Cricketers pub, Turnpin Lane, to find the Art and Craft Market, an open-sided market pavilion surrounded by shops selling textiles, crafts, furniture and needlework. The market in the central space operates on Saturday and Sunday.

Walk 24

Kew Gardens to Hammersmith

Visit the Royal Botanic Gardens at Kew, then stroll beside the Thames at Strand on the Green, see Lord Burlington's Chiswick House and the house where William Hogarth, master of the popular print, lived for 15 years. Rejoin the river along the beautiful walk from Chiswick Mall to Hammersmith.

Allow   6 hours/all day.

Best times   Not Tuesday, when Hogarth's House closed.

ROUTE

Begin at Kew Gardens Station (⊖ and ⇌). Cross footbridge to front of station and walk straight ahead past shops to Lichfield Road. At Kew Road, cross to Victoria Gate and enter **Kew Gardens** ✎ ; open 09.30 to 18.00, glasshouses close 16.30 Monday to Saturday, 17.30 Sunday and holidays, closed 1 January, 25 December. *Admission*.

Follow Route map to exit at Main Gate. Cross Kew Green and turn left over Kew Bridge. Just before end of bridge, turn right down steps to riverside road. Continue along Strand on the Green to City Barge (lunch?), then under railway bridge, and leave river at white house (Strand End), joining Grove Park Road. Take 2nd left into Grove Park Terrace, continue over level crossing and turn right into Fauconberg Road. Keep straight on to Staveley Road and on left turn into grounds of **Chiswick House** ✎ ; villa open Good Friday to 30 September 10.00 to 13.00, 14.00 to 18.00, 1 October to Maundy Thursday 10.00 to 13.00, 14.00 to 16.00, closed 24-25 December.

Follow Route map through gardens to villa. On leaving villa, walk straight ahead and just before gates turn left along The Avenue which curves into straight leafy walk ending at Great West Road. Turn right to **Hogarth's House** ✎ ; open 1 April to 30 September 11.00 to 18.00, Sunday 14.00 to 18.00, closed Tuesday; 1 October to 31 March 11.00 to 16.00, Sunday 14.00 to 16.00, closed Tuesday. Also closed first 2 weeks September, last 3 weeks December.

At exit, turn right to Hogarth roundabout and take underpass to far side, emerging next to George & Devonshire pub. Turn into pretty Church Street. At parish church, take Powell's Walk to the right and go round church to find railed enclosure of Hogarth monument. Leave churchyard down steps to road and walk past Public Drawdock to **Chiswick Mall**. Road to Hammersmith leaves river along Western Terrace and Montrose Villas, and rejoins it at Upper Mall.

Perhaps stop for early end-of-walk refreshment at The Dove, a famous riverside pub, and continue towards Hammersmith Bridge. Walk ends here. Nearest ⊖ Hammersmith (two separate stations, one on Hammersmith and City Line, one on District and Piccadilly Lines).

Leafy Kew

After Gunnersbury Station the Tube from Central London rattles over the iron bridge at Strand on the Green. The river passes in a blur

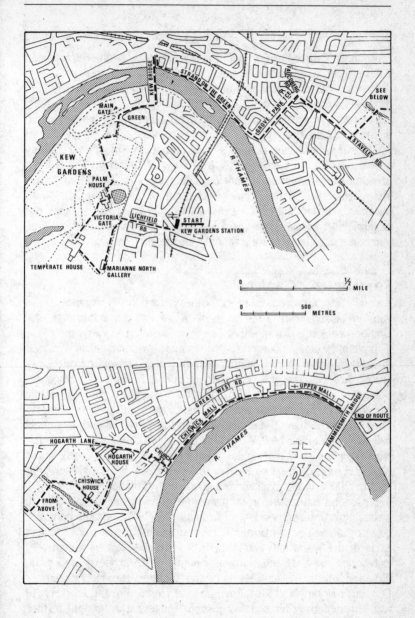

through the latticework of metal, and we dash on to the Surrey bank where decorous suburbia unravels tidy streets and gardens.

Near the station, Lichfield Road has a pleasant run of large villas, the pavements shaded by chestnut trees of notable girth. The only trouble is overhead, where once a minute the latest silver belly whines in on the flightpath to Heathrow.

Aircraft approaching London's chief airport have blighted a six-mile strip across the western suburbs, from Kew to Hounslow. The noise is dreadful. I still remember it from long ago, when I lived in St Margarets, just across the park. That unrelenting whine, deafening when overhead, an air raid of the senses which in a year must block out several hours of human conversation in each house beneath. Next time you boom in to land, spare a thought for the citizens below.

Royal Botanic Gardens

A new Visitor Centre is planned for the Victoria Gate entrance. If the gate is closed, turn right in Kew Road and enter through the Cumberland Gate. From either entrance, turn left towards the stone Temple of Bellona, a domed and pedimented garden building designed in 1760 by Sir William Chambers for Augusta, Dowager Princess of Wales. In spring the grassy bank to its front is brilliant with crocuses.

It was Princess Augusta who inspired the building of the first botanic garden on 3½ hectares (9 acres) of land to the south of the Orangery. She owned the Kew Estate and lived in the White House, a country palace since demolished. When she died in 1772, her son George III, who already owned the neighbouring Richmond Estate, took over at Kew and merged the two estates to form, more or less, the present area of the gardens, in all some 121 hectares (300 acres).

Sir Joseph Banks, the great plant collector who sailed with Captain Cook on his first round-the-world voyage (1768-71), became honorary director of the Botanic Gardens. He sent botanical collectors to many parts of the world and established the name of Kew as a centre of excellence. In 1841 the Gardens became State property under the direction of Sir William Hooker who founded the Department of Economic Botany and Museums, and the Herbarium and Library. He was succeeded by his son, Sir Joseph Hooker, who brought further eminence to the Gardens and founded the Jodrell Laboratory.

The Temple of Bellona is one of the many decorative or purposeful structures dotted through the Gardens. Next on our route is the Flagstaff, at 68.5m (225ft) the tallest in Britain. It weighs 15 tons and was made from the trunk of a single Douglas fir, felled at Copper Canyon, Vancouver Island when about 371 years old. In 1959 the trunk was presented to Kew by the Government of British Columbia, lugged here by road and ship and hauled into position by a detachment of Royal Engineers. It is the third of Kew's great flagstaffs, continuing a tradition which began in 1861.

One of the marvels of these Gardens is the Marianne North Gallery. On its walls, frame against frame, hang 832 paintings of plants, insects and exotic views made by Miss North, who with her paintbox travelled the world between 1871 and 1875, visiting the United States, Canada, Jamaica, Brazil, Japan, Singapore, Indonesia, India, Australia and New Zealand. She presented the paintings to Kew and a gallery to house them, designed by James Ferguson, and herself decorated the doorways with yet more flowers. The gallery opened in 1882.

The paintings radiate an ardent Victorian's enthusiasm for her subject: a little amateurish, boldly coloured and keenly detailed. The viewing eye pops delightedly along the parade: here the Sri Lankan red cotton tree, *Bombax malabaricum*, and a pair of common paradise flycatchers; there a pot of Californian wildflowers; and there, climbing plants from Chile with butterflies. A glowing, hypnotic spectacle.

From the gallery, step across the grass beneath the grey-green fingers of the maples towards the Temperate House. On the left, a vista runs through to the octagonal, 10-storeyed Pagoda, designed by Sir William Chambers in 1761-2. For safety reasons this popular landmark, 49.7m (163ft) high, is not open to the public.

The Temperate House, designed by Decimus Burton, was once the world's largest greenhouse. It consists of a central block with two flanking octagons (1860-62) and two wings (1896-9); it measures 182m (597ft) wide overall and 19.1m (63ft) high in the centre of the main block. It was extensively restored in 1977-80.

The plants kept here are tender woody species, arranged geographically. In the main block are collections from the Old and New Worlds. The outstanding member is the Chilean Wine or Honey Palm, now at 17.7m (58ft) thought to be the world's tallest glasshouse plant. It was raised at Kew in 1846 from seed collected in Chile. Its smooth grey tubular trunk, the texture of a surgical stocking, slants upward to a crown of foliage almost pressing on the apex of the roof.

On leaving, turn left past the north wing and keep straight ahead to the yellow stone Temple of King William (1837). Designed by Sir Jeffry Wyatville, its main decorative feature is a series of iron plaques dedicated to British Army campaigns fought between 1760 and 1815.

Note to the Keepers of the Gardens. You clearly label lots of flowering plants and shrubs. I should also like to know, please, what the trees are called.

Approach Burton's amazing, curved Palm House through the formal Rose Garden. From the central west door, three vistas designed by William Nesfield stretch away to the Pagoda, on the left, ahead along the Lake to the river, and on the right to a large cedar near a place called Beech Clump.

The Palm House, designed in 1845-7 by Decimus Burton and the iron-founder Richard Turner, had reached a sorry state of disrepair by the 1950s. It was patched up but in 1984 had to be closed again for fundamental restoration. Its reopening in 1990 was a great botanical event. Under the new planting plan, there are more deep beds to encourage lush growth, the plants have been regrouped geographically and now live in a single, humid, tropical climate. To see a panorama of this warm, wet forest of foliage, climb one of the spiral staircases to the gallery which tours the building.

Beneath the glazed arcs of the roof, all is damp and fruitful. Blobs of water stand on the spreading fat leaves of the Canary banana, joined by big yellow bell flowers which have plopped off the neighbouring *Allamanda cathartica* and stuck there. A ribbed arm of Lady's Finger sticks out, terminating in a dark, plum-coloured, singularly vicious-looking flower, like a venom-bloated tulip. The names of plants, their rounded shapes and heavy textures combine to suggest hot, lazy fecundity: paw-paws and pink, satin-petalled hibiscus, giant drooping furry fingers, round leaves of sea grape, fronds of coconut and Christmas palm, more hibiscus and the pustular red blooms of *Costus woodsonii*.

Return to underheated England at the main entrance. Facing the parterres and The Pond go left past the Queen's Beasts, in all a row of ten rearing animals, replicas of those which stood outside Westminster Abbey at the time of the Coronation in 1953. Lion, unicorn, griffin, bull, falcon . . . they symbolise various strands of the Queen's ancestry. At the Falcon of the Plantagenets, bear left for a tour of the small but enticing Waterlily House. Our main direction is right to the circular bed with the urn, then left towards the Main Gate (signposted).

This is the Broad Walk, leading to the Orangery past, on the right, Japanese cherries and weeping beech, and Crab Mound on the left. The Orangery (1761) is another creation of Sir William Chambers and has served variously in its original purpose, as a glasshouse, a wood museum, and now as home of the Kew Shop and Orangery Tea Room. From here, bear left across the grass to the Main Gate.

Walk straight ahead past Kew Green towards the river bridge. On the left are the Herbarium and a row of pretty town houses of early Victorian vintage. Pubs too, but I walk on; refreshment is more refreshing beside the river.

Strand on the Green

Cross Kew Bridge towards the unlovely blockhouses of Brentford, rearing upwards and also cramming the horizontal plane to the left, quite out of keeping with the houseboats which loll beneath them at their moorings on the nearby island, Brentford Ait. (The Thames on the upstream side of London has many islands, aits or eyots – the word comes from the Old English for 'islet'.)

Fortunately, we are not going to Brentford. Our concern is with the infinitely prettier reach to the right of the bridge. The riverside walk at Strand on the Green has few rivals in London, save, perhaps, for the Malls we come to later in this walk.

After the warehouse blocks of Pier House (1914), bear right to the footpath which follows the river. The houses beside this old towpath are beautiful, and the view towards the railway bridge has a breadth and brilliance of light unusual in London. I like it best along here when the tide is low and a fat strip of virgin mud unfolds in gentle greenish rills, setting the stranded boats at cockeyed angles.

The houses and cottages, balconied and bay-fronted, are strung with climbing plants and protected by raised steps to keep out floodwaters which regularly rise over the embankment – a reminder that the Thames is still tidal here, and for several miles upstream as far as Teddington Lock. Best known of these waterside residences is Zoffany

House (No.65), where the German-born painter Johann Zoffany lived from 1790 until his death in 1810. Others to note are Compass House and the neck-gabled Dutch House.

The City Barge, just this side of the railway bridge, is a famous tavern dating from 1484. Here may be a good place to stop for lunch. In summer the riverside walk is jammed with jolly drinkers who come out from the city and in from the suburbs. The pub takes its name from the Lord Mayor of London's state barge which had its winter moorings opposite the inn, next to Oliver's Island. For three years it was my local, and very pleasant it was to sit in the window of the upstairs New Bar and watch the light fade at evening.

Through the bridge is the Bull's Head, a rival place. I remember a good night, long ago, when the comedian Tommy Cooper, who lived nearby, was trying to drive golf balls across the river (for charity, I should add), and the sound of each unsuccessful 'splosh' coming back through the dark, tickled him to new heights of lunacy.

Keep on past the almshouses, founded in 1724 'for y use of Poor of Chiswick·for Ever'. At the white house, Strand End, turn inland through the quiet streets of Grove Park, crossing the railway tracks of the Barnes Loop and turning into Staveley Road.

Chiswick House

The gardens of Lord Burlington's Classical mansion (1727-9) are a delightful mixture of wilderness and precisely laid-out paths with architectural terminations. There is something for everyone, from admirers of sphinxes and obelisks to the afternoon man out galloping his Irish setter through the woodland paths. From the entrance, keep straight on past the tree-lined cricket ground to the steep upcurve of Classic Bridge. Cross the canal or river and turn right up the path which leads to the Amphitheatre. This was laid out as the Orange Tree Garden and first painted as such c. 1728 by Pieter Andreas Rysbrack. In his painting, orange trees stand close together in tubs arranged in three concentric rings on the steps of the grass amphitheatre. At the centre is the Obelisk Pond, and on the southern bank rise the white circular body and rectangular portico of the Ionic Temple. In today's version the scene is more rustic, there are fewer tubs and the surreal stillness of Rysbrack's picture is only hinted at.

Walk on to the base of the *patte d'oie* (goose's foot), where in the original version three straight avenues lined by tall hedges radiated away to terminate in distant buildings. Nearby, from a semi-circular point known as the *exedra*, a broad gravelled path leads to the house, flanked by great urns and a pair of non-matching sphinxes.

Chiswick House was designed by the Third Earl of Burlington, whose family had owned the land since 1682. When completed in 1729, it stood next to an older Jacobean house and was then joined to it by a gallery called the Link Building. After Lord Burlington died, in 1753, the old house was pulled down and in 1788 wings were added to the new house, designed by John White. Nearly two hundred years later, after a long period of neglect, Lord Burlington's innovative work as a Classical architect became fashionable again, and in 1956 the wings were demolished and the present building painstakingly restored.

Essentially simple, of two storeys on a square plan with a shallow-domed octagon at the centre, the house has a portico of columns copied from an ancient Roman temple, that of Castor and Pollux in Naples. This was known to Lord Burlington through illustrations by the Italian architect, Andrea Palladio. The idea for the internal octagon comes from a building designed by Palladio, the Villa Almerico (or Rotonda) at Vicenza. Other important contributions to both house and gardens were made by William Kent who, as Horace Walpole noted, was usually 'not only consulted for furniture, as frames of pictures, glasses, tables and chairs, etc., but for plate, for a barge, for a cradle'.

The chief mystery of the house is what it was *for*. It was too small for a lord to live in, and although it had a wine cellar there was no kitchen, and the 'Eating Room' was in the old house. It seems most likely that Lord Burlington built it primarily for aesthetic reasons, to re-create the forms and atmosphere of an ancient Greek house. Having done so, he was happy to use it as a delightful place for receiving guests, and for reading and contemplation. More everyday tasks he performed next-door.

The house is now managed by English Heritage, who provide visitors with a step-by-step sound guide. I have reservations about these earphone-cassette player combos at the best of times, not least because they impose a pace and scope which may not at all fit with the plans of individual visitors. Here at Chiswick they really over-egg the mixture. Near the entrance, in particular, the newly plugged-in have to jerk about all over the place like hyperactive robots: listen to this, look at that – two steps to the left – turn right – go back to where you were – press button to restart commentary . . . and on and on until, I suppose, you spin off the edge and end up in the garden, or drop to the floor from culture fatigue.

Suspecting there was a better way to enjoy the splendours of the interior, I shut the thing off and began a blessedly peaceful tour of the downstairs rooms, grouped around the Lower Tribune or hall at the base of the octagon. Then upstairs to the Tribunal or saloon at the centre of the principal floor, its domed ceiling decorated with a quite extraordinary series of plaster coffers. Turn through the three-room Gallery on the north side – at once cool in its structures and delicate openings, and warm with extravagant gilding and plasterwork – and tour the lavish Velvet Rooms – Red, Blue and Green. The wonderful painted ceilings celebrate the arts and architecture – allegories presiding over the exquisite paintings and sculptures of the owner. The Blue Velvet Room, though small, was perhaps the focal point of this curiously unfunctional house – the exclusive cabinet where Lord Burlington showed his collections of architectural drawings and Dutch landscapes to other deserving connoisseurs.

In Transit

There now follows a quite nasty piece of culture shock, for which our present century is entirely to blame. To the east of the house, follow the curving Avenue, laid out by the enterprising Sixth Duke who also built an ambitious conservatory in the 1820s and founded a menagerie with pheasants and an elephant, adding a giraffe, emus, elks and other exotics. Then the Avenue straightens out . . . and channels us to our doom. By the lodge we are flung, as though from an ejector seat, slap into the metallic bedlam of the Great West Road.

In the 1750s, William Hogarth made a drawing of this view, or one very similar, from an upstairs window in his house which lies just down the road. Called *Mr Ranby's House*, the picture shows a cornfield stretching away to a distant wall, beyond which are two houses and a line of trees, sublimely remote, as though in the middle of nowhere.

Hogarth's House

The home of the great caricaturist is, traffic noise aside, pleasantly calm – a simple, almost dour museum arranged in the rooms where Hogarth lived intermittently with his family from 1749 until his death in 1764.

The house, the artist's 'little country box by the Thames', served mainly as a summer residence to which Hogarth could escape from the business cares of Leicester Fields (now Leicester Square) where he ran his printing press and kept a town house. After falling into disrepair it was restored, refurnished and opened to the public in 1902. It suffered bad damage from bombs in 1940, was again restored and re-opened in 1951; it is now in the care of the London Borough of Hounslow (which also owns the grounds of Chiswick House).

Hogarth, the son of a schoolmaster who worked his way up from apprentice engraver to become a master of popular satirical and moral prints, saw himself as a natural enemy of the upper-class connoisseurship practised by his neighbour Lord Burlington and the other aesthetic authorities of his day. In *The Man of Taste*, on view here, he took a direct swipe at the Third Earl and his collaborator, William Kent.

The collection at Hogarth House covers the walls on both floors. It vividly demonstrates the artist's strengths and weaknesses – his cutting eye for corruption, pretence and excess, also the careless draughtsmanship that often let him down when he ventured beyond his prints into portraiture and history painting. All the most famous series and scenes are here to enjoy: *The Harlot's Progress*; *Marriage à la Mode*; *Gin Lane*; *Credulity, Superstition and Fanaticism*; *The Rake's Progress* – peopled by stupendous grotesques from every compartment of life in eighteenth-century England.

Church Street

Again brave the thunder of the cars and trucks and walk towards the Hogarth roundabout. Everything seems to be called Hogarth around here, and the artist would surely have had something to say about the garish blue-green horror that is the Hogarth Business Park – renaming it 'Hell's Computer Factory' would be a step in the right direction. Go down through the grim but necessary pedestrian underpass and skirt the brewery to Church Street, where a serried frontage of attractive town houses and cottages runs down to the parish church and the river. This was the core of the old fishing hamlet of Chiswick, grouped about the Church of St Nicolas.

In the quiet churchyard a squirrel bounces among the chest tombs and grave slabs close to the Hogarth monument. The pedestal stands behind a railed enclosure, surmounted by an urn and carved with a mask, palette, brushes and book. The inscription, by David Garrick, states:

> If *Genius* fire thee Reader stay
> If *Nature* touch thee drop a Tear
> If neither move thee turn away
> For HOGARTH'S honoured dust lies here.

Chiswick Mall to Hammersmith

Go down steps from the churchyard to the river road, passing the Public Drawdock where boats are pulled up from the water. In 1866 the shipbuilding firm of Thorneycroft had its beginnings near here, at Church Wharf. Along Chiswick Mall are many elegant town houses of much earlier date, with fine riverside gardens across the road. Bedford House was rebuilt *c.*1750 by Edward Russell, son of the Fourth Earl of Bedford. Walpole House has associations with the Walpole family.

Walk on past the tufty, stone-banked slab of Chiswick Eyot. Each stretch of riverside has its own character. The mansions of the Mall give way to the charming modest houses of Western Terrace and Montrose Villas. The porticoed row on the river flank is called Hammersmith Terrace. Blue plaques commemorate several artistic inhabitants of times past, but not yet A.P. Herbert, the 'poet of the river', who died in 1971. (To qualify for a blue plaque, a person must have been dead for twenty years – so A.P.H. is now due his.)

At Upper Mall we rejoin the river. In the distance is an early view of Sir Joseph Bazalgette's Hammersmith Bridge. Two rowing eights pull upstream on a leisurely training run, along the course where, each spring, the University crews of Oxford and Cambridge will sweat and tear limbs from their sockets in search of victory's prize.

Through a modern arch stands Linden House, since 1963 the headquarters of the London Corinthian Sailing Club, founded in 1894 to encourage the 'building and racing of Sailing Boats'. A sight of the Old Ship Inn reminds me of Sunday morning walks with my father which began in West Kensington and invariably terminated outside a pub on this part of the river. Did I really stand here with my glass of ginger beer while he tackled something stronger inside? Probably, but I don't firmly recall this spot.

At the end of Upper Mall West, where the path veers inland, is Kelmscott House, now the home of the William Morris Society. In 1878 Morris rented the house, then known as The Retreat, and renamed it after his Oxfordshire house, Kelmscott Manor. He installed a loom in his bedroom and there began work on his 'Cabbage and Vine' tapestry. Later he converted the coach house into a small factory making 'Hammersmith' carpets, before transferring his main works to Merton Abbey. He died at the house in 1896.

Close by, the rowing eights have come off the river. The boy crews, now in wellington boots, carry their boats across the path and into the boathouse of Latymer Upper School. An underpass beneath the Great West Road links this part of the school to the main building in King Street.

Past The Dove, a famous pub which opened in 1796 as a coffee house, is an open space, the site of Old Creek, the harbour where the medieval village of Hammersmith first took root and sailing barges put in to load and unload. Nearby, on a bench, a white-bearded elder sits – the image of Blake's God the Father – and gazes across the water, seeming to dare an orange autumn sun to set before he is ready. Only the overhead whine of the aircraft, more muted here than at Kew, but still troublesome, brings us back to the present century.

Oh, and the pub where I drank those ginger beers – it must have been the Blue Anchor, closer to Hammersmith Bridge. Now I remember the river wall, and the bar door set flush with the pavement. Here too, as close to the slipway by the bridge as we could get, I was held aloft, aged eight and nine, to see the boat-race crews come past. Me in my Oxford favours – the dark blue rosette with yellow crossed oars – hoping against hope that Oxford would appear first. But always, in those years, it was Cambridge, drat them, shooting the bridge two lengths up and going away.

Walk 25

Windsor

Take the train to the pretty riverside town of Windsor, dominated by the great royal castle. See St George's Chapel and the State Apartments and stroll out to the green avenue of Long Walk. Wander back through the town to the Thames and maybe take a short boat trip or explore the antique shops in Eton High Street.

Allow All day.

Best times Not Sunday.

ROUTE

Getting there Take the train from Waterloo Station to Windsor & Eton Riverside. Check times in advance (071-928 5100). Journey time about 50 minutes.

Begin at railway station ⇌. Turn right past Royal Oak pub and left at George V fountain. Follow Thames Street uphill past Theatre Royal and around next bend. At Queen Victoria statue turn left up Castle Hill to Henry VIII Gateway and enter **Castle precincts** ☞; open 10.00 to 18.15. Interiors open as follows:

St George's Chapel usually 10.00 to 16.00 and Sunday services. *Admission*.

Albert Memorial Chapel 10.00 to 13.00, 14.00 to 15.45, closed Sunday.

State Apartments mid-March to mid-October 10.30 to 17.00, rest of year 10.30 to 15.00; Sunday open early May to mid-October 13.30 to 17.00, closed rest of year, also when Her Majesty is in official residence, usually in April and periods in March, May, June. To check, ring Tourist Information Centre (0753 852010). *Admission*.

Queen Mary's Dolls' House & Exhibition of Drawings 10.30 to 17.00. *Admission*.

For all, last tickets 30 minutes before closing.

From Henry VIII Gateway go ahead through cobbled Church Street and turn right down Church Lane to Guildhall (closed to public). Turn left past Parish Church and left into St Alban's Street. Visit **Exhibition of the Queen's Presents and Royal Carriages** ☞; open 10.30 to 17.00. *Admission*.

At exit turn left and bear left into Park Street. Go through gates at end to **Long Walk**. Follow walk down for approx. 200m and turn right into Park Close leading to Brook Street. Turn right along Sheet Street and left into Victoria Street. Turn right up Madeira Walk and at brick archway bear left alongside gardens made from old churchyard (tombstones against wall). At the road, turn right and continue through passage to Peascod Street, the shopping centre.

Turn right towards Castle and at High Street turn left downhill. At next bend look for arch with bust of Edward VII above. Go left through arch and down steps to gardens of The Goswells. Turn right into Barry Avenue beside river.

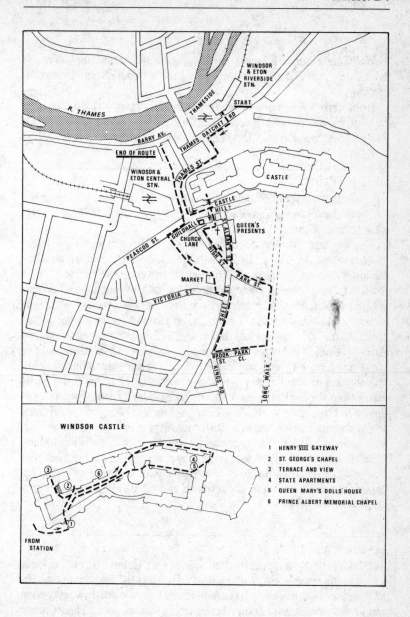

R. THAMES

WINDSOR & ETON RIVERSIDE STN.

THAMESIDE

START

BARRY AV.

END OF ROUTE

THAMES

DATCHET RD.

THAMES ST.

WINDSOR & ETON CENTRAL STN.

CASTLE

CASTLE HILL

PEASCOD ST.

GUILDHALL

CHURCH LANE

QUEEN'S PRESENTS

ST. ALBAN'S ST.

HIGH ST.

MARKET

PARK ST.

VICTORIA ST.

SHEET ST.

BROOK PARK ST. CL.

KINGS RD.

LONG WALK

WINDSOR CASTLE

FROM STATION

1 HENRY VIII GATEWAY
2 ST. GEORGE'S CHAPEL
3 TERRACE AND VIEW
4 STATE APARTMENTS
5 QUEEN MARY'S DOLLS' HOUSE
6 PRINCE ALBERT MEMORIAL CHAPEL

Walk ends here. Nearest refreshments all around, best around bridge to Eton High Street, where many antique shops. Return to station.

Boat trip Two journeys offered at landing stage. 1) To Boveney Lock and Weir, passing Windsor Castle and Racecourse (35 minutes). 2) Extended version past Boveney towards Bray Lock (2 hours).

In the Train

There is another route by rail to Windsor which is quicker but scenically rather barren. It goes from Paddington and you change at Slough to the local train to Windsor Central.

The way from Waterloo to Windsor & Eton Riverside is a good deal more interesting. The train snakes out to the south-western suburbs through Vauxhall – passing fresh mounds of vegetable débris at New Covent Garden market – and on through Clapham Junction to Putney, where the Oxford and Cambridge Boat Race begins. We, though, are in a cutting and must wait until after Richmond Station for a sight of the river. As the train approaches the bridge, look left or upstream towards the centre of town. On past banks of wild flowers near Whitton, and the gorse and fern of Hounslow Heath. Feltham is dire, but soon the fields are populated with horses and flower nurseries along with the usual warehouse sheds. Between Ashford and Staines a farmer is getting in the hay. Then open views of green, passing the lakes and reservoirs which abound here. London's Heathrow Airport is nearby, but we are no longer in London. At Sunnymeads the Thames has shrunk to less than half its width at Waterloo. Datchet is pretty, from the brief glimpse of it you can snatch at the level crossing. The train runs over to the far bank of the river, and suddenly across broad parkland a fine view opens up of Windsor Castle.

To the Castle

At the George V memorial fountain we turn up Thames Street beside a line of castle towers. Curfew or Clewer Tower is the first, completed in 1230 in the reign of Henry III to defend the Castle's north-west corner and in the nineteenth century fitted with a conical roof. Then Garter Tower, used by the Garter King-of-Arms as his administrative centre, and at the corner the Salisbury Tower, named after the Bishops of Salisbury who formerly controlled the Order of the Garter. This knightly order, the highest in the land, was created by Edward III in 1348 and is based at Windsor Castle. Each year, new Knights of the Order are invested in the Throne Room of the Castle and then process behind Her Majesty the Queen to the grand Garter Service in St George's Chapel which lies immediately behind these three towers.

As for Windsor itself, it remains a pretty and well-kept town but now groans more visibly from the pressures of mass tourism. Thirty years ago this part of the street had a bookshop and offered a mixed range of affluent high-street shopping. Now, the emphasis is on fast chicken and burger joints, catering for the crowds who arrive mostly in coaches which deposit their groups at the foot of Castle Hill, by the Queen Victoria statue. In summer the Castle approaches and its precincts can be uncomfortably crowded and some patience may be needed when filing, for instance, through St George's Chapel or the State Apartments.

Henry VIII Gateway

Each morning at 11.00 the Battalion of Foot Guards mounts its
Changing the Guard ceremony. In summer, when the Court is not in
residence, they assemble on the lawn on Castle Hill or on the parade
ground in Lower Ward. When the Queen is living at the Castle, Guard
Mounting takes place in the Quadrangle or Engine Court. The
ceremony is a scaled-down version of the procedure at Buckingham
Palace (see *Walk 3*) as the New Guard relieves the Old and sentries are
posted at strategic points around the five hectares (thirteen acres) of
the Castle precincts. At intervals, the band plays often quite jaunty
numbers to entertain the multi-national throng which gathers.

Enter the Castle at the Henry VIII Gateway. The arms of the king
stand above the narrow archway flanked by stout battlemented turrets.
Henry VIII is one of the principal figures in the evolution of the Castle.
In broad terms, it began as a Norman fortress, built by William I to
guard the western approaches to London and protect the Thames
between London and Wallingford. It expanded under successive
Norman kings, and in the 1340s the Plantagenet Edward III conceived
his idea of reinstituting an Arthurian brotherhood of knights, which
came into being as the Order of the Garter. Henry VIII added buildings
to the Castle and Charles II saw through much renovation and
decoration to medieval rooms which had received little attention for
three hundred years. George IV commissioned Jeffry Wyatt (later
Wyatville) to redesign many rooms and he also altered the walls and
battlements to give the Castle its present silhouette and form. As an
essentially military structure, surrounded by thick grey stone walls and
towers, Windsor lacks the warmth of royal palaces such as Kensington
or Hampton Court. Its true value arises from its close association with
the kings and queens of England, many of whom were born and are
buried here. The history of Windsor runs in intimate parallel with the
history of the nation.

St George's Chapel

Cross Lower Ward, where a sentry comes hard to attention and glares
fiercely at a child who has stepped over the white line in front of his
sentry box. He may be dressed like a chocolate soldier, but that black
modern rifle is for real! The child retreats. St George's Chapel was built
between 1475 and 1528 and contains a fascinating blend of Gothic and

Renaissance styles. Enter and collect a plan which selects twenty-six points of interest. Turn to face the brilliant stained glass of the west window, depicting some seventy-five kings, princes, saints and popes, and, it is thought, the master mason William Vertue who built much of the nave and appears at bottom right holding a hammer.

At the west door, look out to the angled row of Horseshoe Cloister, built by Edward IV (reigned 1461-83) to house the clergy of the new chapel, and now occupied by grace-and-favour residents. The great nave and vault are quietly impressive; the bosses in the ceiling are carved and painted with the arms of Henry VII.

In the north-west corner, the Urswick Chantry of 1507 has a strange marble monument. It dates from 1824 and shows hooded mourners weeping over the premature death of Princess Charlotte, daughter of George IV. She lies beneath a shroud, her body folded with one knee raised as though in natural sleep. Charlotte, the woman who would have been queen, died in childbirth at the age of twenty-one.

The choir is the jewel of the chapel, rich with an extraordinary density of carved wood and stone and bedecked with flamboyant heraldry. This is the spiritual centre of the Garter Knights. Each stall allotted to a living knight is crowned with his banner, helm, crest and sword. On the backs of the stalls, ornate brass and copper plates commemorate past occupants. To the left of the ornate Victorian altar and reredos, a beautifully carved wooden oriel window is set in the wall. It was created by Henry VIII as a gallery for Catherine of Aragon, his first wife.

Step down through the choir; in the Royal Vault beneath the tiled floor are the tombs of George III, George IV and William IV. Further along, a second vault bears the remains of Henry VIII, Jane Seymour (who died giving birth to the future Edward VI), Charles I and an infant child of Queen Anne.

The story of Charles I's burial is haunting. After he was publicly executed outside Banqueting House in 1649, his body and severed head were brought secretly to Windsor during a snowstorm and buried in this vault. More than a hundred and fifty years went by, and then in the early nineteenth century workmen came upon the unexpected coffin. The doctor of George IV was summoned and the lid prised open. The doctor found himself looking at a royal face he knew from Van Dyck's painting. Then, in the sudden exposure to air, the features collapsed and crumbled.

Through the Wards

From St George's Chapel, turn downhill to Horseshoe Cloister and walk past the cluster of half-timbered cottages to the terrace. Here an excellent view unfolds across the rooftops of Windsor and northward to the great Chapel of Eton College. This most famous of boys' boarding schools was founded in 1440 by the pious Henry VI, who founded King's College, Cambridge the following year (see *Walk 31*).

Walk up past the Albert Memorial Chapel, a profusely decorated though strangely inert monument created by Queen Victoria to honour her dead husband. Ahead is the great Round Tower, most famous of landmarks in the Thames Valley. The first fortress here was built on an artificial mound in the reign of William I the Conqueror. The stone building dates from Henry II (1154-89) and was later enlarged by George IV's architect, Jeffry Wyatville, who increased its height and designed the flag turret on top. The floor of the moat is now a rose garden. Turn left through a gate to North Terrace, where George III liked to take a morning promenade. When his health failed and he went insane, the king became virtually a prisoner at Windsor Castle for the last nine years of his life, and died there in 1820.

State Apartments

These suites of private and state rooms have evolved in a gradual refinement of the medieval castle. Much of the Gothic here is Victorian. Anthony Salvin designed the Grand Staircase in 1866, and the pattern of arms decorating the wall is repeated in other rooms. Red ropes usher the visitor next into the King's Dining Room – a brilliant return to the reign of Charles II. Antonio Verrio's ceiling portrays a very unbuttoned banquet surrounded by garlands of fish and poultry, a boar's head and a dead calf, flecks of painted blood everywhere. The carvings by Grinling Gibbons are supremely opulent, in particular in the group surrounding the portrait of Catherine of Braganza, the king's wife.

Continue through the more sober King's Drawing Room to his State Bedchamber, remodelled by Wyatville around the eighteenth-century bed with rich purple and green hangings in which Napoleon III and Empress Eugénie slept during their visit in 1855. In the King's Dressing Room are some outstanding pictures. Above the fireplace hangs the triple portrait (face and two profiles) of Charles I which Van Dyck painted to serve as a model for Bernini's planned bust of the king;

the portrait was sent to Italy for the sculptor to work from. Look also for the Rembrandt: a dark portrait of *An Old Lady 'The Artist's Mother'*.

From the King's Apartments, pass to a set occupied by the Queen: Drawing Room, Ball Room (containing Van Dyck's *Children of Charles I*), Audience Chamber and Presence Chamber. This last is a Charles II room and lavish with a Verrio ceiling, carvings by Grinling Gibbons and Gobelins tapestries of Old Testament scenes, added in the 1780s.

The work of Wyatville resurfaces in the Guard Chamber, decorated with vast lattice and rose patterns of pistols, swords and muskets, and continues in St George's Hall, for which he designed a 'medieval' roof painted with the shields of Garter Knights. A grand room, but somehow cold and unimposing. Continue to the Grand Reception Room and the Garter Throne Room. Here on Garter Day in June each year, the Queen invests the new Knights of the Order.

The Waterloo Chamber continues the tradition of the Waterloo Banquet, held each year at Apsley House until the Duke of Wellington died in 1852 (see *Walk 3*). George V revived the tradition in 1914 and a dinner is still given here in certain years on the anniversary of the battle, 18 June. The walls are lined with Sir Thomas Lawrence's paintings of eminent individuals – warriors, politicians, George IV and Pope Pius VII – associated with the overthrow of Napoleon. In the next and last room, the Grand Vestibule, arms and armour from the Napoleonic period are the principal theme, with a marble statue of Queen Victoria beneath a wooden canopy in imitation Gothic.

Nearby is the entrance to Queen Mary's Dolls' House & Exhibition of Drawings. The purseholder of a family of four or so may begin to baulk at the prospect of yet another set of entrance fees. On the other hand, many children will be at least pacified and perhaps greatly entertained by the giant dolls' house designed in 1923 by Sir Edwin Lutyens for Queen Mary, wife of George V. The Palladian mansion, measuring more than 2.4m (8ft) by 1.5m (5ft), captivates by attention to the smallest detail: each volume in the Library was specially written by authors such as Thomas Hardy, Walter de la Mare, Arnold Bennett and others, and bound separately in leather, each painting executed by artists such as Sir Alfred Munnings and Sir William Orpen.

A further plus is the chance to see the royal collection of drawings, separately displayed. Works from this enormously valuable collection are rotated, as much to spare them from excessive exposure to light as to demonstrate the breadth of drawings held, but a visitor can hope to see fine pieces by Holbein, and many studies of the human figure by Leonardo da Vinci together with some of his allegories, grotesques and battle machines.

Town Buildings

Stroll down to the castle entrance and continue through the cobbled way of Church Street, in the old market centre. The town's Merchants' Guild met formerly at The Three Tuns, built in 1518. Turn down to Guildhall and the Mayor's Parlour, an attractive building completed by Wren in 1689. In High Street, the Parish Church of St John the Baptist was rebuilt in 1820 and contains a large *Last Supper* presented by George III, and operates a brass rubbing centre founded on its collection of reproduction brasses taken from sites throughout southern England.

Exhibition of the Queen's Presents and Royal Carriages

On view in this second curious pairing of royal collections, see some of the original stalls, now occupied by model horses, and a line of royal carriages. These fluctuate as vehicles come in and go out to take part in royal ceremonies. Of the more permanent fixtures, the *Char à Banc* presented to Queen Victoria in 1844 by Louis-Philippe of France is graceful and elegant with four rows of upholstered benches. Here too are King George V's bath chair and the Sandringham Game Cart, pulled by Shire horses or Suffolk Punches and used to pick up the grand hauls of pheasant and hare shot by Edward VII and his guests on the royal estate in Norfolk.

The Queen's Presents room is a small treasure-house of objects given to the Queen on her travels: a little folksy, a little kitsch, the kind of gift Her Majesty accepts with a gracious smile and passes rapidly to an aide. A dragon on a casket wears a lighted red bulb in its mouth (King and Queen of Nepal, 1961). A terrible painting of a ship framed with shiny sea shells is sweetly naive (People of Andros, Bahamas, 1985). Queen Mary's miniature cutlery set is intriguing, though, and I loved the big silver watering can (1961). Well done, the All Indian Institute of Medical Sciences, New Delhi, who hit upon the idea.

Long Walk

The gates at the end of Georgian Park Street give onto an extraordinary vista. Long Walk cuts a broad green swathe for fully 4.8 km (3 miles) from the East Wing of the Castle to a mounted statue of George III on the far horizon, known as the 'Copper Horse'. The part of the Castle seen here is the private and visitors' wing, at its centre the King George IV Gateway flanked by Augusta Tower to the right and Lancaster Tower to the left. It was from Augusta Tower that Edward VIII broadcast his Abdication Speech in December 1936.

Stroll gently downhill through Long Walk, and perhaps be overtaken by one of the clip-clopping horse-drawn carriages which can be hired for rides and seem to give unusual contentment to the hirers. Perhaps, just for a minute, if they half-close their eyes, this is *their* castle they are riding towards . . . the Duke and Duchess of Bloggs, out for a spin in the park.

From Park Close, follow the Route through the backs of Windsor town and arrive eventually at the greens of Windsor and Eton Bowling Club, the putting green and the river, facing Eton College Boathouse. A final choice here: to boat or not to boat? Regular departures from the landing stage offer a relaxing tour on the Thames to Boveney Lock or beyond. 'Don't pay now, just come on board,' cries an amplified voice. A nice way to round off a day in Windsor – and so much more comfortable than *Three Men in a Boat*.

Walk 26

Hampton Court

Take a short train ride to Hampton Court and tour the great Elizabethan palace and grounds. Highlights include the Tudor Kitchens and State Apartments, the Maze, the Mantegna Exhibition and the Great Vine.

Allow All day.

Best times Any day.

ROUTE
Getting there Take the train from Waterloo to Hampton Court (not Hampton Wick). Check times in advance (071-928 5100). Journey time approx. 40 minutes. All-zone Travelcards valid on this line.

Begin at railway station. At the exit, walk ahead to the balustraded bridge and cross river. Turn right at Trophy Gates and go in at left to Ticket Office. **Hampton Court Palace** 👁; open mid-March to mid-October 09.30 to 18.00, Monday opens 10.15; mid-October to mid-March 09.30 to 16.30, Monday opens 10.15 (last tickets 45 minutes before closing time). Tudor Tennis Court and Banqueting House open mid-March to mid-October, closed rest of year. *Admission*. Gardens free, open until dusk or 21.00, whichever is earlier.

Approach Great Gatehouse and cross Base Court to Anne Boleyn's Gateway. In Clock Court, turn left to **Tudor Kitchens Tour**. Return to Anne Boleyn Gateway and go up broad stone staircase to **State Apartments**. Complete tour of Palace interior by visiting **Renaissance Gallery**, entrance at side of Clock Court.

If it is lunchtime, go out through Base Court and turn right to Garden Café or Tiltyard Restaurant. Or continue past these to gate and turn right in Hampton Court Road to excellent mock-Tudor pub, the King's Arms. (Keep Palace ticket with you at all times.)

In afternoon, return to gardens and visit **Maze**. At exit, walk ahead beside Wilderness garden to gate to Broad Walk. Turn right towards Fountain Court and at door on right enter **Royal Tennis Court**.

At exit turn right across garden front of Fountain Court and at corner turn right to Knot Garden. On right is entrance to **Mantegna Exhibition**. Return to Knot Garden and turn right to see the **Great Vine** in its greenhouse.

Turn back a short way past 17C garden on right and turn right to **Banqueting House**. At exit return to main path and turn right. After Pond Garden, turn right through shady walk to **Tijou Gates** beside river.

Return along terrace beside Broad Walk to front of Fountain Court. Stroll along one of the avenues to the Canal and Long Water. Turn back to Palace and walk through Fountain Court and on to Great Gatehouse. Walk ends here. Nearest refreshments in Palace grounds. Return to station.

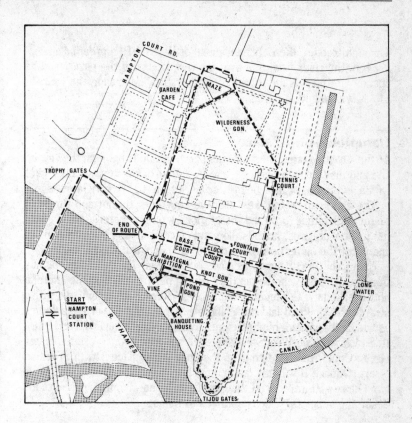

In the Train

From Waterloo the train shares the route to Windsor past New Covent Garden Market, then after Clapham Junction veers south by Wandsworth Common to Wimbledon. Then follows a wedge of featureless suburbia. The long parade of offices, sheds and semi-detached houses is briefly interrupted by the sewage tanks at Berrylands, then comes the place which has the hardest name of all to live with – Surbiton. Trim flowers grow in neat beds on the platform, and fuschias wave their heads in uniform hanging baskets. Then the line swings over an iron bridge to Thames Ditton and all is at once leafier and more spacious, a little old country station bordered by a white paling fence. The train runs on to Hampton Court and terminates there.

Through trees to the right, a glimpse of Henry VIII's great palace.

From the river bridge, a broader view opens of the palace and its chimneypotted roofline. In the other direction, upstream, the weirs at Molesey straddle the Thames.

Hampton Court Palace

At the Trophy Gates, turn into the palace grounds beneath the carved lion and unicorn. Do not forget to buy your ticket now at the Ticket Office and Shop, or face being sent back from the Great Gatehouse.

The approach to the west front is very fine: the jut and thrust of turret and chimneypot, and the glorious stone monsters which guard the moat – dragons, hounds, lion and unicorn. Cross the grassy moat and enter the sumptuous dark red-brick courtyard of Base Court.

Hampton Court Palace was made over to King Henry VIII in 1525 by Cardinal Wolsey, who began the building here in 1514 on the site of a house leased to the Knights Hospitallers. Henry VIII expanded it with a new Great Hall and laid out elaborate gardens, a tiltyard and tennis courts, and a park for hunting game. In the reign of William III and Mary II, Sir Christopher Wren was allowed to pull down Henry VIII's Cloister Green Court, the third court in the line, and replace it with Fountain Court. George II was the last monarch to live at the Palace, and after him George III introduced the gift of grace-and-favour apartments for deserving subjects, which continues to this day.

Tudor Kitchens

Pass through Anne Boleyn's Gateway and in Clock Court turn to see the gilt astronomical clock made for Henry VIII by Nicholas Oursian. Its extraordinary face indicates the hour, the month, the phases of the moon and the time of high water at London Bridge.

In a corner of this court a doorway leads to the Tudor Kitchens Tour. See the wonderful model of the palace kitchens, the largest and most complete set of comparable rooms in Europe, a feeding machine for six hundred guests or more – and in those days they ate till they dropped. A great row of departments included special rooms for pastrymakers and confectioners, boiling rooms and larders, leading to the Great Kitchen aswarm with cooks and assistant cooks and young boys to turn the

spits. The scene is set for a banquet on Midsummer's Day 1542. Then go out and file through back courts where specialist craftsmen toiled in their workshops. From Master Carpenter's Court go into a butcher's room to find a deer on the table and a boar in a bleeding bath. After Fish Court the display is more concentrated, a splendid restoration of the rooms for pie-making and preparing fish and vegetables, and in the Great Kitchen the smell of woodsmoke from a log fire, where a cauldron simmers.

State Apartments

Henry VIII's Great Hall is crowned with a classic among hammerbeam roofs, the work of James Needham, the king's master carver: richly carved pendants drip from it like so many tropical fruit. Around the walls are antlered stags' heads and giant Flemish tapestries (1532-6) portraying events in the life of Abraham. A series of prints on show provides a key to them. Turn through the Horn Room, once an antler store, where food was delivered from the kitchens. From the Watching Chamber, a secondary dining room, go on to the Haunted Gallery. This is from the Wolsey period and is said to be haunted by the ghost of Catherine Howard, fifth wife of Henry VIII, to whom she was married for two years and then was executed. A grace-and-favour resident heard a woman screaming, and claimed she knew at once who it was.

The Chapel Royal is entered from the Royal Pew, an upper gallery. The chapel is a fabulous place: the painted ceiling in blue and gold with carved and gilded pendants, heavenly stars and pairs of gilded angels' heads in the corbels. Repeated through the ceiling is the motto 'DIEU ET MON DROIT', the words spaced with roses and the 'N' inverted. Grinling Gibbons carved the magnificent reredos, creating paired columns with pilasters behind. To the right of the altar, *trompe l'oeil* windows by Thornhill balance the composition.

The Queen's Staircase, in marble, was designed by Wren and incorporates wrought-ironwork by Tijou and painted walls by William Kent, the Classical decorator. A great lantern hangs deep from the ceiling, and on the far wall an allegorical painting by Honthorst features Charles I, his Queen and the Duke of Buckingham as Jupiter, Juno and Apollo (1628).

A dramatic transition occurs at the William and Mary State Apartments built around Wren's Fountain Court. Look out through bevelled windows to see how the view has shifted through more than a century, from Tudor brick to the new Classical perfection in four elegant storeys: the arcade of the cloister, a deep row of pedimented windows, above these a set of bull's eyes, audaciously squared off with lavish stone reliefs, then a set of square windows with patterned corners and a top balustrade to bind the façades together. In the middle of the garden, water spouts from a tinkling, slightly lethargic fountain set in a greenish round pond.

In the Queen's Guard Chamber are Kneller's *Hampton Court Beauties*, a series of portraits of seemingly refined court ladies. Two colossal stone Yeomen of the Guard support the mantel above the fireplace. In the Queen's Presence Chamber is Queen Anne's tall four-poster bed, screened by faded maroon and mustard hangings. The Queen's Private Chapel appears to be a simple panelled room at eye-level, but look up to the dramatic octagonal dome and lantern. Some interesting paintings here include *Flora* (School of Leonardo) who wears a school-of-Mona-Lisa smile, and a pair of cherubs from the same source, a *St Jerome* by Georges de la Tour and a portrait by Annibale Caracci.

After the Queen's Bathing Closet, panelled and furnished with a marble basin and fire surround, move into the Private Dining Room. Here we have turned a corner of the court, and now can look westward to see Wren's eventual solution for merging his own concept with the Tudor palace. On the west side the balustrade is lower and Classical urns parade the roof beneath the line of mellow red-brick chimneys.

Continue through to the rear of the palace and from the Queen's Drawing Room look out to Long Water, the narrow rectangular lake which disappears in the general direction of Kingston, fronted by fan-shaped avenues and linked to the arcs of the Canal. In these rooms are lavish ceilings by Antonio Verrio. In the Public Dining Room is a fireplace carved with the royal coat of arms by Grinling Gibbons, who also designed the bracketed cornice.

Next is the Cumberland Suite, with interesting portraits of ladies of the court by Sir Peter Lely who gives them all remarkably similar lips, as Rossetti was to do in a later age. These rooms contain Wolsey's Closet, a rare surviving Tudor interior: the ceiling has heraldic decoration and on the walls are painted panels, some from the fifteenth century and only discovered during renovation in 1962.

Renaissance Gallery

To complete the palace tour, visit the Renaissance Gallery (entrance at the Classical side of Clock Court). Here see fine Tudor portraits of Edward VI and the panoramic group with Henry VIII, Jane Seymour, the Prince of Wales, Princess Mary and Princess Elizabeth, four monarchs in a row. Adjoining Tudor rooms are plainly adorned with sixteenth-century linenfold panelling, then the pace of the paintings grows a little quicker, arriving at a stunning array of great masters.

The Daniel Mytens canvas of *Charles I and Henrietta Maria* is succeeded by more Tudor royals, then a Holbein portrait of *Johannes Frobenius*, Tintoretto's *Venetian Senator* and portraits by Lorenzo Lotto, Bronzino, Correggio, and a touching *Madonna and Child* by Andrea del Sarto, and Veronese's *Marriage of St Catherine*. Best yet, Raphael's *Portrait of the Artist* and Titian's provocative *The Lovers*. The heroine of *Lucretia*, by Lucas Cranach, points a dagger at her breast in one of the artist's famous treatments of this dramatic theme (the virtuous woman accedes to rape under threat, confesses to her father and husband and then kills herself). Finally, the compelling detail of Pieter Brueghel the Elder's *Massacre of the Innocents*.

Time Out

The hard work is over, it is time for lunch and then the afternoon is free for outdoor games like getting lost in the Maze and trying to understand Real Tennis. As mentioned, the King's Arms in Hampton Court Road is a very sound alternative to one of the palace establishments. It has painted panels of the wives of Henry VIII, and an enterprising food bar. And if the dried flowers on the gantry should put you in mind of Grinling Gibbons, so much the better.

The Maze

The definitive account of life in this Triangle of Confusion occurs in Jerome K. Jerome's *Three Men in a Boat*, Chapter VI, the section summarised as 'Hampton Court Maze – Harris as a guide'. I would add only that the Maze was installed in the late seventeenth century, that the object is to reach the centre and come out again, and that doing so induces extraordinary mass panic in children, compelling them to run with wide-eyed expressions of horror on their faces (largely simulated, of course). And yes, is it not wonderful too how the popular myth has survived that to conquer the Maze you only have to keep turning right.

Royal Tennis
Royal or Real Tennis is an initially bewildering game described briefly in *Walk 20*. Visitors to this court, which dates from 1620 and now hosts the British Open Championships, enter and stand beneath the penthouse roof, on top of which the server lands the ball. A good vantage point, and safe too behind the wire cage from the whizzing ball which has a heavier core than the lawn tennis variety.

Mantegna Exhibition
The formal gardens on the far side of Fountain Court are a delight. The small Knot Garden is bright with flowers enclosed by low clipped hedges, and in the sunken Pond Garden a magnificent display of flowers is set in ordered beds around a tiny pond.

Nearby is the entrance to the Mantegna Exhibition, housed in the Lower Orangery. There are nine canvases in all, and the sequence begins at the far end of the gallery. The paintings are by Andrea Mantegna and date from *c.*1492, and Charles I acquired them in 1629. They celebrate the *Triumphs of Julius Caesar* through a series of incidents recreated in heroic style. Preserving the canvases has been a long-drawn-out struggle since they first suffered serious neglect in the seventeenth century. Modern restorers found that previous efforts to repaint or treat the works had removed so much of the original layer of Mantegna's paint that one of the scenes, *VII The Captives*, has been left uncleaned and now hangs by itself at the top end of the gallery. The other scenes are: *I The Picture Bearers*; *II The Bearers of Standards and Siege Equipment*; *III The Bearers of Trophies and Bullion*; *IV The Vase Bearers*; *V The Elephants*; *VI The Corselet Bearers*; *VIII The Musicians*; *IX Caesar on his Chariot – Great Caesar triumphant.*

The Great Vine
This wonder of the gardens was planted in 1768, and now is trained in its own greenhouse. From just one stem, but what a stem, more than

2m (7ft) in girth at ground level, spreads a massive trellis of vines bearing regularly spaced bunches of black grapes. In a good year the vine in the nineteenth century yielded a crop weighing up to 900kg (2000lb). A patch of ground outside the greenhouse is left uncultivated so the vine roots which have spread beneath it can be freely treated. It is thought these roots may have penetrated to an old cesspit, and have luxuriated down there ever since, hence the Great Vine's exceptional fertility.

Banqueting House

This small battlemented house contains an important Baroque interior. The building was designed either by Wren or his second-in-command William Talman. The ceiling by Verrio depicts an allegory of Arts and Sciences. The surrounding walls are painted grey and gold, as are the mirror frames and the *trompe l'oeil* frames of the wall paintings.

It is an extraordinary room, but prompts the question 'Why build it at all if you live in a huge palace with dining rooms all over the place?' The question answers itself. The Banqueting House was surely made as an escape from the main house and all its pomp and formality. 'Just run us up a little room by the river, will you,' is the sort of instruction William III may well have issued to his architect. Outside, a flock of Canada Geese honk past, low over the water, emphasising that this is a very different place. On the far bank, dozing fishermen nod their agreement.

Tijou Gates and Long Water

Wander through the shady walk and arrive at the great line of ornamental gates created by Jean Tijou for William and Mary to provide a terminus to the Privy Garden. Outside them is Barge Walk, where barges used to be towed, running all the way to Kingston. For a while I thought it would be amusing to continue this walk beside the river, crossing finally at Kingston Bridge, but then it seemed that Hampton Court is so varied in itself and also very self-contained, there was little point in adding an extraneous element.

Besides, we have yet to walk along one of the formal avenues fanning out from Fountain Court, and then stroll reflectively beside the curve of the Canal to the marvellous sheet of Long Water. Perhaps pause here on a bench, alone with a family of piping moorhens.

From here there is no way out to the main park. Turn back, instead, to Fountain Court and see for the first time Cibber's great relief in the pediment of *Hercules Triumphing Over Envy*. Then, producing the entrance ticket one final time, stroll back through the arcade of Wren's marvellous Fountain Court. The perfect ending.

Walk 27

Brighton

Lots of breezy fun at England's best seaside resort. Wander, agreeably lost, in The Lanes, win a cuddly green dog on Palace Pier, take a ride on Volk's Electric Railway and marvel at the outrageous chinoiserie of the Royal Pavilion.
Allow   All day.
Best times   Not Sunday.

ROUTE
Getting there
By train from London Take train from Victoria Station. Check times in advance (071-928 5100); journey time 55 minutes or 1 hour 15 minutes.
By coach from London Take coach from Victoria Coach Station. Check times in advance (071-730 0202); journey time approx. 1 hour 45 minutes.

Begin at Brighton Station ⇄. (Visitors arriving by coach are set down at Pool Valley Bus Station, Old Steine. Walk up North Street to Clock Tower and join walk there.)

Leave station forecourt and walk ahead down Queen's Road to the Clock Tower. Cross North Street to West Street and take 1st left into Duke Street which runs into the maze of streets known as **The Lanes**. Explore at leisure the alleys leading off Ship Street, Prince Albert Street and Market Street. Work through to far side and turn right along East Street to the sea front.

Turn left to **Palace Pier** 👁; open 09.00, 10.00 or 11.00 according to season and demand; usually closes 23.00 up to Easter, 02.00 in summer. Stroll to end and return to promenade.

Turn right to terminus of **Volk's Electric Railway** 👁; open Easter to October, frequent trains to new Marina. Either take a closer look at the Marina (dull, Post-Modernist confection) or return directly to town.

Near Palace Pier is the old **Aquarium**, newly refurbished in style of first 1872 building and operating as the Brighton Sea Life Centre 👁; open 10.00 to 18.00, closes later in summer, closed 25 December. *Admission*.

To visit the **Royal Pavilion** 👁, walk up Old Steine from Palace Pier. On left at No.54 is Tourist Information Centre for further information and booklet with list of guest houses and hotels. Continue towards onion domes on left. Main entrance is through copper-domed arch at far end of gardens. If approaching from The Lanes, go down to East Street and turn left, then cross North Street and go along Pavilion Buildings, past The Pavilion Shop. Pavilion open 10.00 to 17.00, closed 25-26 December. *Admission*.

To visit **Brighton Museum and Art Gallery**, go through copper-domed arch in Pavilion grounds and turn left in Church Street; open 10.00 to 17.45, Sunday 14.00 to 17.00, closed Monday.

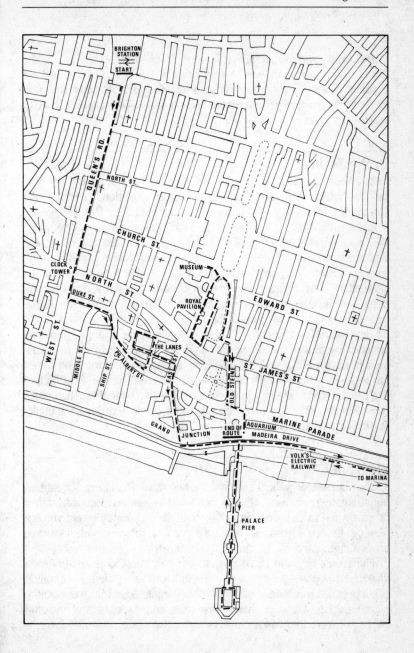

Return to sea front. Walk ends here. Nearest refreshments in The Lanes. To return to railway station, walk W along promenade to West Street. Views from here of West Pier, Grand Hotel and Brighton Centre. Turn right up West Street and continue along Queen's Road to station (or jump on a bus).

In the Train

Out of Victoria, the train crosses the river by Battersea Park and runs on the multi-track way through Clapham Junction, Wandsworth Common and Balham – 'Gateway to the South' in Peter Sellers's satirical travelogue, one of a string of suburbs which mutely compete with each other for the title of 'Most boring place to live in London'. On through further contenders Thornton Heath and Norbury, and then the towers of East Croydon, now a satellite city. Outer suburbia continues along the valley through Purley and Coulsdon, then a deep cutting densely covered in bushes, ivy and stunted trees . . . and the first of the tunnels which burrow through the Surrey Hills and Sussex Downs. In no time we hurtle through Gatwick – famous as the airport where you spend more time in the departure hall than you ever do in the air – then swoop past rolling green fields and scattered red-brick timbered farmhouses. After Haywards Heath and Burgess Hill the great bulk of the Downs looms ahead. On the horizon are two windmills, then more tunnels and suddenly a broad hillside of pastel-coloured houses flanks the final curve into Brighton Station.

The Lanes

At the station exit walk ahead past the bus station and keep straight on for about five minutes. On the horizon the sea sparkles through a narrow gap – much more stimulating than the dilapidated street you are passing. Queen's Road has been in a perpetual depression, an estate agent's nightmare, all the time I have known it.

The Lanes begin in Duke Street, just past the Clock Tower. As a district it is impossible to describe on a linear basis – so full of beckoning side alleys and half-hidden piazzas. In the Middle Ages it was the centre of the fishing village of Brighthelmston, and its tight and twisting alleyways were known locally as twittens. Its modern identity is more commercial: The Lanes is a famous nest of antique shops, jewellers, boutiques, art galleries, novelty shops, restaurants, pubs and seafood bars. For a quick impression, turn right along Ship Street, bear left at the Friends' Meeting House and follow Prince Albert Street around the bend. At the huge cream Town Hall, go left along Market Street. After the Pump House pub explore Brighton Place, site of the old village well, and backtrack left up Meeting House Lane, crammed with jewellers, Prinny's multifarious Antique Gallery and Pecksniffs the Bespoke Perfumery. From Brighton Place an archway leads through to Brighton Square, a modern development with an upstairs café terrace above Casa Rossini. On the north side of The Lanes, the duck-egg blue livery of Hanningtons department store closes the view. Finally, from the Pump House, follow the road downhill and go through the narrow alley past English's Oyster Bar. Turn right in East Street and follow its winding path to the sea.

I love it in The Lanes and can spend hours there – eating, drinking, seeing what's new in the shops, and just watching the world go by. The Lanes express what is special about Brighton – a little eccentric, a little flamboyant, stylish, humorous, unselfconscious. Among places to look out for are:

Shops
Patrick Moorhead Antiques, Ship Street; Graham Webb (period mechanical music), David Hawkins (weapons and chinoiserie), Sue Pearson (antique dolls and teddy bears), The Cat Shop (everything cat-shaped), all Prince Albert Street; Casa Pupo and Mariposa (exuberant pottery), both Brighton Place; the jewellers of Meeting House Lane.

Pubs
The Bath Arms, Union Street (attractive room with good gantry and open fire); The Cricketers Arms, Black Lion Street (gantry recently gone, but all you could want in loud, blowsy Victoriana); Pump House, Market Street (broad bay windows overlooking the throng).

Places to Eat
Browns, Duke Street; Piccolo, Ship Street (pasta-pizza); Food for Friends, Gar's Chinese Restaurant, Pizza Express, all Prince Albert Street; Peter's, Market Street; English's Oyster Bar, off East Street.

Palace Pier and Sea Front

It was a Dr Richard Russell of Lewes who first made sea-bathing popular. In 1750 he published a book advocating the benefits of drinking sea water and bathing in it to cure many diseases, in particular those of the glandular sort. In the early days, sea-bathing was a rigorous exercise – best done early on a cold morning, said the doctors who supported Russell's ideas. Few people could swim, so the well-to-do hired a bathing machine and an attendant 'dipper' who supported their body and plunged them under the waves. Soon the novelist Fanny Burney was writing, 'I have bathed so often as to lose my dread of the operation.'

The Prince of Wales, the future George IV, first came to Brighton in 1783, at the age of twenty-one, to visit his uncle the Duke of Cumberland. He may have come for a cure, but he was anyway bowled over by the pretty town, the bracing air and the freedom it gave him from court life at Windsor. He commissioned the first version of his famous Pavilion in 1787 and the future fame of Brighton was assured. The railway from London opened in 1841 and excursion trains for day-trippers started three years later. For the rest of the century the town expanded fast: more and more hotels and boarding houses, and amusements for the holidaymakers. The West Pier was built in 1866, the Palace Pier in 1899; the Aquarium opened in 1872 and Volk's Electric Railway in 1883. They, The Lanes and the Royal Pavilion are still the biggest attractions in the town (although the West Pier is sadly closed and may be too expensive to restore).

The Palace Pier replaced the older Chain Pier. Its filigree arches and twirly structures reflect something of the Pavilion's style. Its main attractions are food – including, of course, your stick of Brighton Rock; the future – apply at Eva Petulengro's hut near the Palace of Fun; photography – be snapped with your head through a painted board depicting Mr and Mrs Nerd and their daughter, the style very much school of Donald McGill; and just plain fun, at the Palace of Fun and Welcome to the Pleasuredome.

The Palace of Fun is much like any other big amusement arcade. Housed in a tall iron pavilion it has a good central dome decorated with stained-glass rondels of seaside scenes. As someone whose ambition is not to win a huge fluffy green dog, I tend to move on through. The only machine that still exerts a horrible fascination, as it did in childhood, is that one with the sliding trays stacked with silver coins which ease in and out while you work a grabber to seize some of this fabulous wealth for yourself, and never do.

On to the fish-and-chip café and ultimate fun at Welcome to the Pleasuredome, on its right the helter-skelter and on its left Horatio's Bar. Beyond the dome are the rides – dodgems, roundabouts, the Phantom Ghoster.

Volk's Electric Railway

Across the road from Palace Pier, the old Aquarium has had a facelift restoring it to how it looked in 1872. Its new name is the Brighton Sea Life Centre. Up above, in Marine Parade, the bay-fronted houses climb the hill, preserving a proud uniformity with their white, cream and pale yellow façades.

Along the front is the terminus of Volk's Electric Railway. Magnus Volk, the first man in Brighton to install electric lighting in his home, opened the railway in 1883 and in 1896 extended it to the village of Rottingdean on a line of stilts 7.3m (24ft) high which carried it clear of the sea at high tide. Later this section was closed when groynes had to be built to shore up eroding cliffs, and now the railway goes from Palace Pier to Black Rock Pool.

The carriages clank along the back of the beach, passing the anchor of the merchant ship *Athena B* which was safely grounded here in a storm in 1980 after valiant work by the crew of Shoreham lifeboat. The train stops at the Amusement Park and continues towards the waxing grey bastions of the new Marina, curving out to sea. At the station by the Marina, step out for a stroll by Crescent Beach, where nudist bathing is permitted. When this new facility was announced, the car park at Crescent Beach suddenly became the place for trippers to park up for a few hours with their tea flasks and sandwiches.

The Marina itself is disappointing. Unless you have a boat – and the harbour encloses 31 hectares (77 acres) of sheltered water – there is little to see except a few shops and restaurants in a rather dismal Post-Modernist layout. The visual highlights are a Chef & Brewer restaurant got up in black timber to look like an old boathouse, and Leonardo's restaurant, a pink octagonal pavilion, strangely graceless.

Royal Pavilion

Back in town, walk up Old Steine towards the great onion domes of the Royal Pavilion, which early critics likened to the Kremlin in Moscow. The once-fashionable promenade of Old Steine, now more a bus station, was originally common land where the fishermen dried their nets on the stones. Across the gardens the eastern front of the Pavilion basks in the morning sunlight, a grand oriental folly of domes and minarets, a colonnade joined by pierced stone latticework in the Indian manner.

It is fairly appalling to think of the vast sums that the corpulent 'Prinny' lavished on his Xanadu. By 1794 his debts were close to £650,000 and the Government only agreed to settle them provided he married a royal wife (not Mrs Fitzherbert, whom he had secretly married in 1785) and produced an heir to the throne. He agreed, and grumpily married Caroline of Brunswick, who found him as loathsome as he did her. However, it is difficult not to be hugely entertained by the exuberance of the Prince's concept and by the amazing style and opulence of the decorations.

When George first came to Brighton he rented 'a superior farmhouse' on the site. In 1787 he commissioned Henry Holland to transform the house into a Palladian villa. Further extensions followed in 1802, and the interior was gradually refurbished in the Chinese style by Frederick Crace and Sons. In 1803-5 William Porden built the nearby Indian-inspired Dome, as stables for forty horses with accommodation for coachmen and grooms; today it is a concert hall. Then, in the final and grandest phase, John Nash designed the present Pavilion in 1815-22.

Entrance is through the Octagon Hall and Vestibule, the former an elegant room with a canopied ceiling but muted indeed compared with the Corridor beyond. This was where guests assembled for the ceremonial parade into dinner in the Banqueting Room. Its walls and ceiling are crowded with fascinating objects – the pink walls decorated with cerulean-blue foliage, the large Chinese figures, the bamboo and imitation-bamboo furniture. Only the patent stoves are missing, which merely warmed the Prince but stifled his guests.

The Banqueting Room is a vast rectangle, at its centre a dining table with twenty-four chairs set for the dessert course, a dazzling display of silver and silver-gilt. Around the walls are large paintings with Chinese figures and superb tall pedestal lamps in blue Spode porcelain, ormolu and wood. The greatest piece of all is the huge sparkling gasolier with lotus leaves and silver dragons, one ton in weight and suspended from the claws of a great carved dragon. The dragon emerges from a fantastic *trompe l'oeil* ceiling, painted to suggest an Eastern sky filled with painted and three-dimensional plantain leaves.

The Great Kitchen, where the eminent Carème presided in 1816-17, was a model of modernity for its age. It is little changed today. The automatic spit still turns in the bronze-canopied fireplace, and the great *batterie de cuisine* of some 550 copper pieces is ranged around the walls. Here too is the menu for a banquet served on 15 January 1817, which lists 116 dishes.

Return through the Banqueting Room to the South Drawing Room, Saloon and North Drawing Room. These seem almost coolly Classical after the hot colours of the feeding rooms. They contain beautiful Regency furniture with dolphin ornaments, gilt torchères, a couch in the form of an Egyptian river boat on crocodile feet, the ceilings of the drawing rooms supported by slender canopied pillars.

At the far end, the red and gold Music Room is sumptuous and dazzling, wonderfully restored after two recent disasters, an arson attack in 1975 and hurricane damage in 1987. The dome shimmers by the light of its carved and gilded cockleshells, the main gasolier is a glittering pagoda, dragons and serpents adorn the pelmets and the Chinese landscapes on the walls are red and gold: red sky and water, gold everything else, eerie like a photographic negative.

Continue through the King's Apartments, much quieter and reflecting the tastes of the gouty King in old age, when he was more unhealthy than ever and Brighton had grown too noisy for him.

After his death in 1830 the fate of the Pavilion teetered this way and that until the Town bought it in 1850 for £50,000. A great deal of restoration has followed, particularly in the 1950s under the direction of Dr Clifford Musgrave. The Royal Pavilion is still one of the most staggering edifices in Europe, if not the world.

Along the Front

From Palace Pier, stroll along the front for a sight of the West Pier, probably doomed forever, a great section hacked out of it. Those who remember it in its prime say it was finer than the Palace Pier, though perhaps this was because it was patronised by a more genteel or 'naicer' class of holidaymaker who stayed at the big hotels nearby. Alas, it is now rusting and rotting and the costs of restoring it are prohibitive.

Facing the pier is Regency Square, a fine example of what its name describes. It was laid out in 1818, a three-sided enclosure giving all residents a view out to sea from elegant bow-fronted windows, each with its curving canopy. The residents did complain, more than a little, when the West Pier was built, but that is all history now.

Along the promenade are the Brighton Centre, for live events and conferences, and the Grand Hotel (1864), recently famous for the bomb-blast in 1984 during a Conservative Party Conference, from which the building has now recovered. Nearby is Alfred Waterhouse's red-brick Metropole Hotel (1888). My father, by birth an Edwardian who missed being a Victorian by just six days, associated the Metropole with a legendary bell which during the inter-war years sounded on Sunday mornings at about 2 am. This, according to him, was a signal which meant 'All back to your own bedrooms'. Can this be true?

Walk 28

Oxford 'A': South of the Broad

A walk through the historic core of the university city, from the Covered Market to the 'grand' colleges of Christ Church, Magdalen and New. Also to be seen are the High Street, Botanic Garden and Bridge of Sighs.

Allow   6 hours.

Best times   Sunday less good for Christ Church, when College opens 12.45, Picture Gallery 14.00.

Note   Try to spend more than one day in Oxford, spreading Walks 'A' and 'B' across two days.

ROUTE
Getting there
By train from London Take train from Paddington Station to Oxford. Check times in advance (071-387 7070); journey time approx. 1 hour. *By coach from London* Take coach from Victoria Coach Station; coaches also stop on request at Marble Arch (Stop X), Notting Hill Gate and Shepherds Bush (Kensington Hilton). Check times in advance (071-730 0202); journey time approx. 1½ hours.

Begin at Oxford Station ⇌. (Visitors arriving by coach are set down at Gloucester Green Bus Station. Turn left up George Street and right along Cornmarket to join main walk at Carfax, see below.)

Leave station forecourt and turn left into Park End Street. Keep straight on in New Road past Nuffield College and Castle Mound. At top, go through Bonn Square to Queen Street and Carfax. Good view from top of **Carfax Tower** 👁; open 26 March to 28 October, 10.00 to 18.00, Sunday 14.00 to 18.00 (last tickets 17.30). *Admission*.

Continue into High Street and on left enter **Covered Market** 👁. Tour and return to High Street, cross road and turn right to Carfax and left into St Aldate's. On left, at far end of Town Hall block is Museum of Oxford; open 10.00 to 17.00, closed Sunday, Monday. Opposite in St Aldate's is Tourist Information Office for further information and accommodation service.

Continue down St Aldate's and turn right into Pembroke Square to front of Pembroke College. Look back to Tom Tower and main entrance to **Christ Church**; entrance for public is from Broad Walk. To find, go down St Aldate's and turn left into War Memorial Gardens. Keep straight on and turn left to college entrance in Meadow Buildings 👁; college open 09.30 to 18.00, Sunday 12.45 to 17.30, October to 12 April closes 16.30, Hall closed 12.00 to 14.00. *Admission*. Buy combined ticket for Cathedral, Hall and Picture Gallery.

Bear left to **Cathedral** through cloister. On right, Chapter House with bookshop and display of cathedral plate. Enter Cathedral.

Leave at W door to view across Tom Quad. Visit **Hall** on left, reached by fan-vaulted staircase.

From Hall, walk across top of Tom Quad to Peckwater Quad and bear right past Library to Canterbury Quad and **Christ Church Picture Gallery** 👁; open 10.30 to 13.00, 14.00 to 17.30, Sunday 14.00 to

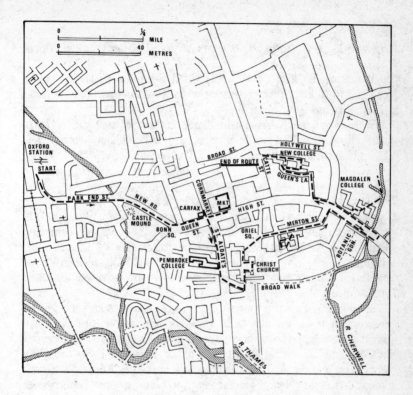

17.30, October to March closes 16.30, closed Christmas and Easter.

Leave Christ Church and from Oriel Square walk ahead along Merton Street to **Merton College** ◉; open Saturday 14.00 to 17.00, Sunday 10.00 to 17.00, October to March closes 16.00.

After visit to Mob Quad and Chapel, return to lodge and turn right along Merton Street and round corner to High Street. Turn right and opposite Magdalen College visit **Botanic Garden** ◉; open 09.00 to 17.00, closed 16.30 in winter, glasshouses open 14.00 to 16.00, closed Good Friday and Christmas.

At exit, turn right to bridge for river views. Cross road to **Magdalen College** ◉; open 14.00 to 18.15.

After visit to Chapel, Cloister Quad, New Building and deer park, return to lodge and turn right up High Street. Turn right into Queen's Lane, past St Edmund Hall, and follow bends to first bridge, where turn right to **New College** 👁 ; open 14.00 to 17.00, in vacations opens 11.00.

Visit Chapel, Cloister and Garden Quad. See medieval lavatory block and return to lodge. Keep straight on in New College Lane, beneath Bridge of Sighs to Catte Street.

Walk ends here. Nearest refreshments: (tea) at Convocation House – to left on far side Radcliffe Square, or The Wykeham – to right and along Holywell; (drinks) The King's Arms on corner Holywell.

In the Train

Now that Oxford is on the Inter-City network you can at least hope to travel in reasonable style and in reasonably civilised company. Paddington is the duchess of the London termini, its concourse in daytime ajostle with itinerant clergymen, titled shoppers, racehorse owners, bogus majors, managing directors and privately educated trainspotters.

The first half of the journey is a fairly tedious spin through the western suburbs – on the left the white-hooded windows of Wormwood Scrubs, the largest prison in Britain – to Slough ('Come, friendly bombs, and fall on Slough/ It isn't fit for humans now' – *Sir John Betjeman*) and through what is laughably known as England's 'Silicon Valley' to Reading. Only now comes the first feeling of real countryside, the train and the Thames together, then after Pangbourne the river cutting and bending on its passage through green meadows, gradually narrowing, all the way to Oxford. A short rush past the southern outskirts and the famous spires glide into view over the ship-like masts of the Ice Rink.

Into Town

From the railway station the way to the centre of, to me, the most beautiful city in England is almost harrowingly ugly. You may as well take a bus to Queen Street and Carfax, the central *quadrifurcus* or four-road crossing. You can catch one in the station forecourt (52) or in Park End Street (40, 41, 42, 43).

To walk this dingy stretch, pitted with carparks like bombsites, go up to the yellow stone Royal Oxford Hotel and keep straight on over the canal where a willow obligingly weeps and coots dive out of sight. Walking serves also to prolong the view of Nuffield College (1949-60), its tower the most undreaming of hulks, topped by a little green spire.

Across the road is Castle Mound ('PRIVATE – KEEP OUT'). The reason is that it falls within the precincts of Oxford Prison. Of the old Castle, a shell keep built on the mound in about 1071, nothing remains. Continue past the cute neo-medieval battlements of County Hall (1841). At the top of the rise go through Bonn Square, noted rendezvous of derelicts, to Queen Street and Carfax.

Carfax Tower

The tower is a landmark too often ignored. In substance it is all that remains of St Martin's Church, demolished in 1820 after it had become unsafe. A large rectangular nave and aisles were added in 1822 but these were pulled down in 1896 to ease the circulation of traffic. A stair turret and buttresses had already been added to the tower to help it stand alone. Above the entrance, the figures of two quarterboys strike bells on the quarter-hour.

The tower is an excellent place to see Oxford from on high. The 99 tightly winding steps may be taken in stages, with a rest at the pictureboard display on the first-floor landing. From the battlements the best view is eastward along the High Street. The nearest prominent spires are those of All Saints Church, since 1975 the library of Lincoln College, and behind it the University Church of St Mary's, where in 1555-6 Archbishop Cranmer and Bishops Latimer and Ridley were tried. To their left is the great dome of the Radcliffe Camera, part of the Bodleian Library. Along the High Street is the low dome of Queen's College gatehouse set in a pedimented screen, then the street makes a pronounced curve and terminates at the river beneath the tall pinnacled tower of Magdalen College.

To the south, the way we go next, is St Aldate's, formerly Fish Street. On the left are the spirelet on the Town Hall and Tom Tower at Christ Church, and on the right the spire of St Aldate's Church.

The random manner in which colleges pop up all over the town helps to illustrate the nature of Oxford University. Like Cambridge, it consists of a group of autonomous colleges, linked federally to the governing body of the University which organises the curricula of the various schools, runs examinations and awards degrees.

Covered Market

Unlike Cambridge, Oxford is an industrial city with a large centre which the University shares with the town. Ever since students first settled here in the eleventh and twelfth centuries the relationship between Town and Gown has oscillated between tolerant and abrasive. Although no serious dust-up has occurred in recent years to match the two-day riots of 1354, when several students were killed, there is always an inclination to think of Town *versus* Gown rather than Town *and* Gown.

One of the most agreeable places where the two meet on good terms is the Covered Market. Browse in the sawdust alleys past straw-hatted butchers and fishmongers hacking and chopping, the strings of fresh hares 'in the fur', the mounds of pigeon, pheasant and haggis exhibiting the gamey tastes of college high tables. Famous institutions include Brown's Café, open at eight in the morning and cherished for its British breakfasts; Cardew & Co., tea and coffee merchants; Palm's Delicatessen and such other old dependables as The Little Bookshop (second-hand), bags and luggage at Delcoy's, pet supplies at Levett's, and dinky boutiques for shoes, hats and chunky knitwear.

St Aldate's

Turn downhill towards the promising bulk of Tom Tower. On the corner of Blue Boar Street, past the Town Hall, is the Museum of Oxford. The history and development of the city are traced at a rather primary school level, symbolised by the flat Norman warrior at the door. Across the road the Tourist Information Office runs a book-a-bed service.

Continue past the Christian bookshop and St Aldate's Church. Next is Pembroke Square and Pembroke College, above the lodge in the corner a Gothicised oriel window with pinnacles. Turn back for a grand view of Tom Tower, the main entrance to Christ Church, completed by Wren in 1681-2: two turrets flanking the arch and the great octagonal tower, all crowned with ogee caps. 'Great Tom', the bell in the tower, rings 101 times at 21.05 every day, commemorating each scholar of the original foundation.

The public must enter the college from Broad Walk, so we continue down the road past the Newman-Mowbray bookshop. Facing the entrance to Memorial Gardens is Alice's Shop, the model for the Old Sheep Shop mentioned by Lewis Carroll (C.L. Dodgson) in *Alice's Adventures in Wonderland*. Dodgson taught mathematics at Christ Church and Alice was Alice Liddell, daughter of the Dean.

Turn through Memorial Gardens to Broad Walk. Above the wall to the left rise the pinnacles of Christ Church Cathedral. The path to the right leads to the college boathouses, and in Eights Week towards the end of May it carries thousands of eager spectators, the men in traditional ties and blazers, the ladies in straw hats and summer dresses, a ritual which absorbs all styles and tastes.

Christ Church

Cardinal Wolsey founded Cardinal College here in 1525, four years before his downfall. Wolsey's plans were taken over by King Henry VIII who founded his Christ Church in 1546, creating a cathedral on the site of St Frideswide's monastery (eighth century) and twelfth-century parish church. Christ Church, by the way, is called just that, never Christ Church College. In Oxford, it is often referred to as 'The House'.

From the turnstile, bear left to the timber-vaulted cloister, part of the old monastery, rebuilt from 1499. On the right the Chapter House serves as a bookshop and has a display of college plate in the central showcases. Here too are an Italian processional cross of 1588 and a panel painting of *The Virgin and Christ Enthroned*, two book covers for the Communion Service and Bible (1632) and Book of Common Prayer (1636) bound in crimson velvet with silver-gilt clasps.

Although small, the Cathedral is densely compartmented with four aisle chapels, all rich in decoration and historic detail, and has outstanding stained glass. From the entrance in the cloister, look left to the *Spes, Caritas, Fides* window by Burne-Jones and Morris, portraying the Three Virtues of Faith, Hope and Charity.

To see the pattern of it all, go to the foot of the nave and look past the twelfth-century columns to the choir and altar. The choir vault by William Orchard (1503) is particularly fine. Working anti-clockwise, the south transept is hung with the Garter Banner of the late Prince Paul of Yugoslavia, a former student, and leads to the Chapel of St Lucy. Here the beautiful east window of 1320 portrays the Martyrdom of Thomas Becket. Nearby are monuments to Cavaliers who died during the Civil War, when for a time Oxford was the capital of Charles I, Christ Church was the seat of his government and the King lived in the Deanery.

The Military Chapel, also known as the Regimental Chapel Royal, has a window with angels by Burne-Jones and Morris. On the north side of the choir is the Lady Chapel with the Shrine to St Frideswide, patron saint of Oxford, and the spectacular tomb-chests of Elizabeth de Montacute (d.1354), Prior Alexander de Sutton (d.1316) and John de Nowers (d.1386). Here is another window by Burne-Jones and Morris, and in the Latin Chapel to the north is a Burne-Jones window depicting scenes from the life of St Frideswide. The north windows contain fourteenth-century glass. Return through the north transept to the nave. In the west window of the north aisle is the Jonah Window by Abraham van Linge (1630s), depicting Jonah in the shadow of the miraculous gourd looking towards the city of Nineveh.

Leave the Cathedral by the west door and look out over Tom Quad, the largest in Oxford, at its centre the Mercury fountain into which Anthony Blanche was manhandled to his evident pleasure in Evelyn Waugh's *Brideshead Revisited*.

The Hall, part of Cardinal Wolsey's foundation, was completed in 1529. In 1644 Charles I opened his Parliament in this room, and Charles II's Oxford Parliament met here in 1681. The broad staircase leading up to it is dominated by the central pier and colossal fan vault which grows out from it in circles of trefoil petals. The long room is panelled to the base of the heraldic glass bearing the names of Deans and distinguished members of the college, with coats of arms and portrait medallions. The hammerbeam roof is richly decorated with devices paying tribute to Cardinal Wolsey. The portraits, all around, are an astonishing gallery of English high office. Inside the door on the right is C.L. Dodgson (Lewis Carroll), then to the left appear the likenesses of bishops, prime ministers, philosophers and men of letters, among them William Penn, John Wesley, W.H. Auden, Lord Amherst and George Canning. Above high table are the founders Wolsey and Henry VIII, and Elizabeth I who arranged studentships for pupils of Westminster School. On the long north wall are Anthony Eden, W.E. Gladstone and John Locke.

Christ Church, as you will have gathered, is an exceptional college, both in grandeur and achievement. It also possesses an eminent Picture

Gallery, reached through the Palladian Peckwater Quad flanked by the great eighteenth-century Library. Housed in Canterbury Quad (1783), the Picture Gallery opened in 1968. A numbered list of the paintings is available at the entrance, overlooked by a School of Holbein portrait of *Henry VIII* (*c.*1545). More than a hundred works from the much larger total collection are assembled in the Primitives Room (early Italian from 1250 to 1500), then the Great Room (Italian, Dutch and German masters, 1500 to *c.*1625), and up steps to the South Room (mostly Italian, seventeenth and eighteenth centuries). Space forbids any detailed description here, though you are likely to find works by Filippino Lippi, Lorenzo Lotto, Tintoretto, Annibale Carracci, Van Dyck, Frans Hals, Domenichino, and works from the Schools and Studios of many Italian masters.

Lunch Break

If it is lunchtime, or lunch seems a good idea while Christ Church Picture Gallery is itself closed for lunch, the nearby options are mainly pubs. Go a short way along Bear Lane to find the Bear (ancient and crowded, with a collection of some five thousand ties on the walls) and the Blue Boar (bar snacks and an upstairs restaurant).

Merton College

The next colleges we see are more typical in scale. We pass between Oriel (founded in 1326 by Edward II) and Corpus Christi (founded in 1517 by Bishop Fox of Winchester) and enter Merton Street, remarkably quiet, the dwindling cobbled way between the stone façades summoning a previous horse-drawn age.

Merton is one of the oldest colleges, founded in 1264 by Walter de Merton, Chancellor of England, and the first to house its students in a collegiate setting. It retains its modest medieval character. Above the gateway (1418) are canopied statues of Henry III and Walter de Merton and a carved panel of John the Baptist with forest animals, including a unicorn.

Bear right through the passage at the side of the Hall and turn right to Mob Quad, the earliest quadrangle in Oxford, completed in the thirteenth century. Here is the famous L-shaped Library, which may be visited on application to the Verger, containing a chained book, ancient manuscripts and an astrolabe said to have been used by William Chaucer.

Continue to the Chapel through a vaulted passage, a marvellous dark and mysterious corner of Oxford. The Chapel is in reality the choir and transepts of a bigger church with a nave and aisles that was never built. The resulting layout gave the model for other college chapels – an ante-chapel formed by the transepts and crossing, leading to the choir and high altar. The choir was begun before 1290 and the east window has fine stained glass with the arms of Edward I, de Merton and others. The altar painting is a *Crucifixion* after Tintoretto.

Returning through Front Quad, look in at the opening on the other side of the Hall which leads to Fellows Quad. In the vault of the gateway are bosses carved with the signs of the Zodiac.

Continue along Merton Street past the entrance to the Real Tennis Court (some of the mysteries of this old racquet game are explained in *Walk 20*), and turn through the dog-leg towards the High Street. On the left is an open quadrangle of the Examination Schools (1882), where students of the University sit their intermediate and final exams: a sombre and terrifying place, to which in their worst nightmares some guilty former students must indefinitely return, bidden by strange inner forces to go back to this dread building and do it all over again.

At the Eastgate Hotel the Gate Bar is an all-day lounge, carpeted and panelled, serving teas, drinks and snacks – useful for getting out of the rain or just for resting weary feet.

Botanic Garden

Going east along 'the High', as they call it here, the famous tower of Magdalen College moves into view at the bend. On May Morning at dawn choristers of the college sing a hymn from the top of the tower, watched by a great throng of dinner-jacketed and party-frocked revellers and the scarcely less bleary-eyed who got up specially for the ceremony.

Turn in through the rusticated gateway of the Botanic Garden, founded in 1621 by the Earl of Derby. The first 'physic garden' in England, its beds and greenhouses contain some 8,000 species from almost every botanical family. Perhaps stroll through the original walled enclosure to the end and turn left by the River Cherwell; across the water is Magdalen School cricket field with a delightful small pavilion. Pass through the wall to the greenhouses. In a magazine article the critic and broadcaster Marghanita Laski recalled coming to the Tropical House as a student to do her reading: 'for it was the only really warm place in the university'. In the first house on the right there is lush warmth indeed, and hot colours: the beautiful pink-mauve flower of the sweet potato, an oil palm, the tangerine-like fruits of *Piper cubeba*, the multiple trunklets of *Pandanus nobilis*. In spring, in the greenhouse by the main building, there are marvellous odours from the collections of daffodils and hyacinth, and, high up, the promise of summer in the yellow flowers of *Acacia gladiiformis*.

Magdalen College

From the lodge, bear right to the Muniments Tower and find the Chapel on the right, before Cloister Quad. The college, whose name is pronounced 'Maudlen', was founded in 1458 by William of Waynflete, Bishop of Winchester. The Chapel follows the Merton plan of ante-chapel and choir, and has interesting glass and furniture in the ante-chapel: the original fifteenth-century stalls with carved misericords and, directly ahead from the entrance, the sepia window by Richard Greenbury (1632). In the choir, the brass eagle of the lectern dates from 1633 and the altar picture, *The Bearing of the Cross* by Francisco Ribalta, is seventeenth-century School of Seville. The impressive screen and reredos are part of L. Cottingham's extensive restorations carried out in 1829-34.

Continue through to atmospheric Cloister Quad where tall grotesque figures of animals and humans decorate the buttresses; they are known as hieroglyphs and were carved in 1509. On the north side of Cloister Quad, break suddenly into an eighteenth-century deer park. The transformation from busy town to apparently remote and spacious countryside is astonishing, one of the most seductive in Oxford. Ahead stands not a Cotswold mansion but New Building (1733), an arcaded Georgian range of twenty-seven bays with a central pediment. To the left, in The Grove, safe behind an iron fence, deer peacefully graze as they have done since 1700. To the right is a pleasant walk beside Holywell Mill Stream, the trees by the water bulging with rooks' nests.

High Street and Queen's Lane

As you walk back up the High Street, one of the best views in the city opens up. In the centre, Queen Caroline's statue stands beneath the domed entrance to Queen's College; beyond the college's elegant Classical screen rises the great dome of the Radcliffe Camera. To the left is a variety of attractive houses in natural stone and coloured façades in white, pink and pale green.

Continue along the High, passing the heavy front of the Examination Schools, decked out on balustrade and gable with enough shields and twirly bits for a Belgian town hall. By the corner of Queen's Lane the view forward has changed. Queen's College is now in the foreground, across the road is University College ('Univ', very old, its antecedents on the site linked, so it has been claimed, with Alfred the Great), and in the distance is the great octagonal spire of St Mary's.

Turn into Queen's Lane, passing St Edmund Hall ('Teddy Hall'), the last surviving medieval hall among the Oxford colleges. The Front Quad is very pretty, with a central well down which after dark undergraduates do unspeakable things. Further along Queen's Lane is the Church of St Peter's-in-the-East, made redundant in 1968 and converted into the hall's Library.

Around the corner in the shady lane bicycles whir along. If gowns are being worn, the long ones are for scholars and exhibitioners, the short ones for commoners.

New College

The oak doors at the entrance to this grand and inspiring college are still the originals of 1386. In niches at the second storey are statues of the Virgin flanked by Gabriel (left) and William of Wykeham, who founded this college in 1379 and Winchester College three years later, where boys were prepared for New College. The two still maintain their close relationship.

Along the north side of Front Quad, to the left, are the Hall and Chapel. From the lodge turn left and left through a passage to the timber-vaulted cloister; beyond it stands the bell-tower. Both date from 1400. Return to the passage and enter the ante-chapel. If there was time to see only one college chapel, this would be my choice – though omitting Christ Church Cathedral would be difficult. In the ante-chapel is Epstein's challenging swathed figure of *Lazarus* (1951). The stained glass is stunning, by which I mean the late fourteenth-century work, in which mysterious abstract patterns surround the central figure in each window. The great west window is much later: designed by Sir Joshua Reynolds and carried out by Thomas Jarvis in 1778-85, it depicts the *Nativity* and the *Seven Virtues* in a rather splashy, water-colourist manner.

Through the great screen, restored in 1877-81 by Sir George Gilbert Scott, the choir and altar are dominated by another successful restoration, the massive reredos, particularly striking when floodlit for an evening concert. Up the altar steps and on the left in a long narrow case is the Founder's Crozier, and nearby is a painting of *St James* by El Greco.

The tradition of music is strong in Oxford. All the college chapels we have seen on this walk stage a number of concerts through the year and New College Chapel is a particularly splendid setting, though *freezing* cold in winter.

Return to Front Quad and walk ahead to Garden Quad. Beyond the wrought-iron screen is the Garden, framed by one of the few sizeable pieces of the old city wall to survive and in the centre the charming mound created in 1623. If, on the way back to Front Quad, you go in at the last door on the left and walk through, you will shortly come to the Long Room adjoining Queen's Lane. This was the college's medieval lavatory. The upper floor has been converted into a gallery for concerts and exhibitions.

Hertford Bridge

Wind through the rest of what was Queen's Lane and has now become New College Lane. On the right at No. 7 is the house of Edmund Halley, Savilian Professor of Geometry from 1703 to 1742. He published the first meteorological chart, and in 1705 predicted the return in 1758 of the comet which is named in his honour.

Ahead is the famous Bridge of Sighs, joining the North Quad of Hertford College to the South Quad on the left-hand side of the lane. Although one of the most famous sights in Oxford, it is a relatively recent design for which Sir Thomas Jackson was responsible; it was completed in 1914.

Our first Oxford walk is done. The second, 'Oxford B', continues from this spot with an exploration of some parts of the Bodleian Library, across the road. Tea-time refreshments are to be had at two nearby establishments: The Wykeham in Holywell (right at the traffic lights) has home-made cakes and cream teas and Convocation House (next to Queen Mary's Church on the far side of Radcliffe Square) has cream teas and self-service. For drinks, the King's Arms (across the road from the traffic lights) is one of the most acceptable pubs in Oxford with small, dingily Dickensian bars beyond the main room. Alternatively, just next to Hertford Bridge is a narrow alley, St Helen's Passage, which leads to The Turf, an old and pretty pub which sells tea in summer and cool drinks all year.

Walk 29

Oxford 'B': Bodleian Library and Museums

Visit the Sheldonian Theatre and Bodleian Library. See the dodo in the University Museum, the Canterbury Quad and gardens of St John's College, and the art treasures of the Ashmolean Museum.

Allow 5 hours.

Best times Not Sunday, Ashmolean Museum closed Monday. Bodleian Library closes 12.30 on Saturday. Ideal start-time for walk: about 10.30, Monday to Saturday.

ROUTE

Getting there See Oxford 'A'. This walk continues from finishing point of Walk 'A'.

Begin at Bridge of Sighs, Catte Street. Cross road, go up steps and ahead to **Sheldonian Theatre** ☞; open 10.00 to 12.45, 14.00 to 16.45, November to February closes 15.45, cupola closes 15 minutes earlier. *Admission* (modest).

After visit to theatre and cupola, bear right into Old Schools Quadrangle of **Bodleian Library**. Entrance to library on right, behind statue of Earl of Pembroke ☞; open 09.00 to 17.00, Saturday 09.00 to 12.30. Visit Divinity School. Guided tours of Divinity School, Convocation House and Duke Humfrey's Library, March to end October, Monday to Friday 10.30, 11.30, 14.00, 15.00, Saturday 10.30, 11.30, November to end February, Wednesday 14.30, Saturday 11.00. *Admission* (*guided tours*).

Leave Old Schools Quadrangle by S arch to Radcliffe Square. Bear right to Brasenose Lane and follow to Turl Street, then turn right to Broad Street. Turn right and walk along past Blackwell's bookshop. Turn left into Parks Road and continue to **University Museum** (opposite Museum Road) ☞; open 12.00 to 17.00. Also visit adjoining **Pitt-Rivers Museum** ☞; open 13.00 to 16.30.

At exit, walk ahead and cross into Museum Road, then through Lamb & Flag Passage to St Giles. Turn left beside walls of **St John's College** and walk to lodge ☞; open 13.00 to 17.00.

After visit to Canterbury Quad and gardens, cross St Giles and turn right and left into Pusey Street. Follow to St John Street. Turn left to Beaumont Street. Optional visit to **Cast Gallery** of Ashmolean Museum in Pusey Lane, off St John Street; open 10.00 to 16.00, Saturday 10.00 to 13.00, closed Sunday, Monday.

At Beaumont Street, turn left to **Ashmolean Museum** ☞; open 10.00 to 16.00, Sunday 14.00 to 16.00, Bank Holiday Monday 14.00 to 17.00. Closed Sunday, Monday, Easter, St Giles Fair in September.

At exit, turn left to St Giles and cross to **Martyrs' Memorial**. Continue to right beside Balliol College. At Broad Street, turn left. A cross in road opposite The Children's Bookshop marks spot where Protestant martyrs burnt for their faith; see also tablet on Balliol wall.

Walk ends here. Nearest refreshments (tea) at Chit Chat, above Boswells, or at Convocation House or The Wykeham (see *Walk 'A'*). To return to bus station, walk down George Street to Gloucester

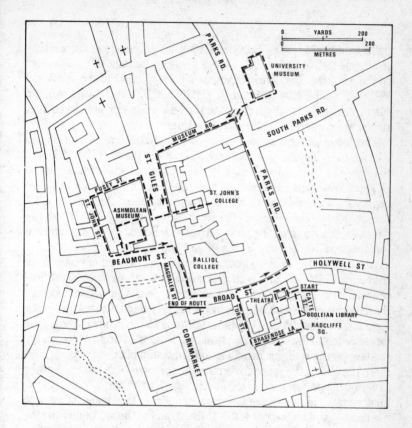

Green Bus Station; for railway station, keep on past bus station and follow Hythe Bridge Street to Park End Street. Buses to railway station stop in High Street and Cornmarket: Nos 40, 41, 42, 43, 52.

Sheldonian Theatre

Across Catte Street stand the buildings of a great institution of learning: the Bodleian Library. First, visit the theatre designed by Wren and built in 1664-7 to house university ceremonies such as matriculation and the awarding of degrees. It is named in honour of Gilbert Sheldon, Archbishop of Canterbury, who funded the building.

Walk through the courtyard between the Clarendon Building, on the right, built in 1711-15 by Hawksmoor for the University Press and now an administrative building, and the Schools Quadrangle of the Bodleian on the left. The Sheldonian faces the Divinity School to the south and we enter by the east door ahead. On its north or right-hand side the semi-circle of the building is repeated in the line of piers on Broad Street surmounted by the heads of Roman emperors.

The focus of the galleried hall is the finely carved, red-cushioned Chancellor's Throne. For an impression of the theatre when full, see the prints by the far door depicting, for example, the installation of the Duke of Wellington as Chancellor in 1834. Try out a backless bench nearby for an idea of how alarmingly uncomfortable the theatre is for concertgoers. The ceiling is the work of Robert Streeter and shows Truth descending on Religion, Arts and Science and casting out Ignorance who falls away by the organ.

At the far door – having bought a plan of the panorama visible from the cupola – turn left and go up a spiralling wooden staircase to the low-beamed attic floor from which the theatre ceiling is suspended. Before the Clarendon Building became available, this room was a paper store for the University Press. Continue upwards to the inside of the cupola for excellent views over the heart of Oxford. Cardinal points are marked on the wall, for matching to the printed plan.

To the east is the route covered in the previous walk, the bell tower of New College rising over Hertford Bridge. To the north, look over the unattractive New Bodleian Library with its recessed upper storeys to the red and yellow brick of Keble College, and to the left of this line the quadrangles and gardens of Trinity and Balliol Colleges fronting on Broad Street ('the Broad'). To the west is the Victorian chapel of Exeter College, its spire modelled on Sainte Chapelle, Paris, from which pan slightly left to Carfax Tower, the spire of All Saints (Lincoln College Library) behind which, a little masked, is Tom Tower at Christ Church. Finally, and best of all, to the south and south-east is a glorious close-up view over the pinnacles of the Bodleian Library and the dome and balustrade of the Radcliffe Camera.

Bodleian Library

To see all of the Bodleian would take a very long time and require taking a job there. Next best is a reader's ticket, though that does not grant entry to some inner rooms and the underground workings where many of the library's 5,450,000 volumes are stored and sent up to the reading rooms on request, a journey for which readers must allow two hours.

In Old Schools Quadrangle, completed in 1619, some of the historic and present functions of the buildings are revealed. On the ground and first floors were the Schools, each labelled above the doorway: Schola Naturalis Philosophiae, Schola Musicae, and so on. Above, on the second floor, were the library rooms of Sir Thomas Bodley's library which first opened nearby in 1602. The Schools remained here until the new Examination Schools in the High Street were ready in 1882, and then the rest of the quadrangle was released to the library.

Principal feature of Old Schools Quadrangle is the great Jacobean Tower of Five Orders. Beneath the canopy on the fourth storey sits James I; on the left stands Fame and on the right the kneeling figure of the University. Facing this grand entrance is the Proscholium, the vestibule to the library, completed a little earlier than the rest of the quadrangle, in 1612. In front of the Proscholium is a statue of William Herbert, Third Earl of Pembroke and Chancellor of the University in 1617-30. The sculptor is thought to be Le Sueur.

Everyone may go into the Proscholium, where a notice gives details of the Bodleian's current appeal for funds to make a single automated catalogue, help with purchases, improve conservation, maintain the buildings and safeguard staff posts. Ponder this when hovering in the bookshop nearby, which has a fascinating assortment of cards, pamphlets and books. There is even a Bodleian umbrella, though the yellow, sludge and white teapot, shaped like the Radcliffe Camera, rather strains the sympathies.

From March to the end of October guided tours take place through the day to the Divinity School, Convocation House and Duke Humfrey's Library, and at other times on a more restricted basis. See Route for details; for further information telephone 0865 277165.

No guide is needed for the Divinity School which lies directly ahead. This is the oldest part of the library. Theology was first among subjects taught and examined at Oxford in the Middle Ages, and the Divinity School was the first school. Building began in 1426 and was completed in 1488. The magnificent vault by William Orchard was the last part of the work, added after the upper floor was built and roofed. Among the objects on view is Drake's chair, made from the timbers of Sir Francis

Drake's ship when it was broken up and presented to the library in 1662.

Beyond the Divinity School is Convocation House (1634-6), built parallel with the Proscholium to form a block in the shape of the letter H. In the upper storey is Duke Humfrey's Library, housing the benefaction of books made by Humfrey, Duke of Gloucester, in 1439-44. The two ends of the H are known as Arts End (1610-12), above the Proscholium, and Selden End (1634-6) above Convocation House. It is a marvellously atmospheric place, the bookcases and shelves almost four hundred years old, the ceiling painted with coats of arms bearing the University motto: *Dominus Illuminatio Mea* (The Lord Be My Light).

In Old Schools Quadrangle is the entrance to the Exhibition Room. Items on show are rotated and special exhibitions mounted. Among the treasures that you may find beneath the cloths protecting the showcases are the *Oxford Chanson de Roland* (second quarter, twelfth century), the earliest English gold-tooled binding (*c.*1519), the *Ashmole Bestiary* (early thirteenth century) and the illuminated *Romance of Alexander* (1338-44).

Leave the quadrangle by the south arch and follow the vaulted passage to Radcliffe Square, at its centre the Radcliffe Camera, the world's first round reading room, designed by James Gibbs after Hawksmoor's original concept of a rotunda and completed in 1749. Although it began as an independent library it was taken over by the Bodleian in 1860.

The square is one of the most perfect anywhere, gloriously varied and united in the greys and pale yellows of the stone. By the entrance to Brasenose Lane enjoy the long sweep of Brasenose College ('BNC', 1509), the nave of St Mary's Church – next to which the first university library was founded in about 1320, the paired Corinthian columns of the Camera and its ribbed dome, the turrets of All Souls' College on the far side – founded in 1438 and admitting no undergraduates, only elected Fellows – and back again to the Bodleian.

Follow shady Brasenose Lane to Turl Street, beside the walls of Exeter College (1314) on the right and first Brasenose then Lincoln College (1427) on the left. The artists and designers William Morris and Sir Edward Burne-Jones were undergraduates together at Exeter, and from their friendship grew many influential projects. On the far side of 'the Turl' is Jesus College (1571), where undergraduates included Beau

Nash and Lawrence of Arabia.

In Broad Street the nearest refreshments are at the White Horse pub, a narrow room sandwiched between Blackwell's Travel Bookshop and its main store (including the underground Norrington Room). Television's Inspector Morse has taken several jars here in the course of his filming duties. An alternative is the King's Arms, mentioned in the previous walk, which has more extensive facilities for coffee drinking and buffet lunching.

From the doorway of the King's Arms, or thereabouts, turn along Parks Road towards the Science area and the University Museum. On the right is Wadham College (1612), founded on the site of an old Augustinian friary. Sir Christopher Wren was a 'gentleman commoner' of the college. On the left is a fine pillared gateway offering views into Trinity College gardens.

University Museum

At the beginning of the Science Area, look to the right down South Parks Road to the modern rotunda and portico of Rhodes House (1929). This is the home of the Rhodes Scholars, set up by the gift of Cecil Rhodes to provide a base each year for about seventy overseas scholars, many from the United States and other usually English-speaking nations.

Opposite Museum Street, turn right around the lawn facing the University Museum. If you have already enjoyed the Natural History Museum in London (*Walk 18*) this lofty galleried hall will strike a familiar chord – the central iron arches in colossal sympathy with the ribs of the prehistoric skeletons arrayed beneath. The presiding figure is the cast of the semi-upright Iguanodon, a giant herbivorous dinosaur.

The museum, completed in 1860, looks after the University's Scientific Collections and is active in both teaching and research. Sections are devoted to the fields of Zoology, Entomology, Geology and Mineralogy. An interesting feature of the arcades is that each polished stone column is made from a different British rock. Around the hall, properly called Museum Court, are statues of famous scientists such as Roger Bacon, who taught in Oxford, and world figures ancient and modern: Aristotle, Hippocrates, Newton, Hunter, Darwin and Linnaeus.

My peculiar favourite is the Oxford Dodo. This flightless innocent from the island of Mauritius was probably imported into Europe in 1638 – just in time, for the dodo went extinct in about 1680. The present specimen, by then stuffed, was bequeathed to Elias Ashmole, founder of the Ashmolean Museum. In 1775, too damaged to keep, it was destroyed. Praise be, the head and left foot were saved. And here they are, in the showcase under John Savery's painting (c.1650) of the beaky, thick-footed animal whose inadequate little tufty wings guaranteed its early retirement from the planet.

Pitt-Rivers Museum

These remarkable ethnographic collections are founded on the gift of General Pitt-Rivers, an army officer turned archaeologist who left them to the University. The museum dates from 1884 and lies through a door at the end of Museum Court. An amazing jumble of objects, grouped in types and gathered from all over the world: masks, statues, outrigger canoes suspended under the gallery, figurines, firearms, ship models, pottery heads, basketry, divining bones, and very much more. The displays of musical instruments, formerly here, have been transferred to the Balfour Building, 60 Banbury Road.

'Yes,' an attendant was saying to new visitors as I left, 'there's most things in here. Witches in bottles, charms against the evil eye, magic dolls . . . ' And launched on a quite separate list of his own.

St Giles and St John's College

Facing the ornate but now dingy Victorian brick of Keble College (1870), walk ahead through Museum Street and the pedestrianised way leading to the cobbles of Lamb & Flag Passage, next to the pub. Turn left into the grand boulevard of St Giles, linking the red-brick mansions of North Oxford to the city centre, and continue beside the walls of St John's College, founded in 1555 by Sir Thomas White, Merchant Taylor, on the site of the suppressed Cistercian College of St Bernard.

Much has changed at my former college. Late at night, or at any other time, you can no longer scale this front wall, then propel yourself sideways, hand-over-hand, along a ledge and swing up on to the Buttery roof. You can no longer do this because the grille on the window nearest the ledge, an essential element in this line of assault, has been removed. But then undergraduates no longer need to climb in anyway. They now have late-gate keys and may come and go as they please. It is up to them. Another great change is that between one-third and half the undergraduates are women, and this too, it is generally accepted, has been a civilising move.

In the lodge, in the week of Torpids – the spring or Hilary Term inter-college boat races – a chalked report on a blackboard had this to say:

'MEN'S 1ST OVERBUMP ON TRINITY. WOMEN'S 2NDS
IN BATTLESHIP MAUREEN BUMPED FOR THE 5TH
TIME MAGDALEN II (SO DID EVERYONE ELSE).
GAUDEAMUS!'

Ahead in the Front Quad, much of it dating from the original founda-tion, is the President's Lodgings. To the left are the Hall and Chapel, both much altered. In the gate tower is a statue of St John by Eric Gill. Go ahead round the grass – never across – and through a fan-vaulted arch to the college's greatest architectural treasure, the Canterbury Quad (1631-6). This is primarily the achievement of William Laud, President of the College between 1611 and 1621 who became Arch-bishop of Canterbury in 1633. The scheme he funded was to in-corporate the Old Library (1596-1601), occupying the south range to the right. There are two elegant arcades, one at each end, and in the central niches are statues by Le Sueur of Charles I and Queen Henrietta Maria. In the plain side ranges the gargoyles and painted drainpipes are almost the only form of decoration. I lived for two years in an attic room off Staircase 3 and look back on the experience as one of enormous pri-vilege, though then I was more concerned, I seem to remember, by the monastic plumbing arrangements which, to find a lavatory, demanded a walk down two flights of stairs, along two sides of the quad and a de-scent into the diagonally opposite basement. Since then, I am happy to say, great feats of sanitary engineering have much improved the student's lot.

Through to the garden, originally laid out by Capability Brown and thought by many to be the finest in Oxford. Ahead is the vast sweep of the main lawn, to the left the rockery and what we called the umbrella tree. Over the rockery wall the blocks of the Thomas White Building, so admirable when it opened in 1975, are streaked and faded; a pity. It is so quiet here, only birdsong intervenes. Just yards from the four-lane traffic of St Giles, you can even hear the sound when a metal label on a tree is caught by a faint breeze and softly taps the branch holding it.

St John Street and Cast Gallery

Cross St Giles and turn right at Blackfriars, the Dominican Priory of the Holy Spirit. In Pusey Street walk beside the low stone block of Regent's Park College, which moved here from Regent's Park in London. St John Street is much better, a splendidly unified street of plain-fronted Georgian houses in honey-coloured stone, when cleaned, with one or two still soot-blackened. Iron cellar gratings are let into the uneven pavement and old 'question-mark' lampposts stand at the roadside, none quite vertical. The charm of the street is augmented by a residents-only parking scheme which on some days leaves it almost completely shorn of vehicles.

At the next left you can take a diversion to the Cast Gallery of the Ashmolean Museum. This stands beyond the gates in Pusey Lane, the entrance up the ramp and to the left. The gallery has some three hundred plaster casts of original statues and reliefs from the Greek and Roman periods. From the fifth century BC are the first accomplished studies of the human figure in the round and sculpture from the Temple of Zeus at Olympia. In the lower gallery are casts from the Parthenon in Athens and Hellenistic works such as the *Winged Victory of Samothrace* (from the Louvre, Paris) and the *Laocoon* (Vatican, Rome). The casts were assembled for the benefit of art historians and art students, some of whom may well be at work behind their easels.

Continue to Beaumont Street, laid out in 1828, as was St John Street. Its finely preserved terraces of three-storey houses, some with discreet pedimented porches and canopied balconies, are much occupied by dentists, accountants and estate agents. At the western end is Worcester College (1714) which has a fine Main Quad with sunken lawn, and a large garden with a swan lake and playing fields beyond.

In the other direction is The Playhouse (1938), once again at the time of writing in the throes of recovery; may this one last. Then comes the Scottish Baronial of the Randolph Hotel (1864), probably the most comfortable in Oxford.

Ashmolean Museum

It began as John Tradescant's 'closet of rarities' and under the guidance of Elias Ashmole the collection was housed in specially built galleries which opened in Broad Street in 1683 – the first public museum in Britain. The present Neo-Classical buildings date from 1845. The Ashmolean contains the University's collections of antiquities, British and European paintings, Oriental art, ceramics, silver and glass and European stringed instruments. It and the Fitzwilliam in Cambridge (*Walk 31*) are like-minded foundations.

At the entrance collect a plan. Ahead are rooms full of Chinese ceramics (52 to 56): marvellously expressive earthenware horses, camels and bullocks with a cart (tomb models, T'ang dynasty, AD 618-905). At the end is a large buddha in carved figwood from North China, *c.*AD 1300.

From here, if you have come this far, routes may vary – and time is always limited somehow. Many will want to see the Alfred Jewel in the Medieval Room (4). It is the most precious surviving example of late Saxon craftsmanship, a thing of wonder to look at: a tiny tear-shaped portrait of an unknown figure. Around the gold frame is an inscription in West Saxon meaning 'Alfred ordered me to be made', hence the association with Alfred the Great who reigned from 871 to 901. The jewel was found in 1693 near a monastery at Athelney in Somerset which was established by Alfred, and it arrived at the Ashmolean in 1718.

The Department of Western Art Galleries is upstairs. In the first room ahead (Fox-Strangeways Gallery, 23) is a fine collection of small paintings and sketches by Rubens. In the Mallet Gallery beyond (22) are large tapestries, and in the showcases drawings by Raphael and Michelangelo. Continue left to Italian paintings in the Fortnum Gallery (21), including works by or attributed to Michelangelo, Giorgione and Joachim de Patenir; Tintoretto's large *Resurrection of Christ*; an exquisite small *St Jerome in the Desert*, possibly by Giovanni Bellini, and a *Virgin and Child* that *is* by him; Piero di Cosimo's *A Forest Fire*; the much reproduced *Portrait of a Young Man* attributed to Domenico Ghirlandaio; Fra Lippo Lippi's *Meeting of SS Joachim and Anna*; a small triptych from the studio of Fra Angelico, *The Virgin and Child Adored by St Dominic with SS Peter and Paul*; a wonderfully intimate *Virgin and Child* by Giovanni di Paolo. Then, on the far wall, is the Uccello: the scampering red figures of *A Hunt in a Forest*, the drama narrowing to a peak in the lean greyhound-like dogs and fragile bounding deer, all beneath the darkest of green forest canopies and a sky of midnight blue.

Next in the Founders Room (20) is a portrait of Elias Ashmole, who took over the collections of the two John Tradescants, father and son, royal gardeners both. Here also is a minutely detailed battle painting of the *Siege and Battle of Pavia 1524-5*, showing the capture of François I, King of France, and much else too: the walls and towers of the embattled city, the tents of the armies, squadrons of heavy armoured cavalry and hedges of pikemen piling in from all angles, the more eminent warriors labelled with explanatory cartouches.

The galleries have a haphazard relationship: coins and medals next to paintings next to musical instruments. To follow the paintings trail, retrace to Fox-Strangeways (23) and go through Weldon (seventeenth-century European, 25) and the Landscape Room (26) to find the Hindley Smith Gallery (27) of nineteenth-century French and some early twentieth-century English artists, including Sickert, Daumier, Courbet, Fantin-Latour, Renoir's lovely *Still Life with Porcelain Figures*, and works by Camille Pissarro; Toulouse-Lautrec's *La Toilette*, a Cézanne of *Auvers-sur-Oise*, a quiet Van Gogh, *Restaurant de la Sirène, Asnières*, Picasso's *Blue Roofs* and Marie Laurençin's fine portrait, *The Artist's Mother*.

Upstairs from the Mallet Gallery (22) are Chambers Hall Room (71), with Tiepolo's *Portrait of a Lady Holding a Macaw* and other works by Watteau, Gainsborough, Reynolds and Zoffany. Then the Combe Gallery (72) summons another roll-call of names: Bonington, Samuel Palmer in his mystical Shoreham period, Millais' famous *Return of the Dove to the Ark*, Martineau's tragic *Christmas Pudding*, Holman Hunt, Burne-Jones, Rossetti. Draw back blue velvet curtains to see watercolours by Turner and Burne-Jones; and pause to see the cabinet which the latter so magnificently painted.

The Martyrs and their Memorial

From the exit turn left through the arch of the Ashmolean's neighbour, the Taylorian Institution for Modern Languages. In St Giles cross to face the tapering Martyrs Memorial, designed by Sir George Gilbert Scott in the Gothic style and erected *c*.1843. Continue along the narrow road flanked by Balliol College and one of the city's larger cycle parks, this next to the Church of St Mary Magdalen. Arrive in Broad Street opposite Dillon's attractive bookshop. To its left are the 'animatronics' of The Oxford Story, a kind of powered waxworks.

In the middle of the road opposite The Children's Bookshop, a cross marks the spot where the Protestant martyrs Hugh Latimer, Bishop of Worcester, and Nicholas Ridley, Bishop of London, were burned at the stake in October 1555. Thomas Cranmer, Archbishop of Canterbury, who had been forced to watch the martyrdom of Latimer and Ridley, was taken out in March 1556 and similarly put to death. A tablet on the Balliol wall records this, though not that Cranmer with enormous willpower held out to the flame his 'offending' hand, with which he had earlier signed his false recantation, until it was consumed. His death came soon after.

Our second Oxford walk is done. For teatime suggestions, see Route, and instructions for returning to bus or railway station. Even more points are to be won by staying overnight in Oxford and progressing on the morrow to Stratford-upon-Avon (see *Walk 30*)

Walk 30

Stratford-upon-Avon

A town trail at the birthplace of William Shakespeare, visiting four houses associated with the poet and his family, the riverside theatres and the church where he is buried.

Allow   All day.

Best times   Any day, except 1 January, Good Friday, 24-26 December. Some houses closed Sunday morning (see panel overleaf).

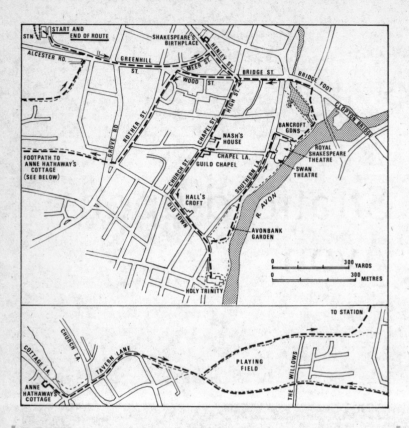

ROUTE
Getting there
By train from London Take train from Paddington Station to Leamington Spa (on Birmingham line). Change to local train to Stratford-upon-Avon. Check times in advance (071-387 7070); journey time approx. 2½ hours.

By coach from London Take coach from Victoria Coach Station. Check times in advance (071-730 0202); journey time approx. 3¼ hours.

By train from Oxford Take train from Oxford to Leamington Spa and change to local train (as from London, above). Check times in advance (0865 722333). Journey time approx. 1½ hours.

By coach from Oxford Take coach from Gloucester Green Bus Station.

Check times in advance (0865 791579); journey time approx. 1½ hours.

Begin at Stratford-upon-Avon Station ⇌ . (Visitors arriving by coach are set down in Bridge Street. Walk up to roundabout, bear right along Henley Street and join main walk at Shakespeare's Birthplace, see below.)

From station exit, bear right past cattle market to join Alcester Road. Follow into Greenhill Street; in row of shops on left, optional visit to Teddy Bear Shop and Museum, open 09.30 to 18.00. *Admission* to Museum.

At American Fountain (pinnacled clock tower), bear left into Meer Street. At junction with Henley Street, **Shakespeare's Birthplace** is beamed cottage opposite, to left. To enter, turn left and walk to Visitor Centre ◉; see panel for Birthplace opening times. *Admission*. Buy combined ticket for all houses a) *without* transport for basic walk, or b) *with* transport to include visit to Mary Arden's House at Wilmcote (5.6km/3 miles) N of Stratford. Follow signs to Birthplace and after visit exit through souvenir shop to Henley Street. Turn left to roundabout and turn right into High Street. Continue past Town Hall into Chapel Street and on left enter **Nash's House/New Place** ◉; see panel for opening times.

Shakespearian Properties Opening Times		1 March-31 October		1 Jan-28/29 Feb 1 Nov-31 Dec	
		Open	Last Entry	Open	Last Entry
Shakespeare's Birthplace	Mon-Sat	09.30	17.30	09.30	16.00
Anne Hathaway's Cottage	Sunday	10.00	17.30	10.30	16.00
Mary Arden's House	Mon-Sat	09.30	17.00	10.00	16.00
Nash's House/ New Place Hall's Croft	Sunday	10.30	17.00	13.30	16.00

Leave Great Garden of New Place via gate to Chapel Lane. Turn right to Guild Chapel and look inside. Turn left along Church Street past Almshouses and left into Old Town. On left visit **Hall's Croft** 👁 ; see panel for opening times.

Continue along Old Town to churchyard of **Holy Trinity Church** 👁 ; open Monday to Saturday 08.30 to 18.00 (summer), 08.30 to 16.00 (winter), Sunday 14.00 to 17.00 and for services. Closed for special services, concerts and rehearsals. *Admission* (modest) to chancel for Shakespeare's tomb.

Exit via churchyard gate and turn right into Avonbank Garden. Walk beside River Avon passing Brass Rubbing Centre; open daily April to October, weekends in March.

Continue to Ferry landing stage and join Southern Lane to **Swan Theatre**. RSC Collection of stage costumes, scenery, etc., open 09.15 to 20.00. *Admission*. Theatre tours sometimes available. Walk round to front of **Royal Shakespeare Theatre** and look in at foyer.

Continue across Bancroft Gardens. Cross bridge next to Canal Basin and see bronze statue of Shakespeare. To right is 14-arched Clopton Bridge. Across road in Bridgefoot is Tourist Information Centre for general information and accommodation service.

Turn left into Bridge Street and continue along Wood Street to American Fountain. Turn left to Rother Street and keep on to gardens on right. Just after gardens, and to right of small triangle in road, take footpath signposted to **Anne Hathaway's Cottage**. Path runs between back gardens of houses to either side, crosses The Willows, an estate road, and continues across playing field. At far side, keep straight on to Tavern Lane. At crossroads with Church Lane, either take Jubilee Footpath across field to Cottage or follow road into Cottage Lane 👁 ; see panel for opening times.

Basic walk ends here. Refreshments in gardens. To return to town, retrace route to Rother Street. To return to station, bear left at entrance to playing field, continue on footpath across The Willows (where take a quick left-right) and keep straight on. At fork with red-brick wall opposite, take left-hand path which emerges on Alcester Road facing cattle market and station.

Royal Leamington Spa

British Rail is periodically criticised for its poor service to Stratford-upon-Avon. It could indeed do better, though I have little sympathy for anyone who would even want to travel to Stratford in the morning, see the town during the day, in the evening take in a play at the Royal Shakespeare Theatre and then expect to get back to London that night. Such frantic tourism is quite against the spirit of *Slow Walks*, and is probably bad for you as well. Far better to go gently to Oxford, spend one or two nights there, and then proceed to Stratford, spending a third night there after the theatre.

At all events you may have an hour or so to kill at Royal Leamington Spa. Rather than mouldering in the station buffet, venture into this placid spa town, a fashionable resort in the early nineteenth century when taking the curative waters was all the rage.

At the station exit, turn left and left through the subway and right at the garage. At Avenue Road, bear left across the road to the Art Gallery. Fifteen minutes should suffice. Among the local pictures and Victorian-Edwardian clutter are a small Jan Brueghel, *Basket of Flowers*; a smallish Malcolm Lowry, *The Mission Room*; and an unpeopled view of *Cookham Rise* by Stanley Spencer.

At exit, turn left to the town centre, crossing the River Leam to the Pump Rooms where the first spa bath was built in 1786. Jephson Gardens, opposite, are named after Dr Henry Jephson, the physician who drew Queen Victoria to visit the town in 1838, thereby securing its royal prefix. Other famous visitors were the Duke of Wellington, Henry Longfellow and Sarah Bernhardt.

Continue along The Parade past the fine houses of Newbold Terrace to the palatial Town Hall (1885) built in pink brick and golden stone. Keep on to Clarendon Avenue (third left after the Town Hall) and turn left to Clarendon Square to find the house at No.4 where Napoleon III lived for a while after the fall of his Empire in the Franco-Prussian War of 1870-1. Return to the station.

The branch line to Stratford travels through Warwick and stops also at the hamlet of Wilmcote. Here you may alight for Mary Arden's House, where Shakespeare's mother lived as a child. However, as trains are once every two hours at best, it may be wiser to continue to Stratford and take a bus out here later. Other attractions at Wilmcote are the museum of farming and country life at Glebe Farm and the Heart of England Falconry.

Into Town

Stratford-upon-Avon is a beautiful, finely preserved market town containing a remarkable number of wattle and daub houses and black and white Tudor buildings made with timber from the Forest of Arden. The main medieval trades were corn, malt and farm animals brought to the cattle market. Stratford is still an important agricultural centre, though the dominant industry surrounds its most famous son, William Shakespeare. From Easter to autumn the town is close to bursting with visitors, open-top buses noisily prowl the sights, and shops, pubs and restaurants with madly Shakespearian names – how about the 'Mistress Quickly Licensed Restaurant' – vie for attention. A degree of patience may be needed to cope with this, and the queueing, jostling and overcrowding at the Shakespearian properties. To avoid the worst excesses, try going out of season. The Bard of Avon industry stops for no man, except on three full and two half-days a year, but going there in, say, February or October should be a lot more comfortable than in the high season.

Shakespeare's Birthplace

Follow the Route from the station. The house where William Shakespeare was born in 1564 is a substantial two-storey wattle and daub house standing alone in Henley Street. The house was purchased in 1847 as a national treasure and the neighbouring houses were pulled down in 1857 to reduce the risk of fire. The Shakespeare family lived in the western section, and William's father John, a glovemaker, used the other part for his business.

Entry is through the gardens at the back, after a call at the ticket desk in the Visitor Centre. Go through to the raftered living room. (Here, as at all the Shakespearian properties, guides are on hand to explain things and answer questions.) An important point to bear in mind is that the furniture was bought in later, in the nineteenth century. Although it includes some Elizabethan and Jacobean pieces, the furniture is there principally to convey the feeling of domestic life in Shakespeare's day. In the museum section there is a documentary exhibition on the history of the house, and in an upstairs room a row of pictures illuminates the difficulty of knowing what the greatest English poet actually looked like. The 'Chandos' version should be the most reliable. Probably by John Taylor, it is the only known portrait painted in Shakespeare's lifetime.

The original is now in the National Portrait Gallery, London (see *Walk 6*). The picture shows a thoughtful man wearing a full beard, his hair thinning on top and worn long at the sides and back. He wears an earring in the only visible ear, the left.

The monument on the wall of Trinity Church, visited later, portrays an older man, more staid, holding a quill in his hand. It seems more like a civic portrait, commemorating the famous poet who in middle age became a lay rector at his parish church. It was made by Gheerart (or Gerard) Janssen, who had a stone mason's yard near the Globe Theatre in London, and was erected in 1623, seven years after Shakespeare's death.

Continue to the room where the poet was probably born. Again, the furniture is only there to illustrate the atmosphere of an Elizabethan bedroom. The cot is a cot of the period, not Shakespeare's cot. On the window glass are scratched the names of well-known visitors to the house – Sir Walter Scott, Thomas Carlyle, Henry Irving, Ellen Terry.

Downstairs the kitchen is full of interesting pieces gathered round the old hearth. In the centre of the room is a curious pivoting 'baby-minder', made to prevent babies from falling in the fire, though there is no evidence that Shakespeare himself was ever clamped into a machine of this sort.

The way out leads through Hornby Cottage, where a book and souvenir shop provides initial exposure to the extraordinary range of goods now roped in to promote the name of Stratford.

The house is not easy for disabled visitors.

Town Centre

At the roundabout at the end of Henley Street, turn right to High Street. The timbered building by the corner, until recently the Tourist Information Office, was once the home of Shakespeare's second daughter, Judith; its cellar served as an early town jail. Continue towards the Town Hall. On the right, just before Ely Street, is Harvard House, home of the mother of John Harvard who founded Harvard University. The Town Hall was built in 1768 in Cotswold stone and the façade in Chapel Street bears a large inscription in capitals: 'GOD SAVE THE KING'. It was originally the Shakespeare Hall and was opened in

1769 by the actor David Garrick as part of the Shakespeare Jubilee celebrations, which he organised.

Nash's House/New Place

The interest here is not so much the house we enter as the ruins in the garden on the corner of Chapel Street and Chapel Lane. New Place was a large town house built for Hugh Clopton, a Lord Mayor of London. Shakespeare bought it in 1597, retired there from about 1610 and died in the house six years later. Drawings on the upstairs landing in Nash House show how both houses were rebuilt as tastes changed and timber-framed buildings were clad in Classical brick and stone. Nash House received the Victorian stucco treatment and a porch was added, but New Place was pulled down in 1759.

In the garden is a well which probably stood in the inner courtyard of New Place, and on the boundary with the Knot Garden the foundations of the old east wall can be clearly seen.

Nash House was the property of Thomas Nash who married Shakespeare's granddaughter Elizabeth Hall. A portrait of the couple hangs in the front hall. When she died in 1676, the Shakespeare line came to an end. The house was bought for preservation in 1862 and the frontage restored to its Elizabethan appearance. Upstairs is the town's local history museum, displaying ancient and medieval relics and an account of David Garrick, the Shakespearian actor, and the Jubilee of 1769.

In the grounds is a replica of an Elizabethan Knot Garden – four beds laid out with low box hedges in a maze-like pattern, the compartments filled with herbs and flowers in brilliant contrasting colours. Beyond is the formal Great Garden, lined with box and yew hedges.

Grammar School and Guildhall

From the garden gate in Chapel Lane, look across to the modern additions at Edward VI Grammar School, refounded in 1553 and which Shakespeare almost certainly attended. The Chapel on the corner also serves the school and is much older. As the medieval Chapel of the Guild of the Holy Cross it was the religious centre of the guild which more or less ruled the town until it was suppressed in 1547. The chapel and all its other possessions were then made over to the town by Royal Charter. Look inside and perhaps hear one of the boy organists at practice. Above the chancel arch is a fresco of *The Day of Judgment*: Christ and the Virgin appear at the top, Heaven on the left and Hell on the right.

In Church Street the old Guildhall, built in 1417, is now the school library. Next is the long range of the Almshouses, its ten bays still occupied by elderly residents. On the other side of the road, a little further down, is Mason's Croft, occupied by the Shakespeare Institute, a scholarly foundation that is part of Birmingham University. Here the romantic novelist Marie Corelli lived between 1901 and 1924. A useful lunch stop is the Windmill pub, with filling bar food.

Hall's Croft

This is the most stylish of the Shakespearian properties. It was bought by John Hall, a doctor who settled in Stratford about 1600 and married Susannah, Shakespeare's elder daughter, in 1607. Their daughter Elizabeth was born the following year. After Shakespeare's death they moved into New Place. The house was much added to in later years and was then comprehensively restored by the Shakespeare Birthplace Trust after 1949.

There are spacious rooms, finely carved Elizabethan and Jacobean furniture, some interesting portraits of the period and a dispensary equipped with apothecaries' jars, herbs and surgical equipment appropriate to Dr Hall and his practice. There is also a good garden with a mulberry tree, herbaceous borders planted with old English flowers and a sundial. It has almost nothing to do with Shakespeare, but is evidently popular – fake, or no – with those who like to amble round old houses breathing 'Beautiful.'

Holy Trinity Church

The quiet street called Old Town was where 'Stradforde', as it was recorded in the Domesday Book of 1086, grew up from a settlement of '21 villagers with a priest and 7 smallholders with 28 ploughs'. The church followed a little more than a century later, much of it being built between 1210 and 1330.

Follow the avenue of limes to the north door. On the inner door of the porch is a thirteenth-century sanctuary ring. A fugitive from justice who managed to reach it could claim protection in the church for thirty-seven days, then had to stand trial if he had not arranged to vanish in the meantime.

This fine church has many treasures and beautiful stained glass. At the far end of the north aisle, the Clopton Chapel contains remarkable tombs to William Clopton (d.1592) and his wife Anne, and George Carew, Earl of Totnes and Baron Clopton (d.1692) and his wife Joyce, Countess of Totnes, daughter of the Cloptons.

Much plainer, though infinitely more celebrated, is the grave of William Shakespeare in the chancel, watched over by the Janssen memorial on the north wall. Here, side by side, are buried Anne, Shakespeare's wife (1556-1623); the poet (1564-1616); Thomas Nash, husband of Elizabeth, the poet's granddaughter (1593-1647); John Hall (1575-1635); and Susannah, the poet's daughter and Hall's wife (1583-1649).

Shakespeare had no wish for his bones to be moved off one day and stored in the charnel house, as often happened in those times. The inscription on his grave is thus a warning:

'Good friend, for Jesu's sake forbear
To dig the dust enclosed here.
Blest be the man that spares these stones,
And curst be he that moves my bones.'

To the left of the altar rail, near the damaged fifteenth-century font, are copies from the parish register recording the baptism and burial of Shakespeare. In 1564: 'April 26 Guilielmus filius Johannes Shakespear.' In 1616: 'April 25 Will Shakespear, gent.'

Royal Shakespeare Theatre

Stroll through Avonbank Gardens beside the river and past the old summerhouse which is now a brass-rubbing centre. The Victorian Gothic theatre was burned down in 1926, to the delight of George Bernard Shaw who disliked the style and sent a telegram of congratulations. Its surviving element faces Southern Lane and houses the Royal Shakespeare Collection of stage props, scenery and costumes, and the 'wooden O' of the Swan Theatre which puts on a varied repertoire of Restoration comedy, new plays, musicals and opera.

The new theatre, by Elizabeth Scott, was built in 1932. Walk round to the front to see the flourishing home of the Royal Shakespeare Company which performs there in an annual festival of his plays between spring and autumn. Seats are prized and generally booked well in advance. For 24-hour Ticket Availability Information, telephone 0789 269191.

Gower Memorial

Cross Bancroft Gardens to the Canal Lock which unites the canal running to Birmingham with the Upper or Warwickshire Avon which flows south-west to the River Severn at Tewkesbury. The old barge trade in coal and manufactures from the Midlands has gone, though pleasure boats still use the canal. Look across to the fourteen-arched Clopton Bridge, built by Sir Hugh Clopton between 1480 and 1490, long and low like the streets of Stratford itself.

On the other side of the canal is the Shakespeare Memorial, a full-sized bronze figure of the poet by Lord Ronald Gower, unveiled in 1888. Shakespeare is surrounded by the figures of Hamlet, Lady Macbeth, Falstaff and Prince Hal.

Anne Hathaway's Cottage

After Rother Street the way out to the cottage at Shottery runs between the backs of houses to a large open playing field, then down Tavern Lane into the village. It takes about twenty minutes, and was very much the route Shakespeare followed when calling on his wife-to-be.

William Shakespeare married Anne Hathaway in 1582, when he was eighteen and she was twenty-five. John Hathaway, her father, was a well-to-do yeoman farmer with more than 20 hectares (50 acres) of land, hence the considerable size of this fascinating cottage which grew from a twelve-roomed cruck-built farmhouse. Its timber frame is based on stone foundations and the walls are mostly wattle and daub panels with some later inserts of brick.

Inside are the hall, where everyone gathered, and William and Anne, so they tell you here, sat side by side on the tilting wooden settle; then the kitchen and its old bake-oven beside the open fireplace, and the buttery for storing farm produce. Upstairs are several former bedrooms; in one stands the canopied Hathaway bedstead, beautifully carved and, from the look of it, hideously uncomfortable to lie on.

The cottage staff deftly funnel you into the commercial sector, which contains no less than three shops, and then you are free to enjoy refreshments outdoors and the beauty of the scented garden and orchard.

Walk 31

Cambridge

The pairing of great university with small market town has
created in Cambridge that rarest of combinations: an intimate
city, and a most beautiful one. After the Botanic Garden,
discover the treasures of the Fitzwilliam Museum, walk
through Great Court at Trinity to the inspiring Wren Library,
wander through the Backs and visit the Gothic wonder of
King's College Chapel.
Allow   All day.
Best times   Tuesday to Friday.

ROUTE
Getting there
By train from London Take train from King's Cross to Cambridge. Check times in advance (071-278 2477); journey time 1hr 10 minutes. *By coach from London* Take coach from Victoria Coach Station. Check times in advance (071-730 0202); journey time approx. 2 hours.

Begin at Cambridge⇄. (Visitors arriving by coach are set down at the Bus Station in Drummer Street. Walk through to Trumpington Street and join walk at Fitzwilliam Museum.)

Check return trains. Station has small tourism centre and can recommend nearby accommodation. At exit, walk ahead in Station Road. At war memorial in Hills Road, cross to **University Botanic Garden** ☞; open May to September 08.00 to 18.00, February, March, October 08.00 to 17.00, November to January 08.00 to 16.00. Sunday opens 10.00 and closes as weekdays above. *Admission (Sunday only)*.

Walk through garden and emerge at Bateman Street exit. Turn left and right along Brookside. At end, bear left to Trumpington Street and follow to **Fitzwilliam Museum** ☞; open 10.00 to 17.00, Sunday 14.15 to 17.00, closed Monday. All galleries open Sunday; on other days Lower Galleries open mornings 10.00 to 14.00 (Egyptian, Greek, Roman, Western Asiatic antiquities, ceramics, glass, textiles, armour), Upper Galleries open afternoons 14.00 to 17.00 (paintings, sculpture, drawings, prints, furniture). Some galleries may be open all day if staff available. *Donation requested*.

At exit, turn left to **Peterhouse**, oldest college in university ☞. Look into front court to see Hall and Chapel. Continue past Little St Mary's Church and turn right along Pembroke Street then left along Free School Lane. In this scientific quarter are several museums, for visiting now or perhaps on second day if staying overnight:

In Downing Street, enter science site through arch and turn right to **Museum of Archaeology and Anthropology** (surveys pre-history of world, local archaeology, new anthropological gallery); open 14.00 to 16.00, Saturday 10.00 to 12.30, closed Sunday.

At entrance to Downing Site, turn left to **Sedgwick Museum of Geology** (Britain's oldest intact geological collection, internationally esteemed collection of fossils), entrance at staircase guarded by stone bears; open 09.00 to 13.00, 14.00 to 17.00, Saturday 10.00 to 13.00, closed Sunday.

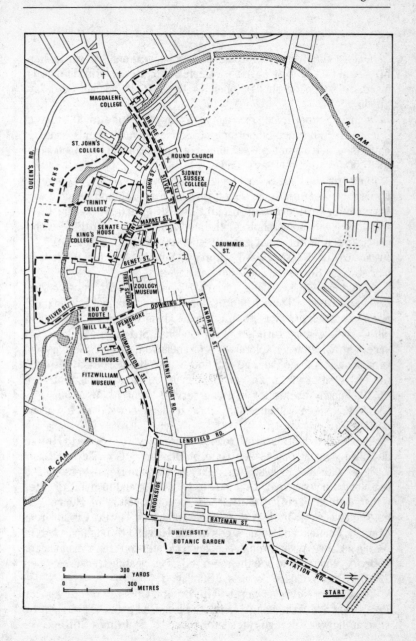

MAGDALENE COLLEGE

BRIDGE ST.

ST. JOHN'S COLLEGE

ROUND CHURCH

QUEEN'S RD.

THE BACKS

ST. JOHN ST.

SILVER S.

SIDNEY SUSSEX COLLEGE

TRINITY COLLEGE

MARKET ST.

SENATE HOUSE

TRINITY LA.

KING'S COLLEGE

DRUMMER ST.

BENET ST.

FREE SCHOOL LA.

ZOOLOGY MUSEUM

SILVER ST.

END OF ROUTE

DOWNING ST.

ST. ANDREW'S ST.

MILL LA.

PEMBROKE ST.

TRUMPINGTON ST.

PETERHOUSE

FITZWILLIAM MUSEUM

TENNIS COURT RD.

R. CAM

LENSFIELD RD.

BROOKSIDE

BATEMAN ST.

UNIVERSITY BOTANIC GARDEN

STATION RD.

START

R. CAM

0   300 YARDS

0   300 METRES

In Downing Street, go through arch opposite Tennis Court Road to **Museum of Zoology** (displays of animal skeletons, marine life, birds, insects, fossils and shells); open 14.15 to 16.45, closed Saturday, Sunday.

In Free School Lane, on right is **Whipple Museum** (history of science told through important collection of instruments used in navigation, astronomy, measurement of time and distance); open 14.00 to 16.00, closed Saturday, Sunday.

Further along Free School Lane, go right through arch of Cavendish Laboratory and turn right. On left is round front of Mond Building with **University Collection of Aerial Photographs** (a working institute and library with some photographs on display; mainly for those with a special interest in the subject); open 09.00 to 13.00, 14.00 to 17.00, Friday closes 16.00, closed Saturday, Sunday, and for 10 days at Christmas – New Year and 2 days at Easter.

At end Free School Lane, turn right along Benet Street. At corner Wheeler Street is Tourist Information Centre for further information, accommodation brochure, etc. Continue along Wheeler Street and at old Corn Exchange turn left along Guildhall Street to **Market Hill street market** ☞. Explore rows of stalls with striped awnings and turn along St Mary's Passage to S door **Church of Great St Mary's,** the University church. **Tower** ☞ open 10.00 to 16.45, last entrance 16.30, Sunday open after morning service about 12.30. *Admission.* Climb 123 steep winding stairs for excellent views over town and colleges.

At exit, turn right and cross road. Go through yard of **Senate House** and turn right at end to see Gate of Honour at Gonville and Caius College, with six sundials. Turn right along Senate House Passage and left along Trinity Street. Continue to post office and turn left to enter Great Gate of **Trinity College** ☞ beneath statue of Henry VIII holding chair-leg. On right see Chapel and Clock Tower. Cross Great Court to fountain and go up steps beside Hall and through passage to Nevile's Court. Walk through echoing S cloister to Wren's magnificent **Library**, and go up to see the room and its fascinating treasures; open 12.00 to 14.00, closed Saturday, Sunday.

Go out from Nevile's Court to **The Backs**. Cross stone bridge over River Cam and walk along avenue to black iron gates. Turn right by stream and walk through gates into grounds of **St John's College** ☞.

Follow path back to river; on left is Gothic Revival New Court, its central tower and battlements nicknamed the 'Wedding Cake'. At next bridge look across to **Bridge of Sighs**, then cross river and turn into Third Court. Walk through to First Court and see Chapel, open 09.00 to 16.00, Saturday closes 12.00, Sunday open for choral services only. Leave college through front Gate Tower and turn to see statue of St John and coat of arms of founder, Lady Margaret Beaufort, mother of Henry VII.

Turn left in St John Street and left into Bridge Street. Cross river to visit **Magdalene College** ☞. In Second Court is the **Pepys Building** housing Samuel Pepys's own library, bequeathed to the college; opening times vary through year and are posted in porter's lodge.

Return to Bridge Street and continue to **Round Church**, then on past Sidney Sussex College. Turn right along Market Street to King's Parade. Enter **King's College** and visit famous Gothic **Chapel** ☞. Opening times as follows:

In term: 1 October to 30 April, 09.30 to 15.45, Sunday 14.00 to 15.00, 16.30 to 17.15; 1 May to 30 September, times as above except Sunday closes 17.45.

Outside term: 1 October to 30 April, 09.30 to 17.00, Sunday 10.30 to 17.00; 1 May to 30 September, 09.30 to 17.45, Sunday 10.30 to 17.45.

Choral services Open in term, weekdays except Monday, 17.30 for Evensong (or Sung Eucharist), Sunday 10.30 for Sung Eucharist (or Matins), 15.30 Evensong.

On leaving chapel, turn right to Backs. Follow path to river, cross bridge and keep on to Queen's Road. Turn left and bear left along sandy footpath towards pointed lead roofs (part of Queens' College). Continue to Silver Street and turn left to bridge; on left is wooden 'Mathematical Bridge'.

Walk ends here, close to two attractive riverside pubs, The Anchor and The Mill, linked by Laundress Lane to rear of Anchor. To return to railway station, walk up Mill Lane to Trumpington Street and turn right. Or, to save feet (a little), walk through Pembroke Street to St Andrew's Street and catch a bus.

In the Train

The fast electric train sways out of King's Cross and hums through tunnels and cuttings, past tower blocks and factories and gaunt Victorian schools to Finsbury Park. On through Hornsey, the fire-damaged façade of Alexandra Palace up on the hill, site of the world's first television transmitter (1936). Then come the sporting suburbs of Southgate, New Barnet and Potters Bar, hothouses of amateur golf, hockey and cricket.

Occasional green fields with sheep give promise of the countryside to come, though the ribbon development persists through Welwyn Garden City to the shiny toytown warehouses of Stevenage. The Hertfordshire landscape is flat and dull, too spattered with housing. One longs to see a wood, but instead gets Hitchin. Then the train wheels east and there, before Letchworth, a burst of open landscape appears, sweeping cornfields to either side. From Baldock to Royston the line runs parallel with the Icknield Way, the ancient trackway linking Salisbury Plain and East Anglia, past woods and parkland and massive farm fields. What hills there are flatten out and the view extends to a far horizon. Then flower fields and orchards, and into Meldreth, Shepreth, Foxton. The train curves through a final bend, past the hangar-like shed of Cambridge University Press and into the station.

The Plan of Action

The curious meandering shape of this walk is dictated by somewhat intractable opening times. Provided a fairly early start is made, you should be able to see much of the university and the town in one day, and visit three quite marvellous places: the Fitzwilliam Museum, the Wren Library in Trinity College, and King's College Chapel. I would then recommend a second day to wander at leisure, out on The Backs – perhaps in a punt – and through one or two other colleges, and maybe visit some of the science museums listed in the Route section.

University Botanic Garden

The garden is a gentle and charming introduction to the town. (Would that Oxford too had a botanic garden, a second one I mean, to lighten that bleak road between the railway station and Carfax.)

At the entrance, take the left fork and follow the earth and gravel path, bearing right at the first open space past the drooping branches of a *Prunus yedoensis*, in spring lustrous with white flowers. Follow the sign left to Martyn Walk, arriving soon at the Conservation Area. In the hedged enclosure is a display of wild flowers in danger – and black-topped wooden memorials to extinct species such as Lamb's succory, last seen in 1970; then a bed of those we need to preserve, the goldilocks aster, cowslip, field wormwood and others.

Continue past the Limestone Mound to the fountain at the head of Main Walk, and follow this avenue past a parade of various conifers, including a mighty Cedar of Lebanon. This is a good, unpompous teaching garden, full of well-labelled plants and plenty of background information on other signboards. It opened here in 1846, instigated by John Stevens Henslow, Professor of Botany and teacher of Charles Darwin.

Turn right around the Rock Garden on Henslow Walk, try the glasshouses if you cannot resist glasshouses, and head along Lynch Walk to the Bateman Street exit, next to a grey-brick canopied villa.

Fitzwilliam Museum

In Trumpington Street the presence of the University grows ever stronger in a growing chain of administrative and academic buildings. Our goal is the white-columned portico of Cambridge's most splendid museum. Its director thinks of it as the finest small museum in Western Europe, and after an hour or so inside you may not wish to disagree with him.

The museum was founded in 1816 by Richard, 7th Viscount Fitzwilliam of Merrion who bequeathed his own connoisseur's collections to the University and also left money to build a museum. It was eventually opened in 1848 and over the next half-century made no great cultural impact although important gifts and bequests arrived from time to time, such as John Ruskin's gift in 1861 of twenty-five Turner watercolours. These considerably expanded Viscount Fitzwilliam's basic collection, strongest in Venetian and Dutch paintings, prints, illuminated manuscripts and music manuscripts.

Under S.C. Cockerell, director between 1908 and 1937, the museum and its collections were enlarged and reorganised in ways thought revolutionary at the time. In its present condition it is like a capacious jewel box subdivided into compartments of startling brilliance. A wonderful place – except that only half of it may be on view when you arrive. The Fitzwilliam is currently so short of cash it can only be confident of opening its Lower Galleries in the morning (antiquities, ceramics, glass, textiles, armour), and its Upper Galleries in the afternoon (paintings, drawings, sculpture, prints, furniture). On Sunday afternoon the whole museum is open.

Not every weekday is run at this breadline level, however, and you may be lucky. It is always worth asking at the front desk. Then collect a copy of the museum's helpful plan and make your way round. Enjoy too the sumptuous marble entrance hall, designed by George Bassevi and completed by E.M. Barry.

The quality of the exhibits is marvellous. In the Dutch Painting gallery, for example, you enter to find, beside the door, not one Berckheyde view but two: the *Groote Kerk, Haarlem* and the *Town Hall, Amsterdam*. There is a Frans Hals, *Portrait of a Man*; a landscape by Jan Brueghel the Elder; a small portrait by Gerrit Dou; a Jan Steen interior and much more. Lift the covers of the central cabinets to find engravings and pen-and-ink pictures by Rembrandt, Rubens and Dürer. In each room, it seems, the Fitzwilliam triumphs over even our most expansive hopes.

Peterhouse

The oldest college in Cambridge is next door: Peterhouse, never Peterhouse College, founded in 1284. Beyond the gallery next to the Chapel is the principal court, and there in the top-left corner is the Hall, the first college building though much altered in the nineteenth century. The great oriel window dates from the 1870s.

The University took root in 1209 when scholars and teachers fled from insupportable conditions at Oxford and settled here in a small community. As the need grew for better facilities, halls and hostels were founded. In the period between 1284 and 1352 six halls or colleges came into being, those now known as Peterhouse, Clare College, Pembroke College, Gonville and Caius College, Trinity Hall and Corpus Christi College. Magdalene College dates from 1428, and in a second wave of building between 1441 and 1475 the original foundations were established of King's, Queens', St Catharine's and Christ's Colleges. These were followed by Jesus, St John's, Trinity, Emmanuel, Sidney

Sussex and Downing. The first colleges for women, Girton and Newnham, were built in the 1870s. In the 'Oxbridge' university system, each college is independent and self-ruling, linked federally to the university's governing body.

The plan of most Cambridge (and Oxford) colleges provides a series of courts with accommodation and common rooms arranged vertically on a staircase system. Entrance is through a main gate containing a porter's lodge, and the chapel and dining hall are usually prominent in the front court.

College dining halls are not generally as accessible to the public as chapels, though at Peterhouse you may be fortunate. Compared with some colleges it is a small, almost intimate room with a Tudor fireplace and Pre-Raphaelite stained glass by William Morris, Sir Edward Burne-Jones and Ford Madox Brown. The Chapel dates from 1628, when Matthew Wren (uncle of Sir Christopher) was Master. It has a coffered ceiling with gilded suns and a Gothic *Pietà* behind the altar.

Adjoining the college is the Church of Little St Mary's (1350-2) which served as the Peterhouse chapel until the college acquired its own. It has a splendid stone font with a wooden cover and the former reredos is by Sir George Gilbert Scott. On the north wall, at the foot of the nave, is the memorial to Rev. Godfrey Washington, a relative of George Washington, who was minister here from 1705 until 1729; the family coat of arms also forms the flag of the District of Columbia.

The Market Town

The core of the town occupies a narrow triangle in the centre of Cambridge. From Peterhouse, our way to it lies along Pembroke Street and Free School Lane, passing sooty walls at the rear of Corpus Christi College. Many scientific institutions are gathered here, and five museums whose specialities are outlined in the Route section. They affirm the University's strong scientific tradition. One of them, the Cavendish Laboratory, is named after a famous Peterhouse man, Henry Cavendish (1731-1810) who determined the composition of the atmosphere and 'weighed the Earth' in consequence of his famous Cavendish Experiment.

Benet Street points the way to the old Corn Exchange, now a concert hall and café-restaurant. Turn along Guildhall Street, past Michael

Ayrton's block-chested sculpture of *Talos*, guardian of Minoan Crete, to find the busy street market. The striped awnings and close rows of stalls selling an appealing mixture of vegetables, antiques, rugs, books, prints and fish – in random order – suggests a way of life little changed in five hundred years.

Now a chance to go up high. In St Mary's Passage is the entrance to the University Church of Great St Mary's (1478). The climb to the top of the Tower, 34.5m (113ft) high, is a tough ascent for all its comparative brevity, though there are resting-places off the steep and tightly winding stairs. On top, a slatted viewing platform raises the visitor's-eye view above the level of the mesh safety fence attached to the battlements.

Fine views extend in all directions: eastward over the awnings of the market; south and westward over King's Parade, King's College Chapel and the brilliant green lawn in front of Senate House. To the north are Gonville and Caius (pronounced Kees) College, a view into Trinity's Great Court and then the mighty square tower of St John's College Chapel.

Back at ground level, cross into Senate House Yard. This is the academic centre of Cambridge, the University being governed by the Council of the Senate. The building is by James Gibbs and dates from 1722.

Through an iron gateway on the far right is one of three fine stone gates built by Dr Caius for the college he refounded in 1557. This is the Gate of Honour, crowned by six sundials, through which students process to their degree ceremony at Senate House. The others are called the Gates of Humility and Virtue and together symbolise the student's path to knowledge.

Continue along Trinity Street, one of the more chic and useful trading streets with a branch of Liberty, then Deighton, Bell, the second-hand and antiquarian booksellers, Heffers bookshop and the Blue Boar, a famous pub now something of a cafeteria, though a possible lunch-stop among several in the area. Also here is St Michael's Church, first built before 1200, which served as chapel of a college, Michaelhouse, before it was dissolved in 1546.

Trinity College

On the outer side of Trinity's Great Gate is a famous statue of Henry VIII holding in his right hand not a sceptre but a chair-leg. Students in the nineteenth century made the substitution, and for some reason this was seen as a good joke, to be perpetuated.

Henry VIII founded the college in 1546, weeks before he died. It is the largest college in Cambridge or Oxford and was first formed by amalgamating two much older colleges, King's Hall and Michaelhouse.

Walk through to Great Court, a quadrangle of awesome size, the creation of Thomas Nevile who became Master in 1593. He preserved the Great Gate (1519), once part of King's Hall, but knocked down much else to provide a huge court with sides measuring roughly 100 yds each. A full circuit of the stone path is 380 yds, and this is the course the future Olympians raced in the movie *Chariots of Fire*. The challenge, for them and any undergraduate who wishes to try, is to get round before the college clock finishes striking twelve. This takes the eighteenth-century clock forty-three seconds; it strikes the hours twice, one round on a high note, the next on a lower.

Bear right to the Chapel, begun in 1554 by Mary Tudor. The ante-chapel has a timber roof with richly painted panels and a series of sculpted monuments commemorating famous Trinity men. Those awarded the largest grade of monument (a grand marble statue) are Francis Bacon (philosopher and scientist), Isaac Barrow (mathematician and teacher of Newton), Lord Macaulay (historian), Lord Tennyson (Poet Laureate), William Whewell (philosopher and Master of Trinity) and, the most imposing, Isaac Newton (scientist) by the French sculptor Louis-François Roubiliac.

At the centre of Great Court is a fine stone fountain, columned and crowned. Beneath its shady ceiling water pours in an eternal, restful-sounding stream through two shell basins with downward-pointing, gargoyle-headed spouts.

Approach the Hall and go up the steps. If the doors are open, take a look at the grand dining hall with gilded hammerbeam roof and, above high table, a portrait of Henry VIII in aggressive pose, legs astride and hands on hips – suggesting, in the context, a man more than slightly concerned about the non-appearance of his dinner.

A *low* door leads through to Nevile's Court, a fine cloistered space finished in 1612. In the north cloister Isaac Newton (who was Lucasian Professor of Mathematics at the University from 1669 until 1701) used the resident echo to calculate the speed of time.

At the far end of the court is Wren's superb Classical library building, completed in 1695. Above the golden stone façade, four figures on the balustrade represent Divinity, Law, Physic and Mathematics, and were carved by Caius Gabriel Cibber. Go upstairs to the Library. Although open to the public for only two hours a day, 12.00 to 14.00 on weekdays, this is possibly the *one* place in Cambridge that no-one should miss.

Projecting from the side walls of the long (57m/190ft) silent room is a procession of stained oak bookcases decorated with limewood carvings by Grinling Gibbons. At the far end, Cipriani's window shows Newton being presented by Fame to George III.

The bookstock here is much as it was in 1820, and is mainly frequented by researchers; later books are kept in a nearby Reading Room. Along each side of the Library are some of its greatest treasures. Beginning with the oldest (first showcase on the left), lift the cloth to see an eighth-century manuscript of the Epistles of St Paul. Next to it is the Winchester Gospels, a spectacular illuminated manuscript of the eleventh century, brightly coloured and thick with gold. Explore here and there among the extraordinary collection of letters, notebooks, manuscripts and printed books. There is a leaf from the first printed book, the Gutenberg Bible of 1456. There are letters signed by Henry VIII, Elizabeth I and Napoleon Bonaparte, and pages from the notebook of Wittgenstein, a Fellow of the College from 1929 to 1951. More soft-centred are A.A. Milne's manuscript pages for *Winnie the Pooh*; the author and his son, Christopher Robin, were both at Trinity.

The Wren Library is a perfect room. To work there for just one week would be excellent, even if the spirit of genius, which surely hovers there, declined to direct one's own pen to finer things.

The Backs to St John's College

The Backs are another marvel of the Cambridge scene. They extend for almost the length of the city's west side, a parade of landscaped college gardens through which winds the River Cam, flowing from south to north. In spring the banks and avenues are fringed with flowering daffodils, narcissi, red tulips, primrose, buttercups, and forget-me-nots which are a heraldic flower of St John's College, symbolising the motto of the founder, Lady Margaret Beaufort: *Souvent Me Souvient*.

Turn out through the gates of Trinity and in through the gates of St John's. Follow the path back to the river, where accomplished punters glide and novices yaw this way and that. The large stone blocks of New Court, to the west of the Cam, are a Gothic Revival extension of St John's and were built in 1831. Of the same date is the famous Bridge of Sighs which links the two parts of the college. It is unglazed, and looks nothing like the even more famous bridge in Venice.

In First Court is the Chapel, designed by Sir George Gilbert Scott in 1869. In front of it, inset in the lawn, are the remains of its predecessor, the Hospital Chapel of St John's. When Lady Margaret Beaufort took the decision shortly before her death in 1509 to found the college, the site was occupied by the Monks of St John. Their buildings were incorporated in the new plans for the college.

In the present ante-chapel are two interesting memorials. Above the old chantry arches is a portrait of Lady Margaret Beaufort at prayer; here she is described by titles acquired through two of her three marriages – Countess of Richmond and Derby. Look also for the double tomb of Dr Hugh Ashton (died 1522), Comptroller to The Lady Margaret. In the upper effigy he is dressed in academic robes; underneath lies a second figure, a gaunt and skeletal corpse.

The college's brick and stone Gate Tower was built in 1516. Go through the arch and look back to see the canopied statue of St John with symbolic gold eagle at his feet. Beneath the figure are the sumptuous arms of Lady Margaret Beaufort. They include a crowned Tudor rose, the Beaufort portcullis and a pair of yales, mythological creatures with the spotted body of an antelope, a goat's head and an elephant's tail. Lady Margaret Beaufort also founded Christ's College and her arms appear above its Great Gate too.

Magdalene College

If time permits before King's College Chapel closes its doors – which in term-time is at 15.45 – follow Bridge Street to the river and visit the pleasant brick-faced courts of Magdalene College, founded in 1428 as a hostel for young monks studying at Cambridge. Its chief attraction for the visitor is the Pepys Building in Second Court which houses the Bibliotheca Pepysiana. This consists of the diarist's own library of 3,000 books which he left 'intire in one body' to his nephew, and then to his old college. The library is sometimes open to the public, chiefly in term-time.

To the left of this building is the Fellows' Garden. It has charming views across to the river and Jesus Green beyond. In one corner is a Victorian pets' cemetery. Small memorial stones commemorate 'A Faithful Cat' which died in May 1892 aged ten years. 'Bumble', an unspecified animal which died the same year, was twelve. Another, 'Ti-Ti', died in 1917. All that mars the intimacy of this garden is the roar of traffic in Chesterton Lane. The college has three other courts across the road: Benson, Mallory and Buckingham.

Return along Bridge Street to the Round Church. When it was built in 1130 the eight sturdy Norman arches defined a circular nave; outside these ran the ambulatory, and that was all. The choir and north aisle were added in the fifteenth century and further restorations and additions in 1841 have converted the church, perhaps unfortunately, into a more orthodox-looking structure.

King's College

The final grand event of this walk is a visit to King's College Chapel, one of the supreme Gothic buildings of Europe.

Enter the college from King's Parade. The front Gatehouse and elegant stone screen are part of William Wilkins's nineteenth-century designs which completed Front Court on this and the south side. The fountain, bearing a statue of Henry VI, the college's founder, dates from 1879. Behind it is the Gibbs Building designed by James Gibbs in 1724.

In 1441, the year after he founded Eton College, Henry VI gave money for the College of St Nicholas to be built on this site. The foundation stone of the Chapel was laid in 1446, the king was deposed in 1461 and work proceeded gradually under the next four kings until its completion in 1536.

Walk past the range of side chapels set between the towering pinnacled buttresses which, with the corner towers, carry the vast weight of the interior vaulting, estimated at 1,875 tons. Inside the ante-chapel there is a sense of colossal space, magically enclosed. To decipher the structure, look up to the ceiling and identify the central bosses of alternating rose and portcullis, the Tudor emblems. To each of these run four half-fans which spring out from the slender pillars framing the great windows.

Much of the stonework and the vaulting was directed by John Wastell, master mason to Henry VII. He worked on the truly grand scale, both in realising the structural concept and in the rich embellishment of the walls and columns. Each Welsh dragon and Richmond greyhound supporting Henry VII's coat of arms and royal crown conveys a massive presence. Roses and portcullises climb the columns to reinforce the glorious unity of the Chapel. In the south-west corner of the ante-chapel, one rose contains the figure of a woman. She is thought to represent the Virgin, to whom the College and Chapel are dedicated.

The dark oak screen supporting the organ is the gift of Henry VIII, and bears his initials and those of Anne Boleyn. He was also responsible for commissioning the glaziers who made almost all the stained-glass windows between 1517 and about 1547. Through the screen the fan-vaulting continues to the East window. The choir stalls are rich in heraldic panelling. This is the home of the Chapel's celebrated choir, composed of sixteen boy choristers and fourteen undergraduates, best known for their Carol Service broadcasts on Christmas Eve.

Behind the altar stands Rubens's *Adoration of the Magi*, originally painted in 1634 as an altarpiece for the Convent of the White Nuns at Louvain, Belgium. It was given to the College in 1961.

To the left of the altar an arch leads through to an exhibition of how the Chapel was built. *Admission*.

So to the Backs Once More

Our walk is virtually done. The Backs are infinitely more pleasant than the crowds on King's Parade, so follow the Route across the Cam and along the footpath to Queens' College. This too is well worth a visit, time permitting. (The College is open from 13.45 to 16.30, entrance in Queens' Lane. *Admission*.) Old Court and Cloister Court are fifteenth-century, and the dazzling white blocks of Cripps Court, beneath the pointed towers now in view, are nearly brand-new. Designed by Powell, Moya and Partners, they date from 1974-81. The College occupies both banks of the Cam, and those passing from one side to the other travel across a wooden bridge, visible from Silver Street. It is usually, if erroneously, known as the 'Mathematical Bridge', and versions of it have stood there since 1749.

At the end of so full a day, it is good to sit outside at The Anchor and idly watch the ducks land on the water and the surface ripple which stirs the punts at their moorings. Should a second glass of beer arrive, it is very good indeed.

Walk 32

Canterbury

Take the route of Chaucer's pilgrims to the beautiful city of Canterbury. Visit the Poor Priests' Hospital and stroll beside the Great Stour. Tour the magnificent Cathedral, and walk the Cloisters where Thomas Becket's murderers gathered for their fatal attack.

Allow   All day.
Best times   Not Sunday.

ROUTE
Getting there
By train from London Take train from Victoria Station to Canterbury East. Check times in advance (071-928 5100); journey time 1 hour 15 minutes, 10 minutes longer if changing at Faversham.
By coach from London Take coach from Victoria Coach Station. Check times in advance (071-730 0202); journey time approx. 2 hours.

Begin at Canterbury East⇌. (Visitors arriving by coach are set down at East Kent Bus Station. Go up to City Wall and walk SW round to East Station.)

Check return trains. Leave station forecourt and walk ahead over footbridge to City Wall. Turn left and at Donjon House keep straight on through alley to **Norman Castle**. Turn right up Castle Street and turn left down Hospital Lane, towards Maynard's Spittal. Turn right up Stour Street and visit **Canterbury Heritage** at Poor Priests' Hospital ✑; open 10.30 to 16.00, closed Sunday in winter, 1 June to 31 October open Sunday 13.30 to 17.00. *Admission*.

At exit turn right and right round Hospital to Greyfriars Gardens. Cross two bridges (Greyfriars on right) and follow Franciscan Way to gateway leading to St Peter's Grove. Keep straight on to Black Griffin Lane and turn right. At Tower Way turn left and cross road to Westgate Gardens; on left is Mayor's Parlour. Turn right beside river to West Gate.

From West Gate walk E into town along St Peter's Street. Keep on past the Old Weavers House and on right visit fascinating **Eastbridge Hospital of St Thomas the Martyr** ✑; open 10.00 to 13.00, 14.00 to 17.00, Sunday opens 11.00.

Keep on along High Street to Mercery Lane. On right at 34 St Margaret's Street is Visitor Information Centre for further information and accommodation guide. Turn left along Mercery Lane to pretty Buttermarket.

Go through Christ Church Gate to Cathedral precincts. Collect Cathedral plan at Welcome Centre on right and enter **Cathedral** ✑; open Easter to September 08.45 to 19.00, October to Easter 08.45 to 17.00, Sunday 12.30 to 14.30, 16.30 to 17.30 (services only at other times). Precincts open 07.00 to 21.00. *Donation requested*.

Follow suggested route through Cathedral and Cloisters and return

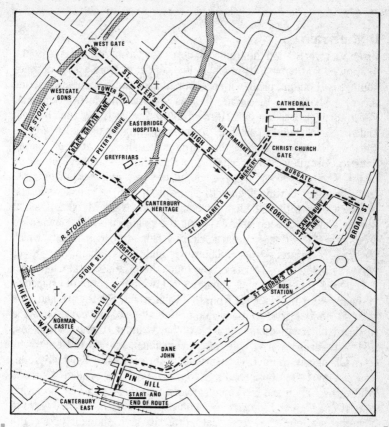

to Christ Church Gate. Turn left along Burgate to Catholic Church of St Thomas of Canterbury.

To visit ruins of **St Augustine's Abbey**, continue along Burgate and cross Broad Street to Church Street St Paul's. Bear right into Longport. Entrance to ruins on left. Opening times erratic, officially 10.00 to 13.00, 14.00 to 16.00. *Admission*. Return to Burgate.

Walk ends here. Nearest refreshments all around. To return to station, turn right along Canterbury Lane. Bear left at tower of church (St George's) where Christopher Marlowe was baptised, and turn right along St George's Lane. Go past Bus Station, cross Watling Street into gardens. Walk towards Dane John Mound, then go up to City Wall and follow Wall Walk round to footbridge leading to station.

In the Train

From Victoria Station the train swings across Grosvenor Bridge by the old power station at Battersea. Below, updated Doré vistas of inner south-east London, bleak with breakers' yards and cement stores, and the dingy backs of Victorian terraces and ugly modern tenements. Filter through Brixton and Herne Hill, after which the run to West Dulwich is a sudden paradise of green playing fields and flowering gardens. By Kent House the gardens are longer and allotments flourish. Bromley South, where the refreshments trolley comes on board. The train picks up speed and hurtles past monotonous estates, then through a cutting lined with silver birch and the carriages at last burst clear into the North Kent countryside. Near Meopham, eight horses stand in a deep hollow. Along the rolling hills, big blown-over trees are stacked like corpses, side by side. Into Rochester, which Dickens rechristened as Dullborough and Cloisterham, the River Medway below, small boats on the mud, then the docks at Chatham.

It begins to feel like a pilgrimage, shadowing the route of Chaucer's company after they set out from the Tabard Inn, Southwark and took the Old Roman Road to the shrine of Becket at Canterbury. Now the fields are filled with crouching apple orchards and tall rows of hop-poles, and oasthouses in each cluster of farm buildings. The North Kent towns from Gillingham to Faversham are not so pretty. After Selling Station, look out on the left for a road sign to Boughton Under Blean. This was where the Canon and his Yeoman joined Chaucer's pilgrims, so giving rise to *The Canon Yeoman's Tale*, an exposure of the wicked ways of alchemists. Soon the great Cathedral rises on the left above the branching River Stour and we glide into Canterbury East.

Into Town

The narrow footbridge from the station leads directly on to the old city wall, which in its preserved state still reaches round the eastern half of the city. A few yards away, past Donjon House, is the keep of Canterbury's Norman castle, built around 1100, its flint and stone façades now under constant siege by vibration from traffic on the ring road.

Walk up Castle Street. The gardens on the right have a curious history. Once the churchyard of St Mary de Castro, they served as a burial ground until the 1850s or so, after the church was demolished (it stood on the site of the White Hart, a cricketers' pub). To create the gardens, the tombstones were taken up and replanted in a row by the churchyard wall. In recent storms, when severe winds caused the ground to lift, bones appeared on the surface.

In Hospital Lane is a long row of red-roofed almshouses known as Maynard and Cotton's Hospital. Maynard, meaning Moneyer, was the first founder, a wealthy merchant with a licence to coin money. The first building dated from 1317, as a plaque declares, 'in the 12 Year of the Reign of King Edward the second'. When it fell into disrepair it was rebuilt and enlarged in 1708 by Leonard Cotton, a well-to-do pewterer.

Canterbury Heritage

Turn right up Stour Street, passing an astonishingly battered cottage, once a stable, which now has a huge front window and does shaky duty as an antique shop. Further up on the left is Canterbury Heritage, housed in the old halls and lodgings of the Poor Priests' Hospital, founded in 1373 as a retirement home for celibate clergymen. The museum tells the history of Canterbury in easy-to-follow sections and makes a useful briefing point at this stage in the walk.

Do not be put off by the vulgar hype which urges 'Follow the Time Globes on a Time Walk through the Story of Canterbury's Heritage'. True, there are some round bits of glass at the entrances to rooms, but all you have to do, thank goodness, is walk round, look at the objects and read the commentaries.

The early rooms tell the story of the first town, peopled by the Cantii, which the Romans called Durovernum Cantiacorum. There are many interesting relics to see, excavated locally: Roman cavalry swords, bronze jugs, a figurine of a mother goddess. Then comes the Pagan section, with Viking and Anglo-Saxon relics. Treasures include the Canterbury Cross, a bronze brooch of the eighth century. It was in this period, in 598, that St Augustine founded his abbey, which for centuries was the burial-place of the Archbishops of Canterbury.

Upstairs, in a room beneath the fine timbered roof, the story of Archbishop Thomas Becket is told. Unpopular with King Henry II, he was murdered in the north transept of Canterbury Cathedral on 29 December 1170, struck down by the swords of three knights,

FitzUrse, de Tracy, and le Bret whose sword broke as it severed the archbishop's scalp.

Becket's body was placed in a marble tomb in the crypt. His death was seen as martyrdom and the crypt was reopened in April 1171 to allow pilgrims to venerate the tomb. He was canonised in 1173 and Canterbury became a place of international pilgrimage, fostering a primitive souvenir trade in hastily cast *ampullae* (flasks), badges and bells. Canterbury water – tinged, they said, with the archbishop's miracle-working blood – was on sale within one year of his murder.

The tomb was moved to the Trinity Chapel next to the Cathedral choir but was destroyed in 1538 during the Reformation. At this time Canterbury suffered severe social upheaval as the communities of monks, nuns and friars were turned out into the secular world. Mary Tudor (reigned 1553-8) firmly reimposed the Catholic faith, and in Canterbury many Protestant heretics were imprisoned in the Castle and burnt at the stake in 'Martyr's Field' outside the city wall. Among the victims of Mary's repression was another archbishop of Canterbury, Thomas Cranmer, who was burnt in Oxford in 1556 (see *Walk 29*).

That, in essence, is the story of Canterbury. Although today there are many more tourists than pilgrims, the chief places of interest in the city all seem connected with Thomas Becket and the Cathedral.

Continue to the timbered Great Hall, where the priests lived. The crown posts are an interesting feature: upright timbers carrying the main weight of the roof down to cross-timbers, or tie-beams, which transfer it outwards to the walls.

Of the other famous Canterbury people celebrated here, the most famous is the unruly playwright Christopher Marlowe. He was born in George Street in 1564 and baptised in St George's Church, the tower of which we come to later. He entered King's School as a scholar in 1579, then went to Cambridge and London. He died at twenty-nine, killed in a tavern fight in Deptford.

Greyfriars and West Gate

Walk round the Poor Priests' Hospital to Greyfriars Gardens, crossing a bridge over the shallow Stour. This riverside walk, the Franciscan Way, was opened in 1990. From the second bridge there is a charming

view of the house once occupied by the Greyfriars, members of the
Franciscan order who first came to Canterbury in 1224 and established
a church and community. The house, built in the thirteenth century, is
all that survives. Two rooms up and two rooms down, it stands astride

the stream. In one of the lower rooms is a trap-door through which, it is said, the friars fished for their supper. The house is sometimes open, about 15.00.

Follow the path beside rows of quiet villas and the low pastel-coloured cottages of Black Griffin Lane, arriving soon at Westgate Gardens. Here is the Mayor's Parlour, a stumpy lodge with castellated tower and a quaint step gable, used for civic receptions. Above the door the shield of Canterbury contains three Cornish choughs (a cousin of the jackdaw) beneath a gold lion of England. The choughs are from the arms attributed to Thomas Becket.

Turn up beside the river to the West Gate, passing the redundant Church of the Holy Cross which is now the Guildhall; across the river is a pleasant row of black and white Tudor houses. The West Gate was the entrance to the city for travellers and pilgrims approaching from London. It was built about 1380 by Henry Yevele, who designed the nave of the Cathedral, and is the last of the old city gates. A few yards outside the city walls is an old coaching inn, the Falstaff Hotel, established in 1403.

Walk east into town along St Peter's Street, passing a huge mural with Pre-Raphaelite aspirations on the wall of the 'olde-worlde' Tea Pot Café which now doubles strangely as the Mother Earth Vegetarian Restaurant. Turnings to the left, on either side of St Peter's Church, lead to the buildings of the old Blackfriars monastery (1234-1538), now in private hands, and to the Marlowe Theatre, a yellow-fronted cultural centre created from the former Odeon cinema.

Keep on past the high-street shops to the Old Weavers House. The picturesque houses beside the river date from c.1500 and were occupied by Huguenot refugees who settled in the city and set up workshops for dyeing and weaving next to this branch of the Stour. River tours depart from the landing stage, beyond which the beam of a reproduction ducking-stool projects over the water.

Eastbridge Hospital

Opposite The Weavers is a fascinating place, the Hospital of St Thomas the Martyr, Eastbridge. Go in through the low pointed arch to the vestibule. To one side is the Chapel of Mother of God the Sign.

The hospital, or hostel, was founded in about 1180 by Edward

Fitzodbold for poor pilgrims. They slept downstairs in the Undercroft, stone-vaulted with arched compartments, lying on rushes spread on the floor. They ate upstairs in the Refectory, a tall pillared hall. On the north wall is an inspirational tempera painting of Christ Blessing. Painted in the thirteenth century, it was hidden for many years behind a chimney and came to light when this was removed in 1879. At the other end of the room, the tiny box-like Minstrels' Gallery is a recent construction (1932), though the painted panels are sixteenth-century and were moved here from the Chapel.

Finally, on the upper floor, they worshipped in the Chapel, which has a fine roof dating from c.1285. When pilgrimages came to an end in 1538 the foundation fell on hard times. The Chapel became a schoolroom for three hundred years and was restored only in 1927. The rest of the hospital was rescued and converted into almshouses in Elizabethan times, and several brothers and sisters still live in small cottages behind the Refectory and in the brick building on East Bridge.

To Buttermarket

In High Street, across the tiny river, is the Royal Museum and Art Gallery. The building has an extraordinary Victorian-Tudor-Gothic front and was built in 1897. It is best known for the cattle paintings of Sidney Cooper, a local artist, and for housing the Buffs Regimental Gallery.

Along on the right is the 'Queen Elizabeth Guest Chamber (1573)'. The Tudor frontage contains an upstairs restaurant, and at pavement level a greengrocer's and Thorntons choc shop. The most interesting features are the Tudor windows and plaster ornaments with cherubs and grapes. Although one of the listed 'sights', it is all rather a mess really, and a fake too, for when the Queen visited Canterbury in 1573 she stayed at St Augustine's Abbey.

In term-time, boys from King's School stand out from the crowd, loping elegantly along in black jacket, wing collar, black tie and striped trousers.

At the next corner on the left, the entrance to Mercery Lane, stone arches in the shop front are the only remains of the Chequers of the Hope, a hostelry with accommodation for a hundred pilgrims which was destroyed by fire in 1860. Go along narrow Mercery Lane towards the splendidly emblazoned Christ Church Gate, the main entrance to the Cathedral precincts. It stands on the far side of a pretty square, Buttermarket, a war memorial at its centre, the shop-fronts preserving the old Tudor atmosphere despite the swarms of visitors who mill about here in summer. On the left in Sun Street is the former Sun Hotel (1503), now a jewellers; a plaque explains that this was once known as The Little Inn 'made famous by Chas. Dickens in his travels through Kent'.

On the façade of Christ Church Gate a row of carved angels hold polychrome shields above a long figure of Christ in Majesty in the central niche. This is a recent addition and in effect replaces the Christ figure destroyed by Puritan idolbreakers in the 1640s. The gate was begun in 1507, the date recorded in the Latin inscription above the archway, and may be a memorial to Prince Arthur, eldest son of Henry VII who died in 1502 aged sixteen.

Canterbury Cathedral

Walk through to the Precincts. A simple plan is available at the Welcome Centre and this proposes a route through the Cathedral. Before going in at the South West Porch, look up at the massive West Towers and the Perpendicular Gothic nave (1377-1405). At the heart of the building is the great Bell Harry Tower, 72m (235ft) high and completed in 1498. Beyond is the early Gothic Quire (choir), rebuilt in 1175-84 over a Romanesque crypt (early twelfth century).

Go in and stand at the foot of the great nave, almost overwhelming in its verticality, as befits England's first cathedral built in the supreme age of glorifying God through the elevation of mighty churches.

A cathedral was established here soon after St Augustine arrived in 597 at the head of a mission from Rome. In 1067 the Saxon cathedral was destroyed by fire and rebuilt by Archbishop Lanfranc between 1070 and 1077. In 1174 the quire was destroyed in another fire and rebuilt. In 1377-1405 the old Lanfranc church, on the site of the present nave and west transepts, was demolished and today's nave took its place.

Beneath the second full arcade on the north side is the Stuart font, made in 1639. Its cover is suspended on an iron frame and worked by pulleys. At the far end, the nave is crossed by a bridge-like strainer arch with fretted decoration. This was inserted in about 1500 to distribute part of the weight from Bell Harry Tower.

To the left of the pulpit, go down steps to the Martyrdom Transept. Here in 1170 the avenging knights burst in from the cloisters and murdered Archbishop Becket, who fell to the pavement just inside the door. This solemn place of pilgrimage is now marked by a dramatically lit modern version of the Altar of Sword's Point, the arms of the black cross pierced by two jagged swords.

Look also for Comper's Royal window (1954) which includes leading figures in the Coronation ceremonies of 1937 and 1953, among them Queen Elizabeth II as a princess, King George VI and the present Queen Mother, and the young Prince Charles and Princess Anne.

On the other side of a stone screen is the Chapel of Our Lady Martyrdom, built in the fifteenth century. It has a fan vault and a beautiful east window decorated with pale green-yellow heraldic designs.

Continue down a flight of steps to the Western Crypt, at its west end the Cathedral Treasury (open Easter-September). The view forward is dominated by the ranks of Romanesque columns, some ornately carved, and low arches leading towards the altar of the Sanctuary of Our Lady Undercroft. Behind the altar is the Eastern Crypt. In this second area the body of Thomas Becket was first buried and remained here until 1220 when it was moved to the Trinity Chapel above, which offered a more appropriate space for the hundreds of pilgrims then converging on Canterbury. At the end of this crypt is the tiny Jesus Chapel with fine early glass and a Gothic vault; between its ribs are the initials 'M' and 'I', for Mary and Jesus.

Go up the steps on the south side to find the Warriors' Chapel of St Michael. A great tomb bears three royal effigies, and the walls bristle with the old colours of the Buffs, the Royal East Kent Regiment.

From the centre of the Cathedral the view down the nave is most striking, and so is the view upwards into Bell Harry Tower. It was built in 1494-1504 by John Wastell, who went on to design the great vault at King's College Chapel, Cambridge (see *Walk 31*). The tower is made of nearly 500,000 bricks faced with stone, and is crowned with an elaborate pattern of fan vaulting and the central lantern with the great curfew bell.

Steps lead up to the Pulpitum Screen and the Gothic Quire. Above the High Altar is the simple marble Chair of St Augustine, where for centuries archbishops have been enthroned. Walk through to the North Ambulatory, passing the ornate polychrome double-decker tomb of Archbishop Chichele (d.1443), the founder of All Soul's College, Oxford. To the east is the Trinity Chapel. At the far end the site of St Thomas's shrine, destroyed in 1538, is marked by a burning candle and an inscription in brass.

Walk back past two notable tombs: that of Archbishop Walter (d.1203) is the oldest in the Cathedral; that of Edward, 'Black Prince' of Wales (d.1376) shows him in full armour with his black shield bearing three ostrich feathers.

Leave the Cathedral by the South Door and turn left around the apse towards the stone and flint buildings of King's School and the remains of the monks' infirmary. Go along Brick Walk and turn right at the next doorway through Dark Entry to the Prior's Gatehouse. Beyond lies the broad expanse of Green Court. The court formerly contained the domestic buildings of the monastery: the Deanery lies to the right, and ahead are the old granary, bakery and brewery. These are now occupied by King's School.

Return to Dark Entry, through which pilgrims may enter the Cathedral at the Dean's Stairs. Ahead and to the right is the Cathedral Library. Step out on the garden side to see the sombre but fascinating Romanesque Water Tower, a buttressed stone building with a pointed roof which once supplied water to the monastery and is still in use.

Keep on to the magnificent Cloisters. On the left, look through the heraldic windows into the Chapter House and the great facing window portraying important figures in the history of the Cathedral. Continue round the Cloister, passing the Becket Door, and return to the entrance to the Precincts.

Dane John Gardens and City Wall

Anything more would be anti-climax. Perhaps seek refreshment in Buttermarket or in the surrounding streets, then continue along Burgate to the Roman Catholic Church of St Thomas. Here beside the road is the tower of St Mary Magdalene, Burgate. After the church was demolished in 1871, a Baroque monument to John Whitfield was placed inside the tower.

From here it is possible to walk through (see Route section) to the ruins of St Augustine's Abbey, founded in 598 and probably the oldest identifiable Christian site in Canterbury. The most conspicuous element is the remains of a great Romanesque abbey church which was demolished in 1538 together with many of the domestic buildings. The principal surviving buildings are the Fyndon Gate in Monastery Street and the Cemetery Gate at the far end of Church Street St Paul's. However, the opening times are inadequate and not to be relied on, which reflects poorly on English Heritage who run the site.

The road back to the railway station passes the tower of another former church, that of St George's. This was wrecked not by Henry VIII's Reformers but by a German bomb in 1942. Christopher Marlowe was baptised here on 26 February 1564.

After the modern shops and the bus station there is a choice of routes. Either walk up on to the City Wall and follow it round to the station, or continue ahead through Dane John Gardens and join the Wall Walk next to the Mound. In these pleasant gardens, laid out in 1790 at the expense of Alderman James Simmons, are a Boer War memorial to the Buffs (East Kent Regiment) and the Imperial Yeomanry of East Kent, and another to Christopher Marlowe. From the top of the Mound, probably part of a pre-Roman defensive system, are attractive views out to the countryside and back to the low brick town and its towering stone Cathedral.

BRIEFING

HISTORY NOTES

The best single place to follow the development of London is at the excellent Museum of London (see *Walk 10*). The following notes outline the evolution of the city and indicate some of the sites and buildings visited during the Slow Walks.

The Roman City

The Romans installed themselves here after the Conquest of AD 43, initially colonising the north bank of the Thames in the area of Cornhill. The first Roman wall to protect 'Londinium' was built at the end of the second century AD and enclosed an area of 134 hectares (330 acres). At the south-east corner was a fort, a forerunner of the Norman Tower. Londinium was the chief administrative centre in Roman Britain until the legions withdrew in 410-11.

See Roman artefacts and other remains in the British Museum (*Walk 9*) and the Museum of London (*Walk 10*). Sections of the wall can be seen at the Tower and on Tower Hill (*Walk 13*) and at St Giles, Cripplegate (*Walk 10*).

Anglo-Saxon Times

The Roman wall survived, and after a period of slumber the city had come to life again when in 597 the Pope sent St Augustine to Britain. St Ethelbert, King of Kent, founded the first version of St Paul's Cathedral in 604. In the next century London grew as a merchant centre, then in 885-6, following a period of decay, Alfred the Great drove out the Danes and restored 'Lunderburh' to the English.

See Remains collected in Museum of London (*Walk 10*).

Medieval London

Edward the Confessor (ruled 1040-65) moved his palace to Westminster and began building a great new church close to a previous

Benedictine abbey. After his success at the Battle of Hastings (1066), William I the Conqueror was crowned in the new Westminster Abbey. He built the Norman keep at the Tower of London which successive monarchs enlarged and strengthened. Astute merchants founded the first City guilds and the first Mayor of London took office in about 1192. By the fourteenth century the leading guilds were the Mercers, Drapers, Goldsmiths, Pepperers (Grocers) and Vintners.

See Westminster Abbey (*Walk 2*), Tower of London (*Walk 13*), Butchers' Hall, Smithfield Market, Cloth Fair and Museum of London (*Walk 10*), Leadenhall Market and Guildhall (*Walk 11*).

Tudor London

The population of London trebled between 1530 and 1600. For Henry VIII it was a great period of palace-building and enlargement of existing palaces: St James's Palace, Hampton Court, Whitehall and Nonsuch (the latter two vanished). The City of Westminster and the City of London were linked by the Strand, a favoured site for noblemen to build mansions beside the river. On the south side of London Bridge, Southwark was made a ward of the City of London and became an entertainment centre with bear and bull-baiting arenas and theatres such as Shakespeare's Globe.

See St James's Palace (*Walk 1*), Hampton Court (*Walk 26*), historic sites in Southwark (*Walk 13*).

The Stuarts

The inflexible Charles I led the Royalist cause to defeat in the Civil War and in 1649 was executed on a scaffold outside Banqueting House, Whitehall. At the Restoration Charles II continued the work of James I, who had opened Hyde Park to the public, by purchasing Green Park and taking his 'constitutionals' amongst his subjects on Constitution Hill. He also redesigned St James's Park.

The Great Plague and Fire of 1665 and 1666 destroyed much of the City of London, and in doing so launched a great age in architecture. Under Sir Christopher Wren fifty new stone churches and a new St Paul's Cathedral arose from the ashes of the medieval timber-built Square Mile. Well-to-do merchants and noblemen moved westward to the healthier fields beyond Charing Cross and great estates were laid out to the north and south of Piccadilly. Wren also designed the Royal Hospital in Chelsea, Greenwich Hospital and the Royal Observatory, and extended Hampton Court Palace.

In 1694 City merchants founded the Bank of England, the base of the modern City's power structure.

See   St James's Park (*Walk 1*) and Green Park (*Walk 3*), Banqueting House (*Walk 2*), St Paul's Cathedral and City (*Walks 10,11*), Royal Hospital, Chelsea (*Walk 26*), Greenwich Hospital (*Walk 23*).

Georgian London

A high period in London architecture. Streets and squares of gracious houses appeared in central districts from Bloomsbury to Mayfair, and the Wren tradition was continued in the elegant churches of James Gibbs, Nicholas Hawksmoor and Thomas Archer. Following the destruction of Whitehall Palace in 1698, the way from Charing Cross to Westminster was redeveloped with such buildings as the Horse Guards and the Treasury. In 1738 construction began of Westminster Bridge, still only the second after London Bridge.

Enlargement of the West End came with John Nash's Regent Street scheme, linking the Prince Regent's palace at Carlton House with the new Regent's Park, ringed by elegant inward-facing terraces. Several Gentlemen's clubs in Pall Mall and St James's Street date from this time (*c.*1820) as do Smirke's buildings at the British Museum.

See   Regent Street and St James's (*Walk 1*), Regent's Park (*Walk 20*), Bloomsbury squares (*Walk 9*), weavers' houses in Spitalfields (*Walk 12*), French eighteenth-century paintings, sculpture and furniture in Wallace Collection (*Walk 19*).

Victorian Times

Queen Victoria was the first monarch to live at Buckingham Palace, moving there from Kensington Palace where she was born in 1819. Her reign coincided with vast growth in the inner and outer suburbs, the arrival of steam railways and from 1863 the Underground. The most important single event was the Great Exhibition of 1851 in Hyde Park, after which South Kensington became the chief site of scientific

museums in London, home also of the Victoria and Albert Museum.
See   Buckingham Palace, Queen's Gallery and Royal Mews (*Walk 3*),
Kensington Palace (*Walk 17*), museums of South Kensington (*Walk
18*).

Twentieth Century

'Modern' London belongs mainly to the period after 1945, when bomb
damage forced widescale repair and the construction of new estates and
individual buildings. The effect on the skyline is most obvious in the
City, now a forest of concrete towers where once only the spires of
Wren's churches and the dome of St Paul's reached above the houses.
The South Bank arts centre is the legacy of the Festival of Britain
(1951). The latest big development is to the east in Docklands, its
flamboyant centre at Canary Wharf in the Isle of Dogs.
See   Mixed development in the City, including new Lloyd's building
(*Walks 10,11*), South Bank (*Walk 14*), Docklands (*Walk 23*).

TRANSPORT
Underground (Tube)

The world's first Underground railway is now maddeningly out of date
in many respects. The decrepit rolling stock, the dismal and grubby
stations and the frequent disruptions to service make travelling by
Tube absurdly unpredictable. I feel most sorry for Londoners who
depend on the thing to get to work and back each day. In harsh winter
weather the whole network comes close to collapse: stations flood,
train doors freeze, huge queues wait to get on the escalators, trains are
cancelled, a 'suspect parcel' at Liverpool Street cuts out the Central
Line. And on and on. Reading the latest disaster on the blackboard by
the ticket office takes on a sinister fascination, as though these
messages are hinting at the onset of doomsday itself, and the bloke on
the street with the 'End is Nigh' sandwich-board is more in touch with
reality than the executives of London Underground Ltd.

For all its faults, however, we are stuck with it. Tubes far outpace
buses through Central London and are the best form of public transport
for getting about the city. The various lines are colour-coded on maps of
the network and in signs at the station. Most central stations are now

fitted with automatic barriers, so travellers must have a valid ticket before beginning a journey. Trains run from approximately 05.30 to midnight, beginning later at weekends (around 07.30). Some stations are closed at weekends and outside peak hours.

Tickets Single-journey tickets are available from ticket offices and machines at the station. A better all-round deal is to buy a Travelcard, valid for use on Tubes, most buses, Network SouthEast trains and the Docklands Light Railway. Greater London has been divided into six travel zones. Before buying a Travelcard, work out from a zone map which zones you intend to travel through and ask for the appropriate Travelcard at the ticket office. Some newsagents also sell them.

One Day Travelcards are available in three versions: two-zone, covering Zones 1-2; four-zone, covering Zones 1-4; and all-zone, covering Zones 1-6. From Monday to Friday you may not use a One Day Travelcard until after 09.30. At weekends and on public holidays there are no time restrictions. Another option is the LT card, a one-day card which may be used before 09.30 but costs a lot more than the ordinary version.

Travelcard Seasons are an even better buy for residents and visitors staying for a week or more. These have no travel-time restrictions and cover any consecutive period of seven days, one month, one year, and odd periods between one month and one year. When you first buy a Travelcard Season, take a passport-sized photograph with you. This goes on a photocard which you then keep in a special wallet with the ticket. For tickets valid for one month or longer, you will need to complete a simple application form.

Buses

The red double-decker bus is a world-famous institution, its top deck offering wonderful views of London's sights and street life. It is a lumbering animal, however, proceeding through the traffic-choked streets at an average speed of about ten miles an hour. If this is of no consequence to you, then go by bus. It must be at least twice as enjoyable as a journey on the Tube.

Night buses are a useful fall-back even if some strange people use them. Look for the night-bus symbol at bus stops, and see the timetables for running times.

Tickets   Buy single-journey tickets from the driver or conductor. Buy Travelcards (see 'Underground' section) at Underground ticket offices and certain newsagents. For ticketing purposes, Bus Zones 4-6 are treated as one zone.

You can use your Travelcard on the red buses and those operated for London Transport by other companies; the latter display a 'London Transport Service' sign on the front of the bus. Travelcards are not valid on Airbus, excursions or other special services.

Trains and Coaches

For out-of-town trips, such as the Slow Walk in Canterbury, you will need to use British Rail. Information about which station to go to is included in the relevant chapters. Inter-City trains operate on some routes and are faster and more comfortable than the standard Network SouthEast trains. British Rail operates its own system of cheap-day return tickets and period returns. The system is frequently changed or modified as new inducements to travel by rail are brought in, so ask at the ticket office for the best deal to suit your needs.

Coaches are a cheaper alternative to rail travel. Services operate from Victoria Coach Station. Journeys to destinations covered in this book usually take about fifty per cent longer than the train time.

Taxis

Not all London's black cabs are black any more, but they are still the highly manoeuvrable vehicles they have always been. Standard taxis are licensed to carry four passengers. Hail them on the street or pick them up at taxi ranks. An orange sign next to the driver's compartment indicates that a taxi is free. Some taxis are on a radio telephone network and their drivers will give you a card with the number to ring.

Fares are not cheap but not unreasonable either. Licensed taxis carry a meter which should be turned down to the minimum fare at the start of the journey. Meters monitor fares for all journeys in the London area. Small extra charges are made for additional passengers and for evening journeys and others beginning after midnight.

For minicab services, refer to the Yellow Pages of the telephone directory. When you book, agree a price and keep the driver to it.

Telephones

Telephone boxes are widely available in the street, in post offices, shops, cafés, restaurants and pubs. Most are operated by the rival companies British Telecom and Mercury. Boxes accept either a range of coins or a Phonecard which you can buy at newsagents. Follow the dialling instructions in the box. Usually these ask the caller to lift the receiver, insert money or card and dial the number. Connection is automatic. On some smaller coinboxes, the caller is asked to press a button on being connected.

London numbers carry one of two prefixes: 071 for inner districts and 081 for outer districts. To dial an 071 number from an 071 telephone you do not need to dial the 071; to dial an 081 number from an 071 telephone you *do* need to dial the 081.

To make an international call, dial 010. Then dial the country code (Netherlands 31, United States 1, etc.) then the area code and number, deleting the first 0 if there is one. Thus the code for Amsterdam is 010-31-20, and for New York City 010-1-212.

Money

Until there is monetary union in the European Community, the £ (pound) sterling is Britain's national currency. Coins are 1 penny (1p), 2 pence (2p), 5p, 10p, 20p, 50p, £1. English notes are £5, £10, £20, £50.

Banks are usually open 09.30 to 15.30 or 16.30, Monday to Friday. Some are open on Saturday morning, but not for cash transactions. Watch out also for public holidays.

Exchange offices are open outside banking hours as follows:
- Heathrow and Gatwick Airports, open every day, 24 hours a day.
- Central London, in railway termini and main tourist areas, open every day until 22.00 or midnight.

Eurocheques and traveller's cheques are easy to change. Take a passport for identification, and with Eurocheques the encashment card as well. Usually, cheques may be cashed up to a limit of £200.

Visitors are advised to bring sterling traveller's cheques which are paid at face value. Currency traveller's cheques have to be converted to sterling and attract a commission.

Most banks and exchange offices accept the major credit cards – American Express, Diners Club, Access, Mastercard and Visa. Take your passport for proof of ID. In central shops and restaurants, cards may or may not be acceptable. If in doubt, ask before you choose or order.

For overseas visitors, it is a good idea to buy at least a first day's supply of sterling notes and coins before you leave home.

Tax-free shopping In Britain some items are exempt from Value Added Tax (VAT) for social reasons. The main ones are food, children's clothes and books.

Tax-free shopping is better value for visitors living outside the EC. Most stores have export bureaux where overseas visitors living outside the EC, and who spend more than £150 in total, can take their receipts and have them stamped. They receive an export form which they hand in with the receipts at Customs on leaving the UK, and receive a refund by cheque.

EC visitors fare less well because VAT rates are broadly similar throughout the Community. All visitors should remember that imported goods valued at more than the local limit should be taken through the 'Goods to Declare' channel on arrival in the home country, and will be subject to excise duty.

Tipping Service may or may not be included in restaurant bills. If nothing about service is stamped or printed on the bill, ask the waiter or waitress. No-one wants to pay twice. After a meal, if you are happy with the service, leave around 10 per cent of the bill.

Tip taxi drivers up to 10 per cent of the fare. Give a hotel porter not less than £1. Leave cloakroom attendants a small tip, say 20p.

Opening Times

Shops usually open from 09.00 or 09.30 to 17.30 or 18.00, and most are closed on Sunday. On Thursday there is late-night shopping in the West End until 20.00. Specialist shops such as antique dealers may not open until 11.00.

Museum hours vary. Some are open every day except certain public holidays; some open only in the afternoon on Sunday, and some close all day on Monday.

Opening times for all main places of interest on Slow Walk routes appear in the appropriate chapter. Winter hours may be shorter than summer hours.

Banking hours are given in 'Money' above.

Cafés open between 09.00 and 11.00 and stay open in the evening according to demand and location. Restaurants usually serve lunch from 12.00 to 14.30 or 15.00 and dinner from 18.00 or later. Most pubs are open from 11.00 to 23.00, but may only serve food between 12.00 and 14.00.

List of Public Holidays

1 January (New Year's Day)
Good Friday
Easter Monday
May bank holiday (1st Monday in May)
Late Spring bank holiday (last Monday in May)
August bank holiday (last Monday in August)
25 December (Christmas Day)
26 December (Boxing Day)

CLOTHING SIZES
For Women

Dresses, knitwear, blouses, coats

GB	10	12	14	16	18	20	22	
Continental	36	38	40	42	44	46	48	
USA	8	10	12	14	16	18	20	

Tights, stockings

GB	8	8½	9	9½	10	10½
Continental	0	1	2	3	4	5
USA	8	8½	9	9½	10	10½

Shoes

GB	3	3½	4	4½	5	5½	6	7	8
Continental	35½	36	36½	37	37½	38	39	40	41
USA	4	4½	5	5½	6	6½	7½	8½	9½

For Men

Shirts

GB	14	14½	15	15½	16	16½	17
Continental	36	37	38	39	40	41	42
USA	14	14½	15	15½	16	16½	17

Sweaters

GB	36	38	40	42	44	46
Continental	46	48	50	52	54	56
USA	36	38	40	42	44	46

Suits

GB	35	36	37	38	39	40	42
Continental	36	38	40	42	44	46	48
USA	35	36	37	38	39	40	42

Shoes

GB	5½	6½	7	8	8½	9½	10½
Continental	39	40	41	42	43	44	45
USA	6	7	7½	8½	9	10	11

Watering Holes

For many years after the cafés and coffee bars of the Sixties had gone into decline, and pubs closed during the afternoon from 15.00 to 17.30, it was difficult to find somewhere to sit down and take a breather. Now most pubs are open all day, from 11.00 until 23.00, and their owners take a much more positive attitude towards food and non-alcoholic refreshments such as coffee and tea. Too many, however, close down their lunch counter at 14.00 and do not reopen it in the evening.

Cafés, with or without a licence to sell alcohol, are again on the increase, and there are plenty of wine bars offering a choice of wines and light meals.

Eating out well is expensive. Compared with Continental and American levels, the price-gap between cheap eating, say at a pizza place, and a full restaurant menu is dauntingly large. Nowadays prices are so high in the better restaurants that many people who once ate there can no longer afford to do so unless they are on expenses.

For the best value and variety in one area, go to Soho or Covent Garden.

Toilets

Public facilities are not as evident as they used to be. Most cafés and all pubs have toilets, though standards of equipment and hygiene vary widely. If a pub has been recently renovated, expect clean modern toilets. If the establishment still rests on its reputation for being darkly atmospheric, the facilities out back may be about as advanced as a Victorian workhouse.

What's On/Further Information

London currently has three listings guides: *Time Out*, *City Limits* and *What's On In London*. I would say the best for general information and its entertainment guide is *Time Out*, which appears each Wednesday. Buy it or one of the others from newsstands and station bookstalls. To keep up with news and local events, buy London's daily newspaper, the *Evening Standard*.

For further background information, look in at the bookshop and information centre of the London Tourist Board in the forecourt of Victoria Station.

London By Night

London is resolutely simple-minded when it comes to nightlife. Music and theatre are what it does best. See a show in one of the West End or fringe theatres, or a concert at the South Bank complex (Royal Festival Hall, Queen Elizabeth Hall, Purcell Room), or at the Barbican, Royal Albert Hall, Wigmore Hall or St John's Smith Square. For jazz and rock venues, see the copious listings in *Time Out*.

Wilder or sleazier forms of nightlife have disappeared almost entirely from view, thanks to a clean-up campaign by the Westminster City Council which closed down a lot of sex establishments in Soho. This has improved the quality of daytime attractions in the area and made life safer for Soho residents. The disadvantage is that, historically, an inventive and freewheeling nightlife never flourishes in an atmosphere of censorship and state intervention. So, in the West End of London many doors are closed which in Amsterdam, Paris, Barcelona and numerous other cities would still be freely open.

Quick London

If you have only a few days to spare, the Slow Walks listed below offer a good introduction to the city and cover many of the main sights and museums.

Day 1   *Walk 2: Whitehall and Westminster*
Day 2   *Walk 6: National Gallery and Covent Garden*
Day 3   *Walk 10: St Paul's and Barbican*
Day 4   *Walk 3: Queen and Country*
Day 5   *Walk 13: The Tower of London and Shakespeare's Southwark*

On Sunday morning, take *Walk 12: Spitalfields* through Petticoat Lane market. Before setting off on any of these walks, make sure that opening times fit with your plans.

INDEX